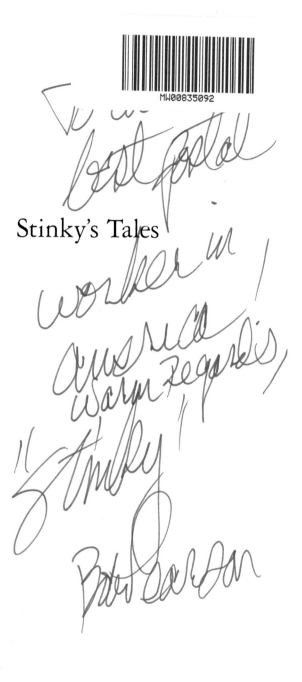

Stinky's Tales

FRONT COVER: The front cover photo was taken when I was one-year old on my father's lap. I am depicted leaning to my right (even then) in front of my father, with my mother's wary eye on my actions, as usual. She did this from birth until I was over forty! My father's mother Hazel and father H.B. Pearson, Sr. stand behind the Adirondack chair. Five-year old brother Dick is next to Isabel. The photo was taken in 1939.

BACK COVER: The back cover photo was taken in 1957 when I was at Michigan State University. Brother Dick is just returning from a tour of duty in Korea with the U.S. Army. Brother Charley and sister Donna ages 5 and 10 respectively are pictured. Our family was at the airport in Rochester, N.Y. Dick was twenty-three and I was eighteen.

To order additional copies, please contact us.
BookSurge, LLC
www.booksurge.com
1-866-308-6235
orders@booksurge.com

BOB
PEARSON

STINKY'S TALES

GROWING UP IN A SMALL VILLAGE IN 1940'S AND 1950'S

2004

Stinky's Tales

CONTENTS

The book is dedicated to my wife, Jan who listened to the whole book as it poured out of my memory in pieces. Her support and encouragement were terrific. Thanks to Gib Sergeant, lifelong friend, who read every word and kept grammar and history on track. Thanks to my brother, Charley and sister, Donna who both gave good advice and who have been along for the ride. Special thanks to "Swede" Erwin, coach, and Elizabeth Bellinger, English Teacher, for their ideas and support. Dedicated to the memory of our class of 1956 at Sodus High School and those who are no longer with us. Thanks to the special adults in Sodus who were such good friends and neighbors. To our children and grandchildren - have a good laugh at what you read here.

INTRODUCTION

The book of reflections about growing up in Sodus, New York during the 1940s and 1950s is a product of many fond memories and many fine influences. The small, farming community located on the shores of Lake Ontario in upstate New York is situated between Rochester to the west and Oswego to the east on Route 104. The village population fifty years ago was two thousand, and graduating classes at the central school were typically about forty to fifty students in size. The village has not grown much since then, although the central school has expanded into newer and larger configurations over a fifty year period.

I was "Stinky" by virtue of falling into a wide drainage ditch emanating from a huge dairy barn one Halloween evening attempting to keep up with an older brother and his cronies. They got away untouched from the prank done by them to a farmer's cow barn. I, by contrast, was affected, in the short term, quite traumatically that October evening over five decades ago, and have heretofore been "Stinky" whenever I show my face inside the county lines. The smell has long disappeared, but the memory lingers in the minds of my peers.

Despite such periodic trauma in my life, Sodus was a pretty darn good place to call home. My career as a teacher, coach and administrator in educational institutions was prompted in no small measure by the influences described within this book. I owe much to my original small town, and was shaped tremendously by many who lived and worked in Sodus.

The book shares reflections whose main purpose could be to help point out some of the special things that have disappeared in our current fast-paced lives. The intent of the book isn't to preach, nor is it to gloat about the wonderful days of yore. Sodus was not perfect, nor were its people. I certainly struggled as a smart-ass adolescent for a long period of time. Fortunately for all involved, good triumphed over puberty in my case. It was the friends in Sodus and special adults who made the difference when I needed the appropriate nudge, cue or paddling. The names mentioned were special to me in many ways and they were involved in multitudinous ways in the lives of others. Sodus residents in those days were more involved than residents in similar communities today. They sat on their front porches hoping someone would come by. Front porches are a thing of the past, as far as social interaction is concerned, but they were active places fifty years ago. People were involved more often with others and especially involved with youngsters. Life was simpler. There seemed to be more simple choices.

Life was especially less ambiguous after World War II. The post-war era was a celebration; it appears, of values tested and true. The village, and the country as a whole, had weathered the storm of war. Dismally, the community had lost its innocence and many of its young men. Something very strong remained despite all the trauma of the war years. The comparisons with current lifestyles and those fifty years ago described in the book are compelling, and can involve the reader in some inevitable conclusions. There are some very insightful memories, as it turns out, because some very special people happened along in my life. These people made for a very unique personal development and for a great community in which to grow.

I invite you into Stinky's life. Have a bit of fun at my expense.

PREFACE

A currently prominent political figure, at the time of this writing a New York U.S. Senator whose name escapes me (but who helped preside over a recent presidential administration characterized by scandal and corruption), is famous for her feeling that "It takes a village to raise a child." As usual, she is wrong, as Dr. Bob Pearson's autobiographical reflections illustrate.

Bob was raised by a strong, devoted, loving family. True, he was surrounded by supporting friends, classmates, and community as documented often. But just as mere participation in sports does not *build* character, but how you play reflects your character, similarly how you interact with your village *reflects* the values learned at home.

The Pearson kid and I have been friends since we made the daily walk home from Kindergarten. We were classmates and teammates. Bob was a member of my wedding party. As adults we lost touch occasionally as a function of geography, but I consider him one of my best lifelong friends. He has, of course, become tremendously successful in his personal and professional life, loved and respected by his family and his students. Comments by his current students, posted on the Internet for all to see, indicate that they feel "Dr. Pearson is the best professor at Berry College."

I am proud to have had a small part in the production of Bob's early memoirs, making incidental suggestions and contributing small points of fact here and there regarding the Sodus community. And, more important, I am proud to be counted among Bob's numerous friends. We share lots of memories.

I'm sure this volume will be enjoyed and cherished by many

generations over the years to come. Would that more of us had the energy, inclination and drive to share our personal histories as he has. Thank you, Bob, for a remarkable accomplishment.

Gib Sergeant (Lester)
Sodus, N.Y. May 2004

***

One of the most satisfying experiences for a retired English Teacher is to find that, during her teaching career, a pupil learned, among other things, to enjoy reading, to appreciate poetry and to find a love of expression in writing. I have been most fortunate to hear from a number of former pupils who learned in my class to love to read books. I have already received two books from a former pupil who has published. He really cannot expect me to read scientific volumes on animal nutrition, but his effort is appreciated.

And now, I await Stinky's Tales. Having previewed the chapter on English at Sodus Central School in the mid '50s, I want to say, "Thank you." Thank you, Bob Pearson, for not saving these words for my memorial service, for allowing me to say, "Thank you."

"Stinky," also known as "Mayor," was identified in his high school year book with this sentence: "I take life as I find it but I don't leave it so." His reputation as an HPE professor at the college level is proof of this omen. He has had a lasting influence on his students and they say so.

I remember the happy high school senior involved in so many activities: music, drama arts, sports, school newspaper and yearbook, and student council where his leadership went county-wide. It was my privilege to be yearbook and student council advisor. Bob Pearson was the designated driver for some of the boys' Saturday night outings. On one Monday morning he confessed to me, "I had seventeen Seven-Ups on Saturday night." He loved FUN. At the same time, he was a self-disciplined teenager. I am sure that his high school years made him the man he is today.

As Henry Adams wrote in the *The Education of Henry Adams:*

"A teacher affects eternity; he can never tell where his influence stops." This is true for me and for Dr. Robert Pearson.

Elizabeth Bellinger (EBB)

Sodus, N.Y. May 2004

***

I feel honored to be able to write something about Bob Pearson.

During my interaction with him, he proved to be a very unique young man. This still applies to him today.

Bob stood apart due to his unwavering principles. He was an outstanding student and athlete admired not only by his peers, but by the faculty with whom he came in contact. His voice was prevalent in student government throughout his student career.

As his coach, I knew that I could count on him to put forth his best effort and as captain work hard at making a cohesive team. Bob was a team player. He didn't worry about individual statistics or being high scorer. He always played by the rules, and put out one hundred percent. His empathy and his sense of honor made him an asset. Though a very serious young man, his sense of humor was infectious, and he knew when to use it.

As an extremely talented, well-grounded, and highly principled individual with his students, athletes and all those with whom he has contact, Bob has been a definite credit to the Berry College faculty and the community in which he lives.

John (Jack, Swede, Coach) C. Erwin

Rochester, N.Y. May 2004

PART ONE
Family

A constant theme for my family during the early years after Dad returned in 1945 from the Navy was meal-time in the kitchen of our century old house. Family bites were very organized and measured in many ways. The meals were very measured in their duration and very predictable in their content. The news would go on the radio in the kitchen at 6PM sharp. After we listened to news and sports, the radio went off and my father would engage us in the discussion of the news and, of course, sports. No phone calls were taken during this time and the whole process would be concluded by 7PM.

The content of the meals would be traditional fare with a heavy emphasis on meat, potatoes, vegetables, and plenty of each. That seemed to be what H.B.P. liked and was used to during his early life with his mother Hazel. This, therefore, dictated our menu. There were at least five of us (and then six once the afterthought named Charley appeared seventeen years after the first-born Dick) and we ate a lot. Isabel (Mom) cooked plenty to spare.

My sister Donna had to be considered a war baby in that she appeared quite soon after H.B. Pearson returned home from navy service. We always used to kid her that the "egg man" Farley Porter was the true father, but she soon did the math when she was old enough to do so. Farley did deliver eggs personally and he also co-sponsored a fantastic mortgage for the "war mother" Isabel. He was not the biological parent for Donna. But Donna must have been conceived during my Dad's first week home from the navy! That is another story for later.

It was in this kitchen that many thoughts and deeds were discussed and planned. It was this family bite time that really shaped much of what I learned about the world via the radio, and then via my father's deliberations on all of it. It also was a time that taught me my manners, my etiquette and my understanding about eating all foods placed before me. What unfolded in the fabric of my family were traditional, conservative values and a commitment to service. Even during the war years and during my father's service time, my mother spent many hours developing our sense of manners and rituals. She was a fine mother and played the father role when so many family men were absent. Fortunately, my family had an uncle and aunt who were special and some interesting grandparents. My mother was a volunteer for several causes. It appears I went along with her out of necessity due to age factors. It did not seem to have any undesirable effects on me. If anything, it kept me out of trouble. When my father returned, I was ready for the lessons he taught and still depended upon Isabel for the rich lessons she taught.

***

Isabel—Queen for every day

Isabel asked the ambulance driver that particular winter day to take her for a long ride before delivering her from the hospital room over to get some therapy for the stroke she had suffered three weeks earlier. The ride through the snow and cold and ample blue sky that day in upstate New York normally would have taken three to four minutes, since the rehab building was adjacent to the hospital. The short ride was easily stretched to a ten minute ride around Newark, New York, and this allowed Isabel the luxury and privacy of dying on her own terms.

"Dizzy Izzy," as my friends lovingly called her, had left the world a much better place by her presence. Her sudden yet predictable absence was monumental to all who knew her and loved her. She had always loved riding and, when she turned fifty, driving. The special love of traveling and riding was passed down to children and grandchildren. Even in death she found her own way to get a ride on a beautiful day!

Even today as I travel I will see something and think Isabel would have loved to have seen that particular view or place. Isabel Pearson was a terrific mother, and for those friends in and around Sodus she was a terrific friend. Izzy would show up with food for shut-ins, and trained her children to consider those people as part of her own private mission to serve them. We grew up knowing that sharing and simple kindnesses were a staple of life, and really never considered any other way. Isabel was literally the unofficial queen of the village. She made her warm way into the lives and hearts of many.

Once she learned how to drive, at the lively age of fifty, hardly a day went by without several people hearing from her via the car horn as she zipped by in her Chevy. Often hardly a month went by without a new Isabel driving story circulating in the village. The queen, it appeared, had a special problem parking, backing up, and pulling into the one car garage (actually a barn) we owned. Izzy performed one of the most incredible driving daily doubles on one day in the winter early in her driving career.

On that winter day she backed out of the barn, down the sloping, snow-covered driveway and smack into the vehicle at the opposite side of the street (but close enough to the driveway to allow for the accident). Her only comment to the Symonds' visitor, who'd parked the car there to deliver something to our neighbors, was that she was sorry but the car had not been there when she pulled in. This explanation was hard to reply to, and as a witness to the comment I merely said to the damaged car owner that my Dad would take care of the matter later.

The day, however, was not over!

As I shoveled out the driveway for the second time that day Mom returned. I signaled for her to park in the street near the big snow banks in front of our house created by successive plowings over the previous three days of snow. I finished the shoveling after Mom had retired to the kitchen of the house. This I knew because Isabel spent many hours a day in the kitchen, and where else would she be when food needed to be prepared? Inevitably it came to pass that the unofficial queen was ready for another foray that same day into the snowy arteries of Sodus. What she did not know was that I had backed the car into the barn so she could merely pull out headfirst into the street. This would solve the dilemma of the previous outing and actually would be much easier. The major flaw in my logic was that Isabel was primed to put the car into reverse and back out, because that is what she had always done since she turned fifty. It did not even cross my teenage brain that Izzy should be briefed on this new routine. She was probably fifty-five at the time so that would be five years of habit; and on that memorable day she went to the barn, got in the car and backed out of the barn as she had done for five years.

You have already figured it out, haven't you? She backed out of the barn right through the rear of the barn. When Dad arrived home, he was very understanding about the whole deal as far as Izzy was concerned. He was, after all, very cognizant of her traits and her distinct talent for the unique and unpredictable. He was not at all sympathetic to my involvement, however! Why in the hell would a person back a car into a barn when this had never been done before? Why didn't I warn the visitor whose car was stacked up on Izzy's runway? Was I not shoveling snow out there when the visitor arrived? Why didn't I warn her? On and on the discourse went over supper.

Isabel finally stopped Pete (Dad) from this line of reasoning by telling him she would not drive in the snow again that winter. For some reason, Dad accepted this token sacrifice on my behalf. Of course, she never stopped driving. She was always interested in driving or riding on snowy, bright winter days.

***

Pete—The frame in the construction

My father visited me and my family when I was about six months away from earning my doctorate at the University of New

Mexico in Albuquerque, New Mexico, in the fall of 1969. He and my mother flew into Colorado, rented a car and drove down into New Mexico and then used Albuquerque as their "base" as the two of them explored Las Vegas, parts of Arizona and many places in New Mexico before flying home to New York State. They had never been west of the Mississippi in their lives. It was an extraordinary experience for them, according to their periodic reports. They checked in with me the way I used to when I traveled. We had switched roles, and it was an interesting time for all of us.

Five months later, as I put the finishing touches on a dissertation and the degree that my father expressed great pride about, my father succumbed to severe flu compounded by some questionable medical treatments. He was gone at age sixty-two. I was glad I had heard of his pride in my accomplishment. During his last night with me and my family, he had told me for the first time in his life that he loved me.

His remarkable emotional moment came after a few beers at a pizza parlor where he was mellowing out with two grandchildren that he had bonded with for what would be the last time. As we sat in the pizza place's big family booth, we enjoyed the end of a great trip for my parents and a near-conclusion to a great educational experience for me.

Son Jack had been adopted in New Mexico, so this visit was my parent's first acquaintance with the three month old kid. They had not seen the chubby Jack during the summer since Jack was adopted in January 1970, shortly after his birth and just prior to the visit from Pete and Isabel.

Older son Jeff, also adopted, had been the apple of my father's eye for three years, so he already knew about the first grandson from my efforts. He did have some nice times with Jeff.

The expressed love from my father out in the New Mexico pizza parlor was nice to hear. His generation of adults expressed love in many ways, but the verbal method was probably the least practiced. In the movie "Hoosiers" Gene Hackman told his basketball team that he loved them on the eve of their championship game. The movie depicted events of the early fifties and that was the era where my high school activities occurred. The scene from the movie did not play out in real life fifties I lived. That is the era when saying "I love you" was not a standard in many families.

I now have learned from all of that fifties mentality and pronounce my love to relatives and friends during phone calls, meals, and on regular occasions. My father probably would admire my efforts at verbalization despite having been tongue-tied for most of his life. His generation merely provided for most of the needs of their families, worked hard, paid their bills, and served their community and nation. They simply did not get syrupy in their dialogues.

My father spent many years serving as mayor of our village. During that era he attempted to use that position as a platform to teach his sons about the dynamics of a small community. He would bring back to our supper table details of episodes occurring in Village Board meetings over which he presided. During certain meals, coming the day after lengthy board meetings of the previous evening, my father would expound for the whole meal (in between bites of Isabel's typical meat and potatoes) about the recent meeting.

Sometimes he would tell us certain actions taken and who would be affected the most. Other times he would deliver verbal pronouncements about certain community figures that were not all that complimentary. We were privy to many things going on in the community that may or may not have been reported in the weekly newspaper, *The Sodus Record*. It was interesting to read the accounts of board meetings after hearing my father's take on the same meetings.

H.B. Pearson was an organized man who took himself seriously and took his jobs very seriously. His death at the relatively young age of sixty-two was a testimony to such a lifestyle. He was the prototype for a "type A" personality before that tag became popular during the seventies and eighties. His energy and zeal for detail propelled him to successful banking, navy, sales and community leader careers. He merely had a tough time telling his family of his love for them.

During many episodes of my life I caught a brief whiff of the love scent coming from him despite his bluster. Often as I played baseball he would sit in his car out along one of the foul lines, watching me play from two hundred feet away. My mother said he did not enjoy mingling with all the parents and kids in the traditional bleachers because they wanted to talk community business, or wanted to make small talk. On both fronts he was not willing to suffer such things lightly. He merely avoided all of it in his seclusion down the third base line.

His love of baseball was manifest, despite the fact that he never played catch with us as kids. That, I guessed, was considered too pedestrian for him, despite his love of the game. He was a blue collar type much of the time, yet he possessed an aura he rather enjoyed propagating. Playing catch was OK for the neighborhood men, but not him. I also concluded that his average ability in the baseball realm probably kept him from exposing that average skill in front of other men or boys. He was a man of great pride. Thus he could not bring himself to play catch. He did swim like a fish, and that impacted upon all of us.

There were times when a particular baseball game had unfolded nicely for me, and I awaited the fatherly assessment upon reaching home. Almost without fail old Herman Blaine would cover the missed bunt attempt, the strikeout or the botched catch prior to delivering a brief, calculated pat on the back for a homer to win the game, a good pitching performance or some other positive event of the day's game. I never was allowed to linger too long in my glories, due to his tactics. I think, as I recall the times, that made me stronger and much less likely to be enamored with my successes. I did feel his love in the way he taught me about life.

Dad's tactics may not have made Dr. Ben Spock proud, but my guess is Dad could care less about that educational "mish-mash." That would be my father's assessment of the "feel good" generation of educators. H.B. was a no-nonsense product of the depression-era.

He was born in 1906 and during his early life he had seen a first Great War, depression and tough times. He had served in the navy during the second Great War and had worked his way up through the banking business to assistant bank manager before being drafted by the navy.

When he returned from military service, our household changed greatly. His return ended a whole lot of stuff tolerated by Mom but not allowed by Dad. His iron control was evident very quickly. As a seven year old I was too young to try any challenges of the new regime. Unfortunately this did not deter my older brother Dick from challenging the new leadership. At age twelve, Dick was on the cusp of becoming a teenager; and from my perspective, he was on the verge of annihilation!

H.B. would come in from his new job at the canning factory as a sales person and sit there at the evening meal and begin a question-answer period. His questions were to the point and were often the type that demanded a mere yes or no. The questions delivered were to assess the work being performed by the yard hands, garbage men, snow-shovelers, and shoppers—we boys being all of those things and more. If the answer was not to his liking, Dad would instantly deliver a response. At best it might be verbally –withering, but in its worst form it was a backhanded swipe at one's head.

The backhanded swipes were often delivered to the eldest son. Dick was rebellious. I was always sitting next to my father at the breakfast nook, a booth he had designed. Dick was on the other side of me away from Dad. Away but not *that* far away! Each parent sat on the end of parallel eight-foot benches. The table separated mother and sister on one side from father and sons on the other. It was a very functional system since under the benches was plenty of storage space for canned goods the family used, courtesy of the canning factory job.

The booth system allowed my father to dictate the terms of any meal. He dictated when a meal would start and when it would finish. In between were the educational moments, the news of the day, and the questions and answers. If Dick failed to deliver an appropriate response to a key question he would occasionally receive a backhanded blow to the side of the head. This was usually enough to keep me from screwing up, and my mother and sister would put their eyes down during the episode so they would not have to witness the brief moment of truth. Sister Donna was young enough to avoid all of this. She and Mom were on the opposite side of the table. It made her life easier.

For most of my life, and even as my older brother was in his last months of life, I tried to get him to tell me why he would not wear a freaking t-shirt to meals when he knew THE question would inevitably come. He would laugh and say something smart-ass. I now conclude it was a turf-war stemming from Dad's absence for two years or so in our young development. Dick was the "man" of the house back then, and upon Dad's return that all changed.

THE question came regularly during the long winter months. Dad would merely say to both of the boys on the bench with him, "Do you have a t-shirt on under your outside shirt or sweater?" This was of HUGE importance to my father. I, for one, never considered life without a t-shirt. To this very day I wear t-shirts of various colors under my shirts and sweaters as a regular routine.

Call it teenage rebellion, call it toughness, or call it stupidity— but Brother Dick would come *sans t-shirt* to many a meal. Many times during these meals, THE question would come out of father's mouth; and when the negative reply came from Dick he would get a backhand. Dismally, for me, I received the elbow in the chops connected to the arm delivering the backhand to Dick.

The education was clear for me and I don't think I appeared without a t-shirt.

Dad changed jobs upon being discharged from the navy. Much of this I contend now was due to the fact that he could not stand in the bank anymore and watch wealth come and go. He probably felt compelled to make his own career, and sales were something he found very dependent upon initiative and not standing and waiting.

His bank job did provide him with a great opportunity to

raise money once for a new organ for the Presbyterian Church. He only attended twice a year but in situations such as soliciting money he was a good member. I sat in the kitchen doing my homework one evening as I eavesdropped on my father's call to a rich local farmer about the need for a new organ for the church. The call was to the point. Dad said as a banker he knew the farmer was one of the wealthiest men in town. As a church member he knew the farmer could help the church. As mayor he merely said he knew the property assessments were probably too low on the man's land. Within three weeks, the church had all the money needed for a new organ. The farmer was the major donor.

My father's influence upon me was manifest despite the lack of "touchy-feely" moments.

As he made some of his last statements to me in Albuquerque, when I was in my thirties and he was five months away from his death, it seemed appropriate that we were all sitting in a booth. In this particular booth I *know* I must have had a t-shirt on. I am sure my oldest son Jeff, sitting in the booth next to my father, had one on also.

***

Tinkling the Ivories—A mother's wish

Mrs. DeSmith had two sons who learned how to play the piano, and after a negotiation with my mother she agreed to try to teach me how to tinkle the ivories. Although my mother was a great pianist she played by ear, which meant she did not read music but merely improvised songs from her innate ability to do such a thing. All who heard her play were in awe of this rare ability. I had heard her play often. She knew she needed to turn my career over to a formal teacher who could teach me music.

When I was in fifth grade, my piano career began at the DeSmith home. I knew David DeSmith and he had a great Hardy Boys collection he had purchased. David and I were in the same class so we hatched a deal. He allowed me to "rent" Hardy Boys books every time I had music lessons. The lessons were once a week so that gave me time in between lessons to read the two or three books I rented at a nickel apiece. I spent an inordinate amount of time reading about the Hardy Boys and did not spend much time practicing piano. If I was going to be confined to the indoors for something, reading seemed more interesting than piano.

My mother tried her best to create interest where there wasn't much. It was sad that my life as a pianist did not develop. It was clearly my own fault. Mrs. DeSmith was a good teacher and my mother was a great role model. She should have known she was fighting an uphill battle based upon some notable piano stories in my life with Isabel.

During the war years Isabel played the piano for the weekly Rotary Club meetings held in the Shannon boarding house on the end of High Street. She got meals for the three of us and some pay for this as the club met at the evening hour once a week. My Mom also worked at the Cotanche Drug Store during the war years as she struggled to make ends meet.

One night, when she was playing the piano for the Rotarians at the Shannon House, I came into the huge dining room where she was playing for the Rotarians. The men sang loudly as Isabel pounded out "Roll Out the Barrel." She did not miss a beat as I told her calmly that I had cut two of Dick's fingers off down the street at our rental home.

My mother's first response was to tell me not to kid her about something so gruesome. She tried to keep playing as the men kept singing. Finally the song ended, and Isabel excused herself from further playing so she could take me home. I was probably six and my brother was eleven. He had two bloody fingers dangling on his right hand. My mother saw them as soon as she made it with me back to our house. Her reaction was shock because Dick had placed his hand in the upstairs bathroom sink and filled it with cold water.

The sink was blood red and Dick was feeling poorly. He was crying and that made me start crying also. I was scared that he would be short two fingers. I was also afraid that Isabel would disown me.

We had been playing during her absence and our game had gotten away from both of us. Dick could torment me at times when he felt the urge. He started tormenting me by throwing things at me. Until I was about thirteen or so I would deal with the situation and try to stay at arm's length away from him when possible. On this particular evening, I grabbed a large kitchen knife and chased him around the house. He stopped throwing and ran. I had switched from defense to offense by merely picking up the kitchen knife.

During the chase I don't think it occurred to me that I could hurt him or myself. My intent was to merely turn the tables on the tormentor. I was now the tormentor. I had him trapped upstairs in the bathroom where he barricaded the door. After a few quiet minutes Dick opened the door a crack, and for whatever reason he slipped two fingers out through the crack to "test" for my presence. I was there with the knife and I sliced it through the air and at the crack with the fingers protruding. I hit flesh and bone and the two fingers started bleeding immediately. At age six I had performed my first armed attack.

My mother would have preferred that her sons had occupied their time with something other than a knife chase. As a pianist Mom could see the possibility of an elder three-fingered son trying to take future piano lessons to no avail, and the other son serving time in a juvenile detention center. She had been yanked from the cheerful, dynamic Rotary group up the street where they had been singing "Roll Out the Barrel." She had to come to a scene of crying sons and much blood. No one was rolling out any barrels on High Street.

Dick's fingers were stitched at the hospital just down the street, and Isabel was not able to return to the Rotary piano she enjoyed so much. Dick's fingers were going to be OK and he could have taken up piano if he wanted to, but that didn't happen. I did take up piano but let it slip. Many times have come and gone where I wish I had stayed the course and learned how to play the piano.

Late in my mother's life she sold our family home and moved into state-supported housing in nearby Newark, New York. The home she picked was a two-bedroom apartment on the second floor. It had no yard, no garage and no upkeep. For her at that stage of her life this was her best choice. She did have a piano, and played it often.

Once when I was visiting her at this new location, she told me to come over to the state home for the aged that was nearby. She played the piano for the group twice a week. Although Isabel was seventy-five, she told me she enjoyed going over there to play for the "old folks." I really enjoyed listening to my mother play the piano since her spectacular ability to play by ear mesmerized me.

As I came in that day, to a room full of people either watching or singing along with her as she played, I came over to tell her I was there. Without missing a beat she asked if I had tried to slice Dick's fingers off again.

***

Driving Miss Izzy- Travails of aiming

Isabel was taught to drive by her eldest son, Dick. Dick was the person assigned to the task because Dad was not at all interested in the project. Isabel figured that it was time to learn how to drive so she could be more self-reliant in the event that her husband became incapacitated. This was very logical of her, since at mid-century in America wives were outliving their husbands by ten to fifteen years. As it turned out, those actuary tables were accurate. My Mom outlived my Dad by eleven years.

Learning how to drive, after nearly fifty years of riding with others, was a sizeable task; and Dick deserved great credit for doing a yeomen job of driver's education. Isabel had to begin with some very basic lessons. The first day, Dick related, she merely sat in the car and refused to even put the keys in the ignition switch. She sat there learning the mirrors, shifting mechanism (automatic transmission), various controls in the car and even how to adjust the seat. She had tried working with the manual transmission on another car, but the magic of the clutch eluded her. It was automatic transmission or bust.

She finally drove after two days of sitting at the wheel in the street in front of the house. Dad had purchased a used Nash American, reasoning that due to its smallness it would be simpler for his wife. The car can only be seen in museums now, but the one Izzy drove was in a junkyard long ago. Since the car was very small, it was easy to park and get in and out of places. Dad was truly perceptive in this choice since she still hit things despite the car's size. She fell in love with her car, and after a week or so Isabel was ready for solo driving on our street. She made the appointment for the driver's test over in Lyons after driving with Dick on her learner's permit.

She went over for the test with high confidence, yet upon her return she brought with her news of a failing score. It was based upon several factors, and over the next few weeks she improved upon them. Her second test was successful and she became a licensed driver in New York State.

Isabel spent the rest of her life interpreting how driving should be in the village and wherever she drove. She always had her gas pumped for her so that was no problem. Garages back then usually came out and serviced the car as it was filled with gas. Isabel loved this aspect of life behind the wheel.

She loved the horn even more. As she traveled at a very slow speed through the community and in the county she would blow the horn at anyone she knew. It did not matter that a car may be in front of her as she spotted a friend on the sidewalk. I have ridden with her when she would blow the horn at a pedestrian on the sidewalk she knew. The person in the car in front of us appeared to get aggravated, yet got over his initial shock at hearing a horn at their rear bumper once he realized it was Isabel. Most knew her reputation.

My friends called her "Izzy the horn blower." I became "Stinky the horn blower" once I drove, because I had learned from the master horn blower of Sodus. Isabel did do a poor job of parking. When streets called for parallel parking, she merely double parked and went in some place. She did not want to parallel park, even though she did it in Lyons one time in order to pass the driving test.

In Sodus, at the time she started driving, there was diagonal parking on certain streets. She liked this but created some tight situations for others when she left plenty of room to open her driver's side door. This meant that the other side of her car was tight against the adjacent car's door of entry! People were more forgiving in that era. People usually knew enough to wait until Isabel moved her car.

Isabel created legends in her driving patterns. Her exploits with our own garage were legendary and are documented elsewhere. What seemed to occur frequently was that my mother would park somewhere in Sodus where a car had never been parked before. She opened up parking areas in a manner that would make Lewis and Clark proud.

She went early to places like school and church, so the sight of her car in unique places was commonplace. The drawback was that others couldn't unload, busses couldn't get in and other drivers started parking next to her. This created a completely new scheme for the particular situation.

Her car upkeep was left to Dick and Ivan Symonds, a nice neighbor who understood Isabel's inexperience. Between the two of them, Isabel's car was kept in driving condition. She did create problems for the car by virtue of her carefree attitude. She never expected a car to stop running. When her car did succumb to brief down periods, she was impatient for its return.

When Isabel drove other women around, and this happened often, they were all like teenagers on an excursion. It was a familiar sight to see three or four fifty to sixty year-old women riding around in Isabel's car. The laughter was noticeable. Other drivers gave the car a wide berth just for good measure.

The only new car Isabel ever received was after the death of my father. Her car was showing its age, and my father had a used car that was ready to be traded. My older brother and I went to the local Chevy dealer and negotiated a trade of the two used Pearson cars for two new Chevrolets. My mother got a Nova and she immediately fell in love with the vehicle. My younger brother got a Chevelle out of the arrangement. Charley was in college and never had a car. Isabel made sure that Charley got a new car during this bleak time for our family. Using the logic that Dad would have ultimately helped Charley get a car anyway, Isabel said to do it now.

Isabel enjoyed the new car but did not like that it was linked to my father's demise. We all helped her get over that as we reminded her that she did not get any cars from Dad for the first thirty years of their marriage. This seemed to help the matter. One of her first trips around town in her new car was to the cemetery, where she wanted to check on some flowers left on the grave of her husband. She parked for a short time in a key road as the two of us checked the flowers. Before we reached the gravesite, Isabel's car in the roadway had already held up a funeral procession going to a freshly dug grave past where Dad was buried.

Dad would have enjoyed that irony and the people in the procession were in no visible rush to hassle Isabel.

***

Field Daze- Firemen and frolic

The two men sat at the table with thousands of dollars lying there in front of them. It was the conclusion of another successful day with many more new "clients." Many of the previous clients had come through again and again, so that the profit margin was, again, very predictable.

I sat there, my eyes transfixed on the piles of money. There was about ten thousand dollars there, according to one of the men. Given that I was still making a dollar a day mowing lawns or fifty cents a day delivering newspapers for my brother, that small fortune in front of my father on our kitchen table was compelling. My father was treasurer for the volunteer firemen, and the other man helping my father count the money was a fellow volunteer fireman. He carried a handgun, and I had never seen that before either. All this culture shock was occurring in my family kitchen late one Saturday night early in my Sodus years.

The new clients were kids who lived in the area around Sodus. They had attended one or more of the four nights of the Sodus Fireman's Field Days. The previous clients were the older kids and the adults who had enjoyed the many rides, eaten the many treats, and tried their collective luck at table games and other events. In every case people had traveled to the field near the central school owned by the firemen. People came from all over the county and some ex-residents traveled many miles to share the experience with friends, who viewed the field days as the premier event of the summer in Sodus.

As my father and his friend counted the money and sacked it up for delivery to the bank they were very impressed with the take. The four days of the field days usually brought in a nice profit for the firemen. The money was used to upgrade the equipment and the firehouse in town. Saturday night was the biggest night and this particular Saturday must have been impressive, even to the treasurer and his friend. I am not sure if the ten thousand dollars represented the take for one night or for the whole four nights. Logically, since the money from the other nights could have been deposited in the bank on Thursday and Friday, this amount in our kitchen was probably Friday and Saturday money. The only bank in Sodus was not usually open on Saturday at the time of my kitchen money-viewing, so this ten thousand dollar effort was still sizeable by any means, even if it was two night's take.

I was allowed to watch from the doorway of the kitchen as the piles of money were scattered all over the breakfast nook. My only thought was about the money. That was more money than I could have ever imagined. Where did it all come from?

My father gave me the answers over time as his treasurer's duties continued over the years. He was originally a banker with Union Trust upon arriving in Sodus in 1936. After getting out of the navy in 1945, he did not return to the bank for very long. His knowledge of banking and money seemed to be the criteria for being treasurer of the firemen, so he persisted as treasurer for several years after leaving the banking business.

My father showed me the bills for the various set-up charges for the field days. He also showed me how the firemen made money on everything from rides to Belgium Waffles. As I asked questions, he either showed or told me the inner workings of field days. It was a mini-lesson in management. I reflect now that he prepared me very casually and very well for management of things in my professional career. As I supervised tourneys and races in my career in sport, the elements of management taught by my father were very helpful.

I consider the education invaluable. I also consider that too few children in the modern era get such lessons based upon real life events such as field days. The interest in field days or events such as carnivals, theme parks and Disneyworld is obviously still a strong thread extending through society today. What gets lost is the involvement of parents and their children with what goes on behind the scenes.

The fun and frolic of the field days of my youth was always tempered with the fact that it would happen once a year and I would be allowed to go to the field days on Saturday and one other night. Thursday night was parade night and Wednesday night was opening night, so those two nights were always appealing. I contend that in the modern era parents give and give and give with very few limitations on the purse-strings. In the modern era, kids would not be asked to consider limits, nor would they typically be told no. My father had no trouble saying no to me—and that was the end of the discussion.

As treasurer he spent his evenings each night right at the main entrance to the field. I did not try to attend the field days when my father knew the nights he had already authorized. My two nights at the event were probably plenty anyway, since money was involved every trip to the field. As I got older and wiser, it dawned on me to drop in on my Dad and see if he needed any food or drinks during his long hours in the administration office.

This became a great strategy, since I ended up getting food and drinks also. It allowed for me to be inside the main office where the money, guns, and action seemed to be. As I waited to get my father's food order I could help play band music on the record player, watch how quickly my father made change, and also hear radio reports filtering in about drunks in the Ladies Auxiliary tent who needed removing!

Recently, a friend at the college where I teach shared information with me he had heard at a meeting as part of a two-day conference he attended. One fact he heard there was that the average family of four went through almost $10,000 attending Disneyworld in Florida for a week. This included airfare, food, housing, admission costs and other related fees.

When my friend Mike told me that set of statistics, I realized from my personal experiences growing up what $10,000 actually looked like. I also knew that during my childhood everything was much cheaper and much less sophisticated. My parents could allow me two nights at the field days and would have to part with very little cash.

Sophistication in entertainment seems to have permeated the lives of our young people. My philosophical question on the matter would be along the lines of, "What will today's children do to top the entertainment of their youth"?

The enjoyment level at Fireman's Field Days was fine, in my opinion, even when I got the opportunity to go to Disneyworld. I knew Orlando was really nice, but I also knew my father wasn't there in the office waiting for me to come get his food order.

***

Plowed In—Snow comes and goes but plows are forever
The snow banks developed overnight as if by some giant's hand. Where the sidewalk met the street in front of our house a six foot high mound of snow appeared, as if by magic. The same scenario, unfortunately, would occur where our driveway met the street. The mounds of snow were the product of a giant truck with an angled plow driven by one of the village's employees. It was

winter in Wayne County, New York State; and a ten inch snowfall overnight led, invariably, to the huge snow banks up and down each street.

During the course of a typical winter the snowfalls and the linked plowings would call for an enormous physical effort in front of every home throughout the village. In retrospect, the numerous snow blowers of today would have been hot items in winters of the forties and fifties. We moved the snow piled in front of our house at the sidewalk and driveway entry points the old fashioned way. We shoveled it!

My older brother and I were the snow removal equipment at 20 High Street. We used shovels and often worked twice a day on days when the plow made two or more runs through the village streets. Sister Donna was not ready to do this work, and Charley was too late in our lives to make any impact on physical work such as snow shoveling. Two ironies about the younger members of the family come to mind. Donna has lived and still does in the snow belt of upstate New York, and she has done plenty of shoveling in her life. Charley lives in New Hampshire, and he too has had his share of snow removal. Theirs has not been an easy snow life in adulthood. By contrast I live in the Sun Belt, and nary a shovel for snow do I possess.

Other than the obvious snow-connected work related to my family home, there was plenty of fun-related work to be done every time the plows created the mounds. We spent an inordinate amount of time digging tunnels into the huge banks of snow. With a creative design a kid could dig into the huge mound from the house side of the pile and then extend a tunnel several feet at a right angle to the entry point. This could accommodate several people. The return of a plow on a street with tunnels facing the street could fill up the entry and create an unsafe proposition for little people. Usually the entry points were where moms inside in the warmth of the house could peer out to see the legs going in and out.

What was fun for many of us was to bring little sister or brother out of the houses and let them explore the tunnels. Invariably the little kids really enjoyed the snow dwelling. Often, when the wind was blowing and the snow was pounding into the exposed faces, the retreat into the snow cave arrangements made us feel like New York State Eskimos. A common condition appeared each winter on young faces. Ruddy complexions dominated. We really looked like Eskimos!

After a few days of using the tunnels and caves, we became bored with the whole deal; and hours of digging were discarded in a few fleeting minutes as we jumped on the tops of the mounds to collapse the tunnels. For some reason this was a joyous event, and I do not ever remember any of us lamenting the loss of our creation. We always knew there would be more mounds coming.

There were times when shoveling and plowing could not keep up with the snowfall. At those times the community became a cocoon of white. Each house became a bastion of warmth in the white, cold, blowing landscape. The winds would whistle and whine in the trees along the front and sides of the house. The drifts would grow by the hour. High winds would create interesting patterns in the new snow depending upon direction, duration and intensity.

School was closed by virtue of announcements made over the radio stations. School officials had identifying codes to use with radio stations in nearby Rochester so that official closings could be announced. The dream we had was to learn how to mimic the voice and use the code words of the principal and shut down the school on our terms. This never happened. When school was closed it was usually a time when the plows were overmatched by hourly snowfall amounts and by wind-driven, drifting snows. Half or more of the students in our central school were bused into the village from the rural areas surrounding the school. Buses were unable to operate where plows could not control the depth of the snow. This simple equation spelled out the rules for closure.

Out in the township, outside the village, the roads were difficult to keep open once the wind and snow combined to form a knockout punch of weather. Snow fences were strung along the fields twenty to forty feet away from the roads. These fences, erected on private land, would help create drifts close to the fences but away from the roads. This theory of wind and snow predictability seems to have worked in most cases. Huge drifts would build up just off the roads. In severe snow and winds, even this age-old tool did not stop the snow.

The closing of school was cause for celebration! We could dig tunnels. We could slide down the packed snow of the nearby steep streets. We could play indoor games when the cold and snow had made it through our winter outfits. A common sight was a dining room filled with boots, sweaters, coats, gloves, mittens, pants and other outdoor gear strung out over the hot air registers and on every piece of furniture. The smell of the outdoors came in with us. As I write this piece, I can vividly remember the particular odor of wet wool and snow melting onto the carpet.

In the winter world, once early morning shoveling was completed and we had to go to school, awareness stayed with us in school about what we might face upon returning home. Once school sports became a big part of our young lives, we faced the possibility of getting home tired from practice and facing the "gifts" from the plows delivered during the school day.

On days like that, we developed extra grit because we knew Dad would be rolling in from work looking for his spot to park off the street. Once Isabel began driving, she usually got the garage. On some mornings when the plows had covered the end of the driveway leading from the garage, Dad might say to leave the driveway alone. This was a relief. It meant less shoveling. It also meant that Mom was in for the snowy day. This was my Dad's design, since he had little faith in her newly acquired driving skills.

We opened up a spot off the street for Dad's car. This was our way of keeping the car off the street away from the plow. The sidewalk was easy to open since that needed just enough space for an adult to get to the sidewalk to deliver mail, milk, eggs or even gifts at Christmas time.

One day my mother convinced me she had to go out after my Dad had departed. Who could argue with the Queen of Sodus? My shovel allowed her an easy exit from the driveway. I went to play basketball that afternoon, and upon returning to High Street I saw Mom's car sitting in the street. She could not return to the infamous garage (she made it that way, not me) because the plows had covered the end of the driveway once again. OK. Here was the dilemma. If I cleared the snow again from the driveway, Dad would probably guess what had transpired. If the car stayed out there, where it was, I was in trouble because he would *know* what had transpired. That would be a clue for me to prepare for my discipline whatever form it took. My Dad was not a patient man, nor did he suffer from any Dr. Spock-related spare the rod remedies.

Something had to be done. In a heartbeat I had a vision of a daredevil answer to the problem I had helped create.

Clearing Dad's normal spot off the street for his anticipated arrival was a good move on my part. It was a good piece of work to have on my resume in the event the situation went sour. It also gave me a spot through which to drive Miss Isabel's car through toward the garage. Using a clock in the mind's eye, I would be coming into Dad's cleared spot at 4 o'clock and would be crossing the yard heading for a driveway area about where 12 o'clock is located. Once reaching 12 o'clock my task was to get the tires to "grab" on the exposed blacktop and then, with a left jerk of the wheel, would shoot into the garage located off the face of the clock straight out from the 12. I sized up the geometry and calculated I could get enough speed up coming from the street to go through where dad would park later. With enough momentum I could cross the yard where there was snow which had been kept from piling up due to the wind currents in the yard. My last and most critical maneuver would be upon reaching the driveway. I would be coming into the driveway at a severe angle from the yard. The ultimate move in pulling this all off would be to jerk the steering wheel to my left and initiate a controlled slide onto the driveway surface. I had cleared a spot where the wheels would hit according to this reckless plan. Then I would merely drive into the garage, shut the door, and get the hell inside the house.

Experts say teenage brains do not fully develop until twenty. I was just beginning my driving career at sixteen. Not realizing my brain was not functioning fully, I started to solve my problem. I started the Chevy and backed up to gather momentum. It was "Twelve O'Clock High" on High Street. And I was aiming at 12 o'clock in the driveway imagery. I had balls as big as grapefruit!

In a blur that I vividly remember to this day, the car went across Dad's parking spot, plowed through the open spaces in the yard, hit the driveway at the spot that had been cleared, jerked into a controlled slide, adjusted and then flew into the garage. I slammed on the brakes and barely nudged the front wall of the garage. It was the same wall that had already taken two severe hits from Isabel's curious driving patterns over the past several months. I had almost joined her in the wall demolition derby. The car was in the barn! I was sweating profusely.

It was over. The parking plan had worked! Feeling smug as departed the garage, I contemplated the three-foot wall on the side of the driveway away from the yard for the first time. What if the controlled slide and wheels-catching-on blacktop maneuver had not worked? Good God! The car certainly would have rolled over into the neighbor's yard, down the embankment. That, my friends, would have been vivid proof of my complicity with Isabel. That is why teenagers probably need a lot of guidance and driving lessons.

I closed the garage door and hustled inside, hoping Dad would not see tire tracks in the snow covered yard when he arrived in the darkened, wintry evening.

As I was removing my cold weather gear, I heard the plow go by.

When Dad arrived thirty minutes later I was shoveling snow where he was to park that night. Many of my shovels of snow were carried and thrown way up in the yard where, for some reason, there were tire tracks leading at an angle towards the driveway. He never saw them. The tire tracks were covered and the fresh snow covered the bare driveway "safety net" I had scraped for the careening Chevy. Isabel took the secret of her outing that day to her place in heaven. Gloomily, she missed my creative driving. Pathetically, I could not brag about the feat until much later. By then it had lost the excitement of the actual event.

Fortunately the plow provided for creativity in the snow in Sodus, one more time.

***

Victory at Sea- A family saga
During the fall of 1952 a television event brought our family together in a compelling manner. When "Victory at Sea" aired in half-hour segments on NBC television in our living room that year, my father set the rules and standards for viewing. He announced that the entire family would watch the much-advertised series each week. His reasoning was formed, in part, by his navy service during the Second World War. Despite his wishes to the contrary, Dad spent the two service years landlocked in Washington, D.C. after his basic training. His first wish was destroyer duty, since he loved the sea and wanted to be in the middle of the action. Other powers decided against the destroyer idea and sent him to Washington.

Other motivations for watching the program came from my father's inherent interest in history, and the series was a rich historical documentary. For twenty-six weeks the program explored the various sea battles that started after Pearl Harbor and commenced with the victories in the European and Asian theatres of war. Titles such as "Ring Around Rabaul," "Mare Nostrum," "Mediterranean Mosaic," and "Melanesian Nightmare" played themselves out right there in our living room week after week. My father would detail his knowledge of a particular program either before or after the viewing. We learned where Rabaul and Melanesia were, what the words Mare and Nostrum meant and how the sheer logistics of the whole World War II effort came about.

My mother sat and watched the series for the reasons of remembrance and respect over losses sustained by local families. She also watched and listened because she loved the Richard Rogers-composed musical score.

Once the program began, all else in the household came to a thirty minute halt. Homework was suspended and phone calls were very brief. Since I grew up hearing tales of the battles and regularly listening to the news, I was quite sophisticated for a teenager in my appreciation for the series. My prevailing thought about the whole series was that the voice of Leonard Graves narrating the program was astounding. Any other voice seemed to pale in comparison with Mr. Graves's voice.

The whole series was black and white and based primarily on combat photographers' efforts in every part of the world. There were scenes never seen before, and each segment caused the viewer to consider the insanity of war. Each scene also caused patriotic Americans to feel very proud and aware of the fact that we were a bastion of democracy. Those feelings from the "Victory at Sea" saga have remained with me through my whole life.

As I reflect upon the lessons learned during the dramatic programs there were many facts. I came to know names like Robert Russell Bennett (music arranger) and Robert Sarnoff (NBC coordinator) as their famous names flashed across our small screen each night. My father explained who these men were. It helped me understand the whole effort more completely. This sounds corny as heck, but when I watch TV now I look to see who narrates, and who directs, and who is responsible for music. It came from a detail-oriented father.

My father's detail work was documented most vividly after his death at the young age of sixty-two. As I went through his paperwork I found logs he had kept over the years on calendars. He had recorded temperatures, weather events, family events and even TV programs such as the Victory at Sea sagas. He felt his schedule was important, and he sure made that evident to those of us in the room. We watched and learned from the man who loved the Navy.

As an aside, another detail I ran across was his listing of salaries over his Sodus lifetime stretching back for thirty-five years. Amazingly, to me, his highest salary in any year was $21,000. I thought back then if I were to ever make a similar amount I would have it made. Guess what? I still work and I passed that high figure long ago. I have it made, but for reasons apart from financial.

Victory at Sea is available in black and white original form as a complete series. My wife purchased this for me a few years ago, and the replay of each of the segments in the six-VHS tapes brings back memories of events fifty years ago.

My mother would invariably make popcorn for the weekly event. I can almost sense the scent of popcorn as I hear the well-designed musical themes even now. This must be a crisscrossing of my sensual wires! As I thought about this episode in my life in Sodus, I know I was struggling then to become an adult. The things we did together were important. It is easy to see the impact of doing things together as a family.

My father sat there engrossed in the program, and we did the same out of respect for our leader. We developed greater respect for the Navy. We appreciated the enjoyment of being together in a warm, comfortable house.

Today when parents get caught up in a materialism that allows them to provide each child with his or her own room and their own TVs, the kids can choose any program they wish to view. Because of such modern largesse, families are drifting apart. My Dad had a different perspective. Although he made about $9,000 in 1952 when Victory at Sea commenced on NBC, we were very wealthy as a family. I learned about some of the hardships endured by some of the guys in Sodus who fought on Guadalcanal. This was good for me.

One of our family's best friends from back in the 1940s in Sodus was Emmett Keefe. He served in the Marine Corps on Guadalcanal, and my father had great respect for what Emmett did in his service to our country. Mr. Keefe contracted malaria in the jungle war and probably was never the same after returning to his farm in Sodus. When we watched the piece on Guadalcanal on Victory at Sea, my Dad told us to salute Emmett next time we saw him in a Memorial Day parade. The veterans like Emmett would walk in the annual parade, despite their ill-fitting uniforms. It made good sense to me to salute the man. It still does today. Thanks, Dad. Thanks, Emmett.

***

The Long Wait—A glove for the decade

The New York Yankees were very successful during the era when I became a baseball fan. My awareness of the Yankees began vividly in 1947. They were on TV, right in Sodus on the huge black and white sets in the English and Bouvia appliance store in the middle of Main Street, playing the Dodgers for the World Series title. The Red Sox won the American League pennant the year before but after that the Yankees won the league title every year after that from 1947 until 1959, except for two Cleveland titles in 1948 and 1954. I became a Yankee fan in 1947 because I could see them beating the Dodgers on TV in one of the best World Series championships ever played. I also like the fact that my Dad was a Yankee fan and we could share that excellence.

The Yankees won in six games in 1947, and the series bore witness to several key images. Al Gionfriddo made a great catch right there on TV in the store off a sure home run by everyone's hero Joe DiMaggio. The voice of Red Barber saying "Back, back, back, back, back goes Gionfriddo....he makes a one handed catch against the bullpen!" is a part of baseball history. I have a recording of the moment. I think I can remember seeing it on TV. I have seen it a dozen times since, so the memory is blurred. This was not a nice part of the series for Yankee fans because Joe was our guy. Other notable events were punctuated by the grace of Phil Rizzuto, the energy of Jackie Robinson (the first black man to play major league ball), the pitching of Bill Bevins, Hugh Casey and the class of Tommy Heinrich, as well as Yogi Berra's appearance for the first time as a Yankee.

I was a Yankee fan, and October life in upstate New York was great. Things stayed like that for me and the Yankees through this successful period, and I grew up proud of their accomplishments. Not until 1964, when Yogi was canned as manager, did I change my loyalties. Yogi came back after a long Yankee dry spell as manager again in the early eighties, and damned if they didn't can him again after just sixteen games of the 1986 season. My love affair with the Yankees was definitely dead. Yogi's bad treatment was too much for me!

The Red Sox were the Yankee haters of the past century, Babe Ruth having supposedly started the curse on the franchise. It was always intriguing to watch the rivalry then, as it is now. In 2003 the Red Sox almost pulled out the American League title, but the Damn Yankees prevailed again. All this Yankee–Red Sox stuff was critical to my development, because I played many years of Sodus baseball using a glove autographed by a Red Sox star. Ironically, as I rooted for the Yankees on TV and the radio and in our own living room, I was playing almost daily April through September with a Boston Red Sox/Bobby Doerr glove. No one knew this because I kept the glove close to me and always deposited it where the label was turned down. A Joe DiMaggio glove would have been much better, if one had been available in the store.

It was the 1947 series that convinced my father to get a TV set. It was the overpowering aura of Yankee baseball in the forties and fifties that energized me to work and play at baseball with my Red Sox glove. The irony was that I ended up with a Red Sox player's autographed model despite my allegiance. This all reminds me of a song about loving the one you are with at that moment.

The baseball glove I got was an autograph model infielder's glove with Bobby Doerr's name scrawled across the leather. Doerr played many years for the Boston Red Sox as an all-star second baseman during the 1940s and early 1950s. Despite the fact that I had pledged my allegiance to the Yankees in 1947, this glove was in Tallman's Hardware window, it was available, and the price of eight dollars seemed very possible. This was to be the first new glove I ever purchased. The anticipation was enormous in that particular spring. As I related the information to my father he listened with interest and then said to go ahead and make a deal for the glove at Tallman's. He advanced me two dollars toward the total purchase price and asked how much I had. The truth was that I had less than needed!

This was my first involvement with a "planned" purchase. I had two dollars of my own and had a predictable buck a week coming in from helping with my brother's paper route. I also had a weekly allowance pouring in of seventy-five cents. The income was projected and the cash on hand was four dollars. I went to Tallman's and held the glove as Bobby Doerr might have done in Fenway Park, waiting for ground balls and line drives. The feel of the new leather and the smell was unforgettable. There was but one dilemma. Mr. Tallman would give me the glove *after* I came up with the remaining four dollars and some cents. He promised to hold the glove and not sell it to anyone else. I would have to wait two weeks before I could get the glove.

Consider all the credit card and credit purchases of today in contrast with that eight dollar item! My father, who was the mayor of the village, had a great reputation for paying bills and living within his means. My Mom had made it through the war years in the 1940s when my Dad was gone by making ends meet working in the drug store just down the street from Tallman's hardware. There was no doubt in Mr. Tallman's mind that the Pearson kid would be good for the glove bill.

This was a great lesson offered up by my father and Mr. Tallman. Bobby Pearson, aspiring Yankee, would wait during the spring baseball season for the new glove until he could afford it! The glove remained in the window for a week and then it was finally removed from view and placed in a drawer. My deepest concern during the week in which it was still in the front window was that someone with the right amount of cash would get my glove.

I should not have worried since Mr. Tallman was a good businessman who kept his word. We had no written contract, and I don't remember any receipts. He knew a good risk when he saw it. The days went by and on at least two occasions I visited the store and put the glove on and pounded my fist into the glove. Anytime in my life that I ever put a baseball glove on, the vivid memory of waiting for the Doerr glove during my childhood comes flooding back.

The infielder's glove was eventually mine; and the old, ragged glove I had been using went by the wayside. In my mind I ventured the guess that I would certainly never, ever make an error on a ball hit within reach of the new glove. It took only a few minutes into the first season with new glove for me to botch a grounder or two, and even drop a sure line drive out. It seemed that I had learned my lessons about purchasing without credit, but still had to work on baseball fundamentals.

As I progressed through the years, my love of baseball never diminished, and eventually the Bobby Doerr glove became too small, too weatherbeaten and finally was discarded. By my fifteenth birthday my father bought a new glove for me and paid about eighteen dollars for it. The new glove was huge compared to the Doerr model. The Doerr glove became part of the collection of sporting goods in our back room where the dog slept. My first glove now became available for any backyard pickup game for anyone wanting to use it. Although I had the new glove, the old one came out on my hand in the backyard games. There was a thing about loyalty. Loyalty only went so far, however, as the old glove never reappeared in games out of our backyard!

Despite its downgrade from the frontline in the Sodus baseball wars, my Doerr model brought many fine memories and from its purchase came many interesting lessons. In today's rush to satisfy a child's every want (forget need), parents overlook easy lessons in management of money and appreciation of delayed gratification. All too often, a child gets what he or she wants immediately, as if this is an inalienable right. What the child then learns is that anything is available at any time. Sometimes this just is not possible and then all hell breaks lose. We now have a society based upon the premises of credit and instant acquisition of material things.

The glove acquisition taught me about appreciation and anticipation. I was really quite proud of myself as I paid off the glove and walked out of the store. The glove never left my sight for that whole summer and became a part of me in a way I shall never forget. As I grew older and still kept the anti-Yankee attitude, it now seems more appropriate to have had a Red Sox glove during those years. Yogi got screwed by the Yankees, and that was all I ever needed.

One of the best recent books about baseball involved a story about three Red Sox players making a trip ("The Teammates," by David Halberstram) to visit a dying Ted Williams in Florida. This trip from Boston to Florida by car is chronicled in the best selling book. The players making the trip were Dominic DiMaggio (Joe's brother), Johnny Pesky (a Red Sox coach even today) and a third ex-Red Sox, Bobby Doerr.

As I read the book I considered my meanderings through the travails of Yogi and the Yankees. I am now a come-lately fan of the Red Sox courtesy of younger brother Charley's influence. I am proud that Tallman's Hardware had the Doerr glove there for sale over fifty years ago and not some Yankee glove!

***

The Mortgage of the Century—6K and no interest

Isabel negotiated the best mortgage ever heard of in Wayne County. She was renting a home on High Street from the manager of the Red and White Food Market, who decided to move into his rental home in 1944 after selling his home located in a nearby community. This created a real problem for our family since Dad was off in the Navy and Mom had two hellions, aged 11 and 6.

The details were revealed in the fifties when the mortgage note was paid off and even by today's low interest loans the one Isabel structured was a beaut! When Dad paid off the note sometime during the fifties, he showed me the original and it was for $6,000 payable to Farley Porter. Farley Porter gave my mother the money to buy the house just up the street from our rental house and Ralph Gage, a local jewelry store owner, moved out of the house on High Street and bought a place just out of town. The $6,000 was evidently paid to Gage and the mortgage for the total was due to Porter after the war was over and Dad was home at zero percent interest! As Dad shared this information with me during my teenage years, the full impact of the deal was beyond my comprehension.

As I reflect on the deal fifty years later, I now realize that two men in the community gave a local woman with two small children a hell of a deal. This was a product of their kindness, the sudden relocation of the Red and White Store manager, the way people thought during the war years, and one other thing.

The other thing was the absolute appreciation of the woman called Isabel and her relationship in a small community with her neighbors. My mother was a cheerful, considerate, kind person who went way out of her way to help others. Her kindnesses were delivered almost up until the day she died. These two men engineered a purchase for our family that kept us on the same street and in the same community for the duration of the war. Our family was not disrupted in any way other than the move two houses up and across the street.

I vaguely remember many people helping move our belongings from one house to the other. It was accomplished in a short time period, because I remember sleeping in the "new" house the day we moved. As I read about families lifted up and moved many miles and cities away during war times for a variety of reasons, this particular move in Sodus was really accomplished in a stress-less manner.

Some of the events during that time are now memories associated with sights and smells. The neighbors across the street from our original rental home on the street did laundry for my mother, since mother worked two or three jobs and we did not own a washer or drier. My mother paid so much per week to get the bulk of the laundry done under the circumstances. On some occasions I recall a clothesline behind our house during the rental time, with sheets flapping in the wind. I surmise Mom did sheets on her own and the smell of the bedding coming in from the line is still vivid.

During winter the sheets had a freshness unduplicated in any other season. During the fall the sheets picked up the smell of burning leaves. The laundry coming back across the street weekly had a story also. The Heiss family doing the laundry for us loved cooking with onions. The laundry was always saturated with the smells of the Heiss kitchen, where our laundry piled up in baskets waiting to be picked up by the Pearson kids.

My mother worked as a piano player for the local Rotary Club meetings once a week at night and for an occasional noon meeting. She worked at one of the local drug stores (Cotanches) and although they did not have the Rexall brands nor did they have all the regional and state papers like the competitors, it still became a second home for us after school. Many times I would go into the back of the counter area where my mother worked the ice cream and sandwich trade. Upon arriving after school, a sandwich and a drink would be available for me. I usually finished off the egg salad or tuna salad from the lunch menu and that held me until supper at six or seven. My brother would join me often, but because he was five years my elder he often had other things to do after school. Sometimes these things were associated with a paper route or lawn mowing/snow shoveling jobs. As I reflect on this pattern now, Isabel merely wanted to know where I was. She also wanted to know Dick was productive.

During the war years the story of Rosie the Riveter was told and retold in America. Isabel was not a riveter, but her third job that I recall was important. She would walk up the long street called Orchard Terrace and sit in a civilian defense trailer at the top of the hill. There she looked out of the windows for airplane activity. During the war there was a fear that the Germans or Japanese might mount some kind of air attack and a phone located in the trailer served as a link with a network of such observation positions across America.

Historians now tell us no air attack ever materialized, but my mother sure knew the profiles of the enemy planes appearing on charts in the trailer. Later, during the Cold War, the same trailer served for a time as an observation post again. This time, the planes on the charts were bigger and were Russian.

There were times when my mother had to have the patience of

a saint due to the constant juggling of kids, jobs, laundry and meals. Although the purchase of the dream house was a solution to the laundry issue it also was a big responsibility. The benefits of laundry room and our first home grown washing and drying were negated somewhat when we managed the huge yard surrounding the house.

Mowing and shoveling now became bigger issues than they were in the rental house with a small yard and very little sidewalk. Another by-product of the one hundred year old, two story house was that rent money did not cover water and heat as before. The house was expensive to maintain compared to a rental unit. We managed by virtue of Isabel's support, navy money coming home, and some creative trading of services. The guy who had the mortgage on the house also delivered eggs to our home. He had permission to pick flowers and lilac blossoms for his wife in exchange for the eggs. Mr. Gage had left us a beautifully landscaped yard with a little bird pool and many seasonal offerings growing in abundant color in the yard. It took us about a decade to turn the scene into an average, upstate New York yard.

We often kidded our little sister that Farley was her real father and the proof was that we got eggs from him. This was certainly not the case, as Isabel was a saint and Farley was harmless. Once the mortgage was paid off we rarely saw Mr. Porter, and his chapter in our war years was over.

The house on High Street stayed in our family from 1944 until 1974, at which time my mother sold the house for $20,000 to a young family. Her sense of community was still intact. She could have sold the house for much more, as the location and thirty year's appreciation would seem to dictate.

Her decision at the time, over the protests of others, was that it was a great deal in 1944, and she wanted to honor that spirit by "helping" a young family. Having lived through the original deal I could see the internal logic connected to a special community. There was a time when people helped one another, and business deals were done with emotion and empathy.

***

Brother's Training Camp—Dick was a dictator

After carefully attaching the rope around the victim's neck and fixing the device below so that the noose pulled tightly but not enough to cause strangling and or neck-breaking functions, the posse rode away down the road. Their job was done and now all that it took was for a loss of balance to start the inevitable final struggle against the rope.

Was this a passage out of a western pulp magazine? Was this a scene from a Saturday western at the local movie theatre? No. This was a scene played out in front of a neighbor's house on High Street where I grew up. I was the "hangee" in this case, and older brother Dick and two of his friends were the hangers. This was not about cattle rustling or a ranch dispute. This matter of a "lynching" was about the older brother and his two cronies being fed up with a younger brother following them around all day. The "posse" rode off down the street on their bikes, and I was left seated on my bike balanced under the tree with the rope around my neck.

At the point in the hanging where the perpetrators disappeared over the horizon, my mother appeared as if on a white horse and released my rope and gave me her vow of revenge upon my older brother. It seems that a neighbor lady had called her to inform her of the occurrence at our version of Owl Creek Bridge. Although she was visibly upset at what had happened, Isabel was unable to seek immediate retribution since she had to wait for Dick to return home before dealing with him.

This hanging event was an escalation of the normal big brother harassment I had come to know. I had been directed to do things that were not good for me or others, but this was to be different. I had peed on electric fences at older brother's direction. Up until now, that was the trump card of abuse. The hanging changed me!

I was so energized at having been given a new lease on my life that I vowed to ride my bike down to the nearby Orbakers ice cream place where the lynch mob was predictably celebrating their recent hanging. Their enjoyment of ice cream without the presence of little brother was to have been their reward for "tying" me up with other things. Their enjoyment was to be short-lived.

In a rare, new initiative for me at a young age, something propelled me with fervor to the ice cream stand. I was pissed off, and as my pedals pumped with all my might I could hardly wait to get there to confront the posse, knowing that I now commanded the trump cards. One, they would not harm me in the ice cream place. Two, Dick and the boys were now aware that Isabel knew first-hand what had happened and that would spell trouble for them. Thirdly, something stirred in me as a result of their actions. That new feeling seemed to empower me in a way I did not understand. It was to be my open rejection of having to be friends with my big brother and I was eager to tell him. The near-hanging caused me to see that.

As his younger brother by five years, I was viewed by Dick with suspicion, and he gave me a real hard time. Without a father at home due to the military service, Dick had semi-free reign as big boy of the house. From the age of five to seven I was victimized by him when Mom was not around. He wanted to be man of the house, but he did not wear the mantle well. Nor did he deserve to wear it, due to his temper.

Although the hanging took place after the war years and when Dad was around in between travels for his job, Dick still was a rebel of sorts. I think Dick and his buddies thought that by loosely tying my hands in front of me and propping me on the seat of my Montgomery Ward bike parked against the tree trunk I would be okay—despite the noose around my neck. The near-hanging did become a turning point in my young life.

As I sat there ignoring the older boys at Orbakers, after my hectic ride to be there when they were still there, my ice cream seemed to taste better. They were all in trouble because by now Isabel would have phoned each mother involved with the posse and they would get their brand of punishment. They could not quite figure how I had the nerve to show up, nor did they understand the power of an outraged mother, however long they tried to avoid the penalty phase of this engagement.

Dick went on to other scrapes with Dad and Mom which, upon reflection, make me think there was something else in all of this pattern that would have a name today. His public hanging of me brought with it some stern rebukes and also a loss of my potential friendship for a period of time. His little brother had other fish to fry, and they would be more fun and tastier than an older brother with a grudge.

As I think about the incident now, and even as I talked it over with him many years later, the whole thing was really stupid. The "safe hang," as it was referred to then, would be troubling to others; and he admitted frustration at my constant presence when he wanted to be with his peers. He also admitted that he was chagrined by it, since it did depict him and his two buddies in bad light for some time afterwards. Another offshoot of the whole matter was the development of compassion for younger kids, whether they were my siblings or other kids. I welcomed friendly little followers when they appeared.

Personality development can be assisted by less than perfect situations in childhood. All events in childhood don't have to be success stories. Development of various good traits coming from difficult times can be chronicled in many lives. Brother Dick probably helped me in ways he could not have imagined. At the same time, he was losing some momentum of his own during that time as he tried to pick on me.

My brother would find ways to create havoc for me. It never dawned on me that such havoc could work both ways until the hanging. After the event Dick's rascal behavior involved getting me into activities less often. Whereas I would do things rather blindly under his watchful eye, previously things were different.

Dick went on to his own choices, and he fathered four beautiful children. Each of them was there for him when he was terminally ill. Each of them became a success in their own lives. I was there with them for my brother when he was ill. I got beyond the hanging, and came back to win over the posse—and their leader.

***

Star Dreams—Planning ahead

Star Super Market came to Sodus as a replacement for what was called the Hart Market and then changed to something else over the years. When I got my first position as a bag boy and stock boy, I became aware of the importance of timeliness and work effort. The timeliness thing came quite rapidly, since this was my first experience with an actual time clock and I had to punch in each day I worked. The work effort was very visible since empty shelves stood out like, well, empty shelves. I discovered I enjoyed doing work like this since one could see progress.

The Star manager was a nice, older man named Mr. Clyde Dick. Mr. Dick came to me one day when I was in the store and asked if I would like to work several hours a week during the summer. I had never been solicited for employment ever before (other than by parents at home); so this event stands out as remarkable. My guess is Isabel mentioned my work ethic to Mr. Dick and that swung the decision my way. Another key factor was that Isabel probably suggested this option to Mr. Dick because she wanted to see me busy during the upcoming summer.

As the reader knows, I had an older brother named Dick; so when I heard that the manager's name was Dick this seemed to be too interesting to pass up. Mr. Dick was a hell of a lot nicer to me at this stage than was older brother Dick. One took great pleasure in tormenting me, and the other took great pains to treat me with patience and respect. This impressed me about the manager and it made me want to work hard.

This early lesson in management style has stood the test of time. If a boss treats employees with respect and consideration for each employee's needs, the work place can be influenced mightily. I learned this in my first summer of hourly employment. I had mowed lawns, shoveled snow and delivered papers for money prior to the market job, but had never seen the money accumulate by being at a place hour after hour. I was thirteen years old and was registered with the social security people. I was in the big time! By doing the math I can calculate that this first hourly position occurred fifty-two years ago! I also can reflect that I have not worked for hourly pay very much in my life since then. Calculating the jobs I have had since the market job I probably should have settled upon hourly pay over the years, since I have worked my share of seventy-hour work-weeks on a set contract.

As I developed into my prime as a bag boy and stock boy, many things came to me in the form of experience. The idea of double bagging made sense very early in my career as a paper bag split apart right on Main Street in the middle of a summer rain storm. I was carrying two bags for a neighbor lady and my embarrassment was profound as canned goods and other items in the bag rolled all over the street and into traffic. After retrieving the items and going back after more bags to repack the items scattered that day, I became very deliberate in the double bag realm in all future bagging. Even today, I double bag garbage out of the summer experience five decades ago.

Another fine lesson was the cultural immersion into Wayne County society in the summer months. Migrant workers shopped on weekends after getting paid, and their groceries were carried (or rolled out—another great application of experience)to their vehicles just like everyone else's groceries. I rather enjoyed this experience, since it took me out of the store. For reasons relating to my mother's lessons about kindness and tolerance, I was never hesitant to carry groceries for anyone.

Sometimes carrying groceries for a migrant worker meant loading up two carts, since one shopper may have been shopping for a dozen people back at the migrant camp. Unloading the bags at the vehicle from the two carts then meant unloading numerous bags into the rear of a pickup truck, or even a flatbed truck occupied by many of the workers. For whatever reason, this was not intimidating to me even though fellow baggers reported to me that they were uneasy with this duty. I went from the market to a job as checker in the orchards when I was older and had to work very closely with migrant workers.

The Star Market set up a lunch rotation of baggers like me so that there would always be a bagger or two in the store at all times. I usually managed to arrange my lunch well after the normal lunch hour. I did not want to go eat lunch at 11:00 AM through 12:30PM, because that seemed to be too close to breakfast and left too much of the day to work. My lunch break would often come at 1:00 or even 1:30PM, when Mr. Dick would come around to say he had noticed I had not checked out for lunch yet. Upon returning to the store after my late lunch, I had only three hours or even less left in my work day. This appealed to my sense of organization.

When I commenced my teaching and coaching career, I seemed to follow the same instincts. I did plenty of work early so that I could be ready for the remainder of the day. This seems to have worked over the years, since I am usually prepared for the unexpected by virtue of having done more than was expected earlier.

In my college years, I ran across a teacher whose name was E. Curtiss Gaylord. It turned out E. Curtiss was a Sodus native who had left to get his schooling and after traveling around he had settled in Brockport, N.Y. Brockport was about eighty miles from Sodus, so he still knew much of what had happened in his home town. Dr. Gaylord left an impression on all he met; he was one of life's unique characters. Whether it was love or hate, people remembered him. I liked the man and saw beyond his eccentricities. Others saw him in a different light since he often challenged one's thinking and often concluded with a statement about certain individuals being "dull tools" or "being unable to let the facts influence their decisions." He could be abrasive but was kind to most.

When Gaylord and I crossed paths, he was the assistant soccer coach at Brockport State and taught health classes. I related the Star Market story to him once when we were talking about work ethic. In telling him I enjoyed doing more than was expected, especially in the mornings on the time clock, he was quickly engaged in my story.

He related the story of his experience in the same home town we shared when he worked at the Red and White—a store bought out in the early sixties. He said he used to work extra hours in the mornings so he could get out of work in the afternoons. He also reminded me that his family name was on a street in Sodus and I could not claim that! My buddy Gib and his family lived on Gaylord Street for many years.

Gaylord's Sodus tale was interesting because we shared the same value about the morning efforts. He then told me of a word he had discovered in his travels. The word was *lagniappe*. The word refers to the act of giving or doing more than is expected. I have taught the word to various students over the years and each time I think of Gaylord, Sodus, and grocery store experiences.

Although Gaylord practiced a very healthy life style and lectured others about the need for scientific nutrition, he succumbed to a heart attack while playing racquetball at Brockport. He was only 47 at the time. His death gave all of his ex-students a brief brush with mortality. We reasoned that if he practiced an excellent life style and still croaked that young, what chance did we have in the midst of our hamburgers, fries and grease-filled lives?

Gaylord told me he had learned the word lagniappe from a store owner in Sodus who had traveled to the Gulf States and New Orleans where lagniappe seems to have originated.

I don't know if Star manager old Clyde Dick was around when E. Curtiss Gaylord was in Sodus but I do know the Red and White manager was. He was the same man who rented his house for several years to my family when we lived on High Street. The longer one lives, the clearer it becomes that paths cross in interesting ways if you are around long enough. Could the Red and White manager have taught the unique word to Gaylord? I will never know. All the parties are gone but they were probably there at a similar time and place and Gaylord did tell me he worked for that market.

My Star Market experience shaped my life-long work attitudes. Clyde Dick treated me in a fair manner and solicited me as a worker. That does not happen many times in one's life. Usually a person has to apply and go through that process involving resumes, interviews and references and then land a job. After being hired by Mr. Dick, I gave my best and developed the lagniappe thing. Although I didn't connect that particular word to what I had subscribed to in my early life at Star, it was evident once Dr. Gaylord explained it to me.

***

Organ Grinder—Can you spare some change?

"Preposterous!" My father uttered the word twice. I knew I was privy to Sodus inside info that would be interesting. I was in the kitchen doing my homework, listening to my father on the family telephone that was nestled in the corner of the dining room. Its location made it possible to sit about anywhere in the downstairs and eavesdrop on any conversation. This was nice when the tables were turned on my father or other family members because usually they absorbed every response of mine when certain "personal" calls came and went from the 5311 phone number. When I consider the mobility of modern phones I envy the modern teenagers since they can speak what I was forced to whisper into the common phone.

Fortunately for me this time I was only six strides away from where my father sat, talking to one of the wealthy farmers of Sodus. Those in the living room were another few steps away and I am sure they were waiting for the punch-line on the current phone call. My Dad was a treasurer in the fire department hierarchy of volunteers, served as mayor of the village and now had just taken on a task for the Presbyterian Church in town. As the operative word in the call progressed from "preposterous" to "bullshit" we heard the church mentioned, so all of us in the intelligence gathering system were hot onto something juicy.

The guy my father had called was a wealthy farmer living along the Lake Road in Sodus and was a regular member of the Presbyterian Church. My father was soliciting money on behalf of Rev. Sapher at the church. Sapher's son was Ed Sapher, a classmate of ours who moved away our senior year, when his father took another church. Before their family move, Sapher Sr. and my father made an unusual alliance in the community. The Reverend was a tall, quiet man of fine oratory abilities, but not a politician underneath the robes. In stark contrast, my father attended church about twice each year with an occasional third visit just to provoke some of the critics that labeled him an Easter/Christmas type of guy. He was a politician and was used to making things happen. I still have a photo of the two men together in front of a sign the two of them promoted on the outskirts of the village welcoming people to "Sodus—Famous for Cherries."

Sapher told my father that the church needed a new organ. At the time I think the cost was fifteen to twenty thousand. My father was appointed the chairperson of a committee to raise the money. Dad's idea of raising money was to call the most influential and one of the wealthiest persons in the church. The word "preposterous" must have been in response to the farmer's refusal to buy the new organ. The gist of the appeal, as far as I remember, was for the farmer to *buy* the organ entirely, right then and there, for the church.

The word "bullshit" was next when the man professed that crops were poor and money was tight. My father related to the man that he (my father) used to work in the Union Trust Bank and had seen the man's account information a few years ago. Pete knew the man could afford the entire cost of the organ, and furthermore, people in the church should know this fact.

I know the church got a new organ soon after that call. My father came to my study area that night and told me how he reasoned our wealthy neighbor could afford the donation. My father wanted me to know that he had not been unduly harsh on the man, since everyone knew the man could afford whatever he gave. Whether the farmer footed the whole bill I never knew, but Dad certainly made the first call on the matter really pay off!

In Sodus the volunteerism was impressive fifty years ago. I would only hope the current citizens have the same ethic that was prevalent back then. My father volunteered to raise money for an organ he heard twice a year and figured the best way to do the deed was to get a man who heard it regularly to make the campaign successful.

My father's direct and gruff way of accomplishing things was part of his personality. My mother, by contrast, was completely different. When Isabel heard the blunt appeal to the donor's bankroll she felt my father had gone too far in pressuring the man that night. I could see both sides of the matter, and realize that either of my parents could have solicited the needed funds from the man that night. Isabel would have accomplished it without tying up the phone. She would have driven to his farm and spoken to the man's wife.

***

Igloo Life- Charley's new home

Igloos were cool. When we first saw pictures of igloos and read stories of the Eskimos living through the winter months in igloos, we were fascinated. The potential for creating an igloo was always present in Sodus during the winter months. The expertise was missing from any igloo development, but several of us had all winter to gain the needed engineering abilities. It took us several attempts, but we finally got the arched roofline by using wooden boards as pillars.

When the igloo issue arose, there was no plan to place my brother Charley in the thing for any period of time. Nor was there prior knowledge that the entrance would get blocked by a plow when the builders went away for a short time. Who knows where we were? Critically, we weren't there when we should have been. As it turns out we all were lucky. Charley was about two at the time and he looked like an Eskimo child once he bundled up in his little parka and boots. He went out often, since he loved the snow and would be very eager to join the older boys.

In the dynamics of constructing an igloo, it is vital to have a couple of flat metal, square snow shovels. This type of shovel allows for making neat, cube-like snow blocks for an igloo. Making the walls at the bottom was easy, and after a couple of hours the circular form was evident. Getting the roof on the igloo was the challenge. Not knowing how the Eskimos did it hampered our efforts. In all the pictures of igloos seen in the National Geographic Magazines collected by Grandfather Pearson over the years, no mention of roofing an igloo ever was mentioned.

Some of the boys on the street had fathers who were handy with wood, and in their cellars were found enough pieces of wood to serve as a frame for the roof of our igloo. Cellars were standard fare in New York State and were critical during the winter months. Garages and barns were freezing cold, but a cellar was usually warmed by the furnace going full blast all winter. My friends worked over the boards in the cellars to get them to the appropriate size and we then fit them into the top of the igloo.

After the boards went on, the shovels worked on the last pieces of cubed snow. These were set in place on the boards. The boards lacked the igloo curvature seen in the magazines but they held all the snow needed for a great roof.

Part of our igloo faced the street and utilized a huge snow bank built up over days of plowing. The front of the igloo had a door hacked out of the bank.

As little Charley ventured out into the snow to play he knew there was something out there that had been an object of a lot of work over the day. He probably had been watching out the front windows of the two story house, and eagerly awaited his chance to see the igloo for himself.

Charley was a cherub that tagged along. My friends and I enjoyed having him with us, and several times Charley helped us actually make contact with those of the opposite sex. He was a chick-magnet, as they say in the modern era. On the day of the igloo, Charley was out in front looking for Eskimos. We were not looking for chicks, or we would have watched him a bit closer.

The streets and snow of Sodus were playgrounds for us all, but the street part required some attention to traffic and plows. Charley crawled into the opening of the igloo and set up camp in the newly constructed house. We lacked adequate supervision for a two year old kid; a plow came along and piled a mound of new snow over the entrance to the igloo.

Was Charley still in there or was he already in the house? No one remembered seeing him go inside the real house. We knew he was seen in the Eskimo house. After the plow went away, we scouted the igloo for the two year old. He responded to our voices and we tunneled back into the igloo from the street. He was happy as could be just sitting there eating snow. Thankfully, he had not ventured out as the plow was passing by the igloo.

As we all went our separate ways and Charley and I went inside, Isabel was happy to see her little snowman. She did not know the little snowman had been sealed away in the igloo out in front of the house. Since he could not describe the impact of what had just happened, I sure wasn't about to do the honors for my mother. By writing this I feel this is a way of getting the guilt off my chest for allowing my little chick-magnet to get snowed in on my watch.

***

Donna's Curiosity—No heat, much noise

Sister Donna was popped into the world of Sodus as a beauty who was also the first female child after two boys. She was patient with her situation over the years despite a lack of privacy and a small house.

Within five months of her birth, she was moved from the parent's bedroom upstairs in the one hundred year old house on High Street to the upstairs hallway between the only two bedrooms in the house. Everyone coming and going to the only bathroom in the house then would have to pass by the crib holding sister Donna. Since there were two boys and two adults sharing this small, seasonably cold space, this became a trick to keep from waking her at those times dictated by bladders, bowels, and, in brother Dick's case, visits to the bathroom to do his hormonally-driven reading.

The only bathroom in the house was also the only heated area upstairs, due to the combined magic of an old, inadequate heating system and my father's Spartan view that the bedrooms did not need heat. The heated bathroom became the reading room, the comfort room and the only reasonable place upstairs from November until late March due to the severity of upstate New York winters. As one might imagine, every night was very interesting as the people and things going bump in the night upstairs combined with the runs past Donna to the heated sanctuary. Donna would rise up in her curious infant mode and no doubt wonder, however infants do that, what the heck was going on upstairs. From her bedtime at about 7:30 PM until midnight, depending upon all the other schedules, Donna would bear witness to some weird looking people dashing to and fro. Since there was no heat upstairs and one could often see one's breath at night up there, people did not dawdle as they scurried past Donna's crib.

After Donna reached an age where she could consume wafers, candy, crackers and other morsels, Dick and I would toss food into the crib, as any big brother should, *en route* to the heat. This would prevent an outcry from the little gal and keep the late evening unfettered by having to rock her back to sleep. Sometimes Dick would have to develop more sophistication in this delivery system since he was trying to keep Donna very quiet for his own teenage reasons. It probably is a miracle that Donna did not gain huge amounts of weight from all this early-age bed feeding. After a few years of all the family living upstairs, Dad developed plans for an addition for Mom and him downstairs.

This became a priority when it was learned that another baby was coming early in the 1950s. The upstairs would not hold the next act, and after the fourth child (named Charley when the gender was discovered the old fashioned way) things upstairs went bump in the night much less often. The downstairs would house the parents and the new kid on the block. The new kid on the block would enter Sodus amid much tittering among the local ladies, since Mom was 45 at the birth of the wonder kid. The upstairs was changed forever!

Events would finally find Donna in charge of her own room after her sixth birthday. By then Dick was out of there for all intents and purposes as he meandered through college (three semesters), the working world, the army, and then his own career as a parent with cold bedrooms and four kids. Donna developed her own style in her semi-privacy upstairs. One must remember that the lone upstairs bathroom still serviced two different genders despite the new downstairs annex with its own bathroom. The difference in gender became a source of new information for me as I developed into manhood. Donna was a princess (some friends called her "Queenie") who took much time getting everything together in the morning as befitting an attractive, dark-haired young girl. She taught me early on that beauty does, in fact, take longer for girls. In my advanced life I now most assuredly know this. This factor is very pronounced in married women. This includes a notable married woman such as my wife. I thank my sister for helping me learn this lesson very early on as I froze my buns waiting for her to exit the steam room called the upstairs bathroom.

It became steamy when all the hot water was used up (downstairs also used hot water!) and baths, showers and hair lingered. Thank you, Donna, for the hard lessons, because they made me tough enough for married life. Donna went on to have two beautiful, intelligent children unaffected by genetic links to cold upstairs conditions, long steam baths, and three very different brothers spread over eighteen years.

***

Breakfast at the Lean-To-Meals under glass

The family cat slowly moved around and stretched as cats do. The back arched in the air and then the front paws extended out in front. Fluffy held each stretch for fifteen seconds or so before settling into a new curled position on the shelf in front of the windows in the kitchen. The sun was pouring in and despite an outside temperature of twenty or so the cat was toasty and warm. She was right there in the middle of the kitchen and her life.

The cat spent most of her hours in the kitchen. Why not? This was where Isabel fed her a steady diet of table scraps, cottage cheese, cheese, some assorted cat food and then, once a month or so, fish. The cat was very plump and contented as could be. Our kitchen was essentially a lean-to attached to the one hundred year old square house on High Street. It was a two storey house and the lean-to served as the kitchen, main eating area, social area, study hall, card table—and cat nap area.

In winter the frozen landscape called our back yard was a dazzling white whenever the sun broke through the grey that often dominated. The windows in the kitchen were frosted over regularly due to high inside temperatures, driven even higher than the rest of the house because of the oven and stove top from which endless amounts of food appeared.

Our family ate all meals there except for some Sunday meals and the big holiday meals associated with Christmas and Thanksgiving. The nook built into half of the kitchen dominated and allowed as many as six people to sit on each side. Under normal conditions, the sitting areas easily handled a family of six and whatever friends were there eating with us.

Fluffy would spend hours in the kitchen sleeping and then at meal time she would merely sit and watch us eat, knowing that at the conclusion of the meal she would reap a harvest of leftovers. At times she would merely stare at the family eating at the table and slightly below her elevated perch on the shelf. It now seems uncanny that we allowed a cat so close to the food and the preparation area, but at the time I never thought anything of it.

The lean-to kitchen was warm, cozy and usually friendly. During times of report card shortcomings, absence of T-shirts in the winter, or any infraction recorded on my father's enormous radar screen, the nook became a jury room and a judge's bench. Food was incidental at those particular times since the jury deliberations and the judge's ruling were accomplished swiftly, which cut off conversation and usually diminished one's appetite. My father was the jury and judge in almost every case tried before the family in the lean-to. In that roll he was the unchallenged authority. There were no appeals on cases heard in the lean-to.

If mother felt something needed to be stated, she would usually pick a time after the storm of the decision had subsided. Her best moves would occur during a dessert course while my father was deeply engaged in a piece of pie with vanilla ice cream on it. She gauged correctly that he was more apt to listen to the appeal, and during these times she successfully accomplished the appeal process on behalf of one of her offspring. My mother should have been a United Nations peacekeeper. Her skills in dealing with certain cases that were seemingly lost were memorable.

I would guess one of her greatest reversals of Pete's prior rulings was when she got my older brother Dick a lighter sentence by using her sister Doris, our aunt, as a substitute for part of the penalty. Isabel told my father that Doris wanted Dick to come to nearby Rochester and do work to help her husband with some chores. Dad seemed to buy into that.

After all was said and done, Isabel then called Aunt Doris to see if they needed Dick because Dick really needed them. Such was the magic of the Queen of Sodus.

Breakfasts were certainly the premier meal of every day, always accompanied by the rising sun coming in the northeast-facing windows. Other meals were not as fortunate; the evening meals six months a year were during the times when it was dark outside. The morning scene was usually an artistic delight since temperatures during winter months overnight could plummet below zero. Sitting there with the cat and with the brightness coming through frozen windows was a unique experience. Any breakfast with Isabel involved choices galore since she loved preparing food and loved stuffing her kids and loved the cat.

There might be pancakes, eggs, bacon, toast, oatmeal and dry cereal at any given breakfast. The dry cereal became her trademark in an era when dry cereal choices were numbered in the low teens in stores. Nowadays there must be one hundred different cereals. Isabel solved that fifty years early. She merely concocted "new" cereals by virtue of mixing the remnants of four or five nearly empty boxes into one box. You may have seen Cheerios on the box, but when you poured the contents out you may very well get Wheaties, Cheerios, Corn Flakes and Pep. Yes, Pep was a cereal for sometime, and when mixed with the others it was a tasty delight. Even today I will mix cereals in the same manner as my mother.

When I do the mixing it brings back a flash of kitchen memories. My wife thinks I am nuts, and she probably is correct. I enjoy the mixing of the cereals and sit there contemplating my next great batch. With all the individual choices in the modern era, the mixed choices are endless.

One day during the recent winter months in Georgia, when our temperatures dipped into the single digits, I was sitting at the kitchen table reflecting upon my cereal mix, courtesy of Isabel's training in the lean-to. I was looking at our kitchen windows and the interesting design created from our low overnight temperatures. My memory flooded back to the warm winter mornings fifty years ago. Just as I sat there looking and thinking of all this, a cat we were baby-sitting for our daughter Holly jumped up on our kitchen table as if on cue. It was Holly's cat and it was not Fluffy—but for that brief instant I was back in the lean-to with the cat waiting for a treat.

***

Newspaper in the Porch—A preacher's lament
During the winter months newsboys would usually place the daily paper in the space between the storm door and the regular door. The double doors provided the best place for the paper to be dropped, since winter weather could make a paper left elsewhere disappear for weeks on end. This could happen if the paper was merely tossed in the driveway or on the sidewalk. Drifting snow, new snowfall and shovels or plows could be death to a daily paper in the Sodus climate.

In the modern era, cars drive by a house and place the paper in a specially marked cylinder for the particular paper. When bad weather occurs, the cylinder does have its advantages even though the things look tacky. Without the car window-level cylinder, modern newsboys toss the paper into the yard, driveway or walk. When it rains news delivery people wrap the paper in plastic to keep it dry, and then they toss it. My brother Dick was a unique newsboy for several reasons, but mostly because he loved to toss papers.

Reverend Shaw lived down on Gaylord Street at the far end of the street, and my brother's route included the preacher's house. Because the route included several streets, Dick figured a way to carry his papers on his bike in a manner that brought him to the preacher's house at the end of the route. I was assigned one of the streets of the route and it was the toughest one. It was uphill all the way. Due to my naivety and exuberance over making a buck and a quarter a week, Dick outsmarted me for a period of time.

When Dick arrived at the last house on his route there were times when he was out of papers. This can happen when the papers are split for the two delivery boys, or when a paper gets tossed where one shouldn't.

Reverend Shaw was an elderly man by this time in the late 1940s and I am not sure what denomination he represented. Whatever his religious attachment, one thing was clear after months of dueling with his paperboy—he wished for evil things to happen to Dick. I know my mother loved Dick and I suppose I did also because younger siblings look up to their older siblings. The good Reverend Shaw developed a very interesting love-hate relationship with my older brother.

His love was for the Rochester *Times Union*. His hate was for any deviation from a routine that brought the paper to his porch. In the winter he wanted it between the doors. In the summer he wanted it either on his porch or on the steps at the very least. My brother ran out of papers often enough that the Shaw man knew the phone number 5311 by heart. That was our simple four-digit number, unchanged for twenty-five years in the rural phone network. Mr. Shaw probably dialed 5311 before my brother's bike disappeared up the hill en route to our home. Shaw reported to Isabel that he was short a paper. Dick invariably would have to go get a paper at the drug store or get an extra one from my bag to take to Rev. Shaw. All this sounds as though it could have been avoided and for some stupid reason it wasn't. I now think Dick was protesting the man's nature and challenged him, even if it meant he had to go back to deliver a paper after the route was completed. I also think Dick "ran out of papers" often enough to make me think even back then that it was on purpose!

The holy war over the paper was out in the open. The next thing that happened was that the paper would end up in the yard, near the street on the driveway, and even up on the Shaw roof once or twice. Each deviation brought on the ringing of the phone up on High Street. Isabel became the intermediary between Rev. Shaw and a rebellious teenage delivery boy who happened to be her eldest son. This ordeal may have been solved in some simple manner such as Shaw picking a different delivery boy, or merely purchasing a paper at the drug store. It could also have been solved if Dick had acquiesced and just delivered the gosh-darn paper where Mr. Shaw desired. I say gosh-darn instead of the words that my father used when he finally got involved. He told Dick to deliver the G.D. paper properly. It brought the Lord's name into the battle of the paper for the first time.

This battle was not yet at its zenith. Summer came and went, and the beautiful fall season still found the paper in the yard when Dick dictated such an event. Mr. Shaw would find the paper out there in his leaves and, sure as death and taxes, the bell at 5311 would ring again. I calculate that Isabel did not pass the information about the preacher's calls to the ears of Mayor Pearson. If she had, the events of the winter would never have occurred.

Winter came to upstate New York in a predictable fashion. One day trees were nearly void of pretty leaves and soccer season was almost over and, bam, there was the first snowfall. People scurried around getting storm windows and doors on their homes. Reverend Shaw put his storm door and storm windows up on his porch.

This was the battleground for the final escalation of the holy war of the papers.

The Rochester paper now needed to be placed in the space between the doors on the front of the Shaw home. This was expected, but every piece of evidence pertaining to news delivery at this particular house over the previous three seasons seemed clear that deviation was to occur.

Sure enough, a paper ended up in the snow-covered yard and it was not wrapped in plastic. 5311. Ordered to deliver the man another paper that was to replace the wet one, brother Dick got a weird look in his eyes and headed down the hill. He was going to deliver a paper. I mean he was going to DELIVER a paper.

Reverend Shaw must have been standing on his small enclosed porch. The storm windows were now in place, the summer screens having been removed. He must have seen first hand what happened since he described it all in vivid detail when he cancelled the paper over the phone with my mother. Dick rolled his bike down the hill, took the heavy paper wrapped in rubber bands, probably saw the good preacher man standing there and then calmly tossed the rolled paper through one of the man's storm windows onto his porch. The paper was where Reverend Shaw wanted.

Not all these stories end with a great moral value connected to good events. My brother was a rogue and he tormented me for a long time in my life. He was mean, and for two of the developmental years when he needed a father figure, Dad was in the military. This isn't a cop-out for Dick but I do think it affected him. He and I developed a good relationship after he got to his senior year and beyond. Although he never was very good at reflecting about where he could have done things differently, he was very good at characterizing his war with the Reverend Shaw.

He told me late in his life that the Reverend Shaw was the most stubborn man he had ever been associated with in his life. He then said something interesting. Dick related that if the two of them could have made it through winter without Mr. Shaw canceling the paper Dick would have made a better effort in the spring. Dick said he respected a battler!

Dick's children Erich, Tracey, Danny and Marlys are all special people and have developed into successful adults. They sit around telling stories about their father that are humorous. As they hear my stories from their father's childhood they sit there and nod with understanding. I wish they could have heard Reverend Shaw.

***

Gertie and the Fruit—Izzy was a peach

Gertie Knapp would be diagnosed and treated for a mental illness if it were the modern era. Since she walked barefoot around our village for several years during my childhood, I came to think of her as a very strange individual. She was unkempt and would scare the crap out of little kids when she appeared in their yards and on their sidewalks. She actually looked like a witch at Halloween. She made some kids cry.

Her major function that all could see was the sale of fruit from a basket she carried. The fruit in the basket was well past its freshness time, and in all frankness it was typically rotten. All in the village who crossed Gertie's path treated her with courtesy or else they did a tack in their path and avoided her.

The woman looked very old to me back in the forties and fifties, yet there were sightings of the woman by my sister and younger brother as they were growing up; so she must have been in good shape from all the walking she did. Her brother owned and operated the local Rexall Drug Store, and her sister lived across the street from us on High Street. Her sister Fauney was eccentric and was a good friend of my mother. Fauney would drive Isabel around the village over the years until Izzy obtained her driver's license. When I say Fauney was a good friend of my mother it was true; but then again I did not know of anyone in the village who was not a friend of Isabel's.

Gertie came up the walk one time during the summer months with her usual basket and supply of "ripe" produce. My mother always bought something from the woman but on this particular summer day my mother invited Gertie to sit up on our screened front porch and have a glass of lemonade. This caught the rest of us by surprise because we thought she was strange and this act was an escalation of the friendship Mom extended when she purchased her produce.

I don't think I remembered ever hearing the woman speak since the transactions occurred on the front steps when Mom bought the fruit. As I hovered in the dining room out of sight, my mother and Gertie carried on a conversation over the lemonades. To say I was thunderstruck would be an understatement. My perception of Gertie was that she couldn't or wouldn't talk. My perception was also one based upon my prejudice over her strange appearance and behavior.

After my mother spent a few minutes with the barefoot woman on our front porch, she came into the house and asked me what was wrong. She saw my stunned look and knew this was related to what had just happened. Perhaps I was ten at the time and had never come across someone like Gertie. Mother merely said that she always liked to help the woman despite her outward appearance. Whether the woman's sister across the street or her successful brother in the drug store ever helped Gertie, no one seemed to know.

My mother theorized that Gertie probably got some help from some relative who probably did so with the knowledge that this kept her away from their homes and workplace. Gertie was rarely seen in the winter months, and most of us concluded that her bare feet and lack of winter gear probably kept her inside. People said she lived in a messy house across town behind the old Sodus school; but no one my mother or I knew ever reported that they had been inside the house.

During mid-century America the mentally ill people of every community were often admitted to institutions filled with similarly-afflicted people. Mental institutions gradually dispensed their human cargo into the main streets of the country as drugs and counseling replaced the hospitals and costs of such institutions became prohibitive.

Gertie was *not* in the Wayne County mental institution through the efforts of some family member. Many in the community would have suggested that for her if not for the druggist and neighbor related to her. There may have been many mentally ill people in our community who were not as visible as the fruit lady. My mother had a theory that the sister across the street was the source of food for the basket-lady, as she was referred to in Sodus. This theory was based upon the knowledge that Fauney and Isabel spent many trips together gathering fruit from local orchards or fruit stands. Some of that fruit was reaching Gertie, who then set off through town peddling the stuff.

The money gained from the sale of fruit could not have amounted to very much. My mother always bought the stuff from Gertie. We would kid my mother about these purchases. After some of those purchases Isabel would wait until the lady left our porch steps, and then Izzy would go deposit the fruit in the garbage barrel out back.

I did not make any judgment about the strange lady and her behavior over the years. This was not encouraged by Isabel where anyone "different" was concerned. Mom's viewpoint, by example, was to treat eccentric or strange people with kindness. Over the years she did this with many people.

We used to have a joke we played on her that went something like this. Isabel was called to the front porch where I or one of my friends would have a ragged towel wrapped around our heads. We would have some green apples or some fruit gathered from someplace in a peck basket. Without saying a word, we would hold the basket up to Isabel standing there smiling at us. She would merely say that we had parents and families to look after us so run along home with the basket.

After one of those Gertie-look-alike visits Isabel would tell us that she felt sorry for the woman and that we shouldn't make fun of her, even if she wasn't all there. As always with this type of respect, Isabel was an incredible teacher. When it came to Gertie's visits, a peach of a woman purchased rotten pears from a friend.

***

The Great Escape—What goes down can't go up

On the side of the front porch was a trellis that held a pretty climbing vine six months a year. Out on the trellis during other months of the year something else could be found. Young boys who slept in the bedroom above the porch roof could be seen coming and going on the trellis if someone were to watch closely. Fortunately, the sight of the Pearson boys clambering up and down the trellis was limited to their friends, and did not include their parents.

There were three girls living just across the street and Dick had the hots for one of them. The other two were too old for me at five years Dick's junior, but for some exotic reason one of the older girls who had to be eight years older than me was teaching me how to kiss. Now most people think that kissing comes as naturally as eating, breathing, or other natural acts—but having had the benefit of professional help in the use of one's lips (and tongue), I must disagree. I not only was being taught how to perform the ritual, but I was being instructed on matters that would bring me success in the dating whirl.

My brother and I were a tandem as we would crawl out of the bedroom through the window, onto the roof and then carefully down the trellis. We were on our way to make-out city just across the street at the Wood house. These trellis exits were not used very often, and after we had tried it successfully for two or three exits, things went wrong in a hurry.

I was the young partner in all this, so my bedtime was usually earlier than Dick's. But on a couple of occasions when Dick had something lined up he actually went to bed earlier than normal so that his exit could be accomplished in time to make his connections. My presence with him insured the pain would be shared should we be discovered. I also think he was providing guidance and training for me that would be crucial to my puberty.

The trellis was very well built, but on one trip down we realized we were breaking the narrow slats in the device. Going back up we experienced more breakage. This was not good since Dad would inspect the thing once a year when storm windows went up or came down on the front porch under the roof at our bedroom windows. Like addicts on some illegal drug that provides pleasure, the trellis was our addiction. We had one more trip down in our future and that was the end of an era.

In climbing down for some extracurricular Halloween mischief we dislodged the trellis from the side of the house. The vine had expired for the season and all that was left was dead vines. The trellis pulled away from the house as we jumped off the thing. This spelled serious trouble because we could not jump back up on the roof.

The problem was so manifest that we cancelled whatever we had in mind in order to get our butts back in through the window up on the roof. The front and back doors were locked for the night; and the dog in the back room meant we couldn't go that way even though the door could be opened when locked.

Two boys about fifteen and ten do not ring the front door bell and ask a parent to let them in the door. We decided that the ladder in the garage would be the answer. We cracked the garage door up enough to get us in the garage. Getting the ladder across the yard from the garage and up against the front porch roof was no problem. We climbed back up to our safe haven. Our Halloween mission had been postponed but we were around to live another day.

One problem. A ladder leaning up against the porch would be very visible to Pete going out at 7AM to work. That would bring havoc into our fragile lives. Have you ever pulled a ladder up onto a roof from up on the roof? We had never done this but after several seemingly noisy tries we got the ladder up there. We now had another problem. What does one do with a ladder once they have it on the roof? It would not fit into the bedroom. It could not disappear. After an inordinate amount of time that was now dragging us away from our night's sleep, we decided to place the ladder flat on the roof and pray that Dad would not see it once he got outside in the morning.

The next morning we awoke waiting for the sound of footsteps coming up the narrow steps leading to the two bedrooms and bathroom in the upstairs of the house that we vowed we would never leave in the middle of the night again. No footsteps came; and once again the two of us had dodged some major league problems.

The caper ended when we were able to distract my mother long enough to get the ladder back into the garage.

That next spring when we took down the storm windows from the porch Dad merely pulled the trellis away from the side of the house where Dick had attached it shortly after our near disaster. He tossed it on the ground and told us to dump it our back. He noted the vine limited the view out the windows and had become a nuisance. I am not sure he realized just how much of a nuisance it had become to us.

***

Rock him long—Rocking Charley in the fifties

Dick and I were in charge of Charley for one of the first times. Our parents had left us there as they traveled somewhere out of town. Charley had come to live with our family about two years previously and for much of that time he loved to sit in front of the black and white TV and rock in his rocking chair. While rocking away he would often doze off after having a sip of beer. He never drank very much. He especially liked to rock, sip and watch the harness racing on the tube from some far-off racing track.

Charley rocked away and fell asleep often. This became a ritual for the two teenagers in the house as we treated old Charley with respect and kindness.

No, Charley was not our aging grandfather who had moved in with us late in his life. Charley was a two-year development called a younger brother. He was an unexpected blessing in our house as not many of us living there thought Isabel had it in her to deliver a kid when she was forty five years old. Heck, her hair had almost gone entirely grey from the travail Dick and I had put her through.

Charley is now a normal, successful father and husband. He is respected in the New Hampshire community he and his family call home. He also is totally unaffected by our bedtime ritual when he was little. There is no evidence of brain damage or alcoholism caused by the small sips of beer when he was two.

Charley is my younger brother and, unlike older brother Dick, Charley presented nothing but pleasure to all after he dropped into our lives unexpectedly. The normal nine months transpired for the conception to birth routinely, but nevertheless when Charley popped out it is said that the delivering doctor slapped Isabel rather than Charley. The slap was for getting into the delivering position as a forty five year old lady with circulation problems in her legs. Of course Dad had something to do with all of this, but no doctor would lecture the mayor of Sodus about his sexual prowess.

Charley became a real talking point and center of attraction in our house and on the street. Dick was about to ease out of the house to begin his college career when Charley was born. Fortunately for me I was still going to be around for several more years to work on the "wonderkinder." Among other things Charley was a fantastic babe-catcher. He was the cute, prototype little brother who brought the girls around in the gym or Knapps Drug Store when I would bring him along.

Early in his existence Charley became the new project for my friends who felt the need to teach young kids new tricks. Jake, Ted, Gib, Ken and others would give Charley simple lessons. One of them ultimately caused problems when Charley hit kindergarten and waved with his middle finger at the boys he knew as they passed him in the halls of our central school. You see, the wave was taught early and he remembered and used it until the kindergarten teacher informed Principal Francis Samuel Hungerford that some older boys were perverting a young lad. After that we all rushed in to teach Charley a "better" wave. His new wave was more acceptable throughout the school.

Charley loved sports and still does. He spent many hours watching from the gym bleachers and then spent many of his own productive hours in the same gym. The gym, now over fifty years old, still serves the students and sports of Sodus.

Among other things that younger brothers pick up on are words, unusual visitors and unusual activities. He, of course, repeated and made verbal observations of things in the presence of our parents. He became a form of early warning system and CIA all rolled into one cherubic package. There were times when Charley saw females in our house that he knew did not belong. There was a time when he was but a toddler and he was able to discern that something was amiss under the breakfast booth we had in our kitchen.

Without Charley my friends and I would never have stumbled upon brother Dick making out with a female neighbor *under* the table in the darkened kitchen. This was the same Dick—pardon the play on words—who had been responsible for my hanging earlier in life. Since Dick was preoccupied and unable to retaliate, we tormented him and then fled. Charley's babysitter was under the table with Dick so we have to conclude Charley was not being taken care of adequately. Wouldn't that bring on DEFACS nowadays?

Younger brother was trained early on to climb the narrow stairs up to the upstairs. This was good for his physical development and also was good when he learned to also carry the morning paper on Saturdays so I could read the sports while Charley tumbled on the bed. We had the beginnings of a beautiful relationship.

The beauty of a younger brother for me was I could train him as I practiced in sports myself. I remember teaching him to swing a golf club—just as I was telling him to swing after I had backed away, he swung a wedge prematurely. There is nothing quite like a wedge behind the ear to draw blood. To this day I am not sure how I made it inside the house without Isabel and/or Charley being aware of the blood dripping down my body. Not wanting to scare either of them, I merely ended the lesson for a while as I retreated to a bathroom.

What a change in life as I reflect upon it all. Brother Dick tried to harm me when I got to be too much of a pest. Charley was never a pest, but experts would no doubt say the thirteen years between us were much less of a problem to us than the five years were to Dick when he confronted me.

Charley remains a best friend despite the miles between

Georgia and New Hampshire. His love of the outdoors and the change of seasons is manifest. His eternal suffering over the Boston Red Sox October failures is noted as I keep waiting to see my Atlanta Braves meet his team in the World Series.

He sits there, sipping a beer, rocking on occasion, and enjoying his life. This is something he seems to enjoy doing. I guess it must be in the blood.

***

Chicken Man—The kids saw him coming

We called him the "chicken man," but really he was an egg man. Farley Porter delivered eggs around Sodus and my mother got two or three dozen every week from him. This was a time in Sodus when there were no huge grocery stores and each of the Main Street stores had limitations. Many people had things delivered regularly. The milkman ran from the local dairy and we received six quarts of milk every other day. The milk then was not skim or one or two percent, but whole milk. With six people drinking and using milk the six quarts went very quickly. The eggs and the milk were always left on the front porch and the dairy provided an insulated container that kept glass milk quarts cool for a time.

When young people saw the chicken man coming they were able to relate to the eating habits of each house based upon the number of eggs delivered. My family had a reputation for being big eaters whether we spoke of eggs, milk and milk products like cottage cheese or even cheese. Some man delivered cheese for a period of time. Fifty years ago food was given as gifts at Christmas, New Years and even Easter.

The egg man was also a co-signer with my mother on the six thousand dollar loan she negotiated to purchase the house on High Street when my father was away in the navy. When Farley came by with eggs, there were some who said he came to see Isabel. People couldn't quite get over the loan Mom negotiated without the help of a bank or banker. If there was any spark of admiration there between the two, it certainly wasn't romance. The eggs came, payment was made, and the man left. Three dozen eggs once a week with a one-minute exchange of money for eggs hardly qualifies as tongue-wagging material!

The exchange of goods between mother and others went on all the time. She gave away flowers and branches cut from lilac bushes when they were in bloom in exchange for vegetables from Mr. Dingman's garden. Dingman was a neighbor who would help Isabel with things around the yard when her sons couldn't. He was kind, quiet and unappreciated by many merely because he kept to himself. My mother had a way of making friendships with that type of person.

When my mother got fruit at a local fruit stand, she would share the goods with others on the street. This type of thing does not exist today very often, and the communities are missing a wonderful piece of life. Another neighbor was a banker and he knew the tax codes front and back. It was not unusual at tax time to see people visiting his home with their arms filled with paperwork.

Kids in the neighborhood grew up with the community ethic described herein, and they took some valuable role-modeling with them into adulthood. Many people owned tractors, and when they equipped the tractor with a plow during winter months you could see them driving around doing much more than any person could expect. The tractor people of the village could be seen late at night plowing out a neighbor's driveway so the cars could get out in the morning.

One morning after greeting the milkman at the porch, I carried two quart bottles in each hand from the porch through the dining room enroute to the kitchen. The milkman delivered six quarts at a time in a carrier suited for that load. My trip to our kitchen with four quarts (remember they were glass) was interrupted briefly as my two swinging arms, each carrying two glass quarts, cracked into each other about halfway through the dining room.

There was an explosion of glass and milk that left the dining room a disaster area. I would never qualify as a delivery man for milk based upon that episode. My mother and I spent a long time bringing the dining room back to normal. The offshoot of this was our family was four quarts short for the next two days unless we called the dairy to get replenished. No one back then even thought about going to the store if somebody would deliver the goods.

Farley Porter delivered three dozen eggs weekly; and would you believe that within a few weeks of the milk mishap I turned Farley's delivery into scrambled eggs in our porch area? The event occurred when I balanced three dozen eggs in my arms and coming through the front door one of the egg cartons slid right out of the stack and there were your basic broken eggs right there on the entry.

In the aftermath of the egg caper I was unable to overcome the label of clumsy. My father reminded me for some time that I broke more food than I ate.

The egg man and others like him have vanished from America. Given how much they did for community good will it seems like a good idea to institute the delivery system again. Farley delivered eggs, co-signed loans and was pleasant. That was a triple play unmatched in the modern era.

***

A Foursome for Cards—Ladies teaching time

By the time I had reached the age of six, my father was in the navy, my older brother had developed his own life style free from a strong fatherly influence, and I was cast under the influence of several ladies in my circle of friends and relatives. Due to the strong influence of my mother and my willingness to cooperate in the family setting with the set of circumstances dealt to us, I became a candidate for table training 101. In the reflective jargon, table training 101 comprised the lessons from older ladies upon my life during the years 1944-1950. It was this six year span when my mother relied upon other women to help with her two boys since she was busy being a family provider, a community helper, and finally in 1946 and 1950 a mother of a daughter (Donna) and son (Charley).

Many times during those years I ended up either with older brother Dick or alone at the home of a variety of women. Usually after one attempt to host both of Isabel's sons, most of the women concluded that one of the boys was possible but not both at the same time. The sibling rivalry thing had reached a peak during this era as near-hangings, assaults with knives, terd-throwing fights (yes, you read that correctly) and various other dandy stunts were perpetrated.

Less of the Pearson boys, therefore, seemed better. We began visiting the ladies alone. My grandmother Hazel saw this as a real chance to make an impact upon me and my development. Dick seemed too old or set in his ways for this one-on-one work. He preferred a different path through his childhood. I would make a visit to nearby Rochester during various times when Isabel got weary of the male dynamic duel in her charge at that time.

Aunt Doris was a great place to visit for either or both of us since she was fun and played games with us and her daughter Judy. Judy was my age, so this was a natural. But the most significant development for me at the card table of life came at Grandmother Hazel's. She was my Dad's mother and was definitely matronly. She also was a terrific "gamer," in the lexicon of the era in which she lived.

When I arrived at Hazel's house she would involve me in card games with her two close friends Mrs. Burnham and Mrs. Johnson. These games started with Rummy at the beginning of this particular foursome. As the ladies saw my learning curve improve, they began educating me to their card ways. As the visits and years evolved I became a real player in the foursome. My visits became a real event since I gave the ladies an easy fourth player. The other two ladies lived right on the street and all three ladies had husbands who were still working as salesmen. Many times I was the only male in the house—or in their lives, for that matter—for days on end, as the husbands traveled widely by car or train. My visits usually were for three days at a time.

The games advanced from Rummy all the way through the full gamut of Canasta, Samba, Hearts, Spades, Pinochle and then include table games such as Michigan Rummy, Checkers, Monopoly,

Sorry, Dominos, and even early attempts at Bridge. Over my grade school years I was being trained by masterful, sweet ladies. Make no mistake the sweet ladies were very influential and very traditional. They pointed my way through early errors in games and in behavior. I learned manners not just for the table games but for life. I became very cognizant of polite expectations vis a vis women. This period of time was etiquette training so often overlooked in contemporary life.

As I progressed through their private laboratory of card experiments, the ladies came to see me as an equal partner at the table games. It became very evident to me that I had a "place" where, despite my age, I was considered an equal. Over the years the ladies provided many hours of entertainment and simple fun. They were doing something they loved to do as they went through casual days as lonely housewives (this was before the time when ladies their age had to work or chose to work). Later, as the two neighbor ladies became widows, the time on their hands increased. My own grandmother became a widow much later than the other two, so Hazel was often the recreation director for the ladies.

Current research tells us that the aging process can be delayed or diminished if seniors would use their hands and minds in concert rather than becoming idle. There is no doubt that the ladies of my early life were very sharp, and it could have been from their card-playing habits. All of the ladies outlived their husbands by twenty to thirty years. In each of their cases, the ladies were sharp as tacks until the day they died.

Current observations show us that there is less involvement between generations than there was in an earlier America. The only thing we see that may be a deviation from the current norm is where, out of necessity, grandparents are raising grandchildren. This is not the casual and relaxed effort described in my childhood between me and my grandmother, however. The modern era has thrown grandchildren from screwed-up parents into the arms of the only people available for these kids. Grandparents provide stability and safety for the kids in the modern era. During my childhood the grandparents could pick and choose their entry and exit points in the lives of the grandchildren.

In my case I had the good fortune of being loved by a busy Mom and then had the back-up love of a wonderful aunt and uncle, and Hazel. Her husband (H.B. Pearson Sr.) was the salesman in her life. He traveled and when arriving home he also did some nice things for me away from the card table. It seems H.B. Sr. was short on patience for me and the ladies when they were all thrown into the deal on the table,

As the card expertise increased, so did my ability to work with numbers in school. I would expect that there is a great correlation between math prowess and card playing ability. It would seem educators should explore this connection as a tactic to improve math scores in elementary schools. There are some people who have a conservative attitude towards card-playing, but once they get by that hang-up I say deal the cards during recess!

In my own life I have taken the opportunity to play card games and table games with my kids, my grandkids and many friends. This serves the socialization and education process amply. It also shuts off the computer, the TV and the video games long enough to talk and laugh together over a common game. I am the proud grandparent of children who knew the difference between a flush and a straight prior to kindergarten. These same kids prefer to play cards with my family and me over other more electronic and exotic choices much of the time.

When one of them learns a new twist to a game under my tutelage it makes me feel very proud. It also reminds me that I am merely paying back the debt I owe to Hazel and the ladies of so long ago. I just know Mrs. Johnson and Mrs. Burnham would take pleasure in seeing the little kids learn table manners. I also know Hazel would take great pleasure in seeing little grandsons Grant and Brady draw a single card to a "full boat" in draw poker! They are in kindergarten and third grade, and their math prowess is growing with each hand of cards.

***

Electric Leak—Aunt Doris was mad

I let out a shriek as my penis tingled with the electrical current traveling up my stream of urine. Was I undergoing a torture at the hands of a sadist? No. I was following an older brother's suggestion to pee on a fence built around a cow pasture near where Aunt Doris and Uncle Don lived.

Once the tingle hit instincts took over I disengaged from the activity. As I peed on my pants brother Dick got a great kick out of my accident. He also scored one more time on me and my painfully slow learning curve. I ultimately began to develop a greater awareness about being gullible and naïve—but the memories of his successes still abound.

There were finally a couple of real life events that brought Dick face to face with the consequences of picking on me; but until they played out I was like most of the other younger brothers around. Younger brothers are fair game for the pranks and humor of the older kids.

One of the ultimate events occurred on the eve of my first big basketball game as a junior high kid. Dick and another friend wrestled with me and my ankle was sprained severely as one of them rolled the ankle over under their full weight. I was so hurt physically and my adrenaline was so engaged that I flew into them with a fury unmatched in my dealings with them ever before. I limped around the living room slugging the crap out of whichever one of them got near me. The two older boys were hurt themselves and shocked at my rage. They did not ever bother me again in the same old way.

Because I missed a week of play and practice, my father was quite pissed off at Dick. Dad was interested to see how I would fare in competition and this prevented him from making that judgment.

Another event involved report cards. Mine was delivered on time and got the requisite signature. Dick's was missing. He had wanted mine to be missing also to cover his story. I refused. It turned out his missing card was "lost"—but after a week a report card with some poor grades listed on it started burning up in the dining room ceiling light. The light was unused except during more formal Sunday meals in the dining room with grandparents. The smell and smoke from the burning heavy paper of the report card stopped the meal and helped end Dick's reign of terror and pranks on me for some time. He then had enough of his own problems with the man of the house.

As visitors at Doris and Don's, we always had a good time. Because they had but one child, they did not know the problems associated with multiples of children. It seems then, as now, a multiple number of children always seems to multiply the discipline and logistics of raising children by a much greater number than just the actual number of children present. When I peed on the electric fence, Doris must have thought her quiet world of one child (Judy) had been invaded by a host of hellions. No aunt would have perceived that one brother would actually try to electrocute a sibling. Of course she had but one child and that little darling was just that...a little darling girl. Judy was always quiet and well-behaved. Her cousins from the hicks were the opposite. They were also boys.

When the tingle went away and Doris asked how all that had occurred, Dick was in trouble again. Upon reflection, I could have tried some of the pranks on a brother four or five years younger if I had one. Fortunately there was a little sister in that age group and she was off-limits for pranks. This advice came from the top, and was adhered to most of the time.

Dick's pranks on me were dealt with and I usually did not suffer for long after being victimized. I did not use such pranks when a younger brother came along because he was twelve years younger. Picking on Charley never seemed to be fair game. Some deviations to the norm did occur when I babysat the little guy. These were usually activated out of a sense of experimentation on a live subject. We never lost him in any of these journeys into science.

Dick got some form of discipline from Doris and Don over the electric fence issue, and if Doris hadn't seen the event first-hand she may not have ever known about it. I usually kept quiet about such things. This came from experience—and the sure knowledge I had to share a room with the older sibling. Intimidation was alive and well for a time. Until Dick saw me as a non-threatening person, and until his interests went in different directions than mine, there was the sibling rivalry thing. Doris handled it well because we always wanted to be with her and Don. They were laid back and permissive to a point.

In the modern era there are rituals that people go through growing up that transcend peeing on an electric fence. In the modern era, many of these events are not supervised or witnessed in any sense, so in the final analysis young people get hurt or killed doing dumb things. The "hands-off" raising of children today usually allows for far more serious consequences of any experiment or prank. There have been dumb things in every era performed under the influence of adolescence. There just seem to be a far greater range of nasty end-results now.

Urinating on a fence was stupid. It did not permanently harm me as far as I can discern. Although I could never have children the old fashioned way for some unknown reason, I hold no grudge against my deceased older brother. He had greater worries anyway. About a week prior to his passing he instructed one of his sons to cremate his body and make damn sure the ashes never got into the family cat's litter box by mistake. Now that would have been quite a prank to settle the electric fence deal!

***

Branding the Buick—Uncle Don's nose knew

By the time Uncle Don had returned to his new car after running an errand for Aunt Doris he knew instantly something was amiss. The new car was occupied by his two nephews Dick and Bob. Bob was the younger of the two at five years of age, whereas Dick at ten should have known better. I was the sweet little Bobby. Dick was, by then, notorious and rebellious. Dick's idea was to "brand" our new shooters—Tom Mix cap pistols brought to Rochester by us when we were on one of our visits to Uncle Don and Aunt Doris' home. Tom Mix was the forerunner of western heroes over the years stretching through Roy Rogers, Gene Autry, John Wayne, and Kevin Costner.

The branding was a routine thing seen in the westerns we watched each Saturday at our Sodus movie house. Here in Rochester, the branding was accomplished by the cigarette lighter in Don's new car. Dick suggested it and I, of course, followed his instructions to the letter. As Dick branded our cap pistols it became very evident that plastic handles would brand, but the byproduct was a terrible smell. Additionally, after the second handle was finished it was also readily apparent that the lighter would not return to the little hole in the dashboard due to an accumulation of melted plastic on it.

At about the same time we struggled with the realities of boyhood experimentation, Uncle Don opened the door to enter his new vehicle. His unusually kind and laid-back demeanor so typical of him was now in a whole new mode. The smell was overpowering and the upholstered seats and head-liner no doubt became permanently host to a smell unlike any other car in Rochester, New York. The cigarette lighter was no longer usable. In an era of smoking and not worrying about the "smoker's car" label at the used car lots, this plastic smell went way over the boundaries.

Don drove the two of us home to Aunt Doris, who would try to explain that these nephew rascals were just being boys; and in contrast to their daughter Judy (our cousin) were quite different and would, in the future, have to be better monitored. It actually turned out to be a matter of Uncle Don (poor henpecked Uncle Don) screwing up because he left us in the car while running the errand.

Uncle Don and Aunt Doris were fixtures in our lives and were present at every notable event to show us their support and love. Contrasted to the modern era where uncles and aunts may be scattered all over or may be uninvolved in the lives of youngsters not in their house, Doris and Don were steady, fun, interested in us and were kind. The events in our lives over the many years were entwined with these special relatives. My mother and Doris were sisters, and a spectacular pair of sisters they were! Don "inherited" us by virtue of marriage, but he never once vowed to disown us, despite the cigarette lighter episode—or any of the other things foisted on him by his nephews.

When Doris passed away it was a closing of a huge chapter in the life of our family. Uncle Don survived her and at 91 still is enjoying some aspects of life, even as his memory fades. It is special for aunts and uncles to connect with kids, and as I age this becomes more of a piece of my life. Uncle Don would play catch with me when he visited when my own father was either away in service or away on post-service travels as a salesman. Don worked at Eastman Kodak, as did many thousands of people in and around Rochester, but he always found time to see us and play with us.

Our own father would be rather distant when it came to play, and he would even chide Don at times about playing with us and "wasting" time playing golf. Don was an excellent golfer and played well into his eighties. Interestingly, my father, a classic type "A" personality, never took up golf and never really played much at all with us as he worked his way through his life and passed away at age 62. Don, by contrast, still lives on at age 91. The golf and his attitude about things would appear to be factors in longevity. This isn't anything new or different in the theories about aging. Aunt Doris would play games with Judy and me and others and have fun while doing so.

Too many adults don't try to play cards or table games with kids because such activities are passé and all too often the kids are alone and nose deep in a computer screen. It is noteworthy that many child-rearing experts in the modern era tell readers and viewers that too many children are left alone in front of their computers and TV sets in their own rooms. The problems between adults and children are often commenced when adults provide every electronic thing the kids want just so they will stay out of the adults' hair! There are many reflections flowing from the special uncle and aunt we had and that includes the memories of the terrible odor in Don's car, the special fun we had in their presence and two wonderful friends that went way beyond being relatives.

We had another uncle and aunt, and it is not even fair to compare the two sets of relatives because the other two had to ask us our names during the one time each year they saw us. It seemed much better to be with Don and Doris even though they took a risk each time they extended their hands in friendship. After all was said and done, they kept coming back over and over for fifty years! So did we!

***

The Sisters Bowerman—Two, too unique

Judy Welch (now Judy Scheifflein) is my cousin. Her mother, Doris Welch, was almost as much of a saint as her sister and my mother Isabel was. They were Isabel and Doris Bowerman, daughters of a railroad engineer who worked long hours and days away from home on his job with the New York Central Railroad. The girls married Herman Pearson and Donald Welch respectively, and stayed married until death did them part. Isabel survived Herman by eleven years but, in a reversal of usual mortality statistics, Doris passed on when well into to her eighties, leaving her husband Donald as a survivor. He is still healthy and is well into his nineties in Albany, New York.

The two sisters were the only family for Laura and Ward Bowerman. In a shocking turn of events for the sisters, they were turned over to Laura's father and mother Arthur and Isabel Nothaker of Rochester, New York, when their mother died. The girls were eight and two at the time. Each time I read or even write that, I am empathetic on their behalf even though the death occurred ninety years ago. In any generation this death would be devastating.

The father Ward, who I was named after, took the little girls to Rochester from their home in Syracuse after the death of their mother. Syracuse was only eighty miles to the east from Rochester, but in the year 1913 it may as well have been two thousand miles. Ward Bowerman went on his way as an engineer and died sometime in the decade of the 1960s. During the time between the death of Isabel's mother at 26 and Ward's death in his eighties, Ward was married again and again and again. We tallied at least four other marriages. He pretty much disappeared from the girls' lives.

The Nothakers did stay in our lives until their deaths when I was very young. Arthur taught me German, and was intrigued that I tried some of the words out on German prisoners of war kept in a camp in Sodus during the war. As grandparents are doing today, they merely raised Isabel and Doris in the absence of their biological parents without much fanfare or recognition.

From the time their father left the girls with his deceased wife's family to bring up and until the time Ward died, all we ever heard from him was an occasional Christmas or birthday card. The two sisters were very close-mouthed over their life history. When they spoke of their elusive father I never heard either of them discredit or disabuse the man. They would have had plenty of reason to, since the signatures on the cards coming over the years changed from Father and Grandfather Ward to Uncle Ward. He no longer claimed the sisters or any of their children.

In a Hallmark moment, the man changed his genetic link and title overnight! This would have pissed most children off but the two sisters never seemed to let this twist in their lives bother them. When I reached the age of seventeen and was preparing to graduate from high school, personal cards were made for each graduate to include in graduation invitations. Although "Uncle" Ward had been sending me cards and small amounts of money at birthdays, I had no illusions of his showing up in Sodus to see me graduate. I had never seen him to remember, although there are pictures of me on his lap when I was two. He must have visited the two daughters at that point at least once since the photographs of the old fart with our cousin Judy, Dick and me are a historical record. That documented visit would have been 27 years after dumping his girls with the grandparents. Although he remarried there was never any thought, according to Isabel, of reuniting the girls with their father and his new wife.

In a display of my new-found rebellious attitude toward what Ward had done many years previously to the sisters Bowerman, I sent along an invitation to my graduation with my personal card inside the invitation. The printed card had Robert **William** Pearson in block letters. He had disowned my mother and now I had erased him by dint of the new personal card.

There was no response ever again after that. Ward disappeared forever in the fog of life and I have kept the original middle name despite my temporary anger. Just prior to my mother's death, she joked that if Ward did leave any estate back when he died I screwed up my potential share with my graduation invitation. We laughed about that for a while. (I wonder if he did leave any money…)

Isabel looked after Doris all the years when they were growing up, and as any big sister would she made Doris her "project" for life. Even as they played cards or socialized over a meal we always seemed to be eating, the two sisters were connected in ways that were entertaining to witness.

For many years Aunt Doris smoked. Isabel never got into that bad habit and, although she would have preferred a non-smoking sister, Isabel was diplomatic. Remember, this was the era when it seemed every adult puffed the nasty things. There were times when Doris would harass Isabel to smoke. In comical moments, Isabel would light up and then choke and cough her way through half a cigarette before giving up. She could never get the lighting up routine. She constantly would light the cigarette halfway up the cigarette since she was farsighted. There were times later in the family circle before Dad's own mother passed away that Doris, Isabel, Grandmother Pearson and a few of us were playing cards in the kitchen after a big meal. The breakfast nook was perfect for cards and table games since the table was smooth vinyl.

During one of these games Doris dared Isabel to light up. Not being content to bug her sister she then would work on Hazel who was Dad's matronly mother of fur piece, fine china and picture perfect housekeeping fame. After a period of time the kitchen filled up with smoke as the three ladies and some of the others puffed away. I enjoyed this a great deal but never wished to smoke (other than the two weeks in 7th grade when I chain-smoked for two weeks during my parents' vacation to Florida and Hazel babysat us). One irony in all these kitchen shenanigans occurred when my father ventured out into the kitchen for something to eat or drink in a break from the game he was watching. Upon reaching the kitchen and bearing witness to the heavy haze hanging over the small room and upon seeing his own mother corrupted by the sisters Bowerman, he stood there and said "Mother!" That was all he said. It was another funny moment.

He must have reflected upon the closeness of the sisters and also the fact that their mother had not been around to corrupt. In fact, the Bowerman mother was merely a distant memory for Isabel. Aunt Doris never recalled her mother. Why would Pete interrupt a moment like this with some of his typical sarcasm?

Doris eventually moved to Florida with Don and, although she was legally blind during her last years, she still went to the swimming pool in the condo complex in Boynton Beach and taught swimming to the seniors. This was a parallel to Isabel playing the piano with her arthritic fingers at the senior home for the "old folks" when she was in her last years.

The two of them were given a terrible, harsh double dose of reality early in their life. Nevertheless, they both became great mothers, fine wives, and wonderful mentors to many around them. They both left a legacy in their wake that is remarkable. Ward Bowerman never knew what he had missed out on.

***

Stop the Day for a Meal—A ritual worth noting

If someone were to ask me to list some things to improve the quality of family life in America as quickly as possible, the absolute first thing I would put on the list would be for each family to have a mealtime that would be practiced and honored every day. This suggestion would be simple, quick and cheap.

I base my opinion upon observations that extend back sixty years. In my opinion, the family meal hour has disappeared from the American way of life to our national detriment. What was a typical event daily when I was a young boy is no longer typical. There are multiple reasons for this modern anomaly.

A possible reason for the disappearance of the family meal hour is linked to both parents working and meal preparation suffering accordingly when parents arrive home simultaneously with the children. Some say it becomes impossible in that scenario to sit down and eat together because the meal must, by necessity, be crammed into the hours after all the family arrives and before the schedules of the evening commence. I contend this can be surmounted, even if pizza is ordered from Dominos. No matter what the arrival time of the members is, there still will be a time for the entire family to sit down and eat together at a table. I contend the absence of the table from most meals has caused an absence of manners, conversation and lessons in life.

My father and mother insisted upon the entire family sitting in the kitchen at the booth for the evening meal. If someone had a practice or a paper route, we just ate a little later. If someone had a game at night, we ate a bit earlier. There was very little that impacted upon the forty—five minutes to one hour of family time at the kitchen table. The phone would not be allowed to intrude into this time because my father would merely answer and say we were eating.

Let's consider the intrusion of the phone into meal-time in the modern era. The phone is like an extended earring that cannot be removed from the ear even during a meal. Cell phones appear in restaurants and certainly at meal times in homes across the USA. This facet of modern life would cause my parents instant indigestion.

The table thing is a simple tool for developing manners and conversation. If a pizza is ordered to overcome lack of meal prep time, it still is possible to eat at a table with certain regulations. Despite the fact that a mother doesn't prepare an evening meal as was the routine in most homes at mid-century does not mean parents have to give up the teachable moments still available. The modern era sees the pizza arriving and then sees everyone grabbing a piece. They then scatter to informal places throughout the home. Usually the TV entertains as the family abrogates their collective possibilities for family growth and structure. Is it little wonder the modern family often lacks structure? This leads us to the encroachment of TV into family time, especially at mealtime.

No child in America in the modern era that I ever knew of has been deprived of TV time. Why then bring the TV into the meal when so many other good results can accrue? When people are being entertained or distracted, the ability to converse disappears with the pizza. I conclude that the presence of the TV keeps parents from having to discipline and to correct and teach eating manners. The TV is a free pass for permissive parents. They have created a "peaceful" compromise. I contend the family is compromised. The free pass may last into early adulthood or until a kid is seen eating like a slob at a public eating situation. Guess where the lessons should have been taught? My parents knew we were instructed in proper eating manners since those were of continued interest through the years. I can remember parents and grandparents debriefing me about some matters of manners seen at church meals or even large family gatherings.

I can vividly remember my father teaching all of us how to drink from a glass. My mother worked on napkin use and proper utensil use. My father specialized in leading the conversation around to all of us once he had delivered his opinion on current and local events.

Without a family meal together, think of all the information that does not get passed along. Kids need to know about adult opinions, and especially those opinions expressed by their parents. By the time I was ten, I could tell another person how my father felt about politicians, what political party Dad voted for and how my mother felt about local village issues. These guiding principles were offered up with the green beans and sweet potatoes. My father especially liked the doctrine of children being seen and not heard unless asked to speak. This didn't always work, but it was good to consider what was about to come out of one's mouth when around my father. At meal-time he wanted stuff going into the mouths and then it would be our turn when we had done our best with the food available.

That brings up a critical difference in the events around my family table and the modern table. My father and mother had three basic tenets for the table during meals. One was to try everything on the table; the second was to finish everything on one's plate; and the third was to eat now because the next meal was going to be breakfast. If a child at 20 High Street went to bed hungry, breakfast opportunities abounded at the same table starting at 6:30 AM. How many families in the modern era have no scheme whatsoever for balanced diets and not wasting food?

It is a recognizable pattern that modern parents take the easy route at meal-time and allow six year olds to dictate what they will or won't eat. This was unheard of in the Pearson home of FDR's and HST's and IKE's era. (We did learn a lot of history with our meals) It is, therefore, not at all surprising that our nation's obesity rates are the highest ever at the same time in our history when six year olds are mapping out their own diets. Some kids in the modern era never come face to face with green vegetables. Other kids never come to appreciate fresh fruit or whole wheat breads.

The ritual called the family meal has vanished during the same fifty-year period that our families have broken up at fantastic rates. The breakdown in teaching table manners and learning how to converse comes during the same period when schools are faced with educating kids with no manners or any conversational abilities!

Every meal ever cooked by my mother was an exciting time. None of us around the table ever knew what was going to come out of the oven or off the stove. She would combine leftovers at an alarming rate. Her casseroles were unmatched and she could never create one like the previous one, since each one was a spontaneous venture. No one in our family ever went hungry. This was due to the efforts of my mother. My father never dwelled upon being empathetic very much in his life and in the post-meal dialogue as he assigned chores in the kitchen he would often say "Nice try, Izzy."

Mother never rebelled at this comment for unknown reasons apparently dealing with harmony or not wanting to upset the family unity achieved through the magic of the mealtime. When I related this comment to my Georgia-born wife Jan, she said it was an inappropriate comment coming from a Yankee.

If the simple act of sitting a family down for an uninterrupted meal would accomplish so much for such a small price, it seems that it would be worth the effort. Families could learn to pray at mealtimes. Families could learn to share highlights and problems with one another.

The definition of a family is a group tied together by their relationships doing group activities. The family structure in my home was alive and well, as we learned and were reprimanded as needed about important lessons in life. Every evening meal was arranged for our growth and welfare, even if we did not always know what was in the evening's casserole dish.

***

Jumping in the House—Cousin Judy and the clowns

Aunt Doris liked giving her sister a relief from the large number of duties involved with raising two boys. Just when Doris thought she had a handle on the kids from Sodus, two more kids joined the family. The total of four kids was in sharp contrast to Doris and Don's small family. They had one child, Judy. She was my age and we became good friends despite the gender thing. There were times when Dick and I would visit Rochester and stay with the Welch family. This was good for Isabel and also gave the Welch home a dose of double trouble. They rarely saw this from their angelic Judy (angelic by comparison to the Pearson boys).

When our paths took us to Rochester, our aunt and uncle were super in their treatment of us. They took us swimming to pools. This was a first for us. In Sodus there weren't any pools. When the water was warm enough people would swim in the bay or, if they had balls of steel, in the lake. When the country boys arrived in the big city they encountered a bit of cultural shock. I can remember going into a huge store called Sibleys in downtown Rochester. There was nothing like that in Sodus. The biggest thing we had was a Western Auto, a Ben Franklin 5&10 and of course Miller& Kramer, which was the only multi-level store in town. M & K sold clothes from the various balconies in the rear of the store. It was a unique layout and the office for the business was nestled back in one of the split levels also. I could never figure out why or how the building arrived at that configuration. My Dad's theory was that the Masonic Lodge was above the store somewhere along Main Street and the many slate pool tables in the lodge required special reinforcement. That explained the store's dimensions.

The Welch family was tied to Eastman Kodak, as were many other families in Rochester and Monroe County. George Eastman created the Kodak Camera and the film industry that supported the use of cameras.

Doris was a great advocate for kids having fun. This trait in both sisters belied the fact that their early life was not all the fun it should have been. When Doris saw her nephews and niece coming, she would bring out games. We played Monopoly, Sorry, Clue, and a variety of table games that have all but disappeared over the past years. We played a game called Michigan Rummy that was a modified gambling game. Adults played with kids and everyone was on equal footing in such games.

Aunts and Uncles entertaining kids in previous generations did not have the benefit of video games, Dish TV, computers, Internet, and multiplex theatres. They merely entertained the old fashion way and that was hands-on *with* the kids. I think that the modern era lacks the personal touch seen in other generations. I would venture a guess that we lost communication with younger generations when we no longer felt compelled to play with them.

When the Pearson boys were beckoned to the city by an enthusiastic aunt, a cousin who was always planning things for us and an uncle who viewed us with a degree of hesitation, we never failed to entertain, shock and pretty much wear out our welcome! After two days Uncle Don would be referring to us as the "clowns."

This came, in part, as each of the Sodus contingent tried to impress the female friends of our cousin. Judy had some pretty friends who visited her house when Dick and I were there. The clowning Don witnessed was usually testosterone-driven country boys trying to show off.

There was a sliding door at the bottom of the staircase leading to the upstairs. We would play elevator with the door but as we continued the game the door slammed harder and harder each time. The door was made almost entirely of glass except for the heavy wooden frame. It is surprising that the thing was not broken during the visits from the Hellions from the hicks.

After we were banned by our uncle from playing that game, we started seeing how many steps we could leap up *and* down from a standing start. The landing at the bottom took our leaps down and was our launching pad for the leaps up. Judy had never thought of this game and she probably was stunned to see how a quiet home could be disrupted so fast. That game had a lifespan of an hour or so after which that activity became off-limits also. Eventually Uncle Don had his home, garage and yard mapped out in a series of "no-clown" zones. He got nervous when we ventured into the attic.

Our old house in Sodus had no attic and this explained the terrific cold up in our bedrooms through the winter months. Don was wise to keep us out of the attic since we discovered things up there even he didn't know were there. The cellar became off limits once we discovered the milk box in the landing leading to the cellar. We placed objects in there, tried to crawl through the opening to no avail, and even tried to get Judy in the passage once.

I think Don perceived a clown stuck in the device and milk deliveries would cease. In the total scope of things Judy would make "trade" visits to Sodus but her absence from Rochester was not admired as much by her mother as our absence from Sodus was by our mother.

We clowned around with Doris and Don because they made us feel very welcome. Our clowning around in our own home was limited in its scope due to the presence of a no-nonsense father.

He did not like games and would only play poker with us on rare occasions. He could not grasp the fact that Isabel, Doris and Don enjoyed playing our games. I think that was Dad's blind spot. It made life too short for him. Uncle Don and Aunt Doris played games and lived long lives. Don played golf up until he was ninety and is alive and well in Albany, N.Y. Aunt Doris was swimming almost up until the month she died at 84. My Dad was gone at age 62 and worked sixty hour work weeks up until three weeks prior to his death. He was robust and should have lived much longer.

As one of the clowns still around, I realize clowning is a part of life. My brother Dick stopped clowning around somewhere along the line and, tragically, he did not live as long as his father did. Dad reached 62, but his eldest son only made it to 61. As I write this piece it dawns on me that it is March 15, 2004. My brother and my fellow clown would be 70 years old today. Happy Birthday, Dick! Don and Doris outlived you, and that shouldn't have happened. Doris and Don stopped smoking except for after special events. Dick smoked right up until the week he died of lung cancer.

***

Sailor's Return—Times changed overnight

The war years for our family concluded about the same time they did for most Americans. VE and VJ Days were celebrated (victory in Europe and victory in Japan) and the men and women came back. Many did not return, though, and Sodus was no different than every other community. The lists of the dead and missing were written in gold letters on a huge board in the middle of town. For several years this was a vivid reminder of the terrible losses out of the wonderful community called Sodus (from native American word *Assorodus* meaning Land of Silvery Water). The Second World War was finally over and my father returned home. Fortunately his name did not go on the sad honor roll down in front of the library.

The celebrations were muted once Dad returned. I think part of that dimension was we were reunited with a man we did not know very well. Consider his dilemma. He was faced with two sons that had changed manifestly in two years. They were also strangers. The house he lived in when he left the village was occupied by the Merhoffs, and we lived in another house up the street. Actually the change in houses was a huge improvement but, upon reflection, Dad had nothing at all to do with the acquisition, the move, the upkeep or even most of the furniture. I think this was a tough thing for him to acknowledge.

He was not pleased with going back to the bank as a teller and he was faced with changing jobs in a market suddenly filled with millions of workers. He explained some of this job thing to me when I was older. I asked him about his reaction after the war about the job situation.

Dad was fortunate that he hooked up with a prince of a man named Ed Burns. Ed and his father owned Alton Canning Company in nearby Alton. The two Burns were the best men my father ever worked for over his lifetime. That tribute came from his lips late in his life over a few beers.

The canning company needed a sales manager and Pete was chosen for the task. Our family was introduced to the Adams Family as a result of the job change. Morton Adams was the boss of the acreage that grew the crops Dad had to sell once the crop was canned. The Adams became our fast friends and the three Adams boys were in on plenty of ballgames, pranks, and fun times. My father also met other fine men like Leo Fletcher, Vinnie VanDamme and other good adult influences. They, again, personified the strength of Sodus. That strength was adults who could and would make a difference in the lives of their children and other children.

When my father exited the navy and started the Alton portion of his career and life, we were treated to a revitalized lifestyle. This was connected to a father being home and more money coming in to the family. The connections with the Alton Canning men and women added a quality to our Sodus life. There were fringe benefits befitting men who were willing to work long hours on salaried positions. Ed Burns made sure there was a cottage at Sodus Point many summers in a row for each salaried employee of the management group. Each family could stay at a cottage right on the beach at the lake for two weeks each.

Other treats from Mr. Burns included dinners for the whole staff at Runds Seafood restaurant in Rochester prior to going to the circus, a pro basketball game, a Red Wing Baseball game. Sometimes we just ate dinner in the city with the whole group. When the office staff all showed up with their kids, the group numbered about forty. Consider the cost of feeding forty people and then footing the bill regularly for their entertainment. It was a significant effort. There were times when a twenty-pound turkey or ham would show up on our front porch in the morning. It was brought there by Ed Burns to acknowledge the work ethic of a navy veteran.

Dad's decision to leave banking was wise when one considers the fringe benefits of working for a wonderful man such as Ed Burns. Not many employers in the modern era provide entertainment and food in a manner done by Ed. My father made a great choice of jobs since he could become a much more important figure in the canning business than he ever could have in banking. He once told me he merely waited his time to change from the bank and when the war concluded it was an appropriate time.

We all became accustomed to the return of our father and husband from the service. Within a short time Donna was born, and five years later Charley's arrival surprised everyone, not the least of which was my mother and father.

As the canning business flourished my father traveled widely up and down the East Coast of the USA; and he often went west as far as Chicago, creating markets for the canned goods pumping out of the expanded factory in Alton. Railroad cars were filled up routinely to accommodate huge orders generated by my father's travels. There were chain food stores now across the land and the canning factory had many accounts for these types of stores in my father's sales region.

The veteran came home and created a whole new life for himself and his family. As one of the kids benefiting from the fringe benefits I say thank goodness for the new job and thank God for the end of the war.

***

Ice Storms- The worst of times / the best of times

The climate in the northeastern United States is an interesting mix of weather patterns that can make people love and hate the weather all in thirty minutes. The documentation of weather anomalies is left to the historians and weather experts. Suffice to say the Wayne County weather was something else.

Winter was the most unforgiving of the four seasons. The other seasons had their rare natural events such as hurricanes, high water, early frosts, muck fires, droughts, and tremendous winds off Lake Ontario. Winter had tons and tons of snow—along with the occasional dreaded ice storm.

It was the ice storm that struck fear and apprehension in the hearts of the residents of the northeast. Ice storms did not allow for fighting back as we could with about any other natural occurrence. Plows could handle snow, but there was no vehicle around configured to work an ice storm. An ice storm had a lifespan of its own dictated by Mother Nature. When the conditions finally warmed, an ice storm ended. Falling temperatures with rain were the precursors of an impending problem. If the falling temperature went below thirty-five and the rain persisted, the ice would begin developing on the trees and wires as soon as the temperature reached the freezing range.

I can recall the few ice storms of my Sodus life with some clarity compared to the numerous snow storms. Snow storms were frequent since Sodus was located in close proximity to the eastern end of Lake Ontario. The lake effect snows hitting Oswego and Watertown to the east of Sodus would invariably dump something on Sodus. This "something" was not always a small amount, as a change in winds would bring the heavy snows to the village right off the lake. Ice storms had no friends, and the ice storms we endured were crippling to the village.

Recently Wayne County lost huge numbers of fruit trees due to a severe ice storm. These things seem to go in cycles. I still have my father's pictures of trees burdened and broken by tons of ice during the nineteen-fifties. When the ice hit, it meant that the workforce of the community would have to do Herculean work to get back to normal. The power lines were hammered by ice during these storms in the previous century. The telephone lines went down and communication using phone, TV and radio would be diminished. Portable radios would be the answer for those families possessing such a radio. In every community generators would spring into action to power certain vital things such as the hospitals, Ham radio operations and heating places such as chicken houses. If animals were left out in the ice, they could starve to death if food couldn't be delivered to them.

On the personal level no basketball games were played nor was school in session. Kids would love days off from school but once the ice came postponed games and cancelled school were of secondary interest. Life threatening events were occurring in our village, and in some cases people were losing their lives due to the ice. Accidents were plentiful as people tried desperately to connect with relatives and other loved ones.

Driving in ice was nearly impossible. I can remember fires that broke out during the ice storms. Fire trucks had a very difficult time getting to the blazes. My father went out as a volunteer fireman on several evenings and the only thing he had going for him was the fact that we lived on a hill. His car would slip and slide all the way to the fire hall, where he would muster there with other volunteers. The fire trucks were equipped for about any contingency, but the ice created very dangerous driving situations.

My father got to drive a fire truck on one trip from the fire hall down Maple Avenue, and at that time on the avenue one could find a concrete island about four feet tall in the middle of the pedestrian crossing. My father clipped the island with the rear of a new fire truck one night while driving in the ice and snow. He was banned from ever driving fire trucks again. The island was removed from the street as if to eradicate any bad memory of the object. I think its removal came at the same time my father was mayor of the village.

Of all my recollections of the ice storms of my childhood, the thing that sticks with me the most was the sound of the storm. The term *storm* is often misused. The ice pilled up on the limbs and lines and then wind would deliver a terrible, double whammy. When I think of the word storm, I think of a weather front moving across land depositing rain and/or snow in great amounts. Ice storms were insidious in nature because they seemed to creep up on the folks.

The sounds of the ice-covered limbs moving and groaning under the weight of their new load were absolutely eerie. Eerie is also a word that could be used when we went out and there was no wind. All the sounds of life were muffled and subdued except for the periodic loud explosions of sixty-year old limbs and trunks. I have heard sounds of gunfire on TV and have even heard tanks fire during a demonstration at Fort Knox, Kentucky. So far I have never heard anything to compare with the explosion of a tree.

My family would go to bed during the height of the ice crisis since the power was out, and even though we had an oil burner the blowers did not function. There was not much to do in the dark during an ice storm. As we all listened to the sounds of the huge trees coming apart in our yard, we said a prayer for the two huge Norwegian Spruce trees in front. They towered over the lot and house. They never let us down. Their limbs bent under the tremendous weights but did not snap. Our jars nailed by their lids up at the top of the trees merely swayed with the rest of the tree. I often wonder if the jars are still there.

Hardwood trees and fruit trees were always the first to go. We had an old apple tree that came apart over three different ice storms over a four or five year period. Eventually we gave up on the old friend and cut the rest down. There were pretty willow and maple trees that slowly degenerated over the same storms.

Clean-up after a storm was a lot of hard work. Every property was affected by the ice. Ice was terribly democratic in nature. It affected everyone in proportion to their lot size and number of trees.

As the community kept coming back after each ice storm, the ice storms became a metaphor for human nature in Wayne County.

I bet the folks of the modern generation have developed their own brand of resilience.

***

Chores, Chores, Chores—Shaping the family

I remember my first attempt at building something all by myself. I was ten or eleven. It was my second building job. My previous construction job started when my lifelong friend Gib and I decided to build a boat in his cellar when we were about six. That project is still behind schedule. This solo job was to be a wooden cover for the garbage and trash cans outside our house under one of the kitchen windows. A path around the back of the house led to the remote spot that was not visited often except for garbage reasons.

Back then, in stark contrast to many families of the modern era, the kids under the common roof had chores to perform. Modest allowances were paid, but the allowances back then came as a result of completing critical tasks for the family and the parents. We seem to miss this educational and habit forming option today as parents rush pell-mell around trying to make the lives of their children easier. As I reflect on my childhood I realize this aspect of my life did not harm me and, in fact, shaped me in a positive manner. No task in my teaching and coaching career was beneath me, and that made me better as a teacher and coach and mentor. I started out in garbage back in Sodus, N.Y. and I never minded marking fields, mowing play areas or even making ice for elementary school children on a nearby recreational area. In every case, kids of some age benefited from my work ethic.

I had an idea for garbage storage and handling that was to be on the cutting edge of lunacy. The job was designed when I was about ten or eleven, and my thought was to cover the cans so animals could not tip them over or move the tops off to scatter the garbage. Another thought I had was to eliminate the need for uncovering the cans when we had heavy snows. This occurred numerous times during the endless winters near the tip of Lake Ontario in what is called the Snow Belt. My design would defeat animals and lake effect snow with one magnificent engineering job.

I went into the job solo because I was quite independent—I was the garbage man for the family in the list of responsibilities and I did not want anyone to dissuade me from my bright idea. As I gathered the requisite nails and 2X4's, my problem was a lack of power tools to deal with the tough job of cutting the plywood to fit the frame I had conceived. My stubbornness and independence were about to take the place of good sense.

After getting the framing lumber cut and formed I felt confident about things until the plywood arrived in my neighbor's truck. I had convinced one of the neighbors to bring the plywood to the house and merely tell the lumber company to bill it to my father. In a small town back then a word was like a signed contract or receipt so this three way transaction was not too unusual.

I had no way to cut the plywood to fit the frame. The old handsaw owned by my family was dull and took all I had just to cut the 2X4's. I never benefited from carpentry education or the use modern tools until I was in my twenties. Both of my sons are very skilled in carpentry because their education came from a grandfather who was not my father. My father did not have any inkling about tools or wood working. I was performing solo back then and I knew it.

How was I to cut the plywood? Plywood sheets then, as now, were 4X8 feet and very hard to manage, even if the carpenter possesses the adequate size. I solved this problem using nature and the fact that the plywood was very thin and would bend easily. It was an eighth or at max a quarter inch thick. My frame was such that it extended out from the house about three feet and was eight feet long. Are you getting a picture here? The top therefore was three feet deep. The open front was eight feet across and that made the full sheet convenient. That decided the size of the can bin. Unfortunately, I had the top sloped *toward* the house where the whole thing was attached. Rather than slope the top *away* from the house so snow and leaves could slide off the device I had created a scheme all by myself where snow and leaves could pile up against the side of the house, under the kitchen window above where the sink was located.

In my last act of this job I merely dropped the sheet of plywood down behind the frame about twelve inches and then attached the remaining three feet of plywood to the frame as the slightly bowed roof. Using four-inch nails I hammered the crap out of the plywood frame and made sure everything was attached to the house. As an aside, the four-inch nails became the universal nail in our home. During the next summer I pounded one of the nails trough the top of a soap box racer built by a few of us and as the nail finished its trip through the top and small framing wood it nestled about two inches into my thigh. After completing the race with my leg bleeding profusely I left the racing to another boy. My blood was quite evident in the racer's shell. I probably was being repaid by fate for the use of four inch nails in my garbage bin job.

The bowed plywood sheet stayed in place on top because I had concrete blocks on it for many months. The plywood warped over the months of weather conditioning. The cans did not get snow on them because of the roof. No one living in the house came around to that side of the house for the winter months. I did all the garbage disposal work and really did not want too many people to see my project. Even then I had my doubts. In movies this might be called foreshadowing. The construction job was done in September to accommodate the winter snows. My system was in place for winter, but was not even acknowledged until spring by anyone in the house. This was fine with me because I was already aware of problems.

When it snowed a lot the kitchen window got covered up with the snow piled on top of the garbage bin. Instead of sliding off, it merely caught in the wedged area I had created. This created a new job for me since I did not want the window to be covered with snow from the bin. Another flaw turned up when I realized I had to tug and pull the garbage cans out from under the slanted roof each time in order to dump stuff into the cans. This was labor intensive in contrast to sweeping light snow off a top to dump under the original system. One more thing popped up in regard to my independently designed bin. The snow and leaves piled against the house for long periods of time due to the slope toward the house. This design for the roof managed to start causing the rotting of the side of the house. Oh yes, one other finer point was evident before too long.

Whenever it rained or snow melted from the sloped roof it ran into the kitchen under the sink following the four-inch nail holes I had pounded in great numbers to hold the whole device against the house in the first place.

We ended up having water in the kitchen, rotted floorboards under the sink, rotted sidewall under the window—and a real credibility problem for my carpentry career. The extra labor of moving the nearly full cans in order to dump additional garbage was a problem. Keeping the window above the bin clear was a new task. Twice a week garbage trucks came by, and that meant I had to haul the cans out of the bin so the workers could get them easily. After my first winter of garbage-intensive work, the whole project took on a real foul odor, figuratively speaking

My father finally took it upon himself to come out to my garbage area to see what the hell was going on. By then many problems had already developed over the winter months. His reaction was quite predictable. My project took on a life of its own as my father realized the plywood he had purchased was not in the garage waiting for a soapbox racer. He also realized the leaks in the kitchen were not God's work in an old house but predictable outpourings based upon dozens of holes punctured in the kitchen wall. He was so mad at me I did not get physical punishment that was the norm back then. Instead I was sentenced to his form of hell for eleven year olds.

Hell hath no fury compared to a dominating father with no interest in carpentry whose eleven-year-old son has caused "five hundred *futzing* dollars" worth of damage to the house. He used futz often, and never once did I hear him say the word that was its oft-used cousin in linguistics. I learned much later, after my father's death, that his top income in his whole life was twenty one thousand dollars. He had kept very methodical records and I discovered his income at about the time of my carpentry exploit was about seven thousand bucks. Can you imagine a child creating damage that would take perhaps seven percent of the gross family income? Can you imagine how a father would view the expense in contrast with the benefits, if any?

My penalty was garbage duty forever in a family where duties tended to rotate around washing and drying dishes, emptying garbage, shoveling snow, mowing grass, raking leaves, picking up groceries, washing cars, and picking up tree limbs and bush trimmings. My garbage career skyrocketed. I also did many of the other chores for long time. It seems as though I was destined to be connected with trash and garbage. Even today I am in charge of those duties in my own home.

My father brought in a local carpenter to dismantle and repair the damage. In a final afterthought as the damage was repaired my father had the carpenter put up a bin with the slope in the correct direction. He also made it a free-standing device, away from the house and with more height to the thing so I could dump trash in the winter without hauling the cans out.

No word was ever passed between me and my father about the damage and the repair or the incredible fact that my father and the carpenter seemed to have incorporated my original idea into the new project. Maybe my father was, in some small way, impressed that I would have the balls to attempt a project he never would have considered doing. That did not remove my name from his futz list.

Sometimes it is just smart strategy to quit when you are behind.

***

Grandparents and Ghosts—Wonderful memories

Grandfather Bowerman turned his two daughters over to the parents of the girls' deceased mother. Their mother had died at age 26. The year she died was 1913. My Great Grandfather Art Nothaker was now the surrogate father to his daughter's children. It sure beat the heck out of an orphanage or DEFACS. My mother and aunt were not tossed on the dump heap of the human condition, as they might be in the modern era. The Nothakers were with a man and wife who loved the girls dearly. I know because I noticed all that when I started tracking my great grandfather around.

Nothaker was a second-generation German, meaning that his parents were from the old country. He clung to the German heritage. His food, language and attitudes reflected the old country. I was too young to discuss things but I was old enough to listen and absorb. At breakfasts he would serve me food that was not of my choosing. I ate it because that is what a five year old did when living with an old man and his wife for several weeks in a summer. I ate sausage, hot dogs and bologna about every morning for breakfast when my mother, brother and I stayed with them for several weeks.

As I reflect upon the dilemma my family had back then, it made sense to have extended stays with close family such as the Nothakers. They served Doris and Isabel for many years and now, during war when one of their "daughters" needed help, they were there again. I never discussed this chapter in our family with my mother since I sensed it was too difficult for her to discuss. The only view I heard her voice on the matter was once when she and my father were in a rare, nasty verbal shouting match.

One thing led to another and then my mother, in defending her grandparents, stated that during the war when we were down on our luck the only relatives to offer a helping hand were the Nothakers. She ranted on and said that my father's parents were strangely mute during the war years out of a perceived fear (Isabel's connotation) that Isabel would want to bring the boys to live with them in the city.

My father was unresponsive to this attack, as I remember, so I gauged that my mother had won that point. I do not recall seeing the Pearson grandparents during the war years hardly at all, yet I vividly remember the Nothakers during the same era. I think my mother hit a tender point about Dad's family in her defense of her "makeshift" family. She never talked about the death of her mother or the disappearance of her father, yet I know that certainly was a part of her mystique.

I am proud of my mother's mental toughness as I remember these matters. During the time we were in the city with that set of grandparents, we were entertained by the clever German and his matronly wife. Art used to take us across Lake Avenue to play at a school. This was near where they lived in a triplex just down the street. The original Aquinas High School was located there. We would play hide and seek with my brother and other kids who lived nearby. Art found a spot behind the school where there was an unusual oddity. I often have wondered if the building is still around and, if so, if the oddity is still there.

Art showed me the one to two foot gap in the rear of the building big enough for a kid to hide. It was shielded by a bush or tree, yet was a tiny column of space neatly bricked up for two stories above the ground. It was as if someone messed up with the design and then they merely bricked the thing up with the gap preserved forever. I hid there several times from the others and Art loved it. He and the other boys couldn't find me. He made them think I had disappeared. They finally caught sight of me coming out of my brick lair one day, so the mystery was solved.

Another thing that was evening entertainment occurred when we would go up into the attic of the big house. Three families lived in the triplex. We would go across the common attic space and make funny noises to scare the neighbors at night. We would retreat to the far side where Art's part of the attic was located. It never dawned on me that such a prank could be accomplished by any of the other residents in the big triplex.

One time late at night somebody or somebodies got revenge on the Sodus visitors and their sponsor in hijinx—Art Nothaker. Remembering that I was five or so at the time, it was possible that I was scarred crapless. During that traumatic experience, Dick and I woke up in a dark, strange room and there were weird noises emanating from the attic above our heads. We were both ready to return to Sodus the next day.

We had plenty of good times with grandparents on both sides of our genetic tree. The Nothakers were my grandparents and that was that. They were much older than the grandparents on Dad's side but that never impacted on me until Art and Isabel died early in my life. The Pearson grandparents did a lot for Dick and me but they missed out, I think, on some of our early years. We were probably not the handful they thought we might have been during the war years.

Then again, maybe we were.

PART TWO
Community

The community impact in the era under scrutiny in my life was tremendous; it was also very enjoyable most of the time. In the dynamics of Sodus there appeared to be the beginnings of what we now call "a bedroom community," coupled with the very traditional farming community work ethic. Many people commuted, driving to nearby Rochester, thirty miles to the west. There they worked for Eastman Kodak and other successful industries in the upstate region.

The farmers were fruit farmers or "muck" farmers, but usually men never combined the two due to the differences in the applications of labor. Fruit people dealt with the whims of the weather, the crop prices when harvested, and such things as migrant laborers, short harvest seasons, and transportation from the farms to the factories and cold storage. Muck farmers were different as was their work place. Muck is rich, decomposed earth, trees and nutrients where there once was swamp-land.

Many people in Sodus were of Dutch descent. These people were no-nonsense, hard-working, family people. New York State was comprised of sixty four unique counties that in turn were comprised of various townships; and then within each township were villages. Sometimes the villages carried the name of the township and other times there were other villages within any given township. The townships were larger than the villages and in my home county we were Town of Sodus, Village of Sodus and part of Wayne County. It would take an hour to drive across the county north to south or east to west. In Wayne County, each town and village appeared to have a unique cultural flavor within the county. The farming communities along the shores of Lake Ontario had a preponderance of Dutch, German and Scandinavian peoples. Further inland from the lake and along the famous Erie Canal were residents of Irish, Italian and Spanish descent. Many of their relatives helped build the famous canal. Wayne County also had a growing population of African-Americans. Many of these people were related to the migrant workers who used to travel between Florida and New York, chasing the various harvest seasons as they sought jobs as fruit pickers.

These multicultural details of the communities made for very interesting sports contests throughout the county. The community life was quite seasonal, based upon the farming and the very distinct change of seasons. Winter was harsh and unforgiving and summer was usually moderate, with an occasional hot spell of two weeks. The other two seasons were Mother Nature's gifts to the residents for making it through the harsh winters. The rewards were numerous as detailed in fall's smells and sights and spring's blooms with vivid greens, lilac and tulip colors. In reality, the impact of this community was probably no different than the other nice, small communities abounding in New York State or anywhere for that matter. However the uniqueness of Sodus was still special to my friends and me.

***

Twelfth Night—A forgotten ritual

Twelve nights after Christmas the gathered Christmas trees went up in a blaze seen for miles and felt for hundreds of yards down by the school parking lot. On January 6th the population of the community gathered at the school to watch the local volunteer firemen set off a huge pile of discarded Christmas trees already dried out and ready to glow in a whole new way. The trees were collected by village workers from the snow banks in front of the homes throughout the community. Some people dragged their trees there by sled if they had let the tree linger in their homes beyond the pickup date.

This eve of Epiphany was a special night in our area. According to many people it was considered bad luck to take the Christmas decorations and trees down prior to the 6th of January. The celebration recognized the gift of the Magi according to tradition. This tradition, going back in history hundreds of years, was a pretty big deal for several reasons. The gathering usually took place on a school night, and that was always a bonus and departure from the school night routines at home. Secondly, the night became a visual and sensatory delight since the dry trees burned fiercely and with nice aromas. A third factor was that in the cold night, laced with hot drinks and donuts for all, the kids got a glimpse of adults gathered in a community celebration of life and the passing holiday season.

Twelfth nights involving huge fires do not occur anywhere to any extent anymore for liability and environmental reasons. Probably communities don't function quite like that anymore, either. Whatever liability problems existed then in my home town were not given much consideration, since the ground was usually covered with many inches of snow and the local firemen were there to start the blaze and then monitor it until its lingering ashes were finally extinguished. The environmental concerns just were not a factor in that era. We did not worry about things such as air quality, ozone layers, and global warming since our trees were disposed of, the warm drinks were great, and the event was over long after the smoke drifted who knows where. We burned leaves during the fall and that occurred with regularity. Since that was safe and fun, why would anyone worry about the January blaze?

The leaf fires of the fall were products of youthful "volunteer" firemen all over the village as we tossed horse chestnuts into the small fires and enjoyed the loud pops resulting from the minor explosions of the chestnuts. We would even save chestnuts for January to toss upon the tree fire, but their pops were indistinguishable due to the roar of the trees burning. The local firemen who tended to the details were, of course, volunteers. As with most small villages across America the volunteer firemen were the mainstays of a safe community.,

My own father served as mayor for many years, worked as

a salesman for a local canning company, and on Twelfth Night was there with his volunteer cronies dressed out in fireman's gear. The sight of our various fathers and local leaders assuming the fire fighter's role was always intriguing. Long before the events of September 2001, firemen were held in special awe and esteem in communities like Sodus. The risk to these local people was always there and in certain fires such as when a big building caught in the downtown district—or when the local Greek restaurateur torched his place every seven years or so for insurance purposes—the risk was great.

The Twelfth Night celebration was a piece of cake for the firemen fire control-wise, and they used this night to rally the troops and new equipment in a show of force reminiscent of the July 4th parades and Firemen's Field Days. After the January night concluded, my father would return to home after we had made the trudge home ourselves, and his arrival was an odor-full reminder of the season one more time. His clothes were permeated with the smells of the burning trees.

My home was on High Street and that was nice except that it involved going up a long, rather steep hill from the village and from school. Going there was a breeze, but the return walks were a test each time. Sliding down this hill took many hours of our winter days when we were not in school, so the location had a fine recreational dividend. Such dividends were paid for by taxing the heart and legs and lungs to get back to the top each wintry trip down the hill with the sled. Reflecting upon such activities now, I realize I had a physically challenging childhood, and because of those endless hours on the hill my constitution is better for it today.

As an aside, the state of children's fitness in the modern era is evidence enough of the void of physical activity in their young lives. The Twelfth Night celebration ended with another climb up the hill with my brother and others, and one more great memory of adults and children experiencing something together that developed greater respect for the community and its dynamics.

***

STINKY'S TALES

Paper Route—A con job that was beneficial

My brother had a paper route that encompassed four streets in our home town:our own street, High Street, plus Gaylord Street and the connecting street called School Street. The one not mentioned above was Orchard Terrace. Orchard Terrace was a long street going perpendicular to High Street—straight up! My brother calculated that I could get a weekly allowance from him if I could help him do his route daily. He assigned to me Orchard Terrace. Of the sixty-five papers he delivered daily (except for Sunday) I did a third of them. My assigned papers were delivered straight up. Thank goodness the extremely heavy Sunday paper had to be purchased at the local drug store!

I received one dollar per week from what I think was Dick's four dollar profit per week. For the one dollar I delivered about twenty papers up the hill, and also collected the weekly paper bill from each of the houses. Considering that the delivery work was up the steepest hill in the village and that I had to walk up carrying a bag with the papers, I had drawn the most difficult part of the route.

After doing this for about a year it finally dawned upon me that Dick was able to ride his bike along the normal streets he had and even ride down the only steep piece of his share of the route on School Street. He was finished with his two thirds of the work for three quarters of the money long before I could get up the hill and finish my share.

At the end of the year I was able, with my mother's assistance, to renegotiate the arrangement. I got more money but had half of the route by adding part of my own street. For my paper route experience, I got minimal pay for maximal work.

The papers on Thursday were extremely heavy. As I calculated it upon reflection later in my life, my brother had given me a great form of physical training. Without knowing it he had given me hill work six days a week where my load probably consisted of ten to twenty pounds of papers, depending upon inserts. By carrying such a load when I was ten and eleven years old, my legs developed faster than they might have under normal events. On Thursdays my legs got a terrific workout. Sport-related training later in life would be easy.

I owe my older brother thanks because he played a part in my leg development. My legs are still holding up today. Although he thought he had bested me in the deliberations over the division of labor, my staying power was terrific. Once again something developed in me for which I may not have even planned.

Because Dick had a different view of things and handled situations with less patience, I was able to gather tips at Christmas from my portion of the route that far exceeded his tips. My mother informed me to not gloat over this fact, and that was good advice. When I found out what his tips were contrasted to mine, my Mother's advice was astute. Dick would have crapped had he known the size of some of my tips. Orchard Terrace was the address for some of the village's wealthiest people. This is something that my entrepreneur brother had overlooked in his original design.

The beauty of life sometimes comes at you long after certain events pan out. In the example of the paper route, I benefited terrifically from a fitness sense. This fitness, I am sure, helped me with whatever sport interests I had over my high school years. Additionally, by enduring the steep street assigned to me, the porch dwellers along the route would see me struggling up the hill with my bag. At Christmas time their memories of my struggles to deliver their papers would open up their pockets.

This experience taught me that true rewards come well after the actual event or events. This credo works for teachers and coaches. I receive rewards continually from people who have been with me earlier in my life. The rewards may not be the monetary tips as they were from the Orchard Terrace dwellers fifty years ago, but they are actually better. The kudos come from ex-students.

***

Fruit Farm Education—A masters in life
After completing my doctorate degree at the age of thirty-

two at The University of New Mexico, I was at the culmination of formal education in my life, but there was something more for me to learn. Despite the terminal degree in my field of study, and despite having a new job starting in the fall, here I was with degree in hand, with a wife and two small children and no money. It was time to return to my roots.

I had spent all my savings, lived on a graduate assistant's salary for two and a half years, and needed summer employment. Knowing that my family had lost our father the previous spring and that my grandmother was on her last legs, I decided to travel across country to my home town to work where I had worked as a teenager over a decade earlier. I called upon my younger brother to put in a word for me. Charley got me a job at the Fruit Farm. His helping me allowed me to remember this was the younger brother I had "mentored" when he was an infant and I was a teenage babysitter.

My brother Charley worked at the Sodus Fruit Farm in the scale house, and through his connections he managed to get me back into the orchards for the sweet and sour cherry season that summer. His job was critical to the whole process since he weighed the farmer's trucks before they dumped cherries into the factory tanks for processing. The water in the tanks was always drained prior to weigh-in so the factory wouldn't be paying for water. When the trucks returned to the scales after dumping cherries at the factory the revised, lighter weight was subtracted from the gross weight tallied when the trucks came in. Charley was the key person in the accounting area, since farmers were paid by the pound. Charley was a college student at the time, and I was merely going to be a field hand out in the orchards. I took the job without reservation since I had done it twice before and rather liked it. Besides, I was in need of money!

My summer work was right back out in the middle of the orchards where migrant labor crews picked cherries and dumped them into the truck tanks my brother was weighing. It was the same job I worked back when I was in high school during the summer months. I had changed over the years educationally, but the job in the orchards was the same. The job allowed me to feed a family this time around whereas before I spent money on dates, ballgames, and sports equipment. I could not help but note the contrast.

There were migrant laborers waiting for me when I arrived in the orchard early in June, just as there had been many years before. Orchards come awake as soon as daylight has drained some of the heavy dew off the trees and ground. If it has not rained and the humidity is low, pickers can get an early start. These first several buckets give the pickers a promising start in their day's work. Migrants were paid by the pails they picked. They had to then sort out the bad cherries and twigs on big trays connected to the huge ice- and water-filled tanks. After sorting, the cherries were dumped into the tank by lifting the big trays. I had to insure that the cherries were not just dumped directly into the tanks, thereby allowing the picker to get back picking as contrasted to the time-consuming sorting job at the tank.

My job, with or without a doctorate, was to record the number of buckets dumped into the tanks. I did this as a teenager and repeated the task as a thirty two year old worker. Each time I did the job, I had to get to know some names and faces and then accurately record the efforts. My lunches were often taken in the fields with the workers since they wanted to keep up the pace of buckets dumped in the tanks. Their pay was determined by their individual efforts. My pay was by the hour, and that could be bumped up by the fact that I worked early in the morning to accommodate the crew and stayed on during lunch to count pails. If we worked weekends we were paid more. Getting to know the crew chief and the crew was very important. My master's degree in worker relations was being honed at the orchards.

The contrast between the orchards of Sodus and the classrooms at New Mexico couldn't have been more defined. I made the same observation when I was in Sodus High School with its very small Black population and I worked with forty Black men and women in the summers. I worked those two other summers while a teenager and learned a great deal about migrants and life then.

One lesson was that people have a common ground no matter what the age, gender or color. My good fortune of being related to a mother who was a people person in a small town certainly helped me in the orchards. Another thing that really helped in the orchards was the common interest in sport, and especially the sport of baseball. Most of my friends played baseball and we grew up loving the sport. The migrants loved baseball. They played on Sundays when they could arrange games and were not picking cherries or other fruit.

Whenever the talk came around to baseball the workers were not only knowledgeable, they were often very passionate about the sport. Despite the need to pick many pails to get their money, they still took a little time to linger at the sorting trays to talk baseball.

More than a few times the crew boss would remind his younger workers that time was fleeting and they needed to pick rather than talk with the "checker," which was my official title.

It was common knowledge that the crew bosses were responsible for getting the crews together, helping transport them to the orchards, and even making sure they got medical attention when needed. Crew bosses did have a great interest in the total number of buckets picked since they got bonuses based upon the performance of their crews. They could not afford to transport and feed a worker from Florida to New York to witness the worker goof off once they arrived. I had to be a part of a team to keep the workers in a productive mode. The only thing the crew bosses did not have to negotiate, it appears, was the housing, Usually large farms provided housing areas very similar to the housing depicted in the movie "Cider House Rules." When I saw the movie I was taken back in time and gained greater appreciation for the work ethic of the pickers and their ability to put up with sub-standard housing for the picking periods in their lives.

It reminded me of the time when Robert F. Kennedy came to Sodus as part of his whirlwind tour of New York State when he was running for the senate in the sixties. One of his stops was at one of the orchards, and while he was making a camera-moment so popular in his campaigning the orchard owner came out with a shotgun and wanted no part of the senate election process that would draw national attention to the way he housed migrant workers. The farm owner was subdued, the story goes, and Kennedy beat a hasty retreat to only end up being assassinated in California while he was a New York Senator running for the presidency in 1968. As terrible as the shooting was, it was fortunate for Sodus this shooting did not occur in the Sodus orchards.

The migrant laborers brought many interesting lessons to me when I was a young man. They did so again when I was a thirty-two years old.

When I was at New Mexico I vowed I would take the inexpensive brief case that I used while going to the classes and dump it in Lake Ontario after filling it with rocks. This was to have been my statement against the observed pretentiousness of many educators in the elevated food chain. I was going to fight the stuffed-shirt image so many educators seemed to get at some point in their lives by throwing the case into the lake.

After going back to the fruit farm orchards for that third summer of work I realized that I would be OK despite the stuffed shirts in my world. I picked a day that summer to dump the briefcase, filled with rocks, into the Lake Ontario waters at the base of the bluffs at the orchards of the fruit farm. Somehow, the migrant workers might have appreciated my solitary act.

***

Evil Empire—Honk's place

Frank Atkinson's place of business kept him on the premises about sixteen hours a day. Like so many business owners of that era and even the modern era, owners had to be there to insure business did not go into the crapper at the hands of an uncaring employee. Frank's place of business was named "Honks" and where that name came from I have never found out. What I did find out, however, was that Honks was off limits to young boys and certainly off limits to all women.

My instructions on the matter were quite explicit and they came from the top. My father was omnipotent in my family and, in my eyes, in the community. He was the mayor, a volunteer fireman, treasurer of the volunteer firemen, successful salesman, navy veteran of World War II, and ruler of the domain called 20 High Street. My father told me early on that I was to stay out of Honks. This included the front part as well as the pool area.

This created a dilemma for me since several of my peers went in there, and my older brother went in there with his friends. Honk was a rotund, short man who looked old at every step of the way in my growing process. Honk's wife was active in the Presbyterian Church where my mother established herself and us as members. My Dad went two or three times per year, but Isabel and her children showed up regularly. We often sat with or near Lavina Atkinson. Lavina was Frank's wife and no one, and I mean no one, would ever put her with him in matrimony. The husband and wife Atkinson were the original odd couple in my life. She was tall, slender and rather pretty. Honk was the absolute opposite.

Somewhere in my childhood en route to manhood I ventured into the smoky den called Honks. The first time was a revelation. Peering out at me from behind a counter nearly as tall as his own five-foot height was Honk. His glasses rested down on his nose and he welcomed me with two words: "Root beer?" Honk sold root beer in frosted mugs for a nickel. I bought one and sat on a worn out stool at a dingy counter and sipped the wonderful drink.

I did not offer up any conversation since I knew I did not belong there, nor did Honk say anything. He seemed to tolerate young men and boys who drank root beer and who played the two pinball machines in the place. His real business was the pool hall in the back.

As I looked out into the back of the place, I could not recognize anyone. A haze hung over the green, felt-topped tables. The smoke prevented me from recognizing any of the men who frequented the business. It seemed that everyone smoked at Honks. That was probably one reason for my father's edict. Coach McGinn often said that people on his teams at Sodus should not be seen in the pool hall. I guess his concern was the smoke. The idle time wasted there probably concerned him also. He desired activities more conducive to sport excellence even though he made few suggestions for our idle time of a sport-specific nature. This was long before the idea of sport camps and specialization occurred. His major concerns were Honk's pool room and girls. Of the two potential evils his players seemed to fear being seen with girls much more than the coach seeing us in Honks.

Once I knew I could get into Honks for a root beer, the other things there became readily apparent to me. There were girly magazines. Honk sold newspapers and also the tabloids of the fifties called the New York newspapers. He also sold all kinds of tobacco products, fishing lures, fruit pies, hats, gloves, and assorted adult male things like decks of cards with nudes on the cards.

The pool tables probably provided the greatest source of funds because it seemed like there were a dozen tables back there. I only went back one time with an older boy, merely as an observer. The smoke lingered permanently since there was no modern air filtration system, nor did the back door get opened during the winter months. Second hand smoke was definitely there, and almost certainly it caused breathing and lung problems for the regular customers. No one worried about second hand smoke back then, because no one even worried about first hand smoke back then.

I would see high school athletes back in the pool area when I was in junior high school and marvel at their courage to defy Coach McGinn's edict about Honks pool room. I also wondered about their common sense. The thought never, ever crossed my mind to ever, ever challenge McGinn's edict on Honk's pool room. The edict on girls was something else!

After getting the root beer fix during several visits, I ultimately became a pinball machine player at a nickel a pop. The machine took my paper route money for many weeks as I underwent a minor's addiction to the game. During a long span of time right there under Honk's gaze we were clever enough to put little pieces of wood under the front legs of the pinball machine. This revelation became common knowledge to all who played the machines and the end result was that the ball would linger on the less-tilted playing surface and allowed for huge scores as the pinball careened off the targets repeatedly. Huge scores were rewarded with free games. Once a guy named Jack Lewis had so many free games on one machine we took turns rotating the free play among eight or nine of us. Within two months or so of this underhanded alteration of the machines on our part Honk caught on. His counter-measure was severe. He banned many of us from the machines for a long time. He also attached them to the floor somehow to eliminate the problem of the less-tilted surface.

Despite the clear-cut violations of the parental and coaching guidelines, young men still frequented the place. The thrill of defiance back then was no doubt the same as today. The difference, pathetically, is that the consequences of defiance today are profound and life-threatening because the risks and places of risk are manifestly different. Honk may have looked sinister, but Lavina turned him into a pussy cat. She even had the brass to walk in the place in broad daylight and get papers. She was the only woman I ever saw in the place. Honk was a whipped man.

I know this for a fact because for two weeks my brother and I lived with Honk and his tall, pretty wife. Living with Honk came about because of the church connection with Lavina and my mother's trip to have surgery on her legs due to varicose veins. Donna was cared for by another family, but Lavina got us. This put me right in there with Honk when he returned from his sixteen hour day at the shop. It also kept me on pins and needles since Honk knew of my participation in his offerings at the store. Lavina did not know this, I thought, since if she had known she would have told Isabel, and then the mayor would have known, and I would be dead.

Upon reflection now it no doubt was quite common knowledge that most of us frequented Honk's place, and Lavina probably considered us prime providers for her taste in fine clothes and fur pieces. Why would she rat us out to the mothers of the Presbyterian

Church if it was bad for business? I guess even back then the bottom line was quite influential to one's philosophy.

Lavina was always interested in our family and us children. Honk and she had no offspring, and this gave us a special friend at birthday and Christmas time. I vividly remember receiving fifty-cent pieces on special occasions from Honk's wife through the years. Guess where these fifty-cent pieces ended up?

Living with Honk for two weeks allowed me to see him "whipped" by his wife as he performed all kinds of duties at home no one ever would have imagined after seeing him in his gruff, unyielding stance at the shop. Honk became a person and not simply an icon. I lost my fear of him ratting me out. My brother and I even started to listen to radio programs with him in his living room at night as we seemed to bond.

As with so many relationships in life, it really does help to see a person in a more complete light. Honk came home to Lavina and made an attempt to be a friend of two boys staying in his house. We were also his customers. No one in my house knew that fact. It was an interesting time to be alive.

***

Gib's Dad and Mom—Stalwarts in the community

I had received the call from Aunt Doris after getting pulled out of a swimming class I was teaching at the University of New Mexico. It was March of my second year of study, and Doris informed me my father had suffered a serious stroke and was in critical condition. My time in New Mexico was nearly over and I would finish the degree and my part-time job in June of 1970. I was 32 and my father was only 61 years old. My father had just visited me in Albuquerque the previous November so his recent visit was foremost on my mind. The thought that he would not see me attain my doctorate and miss that moment of parental pride was a forlorn one.

In a blur of activity I calculated how to reach Rochester, N.Y. as quickly as possible so that I could be with my father before he passed away. As my connections took me from Albuquerque to

Rochester via Denver and Chicago, my thoughts were on my Dad and his recent visit with me and my family in New Mexico. The thoughts also were flowing down memory lane in Sodus.

The plane landed and I presented a brave front for my aunt and uncle and older brother, who met the plane. All through the trip I had avoided the fact that there was little hope for my father. My brother and aunt informed me to be prepared to see my Dad in a much different state than when I had last seen him in November. My brother took me aside and was even more to the point. He told me Dad was a "vegetable" and that I had better be prepared to be shocked at his state.

As prepared as I thought I was for what was awaiting me at the Myers Hospital in Sodus, once inside the place and glimpsing inside the room where Dad was kept alive electronically, I lost it. Suddenly, as if by magic, Gib Sergeant's mother materialized and was hugging me and supporting and directing me to a private waiting room. This was Sodus at its very best. A capable registered nurse, Evelyn Sergeant had been a major factor in the life and death of Sodus. In her long, successful career she had witnessed and helped with most of the births. She was also present for many of the deaths.

She was there for me and my family on this bleak weekend. My father lingered on the machine for another day and finally his heart stopped. I made it in time to witness the last belabored heartbeat, but the memory of Gib's mother helping me get through the initial dark moment was never forgotten.

Evelyn Sergeant was performing her nursing duties for many decades in the hometown we all shared. I departed looking for my career elsewhere and never quite found a couple so integrated into a community as they were. She and her husband, L.H. Sergeant, served many in the village. He was the town clerk and in that capacity he kept records on critical matters, and was also a notary. We called his only son Lawrence Henry for a time until we hit upon other nicknames. Lawrence Henry was known by all and knew just about everything that occurred in the town. Gib did not aspire to carry Lawrence Henry's many duties. Consider that Gib's father's signature was on about every document in the village. Gib fashioned his own identity over the years. In the modern era, sons and daughters of notable people often take a negative turn as if to make their parents angry. This reminds me of a great line on one of the recent television shows to "never date a daughter trying to make her parents mad." I was not aware that Gib actually ever made his parents angry.

There was a time after I had been away from the community for many years when I was trying to sell a car over a weekend spent in Sodus. Without much background for such dealings, I merely called L.H. on a Sunday afternoon and explained my dilemma. Without hesitation he told me to bring the car, the buyer, and my papers to him at his house. He maintained an office at his house for these events and in a span of fifteen minutes I had the paperwork notarized and New York State legal. Consider all the bureaucracy of the modern era in stark contrast to the legal and friendly competence of L.H. Sergeant of mid-twentieth century Sodus.

It seems to me that people like the Sergeants make up the core of what we refer to when we say "Americans." People who serve others for a lifetime and who perform ably without fanfare are our nation's greatest resource. Competence and reliability are two traits that are the mainstays of what we are as a collective people. All too often, these traits are absent today.

There are many people like the Sergeants in our country today. Dismally, there are not enough of them out there. The percentage of "Sergeants" in the current population is too low. As we look around we see more and more disconnected, irresponsible users and takers than ever. The modern villages are not as connected together as before because of the absence of people like the Sergeants. The villages are filled with more and more problem-residents than before. What used to be the exception in the form of criminal violations now becomes the rule. The impact of a society without a preponderance of people like Gib's parents is now scary. This shows up in our schools and in elections.

Check out the voting results in balloting across the country.

114

The percentage of participation is woeful for our republic. Check out attendance at meetings called by school districts. Check out the community work ethic and community involvement. How many people are carrying the ball on these initiatives?

Every era has its problems. The manner in which a population deals with their era impacts upon the history books. During the mid-century the problems were there, but it seemed there were more people willing to help resolve the issues.

There is now an initiative in the nation to "leave no student behind." Before this school matter can be adequately resolved it would appear we would have to resolve that a huge percentage of parents are uninvolved. These parents need to step up and be counted.

There was no doubt in Sodus that the Sergeants cared for their community. Each performed their duties without enough recognition. Parents in great numbers performed their jobs and responsibilities as expected by society in that other era. Few students were "left behind." The ones that were left behind were unwilling to conform to common expectations. There are so many inadequate parents behind students being left behind today that until that is remedied the public schools will be in trouble for a long time.

The Sergeants were at the core of Sodus. They supported the community in numerous ways. Their son Gib served the school district for many years as a counselor. They all have paid their dues and were repaid by the satisfaction that the community remembers them kindly.

I know they were always there for me.

***

Joseph Gaudino—A business man with heart
Joseph Gaudino was right from the old country. He was a wonderful, jolly Italian man who brought his family to Sodus and set up a successful dry cleaning business that even today is still in his family. Joseph has left this earth, but wherever he is there are jolly times.

My father related to Joseph for reasons I never fully understood yet really admired. Joseph was a kind, sharing human being and our families got together when there were opportunities for picnics and big meals. Mr. Guadino liked my father's mother and father, especially after they eventually moved to Sodus when Grandpa Pearson's health began to fail him. He went out of his way to befriend them. My thoughts then and even now relate to empathy from Joseph about family support. He had to leave Italy to find his niche in life. That required courage and he appreciated my father's concern over the elder Pearsons.

Mr. Guadino worked very hard at developing his business. The dry cleaning business had to be tough on workers, due to the chemical odors prevalent in the establishment. Mr. and Mrs. Guadino were very hands-on workers. They raised two children and their son died prematurely. That left a daughter, Mary, who picked up the family friendship trait. Their loss of a son and brother had to be devastating, yet the family was always upbeat. They carried their loss very privately in the eyes of all of us who knew the story.

One time when we were sliding down the hill from Orchard Terrace we decided to go straight when we hit High Street instead of turning. We flashed between the Guadino home and the house next to Joseph's. That took us straight down to Gaylord Street and we ended up almost at the house where Gib Sergeant lived. After sliding several times we started a snowball fight right between the two houses we had just gone between on our sleds.

After we became bored with throwing snowballs at one another, we picked targets. There were huge icicles hanging from Guadino's house roof. This was a common sight all winter when melting snow dripped and then froze as temperatures provided the right opportunity. We targeted the huge icicles. Typical of much of what we did, we did not adequately assess the whole picture. The whole picture included a large picture window right behind some of the biggest icicles.

You are already getting an idea here, I am sure. Needless to say, we picked off the icicles and one of the biggest fell into the picture window and shattered it. As with so many events like this in Sodus I seemed to have launched the shot heard around the neighborhood. My throw took the icicle and the window out in a noisy, shocking moment.

I knew Mr. Guadino and his family, and did not hesitate to go do the right thing. Such ethical behavior did not always occur so quickly. Sometimes it needed a little gentle nudging. As I rang the front door bell I could hear much jibber jabber inside. That was the normal result of having a huge window fall into one's dining room. The Italian words were flying and finally the door opened.

Mrs. Guadino had me come look at the damage since she surmised I had caused it. She, of course, was right. She unleashed a steady stream of Italian words on me, and soon Joseph came in from outdoors where he must have been when I was on his front porch. We did not pass so I surmised he had gone out the back as I came in the front. We met in his dining room where broken glass lay all over, and some of it was in the baby crib beside the huge now smashed window.

There had been a grandbaby in the crib when the break occurred. Incredibly there were no injuries to the baby, who was now in the arms of his mother Mary Guadino (Piekunka). The child does not remember how very close we all came to disaster that day. I was absolutely flabbergasted to see how close I had come to really doing severe damage to the baby.

Joseph Guadino saw his grandchild was OK, calmed his wife and daughter down and spoke very gently to me in broken English. He was very understanding and saw I was quite shaken by the event. He smoothed the matter over and I went back out to a deserted, white landscape. My friends, I am sure, figured they had seen the last of me for the winter.

I went home that day after leaving the Guadino home feeling very fortunate over two distinctly different things. I had not done any harm to the baby with my faulty intelligence and snowball throwing. For that I was truly thankful.

The second piece of this was that Joseph Guadino reached

out to me when I had wronged his home and family, and treated me very kindly. I viewed him with an extra amount of respect and kindness, and whenever my father suggested something for Joseph I was there for that duty. I think Joseph never told my parents that story, because I surely would have received some feedback on the matter—and it would have been in very understandable language.

***

Front Porch Chronicles—Life on display

I took my date up to our screened porch one summer night and I heard voices coming from the darkened porch. The porch on our house was a popular place in summer since there was movement of air through the screens, the dreaded mosquitoes couldn't get in, and it was a nice place to just relax and talk with neighbors. Front porch life has almost disappeared from our culture, and we are remiss because we do not attempt to restore that fabric from our pasts.

My Grandfather Pearson was on the porch and his familiar, loud voice carried across the yard as we approached. The others on the porch could see me and my date due to the streetlight's extended faint light. We could not see into the porch. As we opened the door, I still could not see who was there with my grandfather.

My father reached around the door's threshold and flipped the light switch for the porch light. My father, grandfather and three other men of the street were there, just talking whatever five men talked about fifty years ago. I would guess baseball, weather, crops, village issues and kids. Times haven't changed much, have they?

Once the light went on I was aware of how bright the light was contrasted to the dark. I also was aware that my date was wearing a white dress that was wet from a swim we had taken earlier. She had her suit on under the light dress but it was very revealing. I was bringing her to the house to change, and to get some dry clothes for myself also.

The five men sat and stared at my date for an awkward time and finally my grandfather broke the ice with a smart-ass remark for which he was famous. He shared with all on the porch something like it was a nippy evening for a summer night. Front porches usually were more collegial and friendly than that night.

Front porches were an extended hand of friendship closer to the streets, and since they weren't the living room or dining room of a house they had informality to them leading to their success. I can remember walking downtown from my home on High Street and before reaching my destination several adults would wave and/or say hello. They would also call me by name.

There were times when the porches kept a semblance of order to the village. Young people knew about the porch life and in the dark of the summer nights no one knew who was where. This preempted acts of vandalism and mischief.

The porch could be a positive thing in ways not even imagined. Once I was running home from a date and my route took me past the recreation building in the middle of town. Sitting on the porch that night with Paul Uher, our organized youth director at the time, was a new soccer coach who served on the recreation commission. They were sitting on the porch in the semi-darkness. As I ran by at full sprint in order to make it home before my curfew I heard my name and waved. Uher must have told the new coach who I was, because two weeks later when soccer commenced the coach bragged about my summer training and he hoped everyone ran like I did in the summer!

The men had seen me running one night and that was all it took to shape an impression. My peers gagged, I smiled, and we went about our fall workout.

The porch life in Sodus was special and I had just been made aware of it one more time. When fall arrived and the storm windows went up for the winter months, porches took on a new life. They served as back up cold storage for the food and beverages overflowing the ice boxes and refrigerators. The porches filled up with leftovers during Thanksgiving and Christmas. It was a common routine to visit the home of a friend and never get into the house due to the wonderful food choices sitting there on the porch.

In the spring we did not relish the work of removing the storm windows that were on every window. They went up every fall and served to insulate the old house. We enjoyed putting screens up on the front porch once winter was finished with us out of anticipation for a great summer.

***

A Tailor's Gifts—Dollar diplomacy from Ike Gardner

In the current world of turmoil and religious tumult there were certain small lessons learned in Sodus that guided me through my life. Without a formal training anywhere, I became aware of and respectful of many religions because my friends were scattered through the churches of the community. There were many religious affiliations represented in the village by churches and groups of people. We had, as did many small villages then, churches for Methodist, Episcopalian, Dutch Reform, Catholic, Pentecostal, and my own Presbyterian church. In Wayne County in upstate New York, where Sodus was one of a dozen or so villages, there was a very deep religious history. The Mormon religion has roots in nearby Palmyra, and the Quakers and Shakers had roots there also.

Of all the religions of the region, the one I knew least about was Hebrew. This gap was filled in part by my knowledge of a few Jewish people who resided in the village. One of these people was a doctor whose own son became the victim of persecution as described in another chapter. Another Jewish person was a local tailor whose impression upon me was manifest. As my mother and I went to and from his store over the years, Ike Gardner would wait on us with a cheerful demeanor and would always have something to say to me despite my age. This impressed me then, and has always been a concept firmly engrained in my life.

As I read about the hatred in the Middle East in our troubled post-9/11 era it appears that the only sane solution will ultimately be for people to learn about others different from themselves as neighbors. The lesson should start where we treat kids like people, and find out some things about them as the communication and behavior levels both improve. In Ike Gardner's world, he was a minority and dismally

I don't recall how or where Jewish people such as he and the local doctor worshipped. That was a gap I should have filled in my own version of understanding. To this day the only information I have ever heard was that he would worship "out of town." Compared to the many local churches within walking distance of almost all the homes in the village, this religion struck me as being difficult due to proximity and not due to any prejudice.

It is compelling to recall how so many people walked to church in those days, thereby creating quite a mix as churches let out on Sundays. It was always the Presbyterian unwritten and unplanned "code" that we Presbyterians would get to the Rexall Drugstore ahead of all other worshippers and get the Rochester Democrat and Chronicle Sunday edition, and if you got there real early you could get the New York Times Sunday edition that would be stacked in the corner in limited quantities. Even today as my wife and I go to non-Presbyterian church in Rome, Georgia I will look at my watch and point out at 12:15 that the Presbyterians down the street are already out and getting something to eat.

Let us return to the topic of Ike. Ike Gardner delivered something every Christmas to each house on High Street and Orchard Terrace. That street was aptly named since it was surrounded by orchards at the time. In the years since, the orchards have slowly disappeared and been replaced by homes with a great view of the village. Ike lived way up on the dead-end of Orchard Terrace. Every Christmas season for many years Ike would walk his way down visiting homes on his street, and then go to the homes on my street delivering dollar bills. If a house did not have kids, he passed by. He was making a gift to the children of his friends, neighbors and clients. If your house had kids, each kid inside got a dollar bill hand delivered by this nice business man. As he wished you a Merry Christmas and shook your hand, he allowed for a mutual understanding between adults and children.

He also allowed for an appreciation of a different religion and one whose holy season was different than the holy season being recognized in the homes he visited. His holy season went unrecognized by most, if not all, of those he visited. I regret that during his holy celebration we in my house did not return his favor in some way. It was a product of a lack of understanding and knowledge, and certainly not a product of lack of respect. It does point out that even then we were pretty caught up in our own lives and failed to spot an opportunity to be nice to a person like Ike. Even Isabel, with all her lessons taught and tolerance lived, let this small man slip by unrecognized at "his" time of year.

The dollar bill was very worthwhile in the late forties and early fifties because it bought a lot. One could go to the movies for a quarter. Popcorn was a dime and drinks were a dime also. Fifty cents got ten plays on the pinball machine in Honks—but that episode doesn't fit in with this current religious theme. Ike Gardner was generous and soft-spoken. He knew all the kids' names and the parents, I am sure, picked up on that facet of life as they frequented his store. The dollar at Christmas was certainly a great P.R. move in an era where businesses were much more customer oriented. The era was also way before the chain stores came to villages such as Sodus, and local businesses depended upon loyalty premised in service and friendship. Ike was doing something that he must have concluded was really good for business. Each parent of each recipient of the Christmas dollar no doubt went toward Ike's clothing store for periodic purchases.

Ike was a very kind man, and this Christmas mission was no doubt fun for him even in his advanced years. It was noteworthy that when Ike retired and his son took over the business, the dollar flow ceased and Ike was no longer a fixture on the two residential streets in Sodus at Christmas. It is also noteworthy that the store ultimately was sold and went through a variety of manifestations over the years as businesses struggled to make a go of it on Main Street. Perhaps the dollar idea died when Ike did and the son inherited a dying business. Perhaps the business died when Ike died because he knew something his son never learned.

***

Halloween Chronicles—Clotheslined by a big arm

I opened the window, removed the screen and clambered down the trellis next to the porch. This route was always opened for mischief. Until the trellis failed us one difficult night, Dick and I could get down and out, complete some prank and then return without either parent suspecting the absence. Pete and Izzy's bedroom was located on the diagonally opposite side of the house on the ground floor. We were noiselessly in and out of the second floor without their knowledge—usually.

On one night near Halloween, I conjured up a great scheme. During the winter months preceding this particular Halloween, I had been wronged by our neighbor's wife. An errant snowball in her son's ear caused great consternation to her. She blamed me for Freddie's pain and suffering, and accused me of hitting her son in the ear on purpose. This occurred during one of the numerous snowball fights so common to our climate. From baseball experience, anyone ever batting against me knew my accuracy was always in question. Freddie knew this fact. I knew this fact. Her husband big George knew this fact, because he was one of the several adults in the village who played catch with the kids. Mrs. DeBrine judged me harshly and unfairly. My own mother was influenced unfairly, and my apology had to be made for my mother's sake. I apologized...but I vowed revenge.

By sneaking out late at night and cutting the DeBrines' clothesline, I thought I would have a convenient alibi. I would be in bed when the line was cut. The clothesline was critical to Mrs. DeBrine because she dried clothes out there almost daily. This was a perfect crime. The revenge motive from eight months previously would not be connected to the crime.

I was back up in the bedroom within several minutes of my exit. Two different clotheslines were cut apart and were on the ground next door. My sense of fairness was satisfied. I was asleep in a short time.

Breakfast was served and I could hardly wait to learn of the reaction of the neighbor's wife when the clothes were ready to go out on the lines.

My wait was very short lived.

Mr. George DeBrine was at the door and he wanted to know if I could play catch. This was a bit unusual, since he usually played with us once Freddie and I were already out there. He joined us many times. We used baseballs and footballs depending upon the season. He was a good guy, and a parent who showed great interest in our activities. For him to ask me to play catch without Freddie was very unusual. I could not refuse the invitation. He was a compelling figure of a man. At six foot, four inches, weighing well over two hundred pounds, George was not a man anyone would disagree with over anything. I was to find this out soon.

As we played catch with a baseball we made small talk about the season past and talked about the upcoming season. His son Fred and I both played baseball, and Fred was quite a pitcher. George made the last toss, and just as I was heading back inside he said that he wanted the clothesline replaced by whoever had cut it down by the next morning. His unique, sly confrontational style was unheard of at the time.

It was as if I had been hit by a fastball in the ear. How could he have known of my clandestine mission? How could he have connected the dots so quickly between crime and motivation? How could he think his catching buddy Bobby Pearson could have done such a prank? I covered my true reaction as cleverly as possible and merely said that I would ask around to see about replacing the line. He said thanks and went in. I went in and said thank you God that there was no physical abuse. He had connected the dots.

The line was replaced that night after dark by two of us. George never, ever mentioned the line deal again. I paid for the clothesline out of my savings. I paid for the crime. Crime did not pay. Consequences occurred for my actions and things returned to normal. It was my last clothesline caper.

George taught me a valuable lesson. He assigned the responsibility to one of the biggest pranksters in the village. Despite being Isabel's son and the mayor's son, I did possess a finite reputation. When pranks were pulled, my name came up very quickly on any hit list. My father once told me that the chief of police in Sodus, Con Loveless, kept a black book—and that my name was in there with several of my friends. Nothing much was ever done about the black book and my reflection on the matter was that it may have been a "con" job. It probably did prevent pranks before they started. Call it the fear factor.

George was a good man. He probably knew that I had the balls to pull such a stunt on his wife. His wife was an attractive woman, but was very protective of her two sons. George could put all the clues together rather easily. Once I thought he suspected me, even in his indirect fashion, I was really bothered by the matter. How could I have done this prank to a neighbor like George? How could I do this to someone who played catch with me? My own father could never bring himself to just come out and play catch. George was my buddy even though he was an adult. I respected him. This was an exceptional revelation for an adolescent.

Throughout my own adult years I have always tried to reach out to young people whether it was a game of catch, a game of hoops, or even just a talk. George probably never realized the impact of his manner on me in the clothesline caper. He taught me in that one episode that confrontation can be accomplished in different ways.

There have been numerous times in my coaching and teaching career when I have used the indirect approach to discipline. When I paid for the new line and got it up George was satisfied. He pretty much knew all along what had happened and he let things flow from there. In coaching, training rules usually get broken in some manner. When a coach knows the rules have been broken, one interesting way to deal with the infraction is to let the violators stew in their juices for a spell and let them and their peers work out the remedy.

The new line went up in the neighbor's yard. It provided an interesting lesson for a future teacher/coach.

***

Ivan the Great—A prince of a man

Ivan Symonds came out to the car from inside the large service garage behind the Chevrolet dealership on Main Street in Sodus. His kind demeanor was evident, as always, as he looked at my mother's car door. Ivan took one look at the passenger side door of the Chevy, and knew some of the story without even asking Izzy. She had sprung the door open at a ninety-degree angle while loading stuff into the front seat, and could not return it to its shut position. She was in front of the Western Auto store over on Maple Avenue, and knowing that Ivan and relief was just a long street away down Smith Street she headed his way.

I happened to be at the Chevy place as she came there, because my friends and I had seen the last part of the car door's life while we were down on Smith Street as Isabel made her last turn off that street. We spotted Isabel driving toward the service area. Her passenger door was still sprung open, and she had made a mess of it by hitting other vehicles parked on the street en route to Ivan and help.

Mr. Symonds was service manager at the Chevy place, and no one called him Mister. We called him Ivan and he liked that. The young people of our street, our teams, and our town knew him in many capacities, and in every role he was a gem.

He looked over the door and realized from looking at different colors of paint that Izzy had done some damage along the way. He assured her that the door could be repaired and painted to match, as it turned out. He also assured her that she shouldn't worry because he would take care of it as soon as possible and then bring the car up to our home on High Street when it was finished. Since he walked to work often, like so many in the village, it would be no trouble for him to drive it home after work. Upon hearing that last comment my mother was relieved from the turmoil she had created in the auto world that day in Sodus. Ivan had that way with all he came in contact with in Sodus. No conversation at the Chevy garage that day that I remember ever was made about insurance, costs, time or availability of space in the shop's schedule. This was probably typical of the era and of the great trust people like Isabel had in Ivan. Contrast that episode with a similar event in the modern era! There would be many discussions about details and there would be some lawyer involved somewhere in the mix also.

The car door was repaired rather quickly and all that my father heard from Ivan was that the door was sprung and had done some damage but was being repaired. Ivan and Isabel had their little secret. Who needed the mayor of the village to get involved with his wife's driving? Dizzy Izzy made such things rather commonplace in her trips around the community! The episode was downplayed nicely by our neighbor and friend Ivan.

I heard later that Ivan had taken the added responsibility of visiting the damaged cars and their owners on Smith Street to explain what had happened. I am not sure what happened relative to insurance and those individual, delicate matters but, once again, the extra service touch was delivered by a community member going way beyond the call of duty. I am aware that there may be "Ivans" in every village and community now, but we sure don't see them as readily. He set a standard for Sodus that was notable.

As our group of young people was growing up and we were outdoors almost every day of the year, it was a rare weekend or early evening when Ivan was not to be seen outdoors mingling with neighbors. He also was outdoors watching or joining us in games of catch or shooting hoops. He had a brush haircut for many of the years I knew him and he seemed to "fit" right in with the hair style we seemed to prefer. Actually, our parents seemed to prefer that style of cut as I reflect upon it now. After the Beatles hit the American shores in the following decade, all bets on brush cuts and burr haircuts were off!

Ivan and his wife had four children and son Ken was in our graduating class. Like so many in our class, Ken became a teacher and now is a successful coliseum manager in Fort Wayne. Ken's youngest brother and Ivan's youngest son recently became captain of the USS Ronald Reagan, a new aircraft carrier in our fleet. A measure of any parent is an ability to give each child a chance to excel. Some children take the opportunity and run with it, whereas some drop the ball and struggle. Success seemed to come to many kids in Sodus and behind most of those stories were some interested parents. There were many teachers, adults and coaches involved in the successes; but it started with men like Ivan and their spouses being successful parents.

I got to know Ivan quite well in the PONY League baseball seasons during the summer months. Along with all his duties as a father, husband, service manager, and good neighbor, Ivan also found time to be an assistant coach on a team in the summer baseball for teenage boys.

He was the perfect fit for summer baseball and being with young guys. We all respected him for his demeanor and his ability to relate to us. Many adults would not be at ease with a bunch of hormone-driven rascals speaking with them on a first name basis. Sodus had a fair share of such men, and it made a terrific impact upon us.

The last game of the PONY season occurred at one of the nicest baseball settings anywhere. This game marked the last of three summers of PONY league ball for many of us. In the following summer we would move up to American Legion ball. It also marked the end of having Ivan around us on our team, because we would have another coach at the next level of ball. For this last PONY game we were at Sodus Point. Sodus Point had a nice baseball field overlooking Sodus Bay. In addition to enjoying the view of the boats out on the bay we also knew that the post-game times were going to be filled with the treats of the resort village. Any reader might think we might be talking about female treats. No we were interested in the game and not young ladies! We thought about such things as custard, white hots (these were pork hotdogs indigenous to the Rochester area for a long time before marketed in a wider area) and milkshakes just across the street from the diamond. The girls would come into our lives a little later; but baseball took a front seat before any of our backseat efforts could be explored.

As an added incentive to the nice capstone event for summer

ball, Ivan was to be the head coach since the regular father/head coach could not be there. I was slated to pitch, and for all the normal competitive reasons I wanted to do well. With Ivan coaching it made this evening that much more special to my peers and me. The summer games usually started about six thirty PM so that they could be concluded at or before twilight. This starting time also allowed for people like Ivan to get to the field after work with his son and others on the team.

The evening was to turn sour in a hurry. After working all day throwing boxes off a truck, it turned out that I had the first sore arm of my baseball career. I had two really sore arms from my day's efforts at my summer job. The sore arm(s) came at the worst possible time. I had to summon Ivan to the mound after just two innings of fruitless effort. He was willing to let me "pitch my way out" of the four run deficit I had created by walking five batters, hitting another two and wild pitching two more balls. The other team hadn't hit me yet, but things were really bad. Real bad! Ivan was seeing my struggle in a broad perspective completely unconnected from a particular score. He was going to stick with me no matter what because he had seen better performances from me in the past. In a rare moment of maturity for me, and out of great respect for the adult I so respected, I told Ivan that it was no dice. My arm was shot that day, and I advised that he should get me out of there. This was contrary to my normal stubbornness and yet indicative of how much the neighbor/friend meant to me.

With the same casual manner in which he was to console my mother later in another summer, he put his arm around my shoulder and said that there were good hot dogs down at the "Point" regardless of the final score!

Not many young people today have adults like this in their lives in such a close and supportive manner.

***

Boat People—Baywatch in Sodus Point
Elsie Parsons was married to George (Judge) Parsons; they were

parents to two children, Patty and Bob. The children were seen all over Sodus Point and all over the various boats their popular father and mother owned over the years. George was an original item, and if a writer invented him in a book the Hollywood stars would line up for a chance to play George in a movie. The life in and around the Parsons was always exciting.

There were times at Sodus Point when the Parsons' yacht of that season was launched into the cold waters of Sodus Bay after resting in storage all winter. Most serious boat owners paid to have their large boats stored rather than sitting out in one of the lots near the bay. During the winter months the Hellions of Sodus who were the "crew" of the Parsons' yacht would work on the boat inside a cold, dimly lit storage barn. It was a fair trade for being able to sit on the decks, steer the boat, swim alongside it wherever it went, and travel to Canadian and American ports along Lake Ontario and the St. Lawrence River.

We knew we were blessed to live in the same village with the Parsons family. Elsie was the quiet, solid partner in the marriage as we Hellions saw the pairing. The Judge was the boisterous, outgoing captain of the ship and the family. George reminds me now of what I have learned of Ted Turner while living in Georgia the past twenty-two years. Turner, like the Judge, loved sailing and pleasure boating and shared this love with all around him, as did George. Both men had money and both shared their wealth with those around them. Turner was much wealthier but Parsons was more multifaceted by virtue of his love for playing baseball, law business, courtroom protocol and helping kids get involved with baseball.

There were times when the Judge would announce a cruise to some port along the lake, usually Canada or somewhere in the St. Lawrence River and Thousand Islands. We would all request a few days off from wherever we worked and then muster at the dock behind the Sodus Point Cottage belonging to the Parsons. We brought food from home to sustain us for a few days and baseball gear so we could play baseball wherever we stopped.

We learned how to navigate using maps, understand a depth

gauge, maneuver the yacht using the engines, and read the ship's compass. For many years George and his family owned Chris Craft luxury cruisers forty to fifty feet long. After the kids grew up, they were mature enough to handle a sailboat. The sailboats came in sizes thirty to forty feet long. When George first got involved in sailing he had a series of racing sailboats and became a successful captain of sailing teams.

Some of the great things we shared involved the glowing presence of Elsie Parsons. We would cruise and share the boat and the food we brought. Elsie always supplemented our food from home with her own wholesome meals. One time after we had been traversing the ancient locks of the Rideau Canal in Ontario Province, Canada for a day, Elsie prepared an unforgettable meal. All of us there on that quiet lake watching the sun go down as the water lapped at the sides of our boat remember the meal. We were famished, and the presence of friends in that setting has been etched in our memories.

We were on the forty-five foot cabin cruiser on one of the lakes connected by the one hundred fifty year old series of canals connecting Kingston, Ontario at the eastern end of Lake Ontario with Ottawa, Ontario. We anchored for the evening after making our way north through the locks that operated by chains pulled through an old series of pulleys. We were worn out because of a full day of swimming. Every time we stopped to pull our way through the locks, we would swim. The wind, sun and water took its toll on all of us.

Elsie had quietly prepared a huge pot of stew through the afternoon of fun, and by the time we anchored we were starved. Those of us in the boat consumed all of the contents of the huge pot. Elsie thought the stew would last for two days and we went through it in one hour. She was learning about teenagers. Her children were very young at the time so they were not at yet the appetite levels of her Hellion crew.

When we docked back in Sodus after a trip with the Judge, the mothers and girlfriends would often be eagerly awaiting our arrival. We felt like successful pirates coming back from a rampage in foreign waters. We were lucky teenagers from Sodus who were eager to get back since we all enjoyed our land lives as much as we did our water lives.

The days spent at Sodus Point on the docks, boats, and beaches during the summers of our youth were outstanding memories. Eventually every young person in the community, and probably every young person in Wayne County, would show up at Sodus Point. When I say show up I really should say "show off." Boys would be boys and do crazy things to inspire the attention from girls.

The girls would merely be girls. They would show up in groups riding in convertibles or fast cars, slip into their bathing suits and then preen and strut for the boys. Predictable adolescent bragging took over at the end of the summer, and it was always interesting to hear the Romeos of the village brag about their private lives at the bay. If one tenth of the bragging was real, it still would represent an interesting romantic summer cycle.

I was fortunate to be close to the Parsons family. They followed my life and that of my family with interest and friendship. I was keenly aware of the presence of the Parsons even during the seasons away from the boat people. During the fall George would always have a huge Halloween spectacular in the front parlor of his house where he would be the star. He would dress up like a pirate, usually (and that was appropriate given his reputation on foreign shores), and share candy and joke with the kids daring to enter the parlor. In the winter he would stop by the houses of his Hellions and leave presents. In the spring he was behind baseball banquets and baseball leagues. He was truly a kid at heart. His wife was young at heart, but knew enough to stay out of the bright glare of life's light George lived under.

Every time I visit Sodus Point, it is like a trip down memory lane. The docks and cottages are still there serving the recreation and water sports of the region. The fun connected with water has shaped me in ways I cherish deeply. I feel so strongly about the

Sodus Point and Lake Ontario connection, I have instructed my loved ones to have a party up there some summer after I am gone and then scatter my ashes on the waters of the lake.

***

Simple Numbers—Four for the ages

Several of us collected baseball cards during our formative years. Baseball was a common denominator. It gave us great moments of our youth, and we were free to fly around the base paths and run after balls hit into spacious gaps in our plush, green fields. There were ways we communicated that put discussion into simple numbers. Some were 60, 2130, .406 and 56. Ask any baseball fan what these numbers mean and the answer will be immediate and profound.

These four are but a few of the many that make up baseball lore and history. The four mentioned above refer to Babe Ruth's mighty sixty home runs, Lou Gehrig's magnificent streak of twenty one hundred and thirty consecutive baseball games played without missing a game, Ted Williams' incredible batting average in 1941, and Joe DiMaggio's equally incredible hitting streak in the same year. All of us playing baseball on the field and playing our table baseball games could recite the records.

As teachers and parents look for clues to the educational process involving children and acquisition of knowledge, they should look at the impact of baseball upon the mental processes. How is it that young children acquire numbers of great baseball significance but have no interest in historic or scientific facts?

I once heard or read that a great teacher made the student fall in love with the subject. All else fell into place after the love of the subject was positioned. This must be what occurs with our national pastime. As my friends Gib Sergeant, Ken Symonds, Charley Mossgraber, Don Davis and others spent time together, we would compare stats of players and talk baseball steadily through the baseball seasons of our youth.

Although the television coverage back in the fifties was very limited when we cherished baseball the most, we heard many games on the radio. We would sit around playing cards and listening to games from distant cities. For some reason we picked up games out of St. Louis, Chicago, New York and even Boston. Depending upon the weather we would pick up AM radio broadcasts to whet our listening appetites.

There were other records we saw develop, and Ted Williams stood out even though he was a Red Sox player. Williams spent three years in the military during World War II and served two years during the Korean Conflict. When records are compared, Ted Williams stands out as one of the best ever. In Sodus, Williams was not the favorite star; DiMaggio, Mantle, and the rest of the Yankees and Giants were. This didn't diminish his luster as a baseball giant. Way before the on-base percentage was a stat of choice for baseball fans, I had friends like Ken and Charley who appreciated the fact that Williams was on base nearly fifty percent of the time!

Williams retired in 1960 after his sterling and twice-interrupted career. His career on-base percentage was .483 and that figure has never been bettered by any player. It stands like a Mt. Everest of baseball. This mark was a product of many walks, few strikeouts, and many, many hits. When we played baseball, we liked to copy the batting stances of well known players. Of all the stances and strokes of the era, one we could not copy was Ted Williams's. For one thing, none of us were left-handed; and for another thing, one does not copy a once-in-a-lifetime batting style. None of us hit like Williams even for one at bat. We should not have felt bad, because no one had ever hit like the man.

One of the classic interviews was held prior to Williams's death several years ago. In the interview, the sports announcer was asking Ted what he would have hit against the pitchers of the modern era. Without hesitating Williams noted he would probably hit .300 but he quickly amended the initial statement by adding that he was over seventy now. It was a great baseball moment for a kid like me who was still a kid at heart.

Our terrific friendships in Sodus allowed us to communicate

using baseball as our common language. The statistics of the game were never used by math teachers to make us more interested in the subject, despite the power of our interests. The Sodus teachers stood out in our collective reflections; but the baseball thing didn't get exploited when they had the chance.

There were baseball cards all over the place and the bubble gum cards were the most prominent. There were very valuable baseball cards passed on through the ages as the kids of the forties and fifties shared their hobby with their kids and grandkids.

My mother found the baseball card collection I built over the years and had left in our family home after moving on to college. She gave them away to other kids in Sodus at the time she sold the house and moved out of town. Although her heart was certainly in the right place and I loved her, this one act of community friendship was performed without a good grasp of what the cards were worth.

Despite all our knowledge about Williams, DiMaggio and the great names of baseball during our young years, my mother was not a party to these discussions. The hundreds of Pearson cards went out the door to appreciative kids in a village I loved. Several years ago baseball traders on television were comparing notes about valuable baseball cards from the era I write about. One card was mentioned as being especially valuable. A Mickey Mantle rookie card was worth thousands.

Mickey Mantle was my personal favorite player, and I took pains to collect many of his cards. I remember that I owned two or three of the rookie cards. Those are numbers I particularly remember about baseball.

***

Four Doctors and a Baby—No choices

When I was born in Sodus the year was 1938, and fortunately for me and my mother Dr. Tom Hobbie delivered both of us from a less promising fate. Dr. Tom was the baby doctor of Sodus and the area. He was a magnificent practitioner who waited his whole life for a baby son of his own to take over the name and a promising medical future. No sons came, but he had a basketball team of girls, and each of the five had the opportunity to practice medicine. Whether any of them ever did I do not know. He took great satisfaction from seeing all the sons and daughters of Sodus in action, since he delivered almost every one of them over a period of fifty years.

During an alumni basketball game one winter evening, my mother sat with Dr. Hobbie and his wife to enjoy the forty basketball alumni cavorting in the gym. The gym was packed with people, alumni of all sizes (and shapes quite different from that of their playing years). Dr. Hobbie leaned over to my mother during that game and told her that he had delivered every player on both teams playing basketball that night. Isabel related that story to me after the game; it was something we probably all knew if we had put the thought to words. It took the fine general practitioner to verbalize his own legacy.

His work with mothers and babies over fifty years was noteworthy. At some time in every pregnancy in the village, the pregnant woman would say a little prayer of thanks for Dr. Tom. It was quite common knowledge that some of the other doctors had a constant battle with the bottle. No one wanted to come into Myers Community Hospital and have a doctor show up to deliver a baby when the doctor was under the influence of alcohol.

In a small town there were all manner of clues to the proclivity for the bubbly. If one sat in the drug stores on nearly opposite corners of the village's Main Street in the early mornings, the sight of the town drinkers was common. They would slowly come in to pursue an Alka Seltzer to help them get over a hangover. Many times the men coming in with hangovers were doctors.

The drug store scene was not the monopoly of the medical men described above. There were lawyers, businessmen, farmers, and many others. The number of problem drinkers back then was no doubt similar to any other time in the history of our community or any community in America. As workers and patrons of the drug stores mingled with the hangovers, there were very few secrets in the village.

Drug stores sold many things back then. The main difference between drug stores of the modern era and those of fifty years ago seems to be the quality of confidentiality. If a person bought condoms no one knew it except the person behind the counter where the various products for the purpose were discretely located out of sight. In the modern store, there they are right by the checkout. I suppose this has certain advantages relating to verbalizing one's needs. It is simpler for a guy or gal to merely pick some up and then put them on the conveyor belt with the magazines, toothpaste, cold cream, and beer.

That is another huge difference in the two eras. Beer, vegetables, condoms, Coke, pretzels, greeting cards and drugs are seen flowing across the counters in this century. Long ago, drug stores had a narrower niche. It seemed to be a better system back then because it made people take more quality time, walk into several stores and communicate with a store owner and other customers. Think of the modern era's lack of verbalization.

It is entirely possible to go shopping without ever saying a word to a soul. After collecting the goods, swiping the credit card, signing or collecting a receipt all a person needed to do then was walk out. Is it any wonder our modern society lacks quality communication? Is it also any wonder that people can "live" in a community without really ever feeling they are part of the whole enterprise? A sense of community ceases to exist when people stop talking. Dr. Hobbie helped the community talk and function. A few years ago it was estimated that Dr. Hobbie had delivered 10,000 babies. The man was ninety years old at the time.

Dr. Hobbie was a constant sight around in the hospital as he delivered the goods day after day and year after year. He also had an office in his home that serviced the non-maternity needs of others. The office brought together people of all walks of life. He knew every patient by name, house, and family. He was unique to the practice of medicine despite medicine's storied past. Sodus could not have existed without the man.

The other three doctors practicing in the village all had their faithful patients who, in some cases, overlooked the human frailty of their particular medical man.

The three doctors all served the village's needs and were each different in their own way. Many communities now have numerous doctors and they develop a niche based upon the specialty-driven society in which we live. Some people have four or five doctors depending upon their wealth, ailments, and/or needs.

The people of Sodus at the basketball alumni game should have stopped the whole thing at halftime and honored the good doctor on that winter evening years ago. Sodus finally held a huge recognition for the baby doctor, as we all referred to him, several years ago. I wish they had done it when my Mom was in the gym with the doctor. She always had a special spot in her heart for Dr. Tom. My friends and I were playing that night, and that always entertained my mother—but what was really special that night was forty guys having the same baby doctor!

***

Cookout in the Cafeteria—Where was the phone?

Once upon a time in Sodus, there was a big, two story brick building located on the west end of Main Street. This was the central school. This building ultimately gave way to a modern, sprawling building with wings that housed K-12 under one elongated roof. The old school building maintained its presence on Main Street, reconfigured as a factory for various products over the years. It still stands on the site today, serving some business purpose. The new two-story building, located at the far end of Mill Street, was completed for use at the beginning of the 1950-1951 school year. During the last days of construction, just prior to the building being occupied by all the kids K-12 in the Sodus Township, there was a glitch in the plans. A fire started in the basement and nearly took the whole place down before a single student learned a thing in the structure.

The various one-room and two-room school houses located outside the village limits were prepared to give up their clients for good. The old buildings that served so well for so many years became private homes, businesses and community buildings. The kids living outside the village started riding buses to school. The kids in the village merely altered their walking patterns to accommodate Mill Street rather than Main Street. Back in the mid-century in Sodus, probably eighty percent of the kids in the village walked to school. The old stories about walking miles and miles every day to go to school were not quite accurate. My generation of village residents who were in school at the time did walk a half mile to a mile each way every day. Some students drove once they were in high school, and some parents drove their kids in bad weather. There were no long lines of cars dropping kids as seen in the modern public schools. It was an interesting sight for the kids living outside the village when their buses took them past their peers trudging through the snow towards school. From the warm interior of the school bus no doubt would come a plethora of interesting comments about being lucky to live outside of the village. It would be about the only time such comments would flow, since living in the village allowed for a lot more opportunities than were available over in Joy or Sodus Center. Both of those tiny communities had populations under one hundred.

Many kids in the school had a parent or parents working there. This was common back then in small communities. One great fringe benefit of the huge numbers of citizens serving in the school was that every incident and activity occurring in the school was common knowledge. There were very few secrets in the system. Cafeteria mothers could see and hear many of the things currently of interest as they dished out food. Teachers heard everything going in and out of the teacher's lounge. Merely working in the office or as a custodian opened up very precise lines of information.

When a bond issue was approved and the new school construction began, the whole Town of Sodus anticipated the new school with great enthusiasm. The new cafeteria would be separate from the gym. This was a tremendous development in sharp contrast to the combination situation we used for decades in the old school. The new gym was huge, bright and even had a dividing door to create two gyms from one. We all looked forward to the games, physical education classes and school activities in the gym.

The school was so expansive and bright that as we toured it weeks prior to grand opening we felt we had been delivered to a different planet. There was some small finishing work to be done and the school would be ours to use.

There is much conjecture about what happened next and how it happened; but just before the school was to open its doors to six hundred or so kids, there was a fire.

The fire evidently started in the basement. Some people at the time in the volunteer fire department said that some cleaning rags and cleaning fluids were stored near the furnace area and they ignited. I heard my father say it could have been a cigarette deposited in the wrong place at the wrong time.

The fire began in the basement but then spread upstairs to the cafeteria, locker room for women, storage rooms and to one end of the gymnasium. All of this just before the grand opening was terrible news for all of us. There was a factor that surfaced in the aftermath of the fire that was very unsettling.

There was a watchman on duty all night and although he knew the fire had started rumor had it at the time that the man walked the mile uptown from the school's location to report the fire. Various stories circulated in the aftermath of the fire that the watchman did not know how to use the telephone, or did not know where the telephone was, or could not speak good enough English to report the situation to the operator. Another scenario had the man trying to fight the spreading fire by himself with meager fire fighting equipment. I do not know which scenario was closer to the truth. I heard all the opinions from firemen, teachers, parents and other local residents.

The school fire was a terrible setback for the high hopes of all. If the watchman was incompetent in delivering the message about the fire, then the fire was allowed to spread too far, too fast without the benefit of our excellent volunteer firefighters. The fire set the opening of school back a half year. Fortunately the firemen were able to stop the blaze from spreading through the whole school. The only long term effect we ever noticed when we officially opened the school was that our maple floor at one end of the gym had a ripple from water damage that could not be fixed in time for the opening.

That was a modest disappointment in comparison with what the real disaster that could have been. We were eager to use the new school. The gym floor was a mild irritant; and considering we came from an old school with a floor containing multiple dead spots, rippling boards and mustard and ketchup on the floor this was nothing.

We heard the night watchman was fired, and nothing was ever said about criminal charges if there were any. Our school was finally opened. On one of the first days when we were in the building, several of us went down the back stairs to see where the fire had started many months before. We saw the area but everything was back to normal.

Coming back upstairs from our exploration of the basement area we came across something very interesting. Down near the bottom of the stairs was a phone on the wall. The phone was there about thirty feet from where the rags ignited, according to one of my friends. His father had been with the fireman doing the cleanup. Was this particular phone there the night of the fire? Did the old night watchman really walk all the way to the fire hall and report the fire in person rather than call? What really happened that night?

***

Memorial Days—Parade of memories
Every Memorial Day across America at mid-century there was a parade. In Sodus, the parade was fashioned from something old and something new. As a Cub Scout and Boy Scout, I joined my friends and marched in the lines going down Main Street with the parade concluding at the community cemetery. There were Brownie

Scouts, Girl Scouts, high school bands, majorettes, fire trucks, and an occasional convertible with a notable person.

The others in the parade were the cherished veterans. There were some from World War I very much alive back in the forties and early fifties. The number of these men diminished rapidly as the years rolled by. By the time parades of the seventies and eighties marched down the street, the World War I veterans were gone. The veterans of World War II were numerous, and they marched down the street with the best proud, erect strides they could muster. I was always struck by the wear and tear of the years on the men in the parade. These men reflected what all of us go through as the decades pile up on our bodies. Young people do not appreciate the aging process until they undergo it themselves. I had great respect for what I witnessed in the parade of veterans. Despite the products of aging evidenced by the shuffling feet, the limps, the pot bellies and the slow pace, these men were the keepers of our security gates when we needed them the most.

All of us along the parade route (or at the end of the parade where early marchers waited to see the remainder of the parade flow by) were in awe of the veterans. What made the whole thing very important to us was that the men being honored were our porch buddies, our mechanics, our businessmen and our parents. I was affected by the spirit of it, back then and, thank goodness, I am still affected in the same way when I see a similar parade. Gloomily, we don't seem to have many parades like that anymore. In the race and pace of modern life we seem to ignore some of our critically important heritage.

Tom Brokaw called them "the Greatest Generation" in his best-selling 1998 book. We, in Sodus, called them our fathers, uncles, friends and neighbors. They were the survivors of the ordeals abroad. In every community across the continent, there were the memorials to the dead and missing from conflicts. During my high school years we started seeing Korean War veterans showing up in the ranks of veterans. The Veterans of Foreign Wars was a prominent organization in Sodus. There were activities involving any returning service man or woman. As the VFW and American Legion involved themselves in the community, we saw them in action at Firemen's Field Days, July 4th activities, and knew they had a VFW/American Legion Post where the veterans could meet and play cards.

I became very aware of veterans since my own father had served for two years. As other fathers returned to Sodus, I was interested in asking questions about the war years. My own father counseled me to be very respectful of the privacy of those men coming back from frontline duty. My father told me that these men carried an additional burden. Often they would prefer not to talk about their experiences. They marched on Memorial Day, and they honored their fallen counterparts in the ceremony at the cemetery. Many of the fallen were interred in Sodus. Others had been buried at sea or rested in foreign cemeteries.

When I did get an opportunity to pick the memory of one of the veterans from Wayne County, it invariably came when I was in my twenties and the veteran was under the influence of alcohol. Almost without exception, the interviews that were of great interest to me occurred in bars when I was there with friends for a social gathering. As I slipped away from the noise and drinking and talked with the veteran, it was evident the opportunity to talk was a catharsis for the vet. I was a history buff and did not do too well drinking, so this was a productive enterprise for me. I spoke with three or four veterans in this manner over a period of years. I was always left with an incredible respect for these common men whose bravery was uncommon.

The veterans would squeeze into their old uniforms at parade time, and despite the obvious weight gain most of the men appeared very impressive. The one constant in all the parades was the genuine emotion shown by spectators. Patriotism was alive and well back then. Memories were fresh of the sacrifices made by Sodus men, and there were always tears flowing down female cheeks along the parade route.

Whenever Americans reflect upon our national, regional or

local greatness the Memorial Day parade should be the highlight of our reflection.

***

Parking Lot Babies- Revisiting a Hobbie

The Sodus hospital was named Myers Hospital and at some point was deemed too antiquated and too inefficient for the last part of the twentieth century. The name carried on to a modern, one floor hospital two miles north of the village. The new hospital was located on a high point overlooking the fruit farms and the lake. It was not as easy to get to in emergencies and was not a "walk-in" facility, as it was right there on Main Street and Gaylord Street.

When the hospital succumbed to the bulldozer and wrecking ball, people in the township were sad to see the old building go. It held many of the medical and emotional moments in the history of the community. Dr. Hobbie delivered most of his ten thousand deliveries in the facility. Operations were performed in the old operating room that did not do a very good job of containing the heavy smells of ether. There were times when visitors became affected by surgery unrelated to the visitor. The ether seeped out all over the building.

Once the hospital disappeared, the discussion was then about what to do with the space. A huge parking lot won the day and the new lot served many purposes associated with various businesses in that part of town.

When I visited the parking lot with some of my relatives we joked about the life-related events that had taken place "in the parking lot." I explained to my own children that I had been born right there, where the automobiles now parked. There were many other buildings in Sodus that functioned during the mid-century in different roles than they do in the new century. This happens everywhere in the country, but a small village such as Sodus notes the passage of buildings with more respect than in big cities.

I remember seeing two twenty-five year-old structures being imploded in downtown Atlanta within months of each other. It was very sad to observe. The Omni and Fulton County Stadium both were gone within two months of one another. They had served for twenty-five years and then they made way for the Olympic Stadium expansion into what is now Turner Field, where the Braves play baseball in downtown Atlanta. The Omni served as a venue for the Hawks of the NBA and numerous hockey games and concert activities. It was immediately replaced by the Phillips Arena, where the Thrashers of the NHL and the Hawks of the NBA play.

The Atlanta saga contrasts with the seventy-five years of Myers Hospital and the continued use of the old buildings all along Main Street in Sodus. Even the old bowling alley of my youth still sits there on Maple Avenue, used now for VFW/American Legion. And the old one-room school houses of American history met better fates than did the Omni and Fulton County Stadium. Most of the old schools are still around. Even the old Sodus school stands after nearly one hundred years.

The hospital demolition was a sad day, but the promise of a new facility with no ether smell was something to anticipate with enthusiasm. Nurses and hospital workers were glad to be out of the old three-story building. It was drafty, lacked modern electrical connections and was hard to maintain. Steam heat was wonderful when it was at the right temperature, but many residents had stories of cold or excessively hot stays in the rooms of the old facility.

My mother was involved with many friends at the hospital. I referred to the building earlier as a "walk-in" hospital, and that was a very accurate statement. People would merely walk in to visit others and the nurse or person on duty would wave and give the room number. There were visiting hours, but they were ultimately very flexible due to the presence of people such as my mother.

She would have several people to visit in various rooms and her journey through the facility with me or other kids in tow was a common sight. Why I never became sick from the chronic ether smells I will never know. I enjoyed being my mother's helper on these missions. For reasons connected with my upbringing by powerful women, I was very sympathetic to those friends of my family in the hospital.

My sister recently related an old story about swallowing pennies with a neighborhood friend when the two were very young, ostensibly to study the results of the digestive process on the pennies. She recalled that the pennies came out but they were not greatly changed by the process. If, for some reason, those pennies did not come out when Donna and Tommy DeBrine did their experimentations, it was comforting to know the "walk-in" hospital was just down the street around the corner. Nothing like a stay in the old hospital would have solved a severe money problem my sister might have created.

In a purely modern twist of fate, the local hospital has closed most of its services and now Sodus residents have to drive twenty miles to get help. That is quite a change from the old days. And I am not talking just pennies here!

***

Life in the Yard—A modern EPA dilemma

We would sit out in the yard for picnics, play modified ball games in the thick grass, practice place kicking footballs between two tall bushes and over the hedgerow at the rear of the spacious yard, and maintain the two hundred twenty foot deep lot. The many uses of the yard did have a "price tag" in the form of maintenance. The lot was also one hundred feet wide. The half-acre lot was the scene of many events in our lives. Most vivid were pick-up games among friends, family gatherings and, of course, the routine maintenance.

One thing was unique to our yard and the others bordering the orchards at the rear of our property. We did not seem to have the mosquito infestations and other bugs common to the region, in contrast to other neighborhoods and places like the drive-in theatre and playfields elsewhere.

For a very long time the orchards were sprayed with varieties of chemicals to keep the apples and cherry trees in great shape for their ultimate contribution. When the huge sprayers were pulled through the orchards by the tractors the mist of spray would invariably drift into our yard and onto the bushes and trees there. I firmly believe that we had the same protection from various creatures that the trees in the orchards had received. Never once did any of us consider that we were also living very close to a biochemical problem.

The forties and fifties were not a time to worry about EPA standards since they were not even heard of back then. There were bigger fish to fry, such as getting over World War II, finding a new economic reality for the nation, and considering how to win the Cold War. On the very small stage at Sodus the large issues were always those of the nation, but realistically the problems were high water at the "Point" (Sodus Point), prices and profits for each year's fruit crop, the low water pressure in the village during the summer months (great usage and canning factories going full bore), recovering from storm damage from any of several harsh winters, and even concerns about upcoming sports seasons in the school.

The environment was a case of taking the good with the bad; and the resulting balance was always swayed by the upstate New York fall season. No matter how bad the winters were and how much inconvenience there was in summer over water, the fall season always made up for all else. Fall seasons in our area were magnificent times, with hardwood trees a blaze of color and the smell of burning leaves always in the crisp air. EPA during the forties and fifties? No way. The burning of leaves was an art form and a treat to the senses. The chemicals sprayed right out beyond our field goal practices were a guarantee of good apple crops. The cherries harvested from the trees made the village famous.

For many decades we were the "Cherrytowners" and then, in a move made to insure that our school would not have to be the brunt of crude sexual jokes related to our number one crop, the officials decided upon "Trojans" as a new name. In a flurry of new decision-making based upon belated awareness that "Trojan" was the name for the number one condom in the country, the nickname quickly became "Spartans." It appears there was much more concern about the image and not the environment back then.

The local farmers maintained ponds from which they drew

water to mix with the chemical sprays used in the orchards. My friends and I made such ponds a part of our recreational upbringing with no concern about anything chemical in the water. Our greatest concerns in those "spray" ponds were bloodsuckers and snakes. There was no EPA concerned with those ugly items! A young man not jumping in such a pond (and getting out quickly) was viewed with some degree of circumspect. My guess is very little concentration of chemicals ever went into such ponds, since farmers were pulling water out and would not have wasted chemicals in such a pond.

If there was any concern over the environment it came in the summers, when the beaches at Sodus Point would, periodically, be littered with dead fish (mooneyes) and/or seaweed mixed with dead fish and empty cans and bottles. Even then, there were storms to flush out the system and occasional pick-up efforts by the community forces. Whenever we went swimming we never made any connection between what we knew happened when a "head" on one of the numerous large yachts and sailing vessels was flushed. In the mid-century effluvia from the boats with toilets was pumped right out into the lakes and bays.

It probably is quite amazing that there were not numerous E-coli and other related problems back then.

I can remember being in the water one time while rubbing the side of Judge Parson's yacht with sponges to clean off the waterline scum on his forty five foot Chris Craft cabin cruiser. During my scrubbing what should appear out of the bowels of the boat but a product of the bowels of one of my good friends? This was very gross at the time, and only my proximity to the outlet for the toilet allowed me to see something that was repeated thousands and thousands of times each summer in the bay and lake. This arrangement changed once we saw the Great Lakes going dead from waste deposited in them. Laws were enacted required holding tanks in pleasure boats similar to the ones found in Winnebagos. The EPA finally struck at the lifestyles of the rich and effluent!

Let us return to our back yard pleasures. The yard was huge, and a half acre of grass was a big job with hand mowers. It took several years before H.B. Pearson swung for power equipment in his yard. I was a serf in the system, so I mowed with my brother the hand mower way. Mowing was but one of the many issues to contend with in the spacious yard. Mr. Gage was the previous owner, and he and his wife were masters at landscaping. Inherent in the sale of the house to my mother was the understanding that our family would keep the landscape looking pristine, as did the Gages. Even though they moved to a newer place in the country, Mr. Gage was a jeweler in the village and he would walk around the yard during his lunchtimes. This was nostalgic for him but a headache for me and Dick. This yard was our albatross around our necks, EPA or no EPA.

Much the same as my mother never allowing a quart milk bottle on the table for fear the minister might drop by during mealtime (he never did) she also wanted the yard spotless for the unannounced Gage visits. We did our utmost to maintain the property, and even when Dad returned from service he caught the fever of yard work well done.

Mr. Gage stopped coming by after a few years. This probably was due to his own yard needing work, but more likely it was due to the fact that his prized hand-built goldfish pond no longer was a working part of our yard. Our cat consumed the goldfish regularly and the concrete work developed cracks that eventually became impossible to patch. These things made our jobs a bit easier for the time being.

Dad's return from the navy opened up annual events in spring and fall called trimming and raking, respectively. When your landscaped yard is filled with trees and around the perimeter live all kinds of flourishing bushes, the trim part of the spring became tough. The trees created their chores as the beautiful leaves cascaded down in humungous amounts in the fall. We worked on weekends doing those semi-annual events, so that by Sunday my Dad was exhausted but we still had to finish what we had started on Saturday.

In addition to maintaining the trimming and raking, there

were those times during winter when blizzards and ice storms took down limbs. That clean-up was a bear. Once, during the fifties, a hurricane came through our area on its way towards New England, and that fall storm spectacular preempted the typical mid-winter tree limb problem. We had severe damage, and it took whole trees down all over town, including our yard.

The survival of all the bushes is still evident today despite any abuse they took as field goal posts, poor trimming efforts or years of cursing at their rapid growth.

The trees and bushes evidently benefited greatly from the annual spraying done by the local farmers. Most of the residents in the area during that era seemed to have survived the DDT and whatever else was floating into our picnic area. The EPA may have a huge impact on faming and lawn upkeep now, but back then there was no worry about long-term damage to people or growth.

As I maintain my modest Georgia acreage each year, I consider the various legal chemicals I apply to fight termites, weeds, fire ants and other critters. We never once put anything like these items on our yard, and the grass flourished. The trees never died except by storm damage. The bushes always bloomed and grew. It may have been an EPA nightmare but we never knew it. Ignorance was a part of yard life at mid-century!

***

Politics in the Fire Hall—Lessons in life

My father once took me to a village board meeting held in the upstairs of the fire hall and gave me two pieces of advice. Since he was the mayor *and* my father, this dual authority made quite an impression upon me. He told me to sit there and be quiet. This meant to sit there with my mouth shut and practice my father's best advice for kids. His advice was to be seen and not heard. The other piece of advice for me that particular night was to make mental notes of the process and ask him questions after the meeting. This was the fulfillment of his aspirations for his kids. He wanted us to learn from things around us, whether they happen to be adults, books, history lessons or our teachers and coaches.

I am not sure what prompted my father to take me along, but I remember it as an interesting evening. He probably was taking me along to set some key concepts firmly in my mind about matters in the village. These matters were police reports, recreation reports, and water issues. There was a chronic shortage of water to the village during the summer months of peak use. Until the water problems were solved at mid-century by connecting lines and a pumping station to the ample fresh water supply of Lake Ontario, village meetings focused on water.

I remember feeling uneasy in the meeting I attended. The uneasy feeling came when the police report was delivered. Con Loveless was the police chief, and he lived on the street where we did. The report made me uneasy because there were reports about things that I had some direct and/or indirect knowledge of, and it was as if Mayor H.B. Pearson took me along to sweat a confession out of me right there in the board meeting.

The recreation director reported on the conditions in the community center and the need for greater supervision and utilization of the two-story building. It was located right next to the village library in the center of the village.

I knew of the conditions in the building. During a one-week binge of smoking in my adolescence, spurred on by my parent's trip to Florida, I consumed all of the cigarettes I ever smoked in my life. This was so I could impress whoever was there in the community center. It also allowed me to remain out of sight of the mainstream of Sodus. When you are thirteen years old and smoking two packs a day and the son of well-known parents, smoking has to be done out of sight. I was also an aspiring athlete so the smoking was an aberration for that week. It pointed out how stupid teenagers are regarding their health and welfare. The cellar pool and ping-pong rooms were my hideaways and these rooms filled with the foul smoke of several rebellious teenagers. I provided many of them during that one vacation week.

My grandmother was our babysitter at the time, and she could be conned into allowing my brother and me to go to "meetings" at the community center during times when we should have been home. The one-week smoking venture for me was pure adolescent stupidity. I took the cigarettes from a desk drawer in my father's home office. By the time he and my mother returned from Florida the drawer was nearly empty. This probably meant that I (and some of my friends) had smoked through about fifteen or so packs of cigarettes in a week. My father merely bought more Camels and did not seem to respond to his shortage with outrage.

As I sat listening to the problem of supervision in what used to be my smoking areas in the recreation center, I knew the smoking lamp for me was out. It was out because I hated smoking and it was out because I did not want to piss my father off. He, I think, surmised some packs were missing when he returned from Florida. I think he guessed older brother Dick was the culprit more than me. Nothing could be proven and fortunately for both of us the passage of time erased our fears of being caught

I never smoked cigarettes again after that week. I puff an occasional cigar but do not inhale. I inhaled that week and I suffered from coughing, bad taste, and probably even killed some of the few brain cells I possessed at that time.

Remembering my smoking career and my parents' Florida trip, I see a misspent youth. I see a week of public health ignorance. The village board meeting occurred about the same time as my smoking orgy. I was in about the 7th or 8th grade. I thought the board meeting was for my personal education in a way that screamed of my father's awareness of my teenage activities at the time. He handled things quite well since the end result was successful relative to smoking. His demeanor during that brief period of time was quite different from his normal authoritarian behavior.

The board meeting allowed me to pass on tidbits from the meeting to my peers about police work and Chief Loveless's concerns. Our behavior patterns changed overnight in areas related to Con's duties. Putting it another way, our nighttime teenage antics were curtailed very convincingly by some of my observations. We surmised that our changes were good judgment. We were correct.

Recreation was a big issue in the village then and now. There were avenues of cooperation developed back then that carried on for many years. The school helped with indoor and outdoor facilities. The school provided an occasional bus for recreation purposes. The recreation programs gave kids a wide variety of programs including ice skating, baseball, swimming and basketball. The village board raised the money for the recreation director. I realized that my smoking in my week of smoking unawareness on someone else's domain was not fair. It showed my immaturity and was shortsighted as heck of me.

I was stupid to smoke in the community center and bring potential disfavor to the director from parents and others. The village board meeting and the conversations there made me aware of the much bigger picture. It turned out that my father was brilliant to take me along, whatever his motivation at the time.

When I returned home with him, he sat there smoking a big cigar in his lounge chair, and the debriefing occurred. It was short and sweet. He did the talking and he told me reasons for decisions made at the meeting. He then asked me if I had any comments about the police report or the community recreation report. Here was a moment of truth for me in that evening. With all the teenage poise I could summon I casually said that I had no comments. My glimpse into the inner workings of the village management gave me an awareness I did not possess prior to attending. I was profoundly affected by the trip to the real world.

Later in my life, I registered to vote for the first time in a presidential election. I had to go upstairs over the fire hall where I had spent a mute hour and a half of my young life attending the village board meeting. I registered to vote my party affiliation. I listed it as Democratic so I could vote for John F. Kennedy in good conscience. As a rookie voter, I thought one had to register for the party representing the person one would vote for in the booth.

The lady sitting there was Gail Fitzpatrick's mother and when I turned in the paperwork she looked long and hard at it. Rumor had it that she was a Democrat. There may have been sixteen

Democrats in the whole village at the time. This was Eisenhower country! Rumor also had it that her daughter and I were close friends. This was always the case since the time we had climbed a tree naked together when we were four. We had not climbed naked much since then, so I felt quite innocent. Gail's mother still had a strange look about her. Was she connecting my name and face with her daughter's social life? No. I think her reaction was because my family was Republican.

Mrs. Fitzpatrick did not say a word but it was as if she was connecting the dots in my family political tree. My father was a Republican and so was his father. My mother was a Republican. Since that time in 1960, I have registered Republican every time because the party represents my conservative thinking much more than the Democratic Party does. However, at that moment in the fire house when I registered for the first time, I thought I had once again carried one of my little secrets away from the hall that would irritate my father if he knew the whole truth.

It took me back several years to my previous moment of truth upstairs in the village meeting place.

***

In the Can—Alton Can

During one of my summers after registering for social security as a thirteen year old, I ventured into the canning business. I may have been sixteen at the time and, although I had been kissed, I was definitely new to the canning factory routine. My career was nearly ended on the first day of my employment at Alton Canning Company.

The factory workers assigned to keep me from screwing up the first week gave me too much leeway the first day. They had me go into the loft above the main office, which was a large storage area for labels. The labels were to be taken down from there and matched up with the particular can run in the factory. A can run was what they called the canning process for, say, green beans. The beans grown for and delivered to the canning factory were from acreage all around the small town of Alton in Wayne County. The beans came in at all times day and night, and were processed on bean lines where women worked the beans over. The women picked out the bad ones and sent the others along for canning after clipping bad parts off the bean.

There were labels for several different grocery stores up in the loft storage area; and provided with a list it was easy to match the required labels up with the produce being canned. If Blue Boy green beans had been ordered by a buyer working with my father for sale at grocery stores wanting Blue Boy brand beans, then the Blue Boy label went on the 303 sized can. After cooking and drying the cans were labeled, packed in boxes and then loaded on freight cars or into large trucks. My father promised Blue Boy green beans and the factory delivered them in massive amounts. My father was the sales manager for the factory. He sold green beans. He also sold apple sauce, beets, cherry pie mix, tomato juice, yellow beans and at one time, during a cranberry scare, cherry sauce.

On my first day I merely had to get green bean labels for a particular brand of green beans desired by the buyer. The reader should realize that a Wayne County green bean was a Wayne County green bean, no matter what brand appeared on the can. Anyone comparing different brands of beans coming from Alton would be inaccurate if they could find a difference in beans. There was none. Or there was none until I had my crack at the process during my first day.

The labels should have been green bean labels—but for some reason I delivered yellow wax bean labels to the area where cans were being labeled. I also had to go to lunch after the completion of this simple task so that probably was my excuse for the screw-up. Green beans coming away from the drying area were being labeled yellow wax beans for an hour due to my malfeasance and the presence of Cubans in the factory. The Cubans were cheap labor, and their drawback was a lack of English as their main working tongue.

The Cubans didn't question my choice of labels, nor did the mix-up show up until a food inspector opened a can. The cases of beans already in the freight car were numerous. Guess who went to the freight car to slide the cases to his Cuban friends to re-label? As I was pulling each case out and pushing them along the long rollers back towards the factory, I was aware that this was turning out to be a lot of extra work and was delaying the freight car's departure.

After that episode I checked labels very carefully. The colorful mix of labels in the storage area was interesting. There were labels up there for food products no longer canned by the company. It was someone else's job, however, to dump those. Just the thought of me dumping a pile of labels no longer in use would no doubt bring the product back into production.

Freight cars delivered huge amounts of empty cans that were then filled and returned to the freight car. The factory went through freight cars full of empty cans often during a busy summer of canning the products of Wayne County's farm lands. There were times when I helped empty the huge cars of their cargo. Since it did not happen regularly, it was a diversion from some of the nastier jobs in the factory.

A canning factory runs on adrenalin and overtime during the several runs done during harvesting season. Workers have to work long hours to accommodate the constant deliveries of products to the outside storage areas. There were times when beets piled up or apples appeared in small mountains out behind the factory. Some crops had to be processed immediately, such as the sour cherries for the cold storage. These cherries were canned in fifty pound sized containers and then sent for cold storage until shipped elsewhere.

Some farmers harvested at night to beat the heat or to use more of the working day when the crop was heavy. Many of these farmers worked under lights on their tractors in the fields. When they delivered their goods, they were in no mood for delays in unloading or waiting in line to dump their fruit or vegetables. Some times inexperienced workers such as yours truly would get caught in the verbal crossfire of the dock or dumping foreman and a farmer.

I was sympathetic to the farmers in these cases, since some of my friends and their families were in the farming business. I thought it was entirely logical that a farmer should be able to come in, sign for what he knew he had in his truck and then dump it quickly and be on the way. Sometimes trucks needed to be weighed or crates had to be counted. This always slowed the process down.

Fortunately for Alton Canning Company, and my Dad's boss Ed Burns, I never considered the canning job as a career move. My two summers at the factory were enough to convince me to be a consumer and not a canner. My Dad agreed with this reasoning also. He would remind me as I was going through college that the factory was always looking for young men. This wasn't necessary, as I was committed to completing my teaching degree; but the threat was there anyway. I do still enjoy canned green beans despite my green bean overload.

***

Early Birds Get the News—Early exit from church

As I sit in church services in my current community and gaze longingly at my wrist watch, I reflect upon the days in Sodus when the Presbyterian Church seemed to have the heads-up on religious efficiency. The current situation in my religious life seems to be a battle between the clock and the content of the service. In the current situation, the service wins out almost every time. By the time I glance at the watch, it already is overtime in my ex-Presbyterian existence. In stark contrast to the present situation the Sodus Presbyterian Church of my memories during the fifties allowed us in and out in an hour. Part of this memory may be prejudiced by other factors.

For a long period of time I was assigned to take collection in church with several other boys of the congregation. Usually there were five or six of us. One guy, Harvey DeHond, seemed to be the ringleader of the collection pack. Harvey had this position over the years. No one ever explained his ranking in the ushers' order, but he persisted for years. He rang the bell to summon worshippers to church, and on rare occasions he would allow other mortals the chance to jump up on the rope and ride it until the bell started ringing. This was fun and the purpose of the bell was secondary to the gymnastic skills needed for the job.

Another big difference in collection duty back then compared to today was that we boys disappeared to the nearby drug store for a Coke after collecting the offering. We merely placed the collection plates in the front of the church as the congregation sang "Praise God From Whom All Blessings Flow..." And after the blessings flowed, we were out of there! We timed our cokes at about twenty minutes. That took us away from most of the sermon and we were usually back by 11:50AM. We eased into the rear of the church where Judge Parsons usually sat. He understood young men and enjoyed being a party to our youthful indiscretion. Mothers of ushers occasionally requested their usher sons to stay with them in church in a pew but that was not as exciting as getting a Coke and then getting quietly into the rear of the church. We smiled at all the elders as they departed, thinking we had trumped them at their church.

We were respectful of the positions we held in the church organization and, contrary to what we often told Isabel about the job, we really did a good, honest day's work on behalf of the church. What we told Isabel several times was that one of us had slipped a twenty or a ten out of the plate prior to taking it back. She knew that was not the case, yet each time we made that type of story up she would react predictably. Her temporary reaction was shock, and then an awareness that she had been taken in one more time. She would quickly brush all that aside and inform all who could hear that she prayed for us a lot. She certainly must have done that often!

Whether we were ushers or whether we sat with our mother and our grandmother, we always seemed to be out of church in less than an hour. The Coke made it go faster, it seemed. Since my Dad only attended twice a year, his view was that the preacher must have known the worshippers wanted the reasonably-timed service. This allowed them to get the New York Times after church before any other denomination in town. The paper was delivered in limited amounts on Sundays to the Rexall Drug Store. The papers would come in about 10AM and be sold out by 12:30PM. If some churches kept their worshippers in the pews overtime (using my father's jargon), some worshippers would not have access to the Times that week. Presbyterians were practical people, and it seemed we regularly beat the other church-goers in the community to the printed word out of New York City.

We assigned arbitrary nicknames to each of the several churches in the village. We were neither religious zealots nor were we agnostics. We were young and restless! Our classifications were not meant to harm or to be disrespectful to any church or worshipper.

The Catholics were easy targets. Because of religious instruction all through the school year that got our Catholic peers out of the last period of school once a week, the rest of us were downright envious. During World Series play in the fall when the series was on during the afternoon hours, our Catholic friends were over in the church watching the games while we idled the last period away locked in study hall. The "mackerel snappers," as we called the Catholics, got special treatment, we concluded. We also concluded that we were glad our churches did not do the afternoon stuff because once a week was sufficient.

The "minnow munchers" were the Episcopalians. The minnows were smaller fish than the mackerel. Since the mackerels were bigger than minnows in our juvenile religious metaphors the label seemed accurate since the Catholics in town were more visible. Bingo and the World Series "passes" from school tended to make a religious group more visible.

There were names for the Dutch Reform and the Methodist church members playing on the actual names of church-goers at those churches. Many of the muck farmers attended the Dutch Reform so they became the "onion eaters." The Methodists were Big Sam's Singers, named after the principal of our school, Sam Hungerford. He was a notable singer at the church and in the school swing choir so this name was really appropriate.

There were "Holy Rollers," based on the fact that some of our friends said worshippers rolled in the aisles. Whether this happened or not I do not know, but the word of a friend back then was "gospel" so we believed that stuff really happened. There were "Shakers" who had a significant history in the county we lived in so when the word came down from our peer-experts that those people actually could be seen shaking when they worshipped, we believed.

In the Wayne County, New York history of religion, the Mormons stand out, especially because of the annual world-wide return of believers to the area near Palmyra where founder Joseph Smith was said to have met the Angel Moroni. Every summer Palmyra hosts tens of thousands of visitors to witness the outdoor pageant playing out for a week. Growing up in Sodus gave us plenty of religious diversity so we did not need to rag on the Mormons. The nearest Mormon Church was twenty miles away, so we focused on the local folks.

It never dawned on those of us who were Presbyterians to even consider someone, somewhere in town had a nickname for us. It also, pathetically, never dawned on us just how narrow our religious view was back then. I knew Jewish people but never knew where they worshipped. I knew there were Baptists but did not know much about the religion until much later in my life when I moved to the south. My wife has spent endless hours trying her best to overcome the particular brand of religion my friends in the ushering corps and I grew to love. She is still fighting an uphill battle despite numerous years of reform.

One story from my youth my wife heard about a few years ago pertained to church camp. Presbyterian Church Camp brought many of the youngsters of the county churches together at a scout camp rented by the churches for a week during the summer. The camp was located on Seneca Lake (one of the Finger Lakes) and was normally used by Boy Scouts. I was there with the Boy Scouts once, and this proved to be very helpful for the two summers I was there with my fellow Presbyterians.

All the trails were on a scout map and the tents of the girls of the Presbyterian camp were very easy to locate with the scout map—especially at night. In the second of my religious summer camping experiences I was invited to leave the campgrounds prematurely for behavior unbecoming an avid Presbyterian. I did not go alone; but that was of little consequence to my mother. She banned me from taking up the offering in church for a long period of time. My "pew time" was a tough penalty for what was a rather innocent tent visit. Of course, innocence is not always provable.

As I sit in a Baptist Church in my current sun-belt hometown, the Presbyterian itch sets in about noon and by twelve-twenty I become a pest. If the service goes double overtime, using my father's analogy from long ago, I actually have to get up and leave the church by twelve-thirty.

The New York Times newspapers are in short supply in Rome, Georgia and if a person doesn't get them by 12:30 or so that person runs the risk of missing the New York news for that week! Some habits are just hard to break.

***

Lavina So Fina— Honk's babe

When I get an opportunity, I try to treat young kids in my family to unexpected little gifts or money in an envelope at birthdays or on special days. This comes from an historic appreciation of similar little gifts I received when I was young. I was the recipient of gifts from loved ones and even a local businessman who came to the front door of our house at Christmas with a dollar for each kid in the house. All of this is documented in other chapters; one of the more memorable persons in my life for gifts was Lavina Atkinson. Now Lavina had an unusual first name but her uniqueness did not stop with her first name. She was the wife of Honk, the local pool hall and pinball proprietor. They were as different as day and night.

Mrs. Atkinson was tall, stately and rather attractive. Honk was no beauty. He was short, plump and growled a lot. He was no imitation Santa Claus. No one would ever get Frank Atkinson to play Santa in a store at Christmas. As Honk, he came across as gruff, blunt, and business-like.

Mrs. Honk, as we often called Lavina, was very kind and

considerate. The thing I remember after all these years is her numerous visits to our home and, upon departing, she gave Dick and me each fifty cents. That was a lot of change from a friend of Mom's in the 1940s. Dick and I even pretended to get along nicely when the lady was there so we wouldn't screw up our fifty cent gift.

Lavina volunteered to take care of Dick and me on a couple of occasions when Isabel was in the hospital. This was fun for us, and we were treated royally by Honk's wife. There were many adults in the community who took a great interest in both of us when we were little. Dick and I were chums until Dick tired of me. This did not seem to happen in Lavina's presence, nor did it occur when my grandmother was in charge. When other people watched over us, though, the sibling rivalry got intense.

The interesting thing about growing up in the proximity of siblings is that a person always has a friend for certain games. These usually were table and card games but included catch, shooting baskets, swimming and hiking. Brothers and/or sisters provided an excuse to get out and do something if it appeared there was a unity of purpose. The old adage about safety in numbers operated then, and Isabel figured Dick would look after me. This calculation was short-circuited several times when my older brother opted for separation from his sibling rival. Lavina and Grandmother Pearson served to shield me from those times since Dick respected their latent power. Dick saw through Isabel and knew he could ditch me once he got away from the effective range of our mother.

I had some friends who were only children and I marveled, even then, at their neat, orderly lives. They never had to wonder where something was since their mothers and fathers provided a safe haven for their belongings. By contrast, in my house something important needed to be hidden under clothes or kept in a box somewhere in the house.

Lavina Atkinson always left money for Dick if he was not there so there would be equality under our roof. When Donna was born, I think she may have benefited from our mother's friend's generosity but by the time Charley came along he was not on the Atkinson gravy train. It had ceased running for whatever reasons things like that cease. On the occasion of one of the visits from Lavina, I had one of the childhood diseases and was stuck in the house away from my family and friends. Fear of measles, mumps and chickenpox could be a social isolator in those days since the childhood diseases swept through schools and families quickly.

I was stuck away in our downstairs where my father would put a home office once he got out of the navy. Since there was a cot there with me on it, I realize that this memory came during the 1943-1945 era when Dad was away. I, therefore, must have been about five or six. As I reclined in the warmth of the room sitting right over the furnace and where the afternoon sun streamed in during winter months when the sun was low in the sky, in strode Lavina.

She had no evident fear of the childhood disease I possessed at the time and furthermore she made a big deal of staying in there with me for several minutes. What I remember the best was the four half dollars that the fine lady dropped on my covers as she departed. This was an unheard of bonanza of silver. I was feeling better in a heartbeat due to her generosity. It was more than I had ever received from anyone. Bear in mind this event occurred when times were tough during the war years, and not that long after America and Sodus emerged from the Great Depression. It would be, I think, the equivalent of receiving twenty or thirty dollars from a family friend in the modern era. How often does that small gesture appear out of the blue today? Money does not solve all problems, nor is it the thing that makes friendships stronger. It does something for young kids when the gift is unannounced, unexpected and given with love.

In an irony of small town dynamics, I developed a passion for pinball machines in my adolescence. The pinball machines were located in a business establishment right in the middle of Main Street. It was called Honks. As I stood there playing the Honk man's pinball machines for some of the endless hours of my misspent adolescence, it never dawned on me I was giving him all the money and then some that his wife dropped on me when I was little.

***

Vets Return—Don't ask

There were many World War II veterans that I earnestly wished to speak to about their experiences. As an avid history buff, I really wanted to find out about places and stories associated with war. This interest in history no doubt came as a product of growing up during that era. It also came as a product of knowing about prisoners of war in the nearby camp down on the lake, visiting my Dad at Sampson naval base, listening to the radio news about the war and being aware of all the men from my home town who served.

Growing up in Sodus made me aware of a VFW outfit (Veterans of Foreign Wars) and an American Legion. The VFW had a tent for many years at various events, and the wives associated with the VFW members "manned" the tent selling food or other things. The American Legion was active in sponsoring baseball for young boys too old for Little League and Babe Ruth League. I appreciated the fact that several of us got an opportunity to play far and wide around Wayne County and beyond through the generosity of the Legion. During these community efforts there were very few opportunities to "interview" vets.

My father was quite adamant about me staying out of the veterans' personal and private war experiences. Only after I was able to go into bars when I was older did I begin to hear some of the stories. It was in that setting that the veterans opened up.

There was one man from Wolcott who told me stories about submarine duty in the Pacific. The man was a dairy farmer then, and no one seemed to mention his World War II experience. We were at a bar once during a celebration of the 4th of July down on Sodus Bay. He started drinking after lunch at a huge picnic, and by nine or ten PM he was telling many interesting stories of the submarine experience. His drinking prowess was the stuff of legends, and he did not fail to meet expectations that particular day.

My father was not there, and I ignored his advice from my early childhood since I was, by then, my own person. The stories coming from the submarine veteran that day were stories I had only read about in magazines and books or heard about on the popular series, Victory at Sea, while sitting with my family watching TV. The dairy man's stories delved into failures of torpedoes early in the war that were fired from his sub. He was still bitter after nearly two decades of that recollection. His submarine was put at terrible risk, he explained, when torpedoes failed to explode upon hitting a target. The target then became the pursuer and the sub took a beating on several occasions when this happened. This, then, was the nub of the logic my father had counseled me about. The bitterness the man carried was measurable. He had risked his life in the service of his country and his country couldn't develop a workable torpedo. How in hell could I deal with what my questions had brought up? I was like a dredge bringing up items no one knew how to deal with once the items were on the barge! My father was correct one more time. It always amazed me as I got closer to twenty-one how absolutely bright my father was and how my intelligence had seemed to wane with age. It was if he was getting smarter and I was getting dumber. This seemed to happen to a lot of my teenage friends, also. It had to be something in the Sodus drinking water.

Once I explored the undersea stories of the man under the influence, I could not easily extract myself. I was not an historic participant in this trip down memory lane, yet was attracted to the stories as a moth is to light. The veteran could not seem to stop nor did I want him to stop. Finally his wife sensed it was time to take the man home. She had been passively watching from long range. The wife came and took him gently by the arm and got him to their car. She counseled me that the stories were too difficult for him usually, and he had been drinking too long that day. She said he exposed that vein of recollection on rare occasions. It came with drinking and patriotic times. She commended me for being a good listener. I was praised about my listening abilities, but the woman should have known I was not too passive in the matter. The woman was not critical of me. Her drunk, weeping husband went to his car and was aimed into the passenger seat. There was no driving for the submariner that night despite many safe undersea missions.

I never shared that story with my father because he probably would have been pissed at me. What came out of this college student's mind were probing questions based upon my own childhood education. What came from the sailor were difficult thoughts from a period when he had been my age.

There was one other incident similar to the submariner story and this came shortly after his undersea adventures were disclosed. The farmer from the submarine story had a neighbor who lived just down the road on Route 104 near the Town of Huron. Unbeknownst to me at that time, the neighbor was a certified war hero as was the submariner. The Huron man was called a Pathfinder—this was the term given to the first paratroops parachuted into France in the dark hours before the D-Day landings on the coast of France.

I was summoned over to sit at a table in a bar, again down on Sodus Bay, where the ex-paratrooper was retelling the trauma of jumping at night behind enemy lines. Was it the water and the peaceful atmosphere that brought these stories to the fore? I think not. I guessed correctly that these two men loosened their grip on the stored, unpleasant memories when the beer soaked their brains sufficiently.

Serving as a Pathfinder was terrible duty, it turns out, since these few men were responsible for lighting drop zones in the midst of the enemy so that the waves of planes following them could deposit the jumpers in the correct place. Many Pathfinders never lived beyond the day they floated down from the darkened skies over France. The man telling the story explained that about eighty percent of his particular group did not survive that first day in combat.

Again I was mesmerized. This local man was a true to life hero and no one seemed to know it prior to this moment of truth in the bar. I sat in awe of the man and did little to interrupt the stories. Other, older men were there with him. I followed a piece of my father's historic advice. I was seen and not heard.

Once again the flood of memories was a strain on the man; he, too, left the bar in tears after sharing terrible memories with his friends and me.

Again, my father never knew I had listened into the private reflections of a war hero. Later in my life I thought I might explain what had happened on those two occasions but I could not bring myself to broach the topic with my father. Despite the fact that my father would surely have forgiven my youthful exuberances in the matters related to the two veterans, I still could not bring myself to point out I had ignored his advice.

While student teaching during my senior year in college, I heard some good advice from a mentor. His advice mirrored something my Dad had been telling me since he returned from the relative calm of his wartime navy service. Both men were respected men in their generation. Each told me the same thing in a different manner.

The mentor was the Lyons, New York high school basketball coach and physical education teacher named Richard Blackwell. Dick was a successful coach who turned out many fine teams. He coached Syracuse University basketball coach Jim Boeheim when Boeheim was in Lyons School. During my semester of appreciating and learning from Coach Blackwell, something came up about him being a paratrooper. Coach Blackwell was a relatively short man and he merely explained there were ways to look taller in order to qualify for the paratroop service. He did not speak of these ways nor did he dwell on the fact that he was a veteran. He, like most men of that generation, was tight lipped about his service.

He was a no-nonsense type guy and ran a tight ship at Lyons. Even student teachers like me scrubbed the locker room floors after big classes with a large squeegee. Dick Blackwell did it himself, so he felt we should and could do this also. He did not want any kid falling in the water from after shower periods of another class. He was a mentor and leader by example. The ex-paratrooper merely did his duty as he saw it.

On one occasion he offered up sound advice about life and coaching that related to something my Dad taught me also. Coach Blackwell said coaches don't enjoy talking about their losses and people should not ask stupid questions after losing games. He then added that this was similar to why military veterans did not like to talk about war service. Such men did not like to talk about losses too emotional to deal with much, the same as a coach didn't like it. The veterans were filled with knowledge about losses far more heart wrenching than losing at sports. Coach Dick Blackwell and H.B. Pearson were members of the old school. They both tried to give me good advice.

***

Con Game—Police state

One of the two big houses at the end of High Street was occupied by police chief Con Loveless. He served as chief for many, many years and finally gave up the post to a series of replacements including Don Davis, a classmate of mine.

When we were in school, if someone had told us that Don Davis would be police chief in Sodus, New York, we would have taken that person in for rabies testing.

Chief Loveless was a quiet, unassuming man who kept things under control in the village during his tenure in office. His niece was a classmate of ours. We always tried to pick her brain, thinking we could get insight into the chief's operational patterns. We wondered how long he stayed in the cruiser at the middle of town. Did he go home to bed at eleven PM? Who was in charge of the police business during the middle of the day? Did the chief work eighteen hour shifts? His niece Doris did not know enough about her uncle. He lived a shadowy life and that meant we did not know when to pull future pranks.

Crime rates were much lower back then for a multitude of reasons. Crime in the village was nearly nonexistent, and I personally don't remember hearing or reading about many incidents. The only things I recall were during summer months when Sodus and Sodus Point were overflowing with migrants and summer residents respectively. Sodus was where migrants shopped with their pay from picking crops. On certain occasions alcohol and the close nature of the housing arrangements created scenarios for violence in labor camps or in the overloaded vehicles traveling to and fro in the village.

Sodus Point's crime seemed to be influenced by the huge influx of cottagers and weekend visitors. Alcohol, again as in Sodus, was the primary causative agent in Sodus Point crime statistics. People consumed too much alcohol, were packed into a tiny area called the strip in Sodus Point, and by midnight any Friday or Saturday night trouble could brew up.

Con Loveless was usually spotted sitting in his police cruiser right in the center of the village of Sodus. His counterpart in Sodus Point would drive around looking for aberrations in behavior whereas Con waited for something to come to him. Con's mid-town location was predictable and logical. People always knew where to find him and there were three bars easily visible from his location. The police counterpart to Con at the Point irritated many by virtue of his search for minor traffic infractions. Con did not sweat the small stuff about stop signs or red lights. In fact there were perhaps five stop signs and one red light in the village, so this was an easy task.

The bars of Sodus were quite numerous given the small population. Sodus Point had more drinking places by a narrow margin but in summer months the population swelled to nearly ten thousand during certain weeks and months. Con did not have to manage such a population increase in the village. Any temporary increase was due to the migrants, but they melted away by nightfall to entertain themselves at their own camps. State Police would monitor the camps and go in to clean up any nasty crimes perpetrated.

Our teenagers rarely got into serious trouble, but we and many other teens found ways to go to the edge of trouble and then pull back. Con ignored Halloween and most pranks that came and went without serious harm to anyone. Other than the brief flirtation with BB guns and streetlights, for a while my peers and I did not come up on Con's primitive radar screen in the village.

My father came in once from a village board meeting and

mentioned that Con was keeping a "black book" in the village. This book contained the names of young people and various unsolved acts of vandalism. His goal, according the mayor, was to connect the acts with the names. Was there a real black book or not? I do not know. The possibility of such a thing was sufficient to send waves of apprehension into the ranks of teenagers in Sodus. As the "mole" inside the village board I helped keep my peers alerted to the police activities. I truly believed Con had such a book at the time. My fear was that the High Street neighborhood he lived in and shared with me would cough up some details of severed clotheslines, fractured street lights, leaves dumped on front porches, or snow piled up in front of exit doors to houses. If Con kept a tally of these matters and then delivered the black book contents to the mayor, the end result would be predictable.

My father no doubt had a pretty good idea of my proclivity for pranks. He also knew most of my pranks were quite harmless in contrast to big problems such as DUI, fighting, and migrant laborers with alcohol and knives. Con may or may not have known as much as we gave him credit for, but we were never pulled in for questioning. One time Con invited a couple of my buddies into the police cruiser for a discussion of unsolved events. In that scenario my buddies were pure as the driven snow. They did report the presence of a black book lying on the front seat of the police cruiser.

***

Green's Hill—Jack and Jill and Charley and Donna

Green's Hill is one of the prominent hills in and around Sodus. Green's Hill was located on the western edge of the village, and was the site of the reservoir for the community until the lake water started pouring into the system in the mid-century. There were times when the reservoir approached crisis levels in certain summers. Due to these crisis situations, the connection to the lake was a no-brainer. The reservoir is still there, serving to keep the water pressure constant.

The eastern side of the village is framed by Orchard Terrace, the long sloping hill built up through the old orchards, which have been reduced by home lots dotting the length of the street. There are small hills to the south including Brantling Hill, which has been the location of a rare ski slope in the area. To the north of the village is a sloping plain filled with fruit orchards leading to the great body of water named Lake Ontario.

It was Green's Hill that fascinated the residents back then. I wonder if people still hike up there now; It was the place we hiked to when we were little. The paths up the hill were steep, and at one time there were cows grazing on the hillsides. On the occasions I went up the hill we either followed the rough dirt road used by village waterworks vehicles to check the reservoir, or we went straight up from a place along old Route 104 bisecting the village on a west to east axis.

Once we reached the summit of the hill we felt we were on top of the world. Since most of my friends and I had not seen much else in the form of hills, at the time we started climbing the hill this sensation was understandable. As I got older and was able to travel with my parents and friends to other areas of New York State such as the Adirondacks and the Catskills, I began to realize how small "my" big hill was in contrast to the mountains in the state.

This fact of growing up geographically did not diminish the fond memories of hiking the Sodus hill. Can you imagine how a trip out to the Rockies at that age and stage in my life would impact upon me? What would that contrast have done to me?

I took my little brother and sister up the Green's Hill once when I was in college to share the climb with them and to revisit my childhood. As we neared the top and got within viewing distance of the reservoir and the excellent view of the lake six miles north my young guests were not nearly as impressed as I thought they would be at that moment. It dawned on me that they had benefited from the mobility afforded to them in the family auto that I did not enjoy at a similar age.

When I was their ages I thought Green's Hill was as good as it got. Once they got a taste of the Adirondacks and Catskills in their early childhood, how could this tame old hill entertain them? My early childhood was shaped by the years 1938-1945 when our family was quite limited in travel by money and the war. Rationing was a fact of life from 1941-1945, and my Dad's absence in service of the country was a limiting factor in our experiences. My younger siblings were much "luckier" than Dick and I because those limitations of our childhood had disappeared from their lives.

For me, Green's Hill became a metaphor for many events in our lives. The hike up the hill ignited nostalgic thoughts only I could appreciate. When the hike with Charley and Donna occurred, Dick was already on his way to serving in the army and then becoming a New York State Trooper. As much as my younger siblings were hot, thirsty, tired and somewhat bored with the climb, I was feeling different feelings. My longer legs and athletic background made the hill an easy climb for me. The physical part for me was easier because I had done the climb many times before, even at their ages. My outdoor life and lack of transportation in my youth gave me a decided mental and physical advantage over my younger siblings.

It dawned upon me on the top of Green's Hill that my brother and sister were merely showing signs of what was their life style in sharp contrast to that lifestyle I lived. They had TV and I had the radio at their ages. They had trips to various places and I stayed in Sodus most of the time. They had more organized activities such as Little League and Brownie Scouts whereas my peers and I only got a smattering of some of those things.

I love my siblings and did not think any unkindly thoughts on the climb. By accident of nature and genetics I am a reflective person. The comparisons between siblings and generations are therefore always unique to me. We often refer to a generation gap but I contend, based upon my experience with my younger siblings, that there is such a thing as a half-generation gap.

This half-generation gap is possible due to the rapid changes in technology and technology's impact upon society. Green's Hill was somewhat boring due to the advent of great TV programs showing mountains. The climb was tiring because the kids did not climb almost every day of their lives, as Dick and I had. We climbed hills about every day. We walked to school and that included up and down some large inclines. We climbed trees like crazy, because that seemed to be popular back then. We were outdoors many hours a day even in winter. Although memories of table games and cards are numerous, it is the lure of the outdoors that stands out more than anything in childhood play.

As a Health and Physical Education teacher for my whole adult life and as a coach for much of my professional teaching career, I can see terrific changes related to the metaphor of Green's Hill. The students of the modern era reflect more and more the conditions of my siblings' youth. The gap between the Pearson kids' recreational and activity patterns was noticeable. The differences between Charley and Donna and their young activity years is even more stark a contrast with the modern era. My brother and sister were very interested in the outdoors and in games and play. Both of them spent many hours outside when weather permitted. Donna loved the beach and Charley would go out and shoot baskets by the hour. They merely were normal reflections of their era. I reflected my era in ways much different from the next half-generation or generation.

What we have now is a very sad contrast with either of the time periods represented by my brother and sister and by my older brother and me. Kids of today, by in large, would not go up Green's Hill, nor would anyone convince them to. The parents probably wouldn't allow it. Some lawyer would probably sue like crazy if Jack and Jill "came tumbling down" the hill. No one was going to sue me if Charley and Donna tumbled down, since my mother gave the climb her blessing. Perhaps most kids today would need a uniform with a sponsor's name on it and their own number in order to make a climb.

From a pure coaching perspective, I see coaches in the modern era taking their athletes through pre-season training, post-season training and year-long exposure to the sport of choice. I do see much better technical training and much better strategy, tactics, and personal development in sports. Weight training and sport camps flourish. Specialization is rampant. Many coaches in the modern era simply cannot depend upon many of their students climbing their version of Green's Hill during the off-season as a regular routine.

What I do not see in the modern era is a versatile athlete, jack-of-all trades type person who is fit all year long. Those people were quite ready for any sport by virtue of the many physical things in life that are not present or sought in the modern era. Another thing I *do* see, however, in the modern era is the presence of female athletes that were not there when I grew up. This lack of female sport and games was a gender-specific shortcoming that parents, leaders and coaches did not seem to worry about back in mid-century America. Until 1973 and Title IX, people did not always do the logical, ethical thing.

Charley was quite young when I forced his short legs up the hill. He would recover to lead an active life in and out. Donna never had much of a chance to play sports so her gender really had to try to find activity where they could. I should have seen the handwriting on the sociological and physical wall before I got to the top of the reservoir that day.

***

Ten Bars—And we aren't talking candy
In the analysis of problems in society then and now, a common causative ingredient is alcohol. From the taverns and home made booze of pre-Revolutionary America up to the sports bars and multiple brews of this era, our country has paid a high price for alcohol. Sodus was no different.

Counting the various seedy locations around town, Sodus had at least six bars and probably more counting seasonal applications to better serve those interested patrons. The patrons of the numerous bars were a unique mix of Sodus residents. No one socioeconomic grouping had the monopoly on alcohol problems. This mirrored the national dynamic associated with drinking.

Doctors, farmers, merchants, builders, teachers and citizens of all walks of life were afflicted with alcoholism and the various ancillary diseases associated with drinking. It probably can be said, with a high degree of accuracy, that alcoholism is a truly democratic problem. It hits every nook and cranny of American life. It did in Sodus.

In Sodus some of the problem drinkers would appear at their bar of choice rather early in the day. After that, whatever else happened seemed to be dictated by the rhythm of their drinking. It was common knowledge that some of the problem drinkers did so in the privacy of their homes and then they sometimes would appear, under the influence, at incongruous places. Bowling brought out some of them. During the winter the leagues were popular recreation, and the bowling alley leagues saw their share of problem drinkers. Women in Sodus with drinking problems could not easily frequent the bars; but there were a few female drinkers who would be evident at the bowling alley.

Bar owners had their steady customers and these people must have made a good living because some of the bar owners owned a lot of real estate and other businesses. One of the bar owners sold beer at night and Pontiacs during the day. If a person sat around downtown, as did the police chief, a clear pattern of frequency to and from the drinking establishments would be evident. There were stories abounding about wives going to a particular bar at a particular time and intercepting their husbands before too much money and time could be spent at that favorite haunt. Sometimes wives would come in during delicate times and some bar operators became experts at deflecting marital disputes.

There were some lawyers and doctors who depended upon their favorite barkeep to help get the professionals to their next appointment. Everyone in town seemed to know who had the drinking problems, and the bar operators knew much more.

Fortunately for the local residents, traffic was not a problem and therefore drunk drivers had the roads to themselves much of the time. There were still drunk driving accidents, and lives were forever altered by these acts of irresponsibility by the drivers. There were times when drunks were driven home by bar patrons and even the police chief.

As new drinkers came of age, it was always disturbing to see a young person take the wrong drinking turn in the road of life. Some of my classmates could not handle drinking. We lost a couple of our best friends and finest people to drunk-driving accidents shortly after they came of legal age. During events such as July 4th, Fireman's Field Days, Christmas and other community celebrations, the problem drinkers would turn up with their slurred speech and foul breath.

Many drinkers tipped their bottles in the privacy of their homes or offices. These were the neighbors we often wondered about. Their lives were very quiet and private. Once in a while we would spend the night with friends someplace and during that overnight we would glimpse into the drinking habits of someone's parent or relative. These times could be sources of embarrassment for all of the young people there.

Unlike many incidents depicted in the news in reference to problem drinkers, Sodus did seem to allow the drinkers an extra wide berth to avoid trouble. Even the migrants with drinking problems took their problems back to the relative privacy of their camps. I did not know of any neighbors who beat their wives or any examples of ugly drunks among my friends who did drink. My drinking friends seemed to be happy when they drank. I contend it was the relative tranquility of our home town that kept them in a good mood even when they did overdo the alcohol consumption.

**

My First SOB—Welcome to the real world

I was buried in the beet bin up to my waist. My clothes were red, my skin was turning red and the heat was oppressive. My job in the canning factory was to do about every nasty job that came along for one summer. I was paid about fifty cents an hour, and every day there made me more determined than ever to get a college education and avoid this type of life work.

My father worked as a salesman for the Alton Canning Company. In his duties he traveled to many locations making contracts to sell large amounts of canned goods. He dealt in freight car loads of green beans, beets, apple sauce and any other product canned from the products sold by the farmers to the company. The whole thing was complicated by weather, demand, and the whims of the purchasers. My Dad was a fine salesman and could sell the products of the factory under any circumstance. He was a management person who showed up to work in neat slacks and pressed shirts. He traveled in a business suit. His son was given a job because of his position.

Once I was told I could work in the factory I left the protective bubble created by my Dad and his close management friends Mort Adams, Leo Fletcher and a wonderful boss, Ed Burns. Despite being on close terms with the management types for my young life, in the business I was about to go into harm's way. For that summer of my discontent I would be removed from such things as management trips with the Adams, Fletchers and Burns to Red Wing baseball games, Shrine Circus, Royal basketball games and meals at Rund's Restaurant, all at the generosity of Ed Burns.

My new mentor was the first S.O.B. in my existence. His name was "Tom Smith." The name is different because no one out there would like to hear about their grandfather or great grandfather being a son of a bitch.

Tom told me about the new rules in my life on the first day out in the factory. Despite the presence of such wonderful adults in the management team up in the front of the huge canning factory in their neat and inviting offices, Tom informed me, he never wanted to see me up there while I worked that summer. As it turns out, part of his logic was that he would not want a fifteen year old to blow the whistle on his tactics in the factory.

The factory had to be run with a firm hand since the employees were a mix of migrants, Cubans, seasonal people and several women sorters on the sorting tables. Oh yes, there were three high school kids who were eventually going to go on to college. If they did not know it when they worked at the factory under Tom's steady and mean spirited hand that summer, they sure as hell would know they were college bound *after* that summer.

My father probably knew more about Tom than he let on, and perhaps felt this would be a great growing experience for the prankster from High Street. Fathers often have the capacity for "tough love." Mothers are less tough with their love. If Isabel knew a tenth of what I was going to go through that summer, she would have pressured my father to get me out of there. I vowed not to let the S.O.B break my spirit. This was to be a crucible for me. Whether Tom knew it or not, he was going to make me stronger and more stubborn than ever. My brother Dick's harsh sibling treatment of me was nothing contrasted to Tom's treatment.

Tom was a high school dropout, I found out later. He resented the high school kids who were going to go farther than he had. He resented the front office personnel because of their success, homes, families, cars, friends and even their hours. Tom had to be out there in the factory sixteen hours a day, six days a week. He was a necessary person doing a dirty job. I guess he chose to be an S.O.B because it was his basic nature. He loved it when the peak times called for extending the workers' schedules.

Some of the things I endured that summer were tasks usually given to migrant workers and Cubans. Tom relished giving me jobs usually associated with the migrants. I believe that he was a severe racist, but my presence in his domain gave him a new target for his prejudice that summer. My nature was a friendly nature. I did not get the nickname "Smiler" by accident. My life was a happy life. I found migrants and factory workers interesting. When I worked with them in the factory or side by side with them in the fruit orchards in other summers, we always could find some common ground. Despite an occasional car ride around throwing fruit and vegetables with my friends, I did not consider myself intolerant or racist. I was a delinquent at times, but not a racist.

The factory ran overtime at certain times because freshly picked crops came pouring in based upon harvest schedules and weather conditions. One farmer that summer started harvesting his beans at night using huge lights on his tractors. With the twenty-four hour nature of the harvesting end of things the factory had to adjust. Normally the factory could catch up at night even if the crops delivered during the previous day were overwhelming. When crops were overwhelming, people had to get into the beets or actually move apples so the machinery of the conveyor belts would not jam up. The workers were pushed very hard during times like this. The guy harvesting at night meant that the fever pitch of a busy night carried over into the daylight hours.

Tom wanted his crews on a sixteen hour work schedule due to the intense nature of the crops pouring in for processing during peak times. In a way he was responding to the heavy demands for the finished canned goods product already sold to large grocery chains by the factory salesman—my Dad. Tom had to keep his people busy to can the goods. I was a cog in the operational wheel for that summer. I kicked beets, moved apples, hustled sugar bags onto a platform, picked up garbage, pushed beans with a shovel and basically kept busy.

Mistakes happened when people were pushed hard during the sixteen-hour work efforts. Although such peak times occurred twice for only two weeks at a time over the twelve week summer, they were ugly weeks. Several times accidents happened that were avoidable in a normal scheme. Tractor operators backed over people and objects at night out in the dimly lit delivery areas. Workers lost fingers in the lines and in the can room a couple of times.

One time a Cuban worker was working in the huge loft above where the forty-pound sour cherry cans were being capped after receiving about five pounds of sugar per can. His main job was to dump sugar into a huge funnel which then dumped the estimated amounts into each can going by en route to the cold storage where the cans would be frozen for future consumption. Large trucks would take the cans in large lots to the cold storage. After several hours of working up there the Cuban had to be replaced. He had been up there all night on one of the late shifts in the factory.

When I replaced him I noticed the writing on the fifty pound 'sugar bag." It was not sugar. It was salt. I stopped the canning line to put a stop to the salt distribution into the sour cherries going to cold storage. Tom was there in an instant. I showed him the remaining bags on the loft where salt bags had been poured into sour cherries all that night and then gone to the cold.

The plant S.O.B went nuts on me! I had just arrived at work from home after getting six hours sleep due to the sixteen hour mandated work schedule for that two-week period. He blamed me for not being there through the night when the salt bags had been put on the loft by the Cubans who could not read English. They moved salt bags from the warehouse to the loft when they should have moved sugar. The damage was done. I was there and the Cubans had departed. I took verbal abuse for the mistake. After a long delay in the processing of the cherries for the cold storage due to Tom's lengthy diatribe, other factory regulars moved in to get things going. A tall factory worker actually had to remove Tom bodily from my work space because he felt he would harm me. Another of the factory regulars told me later that once Tom got into that unproductive, hateful mode, somebody had to divert him or he would go nuts.

I was told many years later that Tom died a lengthy, horrible death due to cancer. That was too bad; but his treatment of his fellow man was terrible.

Once the sugar replaced the salt on the supply loft things were back to normal that summer in the factory.

There was one other fine point. The cold storage was freezing sour cherries with five pounds of salt on them not sugar as needed. The trucks had run all night with the new mix of cherries and salt.

Back in mid-century, corporate America had to deal with problems pertaining to profit and production just as today. It intrigued me that there was a two to three hour discussion about what action was required. I knew I would tell Mr. Burns about the salt if the decision had been in favor of a cover-up.

Tom, true to form, evidently was willing to let the whole thing go and let the future consumer of that batch of cherries take his or her chances with salted cherries. I heard this from an assistant plant foreman who was a good fellow but never had authority.

Ultimately, the entire batch was removed from cold storage and dumped out back in the canning factory dump. I was the dumper. I spent three days dumping the cans into a huge, red pile of salted cherries so that the cans could be used again.

Tom blamed me for the damage, and fortunately the Cubans kept their jobs. I cleaned up the mess and in his eyes was punished for not being in the loft when the damage was done. I was home sleeping at the time after sixteen hours of putting up with Tom Smith.

He was my first S.O.B. and he was true to form to my last day on the temporary job. I learned a lot about management from him.

In my dealings with people during peak times in my career, I would sometimes think about how Tom would have responded. I then did the opposite.

***

Messinger—Perry was a cheese man

"Helluva Good Cheese" is a brand of New York cheese originally developed in Sodus. The cheese products with the unique name on it were created by a man named Perry Messinger, a local resident with a creative flare. For many years the little company went along as a special company in the local area. Finally, after the company changed hands, the products were shipped to an expanded trading area. The Sodus cheese, along with horse radish, dips, and other items became known regionally. During the past Christmas season of 2003 while in Atlanta some people heard that I was originally from Sodus, New York. They were consumers of "Helluva Good Cheese!" They purchased the cheese in Atlanta, Georgia. I was impressed because I had known the founder of the company. He also had known me. I was a visitor in his living room one summer night.

Perry Messinger was on old man when I was a young boy. As I grew older and reached my teens Perry was still an old man. Some men just look old even when they are middle aged. He must have been one of those people. Perry lived just off Main Street in Sodus, and we went by his house daily. Perry puttered around making his home made cheese; he was also a Justice of the Peace. I am not sure what other work he did, but he was out on the porch a lot and was usually very friendly. I say usually because there was a night in my adolescence when Perry gave me a gift for life, and it wasn't some of his cheese.

Perry's role as a Justice of the Peace was important since he could deal with certain infractions of the civil code without making the arresting officer have to go to a court later for a court hearing. State Troopers of our area knew Perry well and brought their arrests to Perry for speedy justice.

The night I ended up in the living room of the "Helluva Good Cheese" man was not one of my more memorable nights. After taking a date to her home after a visit to the drive-in theatre one hot summer night, I was speeding through Sodus on my way home. This was because I was very late getting Isabel's car home. I was late for reasons not connected to the length of the movie that night so the "movie lasted a long time" excuse would not work. Nevertheless a problem was about to occur should my father be home from a long trip. Whereas Isabel slept soundly when children were still out, my Dad would not sleep until all were home.

Luckily for me, my father was not back from his trip so my late arrival was no problem where he was involved. Unfortunately for me there would be another problem. A New York State Trooper saw me fly by where he was parked off of Main Street, and gave chase. The trooper turned on the flashing lights as I rounded the turn going down High Street from Main Street and I saw that but decided to merely park in front of my house and meet my punishment The trouble was I knew where my house was and was almost there but the trooper was in uncommon territory. Rather than run the risk of me getting away from him in a neighborhood he did not know he then turned on the siren!

When a siren went off in Sodus, it usually meant it was noon or there was a fire. The trooper's siren woke everyone up on my end of the street including my mother. She was out there at the car door before the trooper could get out of his car. Since it was 3AM, my mother was rather hostile standing there in her bathrobe and nightgown. Other women were out there along with their inquisitive husbands. I had brought the whole quiet night to a screeching halt with my race to get home.

The trooper assured my mother that my only crime was speeding. She informed him that my additional crime was stupidity. They both agreed on that, and Isabel returned to the house to await her chance at me alone.

The Justice of the Peace was aroused from his sleep to deal with my speeding ticket. This did not put him in a jovial mood, regardless of how successful his cheese was selling locally! The trooper took me to his home in the police car so that my car would stay put with my mother looking out at it until I returned.

As I stood there before him in his living room where he had a desk and one of those legal looking green lights over the papers on his desk he merely looked at me over the tops of his glasses. His next question floored me because I was expecting something relating to speeding, trying to run, or an inquiry about my wonderful mother. Everyone always asked about my mother.

The cheese man's legal question that night was: "Where have you been and with whom?" Thinking I had robbed a bank or turned over an outhouse or two was on his mind, and his question would solve other crimes that night. My response was typically adolescent at sixteen. I told him I was with Glenda Smith and time got away from us on her side porch. He finally fined me some reasonable amount and sent me back out to the officer's car with the officer instructed to take me home. As I left his porch he told me never to return as a legal case. His advice was heeded.

On the way home the trooper told me he felt bad that he had turned on the siren and caused me that additional trouble. The sympathetic trooper then offered up that he should not have awakened the Justice of the Peace for the speeding ticket either. I agreed on both issues, but the damage had been done.

Isabel lectured me on various topics including the neighbors' opinion of us after this event. I tried to calm her down but she was not pleased. She took the car away for a month (it was hers to share with me) and then informed me she was going to call Glenda's parents in the morning to see if they were aware of the lateness of the date the previous evening.

That last threat caused some high intensity deliberations on my part since that part of the evening did not need more scrutiny.

Despite upsetting the Queen of Sodus and despite waking the King of cheese early in the morning for a speeding violation, my misery that night ended with a restless sleep. Nothing ever came up again about the threat to call some girl's parents; my guess is enough damage had been done in my mother's eyes.

I still buy and enjoy "Helluva Good Cheese" when I can get it. Most of my memories of Perry Messinger are very pleasant ones.

***

Operators in Charge—Telephone simplicity

In Sodus during the mid-century a person could dial 0 and get a human voice. When the human voice answered, it usually knew the person who was calling. Operators in Sodus were Soduskans who probably knew everything that was going on in the village. Every home had a phone with a four-digit number. By the time I was twelve I could recite numerous four-digit numbers listed for the phones of my friends. A phone book was printed periodically, but since there was very little turnover in numbers and people did not move as they do in the modern era, there was really no reason to keep printing a new book.

Our 5311 number stayed with our family for two decades. Operators had an uncanny ability to remember phone numbers. I guess they were constantly using the numbers so it was reasonable to expect they would be good at recall. When my friends and I would sit together and talk about baseball stats—and a baseball card was a big item—we entertained ourselves by reciting batting averages for players from the previous years. The operators were most valuable players in the Sodus number leagues for other reasons.

When there was a fire or an emergency, the operator was the 911 call of the era fifty years ago. When a person dialed the operator, something was set in motion immediately by a person who knew the village, the streets, and the people. There were instances when operators called neighbors to get others alerted to emergency situations at a neighbor's home. Sometimes operators knew where key people were at any given time and this eliminated costly delays. One time the operator called our home and told my father about a tree the operator had heard had fallen into a nearby driveway. She wanted my father to go next door and check on the driveway to see if her father's car had been hit by the tree. My father was bowling with friends and she knew he wasn't there. The reason I remember this is because I was the scout who went into the storm's fury to check on the fallen tree.

In the modern era there are very few operators and when you do get one on telephone they do not know anything about the local situation. We have paid the price for the computerized era of phones. Phones are now fast, mobile and very convenient. They lack personality and intrude into lives in ways they never did before. I suppose there are plenty of examples of cell phones being damn helpful in certain situations. Operators were our eyes and ears of the night.

The fire department depended upon phone access to key volunteer firemen. When there was a fire and volunteers were needed, the blaring siren mounted on the roof of the fire hall on Mill Street would beckon the volunteers. Often key phone calls were made to make sure all the key volunteers knew about the crisis.

My brother Dick could be nice to me at times, so my life was not always in jeopardy. Usually he would share and look out for me when the situation called for it. He related an interesting story about an operator in Sodus he knew. This operator was a graduate of the school and many knew her. She evidently was a very competent operator since she held the job a long time. When Dick and some of his friends met with her and other girls when they were of driving age but not drinking age the operator would shine.

After a few drinks this gal would begin to detail things she had overheard on the party lines in existence in the community. Since our house was on a private line, Dick suggested that at least this operator had never listened to 5311. Wrong!

She explained that she could listen in anywhere in the system. In fact, she said, not all the private lines were totally private. It was possible to mix calls into the system where private lines were functioning. This happened on occasion when we were using the phone in our house, so this now sounded logical.

As the drinks flowed the operator could recite about every number in the village. The guys and other girls, Dick said, could yell out a name and the operator would respond with the number. She had another trick or two to beguile the boys.

She could outline details of who in the community was sleeping with whom, if that stuff went on sixty years ago. I imagine it did so; when Dick would come in from an evening out with the gang (including the operator) he woke me to inform me of the juicy gossip. This seemed to create a bond between us that provided some new common ground for us as brothers. After he debriefed and fell asleep, I would lay awake contemplating who and what I could retell the following day. In some cases the operator had blown the whistle on some of my friend's parents.

The operator could also beguile the boys in other ways that brought greater community cohesiveness. According to my brother (and remember-this was late at night after he began enjoying the bubbly a bit) the operator could overhear verbal messages pertaining to trysts that were planned. She, he said-she said, would then make a call to a particular number asking to leave a message for a certain male. This would create a fragile environment for the tryst and the operator would merely go back to work connecting calls. If this happened, and Dick swore it did, then who knows what community harmony was created?

Nothing like that exists in today's phone systems since we now have caller ID and phones with pictures. I can recall the point in time when the local switchboard disappeared and the operators went their way. I know of one who would be able to write a hell of a book about Sodus.

***

Untouchables—The Red and White reach

Norm Merhoff grabbed his extension pole and within a few minutes had filled my mother's order from the list she handed him in the Red and White Store. I accompanied my mother on trips to the stores of Sodus and helped carry groceries back up from Main Street to High Street. Isabel and I would use a cart or a bike with a basket on the front. Dick and I took turns carrying the goods for our mother; until she learned to drive later in her life, she did plenty of walking.

The unique thing at the Red and White was that the orders were filled by the shop keeper or his workers behind their big counters. Nearly all the items in the store were stocked on the high shelves and an extension pole was employed to grab boxes and cans for the customer. I do remember some items in the store that were within reach of the customer in the actual customer area, but by in large the work was done by Mr. Merhoff and the Red and White staff. It brings back memories of the constant dialog with customers so lacking in the modern, wide aisles of the super markets. When a customer shops in the modern store the only worker the shopper is compelled to speak to is the checkout person.

The old time stores have vanished from America due to the many logical reasons associated with quickness, customer convenience and ease of shelf replenishment. As the Merhoffs gave up their interest in the Red and White and as newer, bigger stores moved into Sodus, the shopping style and rhythm of customer/ owner relationships changed forever.

There were several unique memories associated with stores in Sodus that linger with me. Most have few modern counterparts. The DeHond Bakery was located just off Main Street yet was on the main route day after day for many people. Once inside the place a person was inundated with beautiful smells of freshly baked delights. Cinnamon covered items were my first choices, followed by items filled with strawberry, cherry or apple filling. On certain visits to the bakery, we were escorted there by Harvey DeHond, the owner's son and only child. If you were fortunate enough to travel to this wonderland of bread, doughnuts, and pastries with the son of the Pastry-King of Sodus, a special tour through the kitchen was possible.

In the rear of the store were large ovens. Sometimes they were still processing treats in the late morning and even at times in the afternoon. The damaged goods that failed to gain approval of the cook earlier in the day were available for free on tours with the DeHond boy. Here, then, was where a trio of ten and twelve year old boys could eat their way through an enormous amount of bakery "scraps."

The DeHonds were Dutch, and my mother loved going in there to talk with Mrs. DeHond. Isabel would load up with breakfast goodies for the Pearson table. Traveling through Sodus by going store to store was a trip down a communication network. During a trip to the bakery the Dutch-speak was evident and on the same day a stop at the dry cleaners found us talking to an Italian immigrant.

There were many first and second generation Dutch and German shop-keepers and farmers. It was an interesting time when the husbands and wives got excited and started jibber-jabbering in their original dialect. We would stand back and absorb this treat. Probably the best time for our peer group had been when Jake's parents got going in their house when a bunch of us were there. Donald (Jake Jr.) would interpret some of what he thought was going on but even our jovial Don could not quite figure what the heck they were saying.

Customer service was the forte of the local drug stores just as was the case with the Red and White. Much of what the shopper needed was behind the counter. Condoms were always behind the counter in the drug store, and only the very bravest of young men dared order up some condoms. Contrasted to the modern era when the "rubbers" are right at the checkout counter, back in Sodus they were hard to find according to those in the know. There was a mystique associated with buying condoms.

When our high school resident doctor-to-be David Hungerford took a job at Rexall Drug Store, we learned more about condoms. He described where and how they were stored behind the counter near the tobacco section. Word in the locker room back then was that Sammy Junior (F.S. Hungerford's eldest son) pricked a tiny hole in some condom packages thereby allowing future tiny sperm to flow unimpeded toward their ultimate goal. This turned out to be false, based upon Dr. David Hungerford's testimony on the matter at a reunion. I believed the good doctor then and even now but my father did have condoms from the drug store and we did have a surprise little brother when mother was forty five, so that locker room rumor might have a believer in my house! David went on to be a famous doctor at Johns Hopkins in Baltimore so I side with him and not the know-it-alls in the locker room. Ah, you ask how I knew my father used condoms from the drugstore. I was at a magazine rack near the tobacco area at a time when he purchased some condoms and cigarettes. I took some of his cigarettes once during a one week binge in the junior high years and I "borrowed" two of Dad's condoms when I was in high school for laboratory experiments.

As with most teenage boys at the time we all carried a condom with us in our wallets if only for purposes of showing off. The identifying circle shape profiled in a wallet enhanced one's reputation at the time in the locker rooms. Locker room bragging rights were not usually backed up at the drive-in or elsewhere. Like most of my friend's condoms, the things eventually aged in the wallet, still in the package.

Discussing customer service was a prime piece for training in any business. Business operators made sure their workers were aware of and could practice public relations. Even when a person went to the movie, went bowling or even went for a haircut, there was a personal touch to every exchange of services and money. The lady who operated the movie theatre knew each kid and could converse with them about family and events that were relevant. The bowling alley proprietors knew almost every bowler in the village and their handicap.

The barber shops were almost carbon copies of barber shops depicted in the movies from the era. The movie "Hoosiers" has a barber shop scene in it that could have been taken right out of Sodus. Everyone seemed to visit the barber shop and everyone had an opinion once they were in there. As youngsters we absorbed the exchanges and got our ears lowered. Sometimes people just came in to the shops just to get up to date news about sports, crops, and politics.

One memorable trip to a barber shop brought back the voice of a deceased classmate and teammate of ours, Donald Virts. Donald was one of the best athletes in Sodus history and he died as a result of injuries in an automobile accident when he was just in his twenties. The barbershop, located down in the basement under Honk's store on Main Street, had two or three barbers most of the time when I was young. One of the barbers taped conversations with various customers as they visited the shop. Donald was on an audio tape, the barber discovered, when Donald was a teenager shooting the bull with the barbers and some other customers. It was a haunting visit with an old friend sorely missed by his classmates.

Sodus was blessed with hard-working store owners. Customers were blessed because the groceries, baked goods and services came with smiles and conversation appropriate to the shopper's life. When I remember the smells of the bakery and the smiles from the shop owners, it is truly a remarkable experience down memory lane. I wish that every shop owner did audio tapes of their customers back then, because one never knows when a voice may never be heard again.

***

RG&E Over TV—Nothing is Private
The winter storm was blowing in from the lake, as they

usually did in the upstate New York section near the end of Lake Ontario. It was probably a Friday or Saturday night as I remember the interesting, vulgar evening because we were up late watching TV and listening to the howling winds and looking out our front windows to check the streetlight every so often. If the streetlight was visible then the snow was not quite a true blizzard. If we could not see the streetlight located one hundred feet away at the corner of our front yard on the street, then we were in for another dandy storm. The TV worked and the streetlight was still visible; so power and storm conditions were not in a crisis mode quite yet.

All of the sudden the sound for the program on black and white television (one of the three channels available using our straining antenna strapped to the one hundred year old chimney up on the roof) stopped and in its place we heard the voice of a neighbor. The neighbor worked for Rochester Gas and Electric and he was on a telephone pole somewhere in the neighborhood being battered around in the swirling snow.

Ralph, as he was known by one and all, was strapped to a pole up on Orchard Terrace checking the lines to find a possible break depriving the upper reaches of the street of power. He was communicating with some device hooked directly into the pole trying to explain to his partner on the ground or somewhere nearby what he had found up on the pole.

The fact that the rest of the neighborhood had power was amazing considering the powerful blasts from the wind but what was really amazing was that Ralph was out in the stuff and on a pole no less! He evidently had found something amiss but what transpired was a glimpse into the adult world of dedicated power line workers that kids would usually never have experienced.

Ralph carried on a five-minute discussion with the other person and in describing the break and the storm and line situation he used about every adult four-letter word available. As we in my family sat in the living room watching some program but listening to Ralph's energized and salty language over-riding the original program, no one moved to turn the sound down. It was as if we all were at the pole hanging there in the wind bearing witness to what real repair guys talk about.

We were told later that the communications between linemen in those situations may carry into a television audio if the pole talk was close enough geographically to the television set. This evidently occurred that evening as we all got a glimpse into the dangerous job performed by a neighbor. It was as if my father, out of respect for Ralph's work, did not make a move to turn the sound down. My mother would not have turned the sound down unless my father told her it was OK. That was part of Isabel's role, and that definitely was part of my father's role in our home. So we sat for five minutes and got educated compliments of RG&E.

As I reflect upon that curious evening many decades ago I am reminded that in the small community, and all other communities big and small, normal people perform very important tasks for the community. Ralph could have begged off and waited until the fury of the wind abated, but there were people without electricity and he and a partner were trying to make it right. Despite Ralph's vocabulary he was a vital community cog that night. No one else around had his knowledge and skill to climb the pole up in the storm that night.

The episode came and went and the electricity was restored in due time as it always was the several times per winter. Ralph went on to retire from RG&E and I am not sure he ever knew of the number of people hearing his dialogue with his co-worker that wintry evening. I wish I had taken time when I reached adulthood to connect with Ralph and share this story with him. My friends around the neighborhood either did not hear the communication or were otherwise occupied that evening. As I retold the story embellished with all the four-letter words I had heard *on television* that evening, my friends could not quite believe me. I wish I had been able to explain to Ralph that my family was in awe of his workmanship on the pole in the storm. I also would have liked to share the other part of the story with him because he would have had a good laugh.

In the small towns around our country and in the bigger population centers it seems as though we have many able, brave men and women who serve us in numerous ways. Ralph was such a man, as was my own father. Numerous men took risks in their jobs for the people of the community. Many of these men were members of the "Greatest Generation," the tab attributed to them by Tom Brokaw. By virtue of serving in World War II and then taking jobs such as linemen, policemen, volunteer firemen, elected officials, teachers, or even snowplow operators, our adults paid their dues in our democracy many times over.

The snowstorm raged on for a couple of days in Sodus and the downed line was repaired in part due to the discussion and planning of two able men out there in the storm. My family and I listened in on the operation for part of one evening. I came away entertained by adult-speak coming out of the television set. I also was impacted because my parents chose to let the local audio documentary about fixing a power line up on Orchard Terrace play out in our living room. We actually came together as a family in a unique and strange way that night. Ralph and his coarse language formed a vision of service by a lineman that night in the storm that seemed to characterize what went in the community regularly.

**

The Fruit Stand Battle- Everyone is a winner

Sodus was known state-wide for its fruit harvests. In addition to being "famous for cherries," our home town was an apple center during the fall. Trees loaded with cherries and apples abounded all along the ridge and lake roads running parallel to one another and parallel to the lake. Fruit buyers flocked to the area every year to buy the harvests. In addition to the sea of red fruit hanging on the trees around Sodus, one could also find peaches, plums, and pears in the same areas.

It was the cherry crop, first the sweet cherries then the sours, that brought the migrant workers, farmers, canners and distribution people to prime focus early in June. After the cherries were all picked in late July (and later in the century shook from the trees), the apple crop became the focus in the fall of all the talent used in the cherry harvest. Often, migrant workers marked time waiting for the apple harvest by picking various other crops. Some migrants worked in fruit and vegetable harvests throughout the county during their time in New York State.

When the various crops were picked, the fruit stands of the area operated at full blast, selling that portion of the harvest not designated for the factories. I am not sure what percentage of the crops went for sale at these businesses, but given the number of establishments in the area, the percentage must have been impressive.

There was excitement everyday at the mom and pop fruit stands up and down the roads leading to and from the orchards. Young family members and grandparents stood watch over the family-run businesses that sold fresh produce. The consumers watched the ebb and flow of products daily, and often timed visits to their favorite stand to coincide with closing time. At closing there were great bargains to be had. This was the result of the constant turnover daily and the lack of abundant refrigeration at the roadside stands. My mother would drive around looking for various bargains once she got into her driving mode. Prior to her driving career she and some of her bridge-playing chums would share rides together looking for special items.

Things such as watermelons brought in from outside the county would bring buyers to certain stands. If a buyer could obtain watermelons, cherries, grapes, cantaloupes and fresh beans all in one visit, that created great loyalties to some farmers. Once one farmer heard some competitor was getting nice melons from a particular source and these melons were bringing in the purchasers, guess what happened? That farmer began dealing in melons to attract his or her share of the market. Some people drove twenty to thirty miles on round trips to get just the right collection of produce. The locals could get great bargains by merely mentioning that someone carried the same fruit elsewhere at a lower price. This did not happen too often, because the sellers were in a bargaining mood daily.

When my Mom and her friends hit the roads looking for bargains for their canning and meals, the price of gas per gallon was about fifteen to twenty cents per gallon. A woman could fill her tank for three dollars. This is not the case anymore. A person driving around very long looking for a bargain better look at gasoline and not fruit at two bucks a gallon!

The trick in shopping at the fruit stands was to hit the places when the produce was fresh *and* abundant. During certain summer and fall harvests that had been adversely affected by weather, bargains were limited. Shoppers had to be cognizant of the costs of operating a fruit business, and still try to be sensitive to the farmer's balance sheet. Many fruit stands were operated by young or old people not able to do heavy work but still expected to help the profit margin.

A farmer friend of mine once put it very succinctly. The farms depended upon Mother Nature for a crop and harvest season of sufficient length and quality to make up for owning the acreage when it was covered with snow half the year! That was a profound thought. There are very few businesses with the complexities of weather and labor all locked into such a short season.

Traveling around the county was a delight for city dwellers. People from Syracuse and Rochester would be seen driving around our village and county on weekends looking for our crops to take home with them. For many of these people, the presence of fruit stands loaded with the wonders of Sodus trees and Wayne County land gave them a weekend trip worth noting in their city lives.

There were times when sales of cheese, antiques, sewn goods and even books accompanied the daily sales offerings of the various farms. For the city dwellers, these stops turned into a cornucopia of Wayne County's best.

As I grew up and made the move from my home town to other locations associated with my jobs, one of the things I missed was the rhythm of the seasons. I missed the fresh fruit and vegetables associated with that fantastic time of the year.

There came a time when bigger stores were able to offer fresh produce at reasonable prices by virtue of a fleet of delivery trucks operating throughout the county. I got to know the son of one of the produce delivery business owners. I wondered how his father's business could "beat" the tried and true fruit stands dotting our countryside. My friend gave me an answer his father would not want to have heard. He said that the fruit stands still offered the best deals and the best produce—bar none. That made sense to me. It also appealed to my inner sense of simplicity and loyalty.

***

Church Camp—Suspended animation

I was on a stretcher being carried by four adult counselors. They were carrying my stretcher on a narrow foot-bridge across a ravine at Camp Babcock Hovey near Geneva, New York. During the morning hours at the Presbyterian Church Camp, I was felled by severe stomach cramps. Our church in Sodus sent us over to the leased Boy Scout camp for a week and I had cramps. I wasn't even a female. Other Presbyterian Churches in the area sent their young boys and girls to the campground to share fellowship with the peers from other communities. Did it cross my mind that I would be sent home early from the campground? If it had been just Boy Scouts and not co-ed church camp I might still be there because it wasn't the cramps that did me in.

I had spent a week with my friends from church at the same outdoor area a year earlier. There was no stomach problem then. There was no problem associated with nighttime visits to girls' tents the first year either. These things *did* occur during the second summer of camp. History will show an abbreviated week for me based upon a fear of my stomach problems. Whether it was food poisoning or a problem appendix that had to be removed several months later in a similar attack, I am not sure. At the time counselors felt it was breakfast bacon that was bad. A head counselor felt I had been bad also.

These counselors also felt that nocturnal trips through the woods from the boys' campsite to that of the girls was something they could not allow. If I were a betting man, my money would be on the vote of the counselors deciding to use my stomach problem as a pretext to evicting me from camp that summer.

Presbyterian Reverend Ed Sapher was beckoned by phone to travel the fifty miles from Sodus to Geneva to pluck me from the camp and deliver me to my home. Preachers did things such as this to facilitate a successful camp experience. There was no changing the decision to evict me, despite the fact that my stomach pain subsided by afternoon that day. I was home before dark that evening, and my mother wondered about my stomach. Rev. Sapher mentioned the attack and the stretcher and the pain, and the Presbyterian's concern for my stomach. Fortunately for me, he did not mention the other facet of my camp experience that summer.

In the grand scheme of things I merely performed at camp at a level commensurate with my "training" in Sodus. As a prankster and hellion who was known to sneak around at night with my older brother, the campsite was easy pickings. It got totally dark there at night and if a person had a flashlight the pitch-black trails were user-friendly. The only artificial light was around the main buildings and on a couple of poles near the ravine in the middle of camp where bridges spanned the gorge. Scouts did night outings but the Presbyterians were supposed to hit the tents and cots at dark and remain there all night. Some of us merely practiced scouting at a church camp. It seemed to be a logical use of the night.

I was with a new friend from Marion, New York and another lad from one of the other county communities. We slipped out of the tent with our flashlights and crept and stumbled down a dark trail. We climbed up a path leading toward our destination. On that night we were bound for a tent area known to be occupied by some "hot" girls from Lyons who had a very "understanding" counselor. If nothing else we planned to swipe some of their clothes off a clothesline or their tent as proof of our daring.

Collecting artifacts from the female civilization was always a part of our testosterone-charged teenage experience. We envisioned that a couple of items from a clothesline would cement our reputations as lady-killers with our Presbyterian buddies back in the boys' tent area in the morning. None of us ever imagined that the raid would turn into a longer visit.

As we approached the tent area it seems things were going just fine without us. Some girls were having a campfire. It seems the counselors were not there. The three of us hooked up with the Lyons girls around the fire. We also hooked up with the Ontario girls and the Wolcott girls. We were visiting an off-limits site late at night surrounded by girls unhampered by older counselors and toasting marshmallows and our heroic efforts. I have no idea where the counselors were that night, but their absence created a false sense of security for us. They were out there on their way back to the girls.

After a visit of an undetermined length of time we were about to hightail it out of there when major league flashlights came on. The counselors and one of the women serving as a nurse suddenly appeared and we were busted. After a quick lecture and a promise to return to where we belonged the evening ended.

The next morning breakfast came and went, various meetings were held and then my cramps hit. I was in agony. My agony was to increase once the counselors detailed our antics of the previous evening. They did not give us a free pass. Sure enough, word got around that three boys were in the girls' camp and the camp director had to do something. I helped him solve the matter relating to my nighttime mission. I was out of there on a stretcher.

Long after that night, I learned from my friend from Marion that he heard I was blamed for the escapade. He and the other boy got off with a reprimand over the night foray into the target zone. I was removed from camp and it appears that was all it took to set an example for the others. My stomach was a convenient issue and I was history at Babcock Hovey!

Later that year I was transported to Lyons to have my appendix removed. It seems there were no surgeons available in Sodus to do the job. Maybe my father did not trust the alcohol-related reputations of some of the doctors. When my tricky appendix was finally removed in the Lyons hospital that following fall, some Sodus girls came and visited me in the hospital. They wanted to see my scar. Since I was in Lyons I felt I should save that viewing for the "hot girls" from Lyons. These girls were the focus of our nighttime trek of the previous summer. I did not show off my new scar because they didn't even bother to visit me.

***

Mayor Pearson—Shaping the orchards

My Dad was a dominant personality his whole life. He exuded confidence and saw most things through a prism of black and white with very little gray in between. His opinions on everything were dominant in our home and in my life. No one in our house disagreed with Dad; and very few in the community dared do so, either. He railroaded some things through the village board by dint of his personality and debating skills. Some orchards along the lake ultimately became the home for water lines and a pump house. Winning approval for this slight change was critical. The space in the life of the orchards sacrificed for water lines was very modest contrasted to the change in water conditions uptown.

A chronic problem in the village during the summer months was the lack of water until a lake water project was finally approved and built. Until the waters of Lake Ontario started flowing through the filtration plant and into the water lines leading to the village in the 1950s, Sodus was struggling with shortage of water.

My father worked with farmers, construction workers, water workers, and everyday citizens to accomplish the task of harnessing the great power of free water from one of the greatest natural sources of water on earth. There was a hesitation to do the task because it had never been done in Sodus before, despite the arguments for the project.

Pipelines had to be laid across private lands and parcels of orchards claimed for the community project. Special bonds had to be passed to finance the project, and upstate Republicans were careful with their money when it came to taxation and bond issues. School bonds passed with great support until the 1980s, when each successive bond issue was up for grabs. Water bonds were tricky until persuasion won the day. My father did a yeoman's job of persuading the dissenting factions to buy into the project. He cajoled some, harassed others, and fought very effectively with other key participants to win the battle of the water.

Sodus benefited immediately, since canning factories had no limitations on water. Fires were fought more successfully as contrasted with times in summer when water pressures were low. Homes had water pressure and water as needed in any season. The reservoir was always high and had plenty in reserve. New homes on Orchard Terrace had water and pressure all the way up the hill, where there had been a problem prior to tapping Ontario's magnificent supply.

People started installing swimming pools where it had never made sense before. The family living just down the street on High Street from us stuck a nice in-ground pool behind their house. My father editorialized that it was foolish to install an expensive pool when a person could drive five miles and swim for free. He also had to acknowledge that his efforts as a pro-water mayor had created a more liberal application of water use and thus the existence of swimming pools five miles from the lake.

At some time shortly before his premature death at age 62 my father admitted to me and others that his efforts with the community team to bring water from the lake into the village was one of his life's premier accomplishments. Historically it seems to be a no-brainer, but sixty years ago the dynamics of decision-making was a bit different. There were capable water experts in the fifties in New York. Other communities were already on lake water up and down the shores of Ontario. The decision to use water from the lake in the 1950s appears as an easy decision now. Now that water users have had the benefit of Ontario's water for almost sixty years, the decision seems to be a real good one. The hesitation to pull the trigger on such a project back in the previous century extended for a few years.

Some fruit orchards were changed by the incisions for the water line but the huge change was at the tap up in Sodus. I can remember getting ready to shower in my home during the summer and the trickle coming out of the shower-head was sobering. A water tower was constructed on top of Orchard Terrace at one point in an attempt to maintain the water pressure. After the lake water was flowing through the water mains of Sodus, everyone was in agreement. Sodus had solved a huge problem. Every naysayer must have enjoyed a good shower!

***

Bert Munzner- First Prejudice
When I was in about fifth grade and had started to play basketball, some of my heroes were older boys playing in the high school. I could see them playing on Friday evenings in the old gym at the school from my perch high up in the balcony that went along each side of the gym. I got to know them by name and number and finally as a person when they were passing in and out of the gym during school days and practices.

The beauty of a central school was that everyone was under one roof. In a small community, the school was the center of the universe—it was the largest building and was the scene of games, graduations, plays and numerous community events like auctions, craft shows, scout meetings, recreation basketball, dinners for Rotary and Masonic money makers and, of course, the classes held there from the day after Labor Day until mid-June. Until I was in seventh grade the central school did not exist in its full glory. There were rural schools out in the surrounding areas around Sodus. These were the famous one-room school houses.

Around Sodus the locations were Sodus Point, Alton, Wallington, Sodus Center and Joy. All of those schools had one teacher who was the teacher for the kids for the first six years of education. Kindergarten was in operation in the village but the surrounding areas were not completely unified on the kindergarten offering. The seventh grade finally brought all the characters together in the large school in the village. The kids then stayed until graduation or drop-out. There did not seem to be many drop-outs to my recollection. Other than the military there weren't many options for a drop-out.

Once I reached fifth grade, my basketball role models were the boys who came to the village from the outlying schools and those boys who grew up in the village. As I learned more and more about basketball, it became readily apparent that I had a sport that was plenty of fun. James Naismith invented the game at the Springfield, Massachusetts YMCA where he taught. It was a sport for members who could not get outside during the fierce winter weather. That same type weather drove us all into the small Sodus gym.

Basketball fit Sodus and every other community across America like a hand in a glove during the winter months. The movie "Hoosiers," depicting a small high school in Indiana during the early fifties, mirrors Sodus very closely. Our school colors were even the same purple and gold of the movie fame. Our teams did not win the state championship, but we were always quite competitive. My early heroes on the court seemed to have a great existence. These guys were the athletic leaders of our community. They were also surrounded by cheerleaders after the games. Both of those things appealed to me, even though puberty had not yet quite taken my body captive.

One of my early role models was a young man named Manfred von Schiller, who was one of the best athletes in the whole school in every sport. Later in my life our paths would cross on the college soccer field at Brockport State, where we were on the same soccer team for three years. He had done a stint in the Air Force, and my graduation from high school coincided with his departure from the military. He and I became good friends and it was fun seeing him in a different light than when I first knew of him and his high school abilities.

There were other older boys on the basketball team that I knew from my neighborhood and from watching the team. One young man whose name was Sam Bell was about the only Black in our school, so his progress in sports was easy to monitor. Eventually Sodus became the school of choice for more and more minorities who decided to remain in Sodus all through the year. Many of the Blacks were children of migrant workers who tired of the trips between Florida and New York; so they settled at one end of the trip or the other. Most settled in Florida due to the winter weather in New York. They were way ahead of the learning curve. It took white people many more years to discover the beauty of the Sunbelt in the winter months!

Until the late 1950s and early 1960s, the school was not a picture of multi-culturalism. The current advocates of multi-culturalism would consider Wayne County schools ineffective. Those advocates knew nothing about the ethnic differences we lived with in the county either. Some ethnic differences created problems.

I personally wanted our only Black person to succeed for the same reasons that people cheer for any underdog. Bell played sparingly, but when he did he had the support of his team and the community. He was respected for his abilities and team effort, and his race was not an issue.

The ethnicity of my friend von Schiller was not a problem, because von Schiller played a lot and was always a leader in every game. His father was a local fruit farmer, and we were told by our parents that his father had been a flier with the German Air Force during World War I. This did not bother any of our fans because many were second or third generation Germans and that particular war was over long ago. There was no prejudice against this family or the Black young man.

The reasons for this were the acceptance by the team of the von Schillers and Bell out of respect for their abilities and team play. Bell was a strong young man. Each of the von Schillers had a physical presence and that included their weathered ex-flier father. The elder von Schiller lived to be well over ninety.

Manfred von Schiller and his younger brother Erich were Sodus stalwarts in every sport, and the only prejudice against them

I saw occurred when Sodus defeated some other team on their court or field out in Wayne County. Opposing fans would often single out the best players from our teams to razz. It was usually the von Schiller boys. Not much has changed in a half century of sport in America.

There was a notable prejudice, however. I was aware of it early in my career as I watched the older boys play. Sodus had four doctors and one of them was a Jewish doctor. Dr. Munzner's medical practice was successful, and he was accepted in the community because, like the von Schillers and Sam Bell, he performed and made a name for himself. Dr. Munzner had a son named Bert who was small, bespectacled and, of course, Jewish. Bert was a sub on the JV team and was no threat to anyone. Someone hated him for his ethnic roots, however. He was not accepted.

The prejudice I became aware of came after a basketball game one night. The prejudice was anti-Semitism. Reports abounded that the aggressor in the matter called Bert a Jew and other names as he beat on him. Bert's only mistake, according to reports, was being somewhere after a game where Vince could take out frustrations on him, for God knows what initial reasons. Vince (the aggressor) beat the crap out of the junior varsity player, whose only mistake was to be born into a Jewish family. Perhaps if he had been an integral part of the varsity and made a name for himself, things may have gone better for him. I doubt this, though. If he was on the varsity and was taking playing time away from Vince (who was a sub on the varsity squad), violence would probably have occurred anyway.

The consequences were quite profound after the attack. The attacker was expelled from school. He was accepted into another school nearby with a long list of rules that he managed to violate quickly. He did not last long there, either. The different school was so close to our community that the incident had a difficult time disappearing. The word of his Sodus expulsion flashed through our school. Most in the town were behind Principal Francis Samuel's quick and just decision. Most were repulsed by the attack. Persecution of Jews was too recent a memory for the adults. The fragile Jewish lad was treated as if he were in Nazi Germany by Vince. The Germans in town were offended, as were all others.

I can remember being offended by the act way back then, and can remember hearing different things about the incident as I grew older. I was not sophisticated enough yet to appreciate the nuances of hatred. I just knew I was sad to think someone got beat up for no apparent reason. The immediate result was the transfer of the attacker to another school. But another sad result was the transfer of the Munzner boy elsewhere. Since Vince was hovering in the background of Wayne County, the doctor-father probably spared his son more attacks. Vince's older brother stayed in school and performed well in his last year. My friend Manfred told me later that the older brother was appalled by his younger brother's actions. This must have made for interesting family discussions back then, when Manfred's teammate discussed his success at Sodus with his idiot brother who by then had been expelled from yet another school. In modern vernacular the younger brother could be called a "redneck."

I was bothered by the incident back then because it tarnished what was a nice feeling about older boys in my life. It turned out that not all of the varsity boys were worthy of the role model image assigned to them by younger fans. Vince made the decision very easy for us.

This lesson was a good one to learn early in my life, since young boys need to know there are bad people out there—even in sports. The term role model is probably overused. In the modern era, as it was fifty years ago, the actions of a person certainly must dictate the worthiness of his or her success as a role model. Vince was a jerk way back then and continued to be one as the years went by. He was in trouble for many years. I never knew or cared what became of him after his high school years, but did hear he started fights wherever he went.

The von Schillers, Munzners and Bells of Sodus all figured out how to exist, and Sodus would have been even better if Bert did not have to go to school out of town because of fear of a redneck. They all were interesting people. One of them was a terrible role model.

PART THREE
Friends

Everyone has a memorable friend or friends surviving the moves, the separation times, the interest changes evident in life. These friends may stand the test of time and be there in adult life. More often, such childhood friends appear in the storyline of one's life and then they fade from view in adulthood. In my own life I have had some friends fitting into the lifelong status, and some fitting into the faded but memorable category. These people used to go by the names Redhead, Lester, Smiley Ape, Humus, Sarge, Dusty, General, Sammy, Fluta, Dunc, Dickhead, Poopy, Root, Ears, Preacher, Curly, Post, Pop, Jake, Kingston, Willie, Deacon, Bung, Soup, Hunter, Charley the Moss, Gumpert, Lexington (an aircraft carrier in WWII, nicknamed flattop—figure it out), and numerous others. Some of the other names were quite raunchy, and were not used openly except in the locker room. Sometimes the names popped out of an incident. Some friends had multiple names. Other times, the name came out of a parent's name or job. Sometimes it was the middle name of some relative, or even a weird name picked up from some obscure source.

These names have hung on people over the years much like Spanish moss hangs on southern trees! Often, it seems, the titles were assigned by coach and teacher Slim McGinn, whose name appears a few times on my trips down memory lane. He was a fixture in the school for much of our time there. Coaches across our country have always had the knack of giving a nickname to a particular student and having that name stick for life. This happened in Sodus also. Some of these names have stood the test of time, and even today I often sign off with one of my all time great nicknames, Stinky, when I communicate with my lifelong friend, Lester. *Stinky's Tales* evolved from some great memories linked to that particular nickname and many others.

The story behind the Stinky name can be found earlier in the book. Some of my assigned names other than Bobby (which has still followed me to this day when certain family members or Swede Erwin talk to me) were Mayor (after my father), Smiler (bestowed by David Cooper, an English teacher who thought I smiled a lot), and Ward (my given middle name, but few used it nor did I claim it very readily). The particular grandfather (my mother's father) with that name had five wives and a reputation associated with the New York Central Railroad that seemed to grow vividly at each retelling. Ward also left my mother and her sister Doris after the death of his wife and the girls' mother when the girls were very young. I never could quite figure that one out!

Everyone has probably been bestowed with a nickname somewhere along the way. What seems unique is that so many adults and others in my life felt involved enough with me to label me in a non-threatening, friendly way. Does that happen in the modern era? Probably not! For many reasons, I conclude this just is not done. I would have missed the labels now that I have grown accustomed to them. I would have missed the fond associations related to the nicknames also. The friends and their names have been fond memories, and despite the several decades in between the present and the formative years, these memories remain a part of a good life.

The more friends one can have, the more enriched one's life can be. In the modern era too many kids have too few friends. This is a product of several trends and some that are not all that nice.

***

Hitch and Swim—Six miles of asphalt

It was hot and the asphalt was doubly so as my Converse All-Star shoes began the first walk down Maple Avenue with my thumb out. This was the first time I ever hitched a ride in my life. I was probably about thirteen at the time and felt very majestic in my new-found independence during the hot days of summer in Sodus. Isabel, the queen of our family and my esteemed mother, did not have a clue that I was hitch hiking to the "Point." The "Point" was Sodus Point, six miles from the Village of Sodus and occupied by perhaps eight hundred people in the school year—but ten times that in the summer months on any given weekend.

My mother envisioned me riding the recreation bus from the community center to the beaches adjoining Lake Ontario rather than doing this less-recognized version of getting to the water. The trouble with the bus was it started at the recreation center, traveled the winding roads to the beaches, but stopped often to gather swimmers and non-swimmers for swimming and/or lessons, as desired by the bus riders. There was a roll call, and if you went you came back. When you came back the route was the reverse of the route going and, of course, as slow and deliberate as the trip to the beaches.

I was hitchhiking for the first time and getting there faster and coming back whenever the urge grabbed me. This certainly beat the bus! All I needed was a thumbing instinct and my towel. I walked for about a mile down Maple Avenue, passing friends' houses and civilization as I remembered it. Leaving the village on foot was a first for me since cars, buses and bikes had usually been my choice of travel. Leaving town in this fashion gave me great insight into various heretofore-unnoticed sights of the oft-used route to the Point. There were old people on their porches I had never noticed before; and there were workers never observed before at various job sites lining the road beyond the village. Many trucks went in and out of the cold storage, which was (pardon the play on words) a hotbed of activity in summer months. Farmers brought their sweet cherries there for freezing in forty pound containers, and many other people rented units in the private freezing areas.

Additionally, I was made aware of the number of cars going by me with very little interest in my thumb and obvious towel. Could this be a bad idea? I knew of many others who told of how easy it was to hitchhike, and therefore my experience should surely mirror theirs, shouldn't it? How could I not be recognized as an "easy rider" bound for one of the greatest fresh water swimming holes known to man? After about two miles of the hot asphalt on this initial hitching attempt of my young career, lo and behold a convertible stopped to gather me up. Just before this historic moment, I had envisioned that I could walk the six miles in the heat, swallow my pride and then try to get a ride with someone I knew coming back later. The bus would be out as an option because of the pride factor; plus, it would have to be recorded somewhere that I did not ride down with the bus. This would not be acceptable, since my father was the mayor and he knew of about everything going on in the village. No, it was hitchhike or bust.

Let's return to the convertible. The convertible was driven by the older sister of one of my friends from my summer baseball team in PONY League. She was a wonderful choice for my first-ever attempt to beat the bus system. Janice (seventeen and one of the inspirational knockout beauties of Sodus) had her own car and would have as many boys chasing her once she arrived at the beach as I would have chasing me in a game of dodge ball in Slim McGinn's P.E. classes during the school year. The absolute beauty of my good fortune and the beauty of the day and the month and the year and my life in general were now incredible. She was driving in her bathing suit! I rode with her the remaining four miles of the journey in teenage splendor. She engaged in baseball talk and I admired the way she drove the car and the way she sat there.

Many saw us as we arrived at the parking lot. Nearly every set of eyes was on the driver, but it was not completely overlooked that Stinky Pearson was riding right there with her! We pulled into the parking lot at the main beach, and it was clear to me I was there ahead of the bus, ahead of my peers in style of arrival, and also way out of my league that day. Nary was a hair on my burr haircut touched from all the wind blowing on us during the drive. By stark contrast my hormones were severely affected. Amazingly, Janice said that she drove to the beach almost every day, and suggested that

I should consider riding with her each time she saw me out there on the road with my thumb and towel. Incredibly for me, she even suggested that I ride back with her that very day when she left. She gave me the time of her estimated return to the village. This was a no-brainer of a decision for me. I would adjust my schedule to hers without a second thought.

This was a whole new ballgame for me, even though my hormones were in overload and I (and everyone in town) knew Janice had many "major league" boyfriends. The summer came and went, and I caught the convertible ride several times when others did not pick me up earlier. I even rode the bus a few times just to get my name on the books in the event my father ever checked such things. When I was older, I began to ride my bike to Sodus Point in order to have mobility once I arrived there. It seemed that such mobility paid dividends; and once a person got tired of swimming the choices were hot dogs at Carl's and ice cream across the street at the Proseus ice cream stand. Once during a rainstorm while peddling through the torrent I was picked up by, of all things, the bus. The bus was nearly empty that particular day and Paul Uher, the super recreation leader and the usual bus driver, stopped to check the wet human he had observed in the road. He welcomed me into the dry and now-comfortable bus.

The hitchhiking ended during my teenage years when a boy from nearby Webster was found dead near the highway after a person picked him up while the boy was hitchhiking. The evil man molested him and then killed him before dumping his body in Wayne County not far from Sodus. After many months, the criminal was arrested and he confessed to the crime and two others like the one in Wayne County.

Isabel never seemed to suspect that I was going in harm's way for a couple of summers and luckily I was never picked up by anyone dangerous. The mayor never said anything, but I always felt he knew much more than he let on. The convertible rides were an exceptional and simple experience in an era when hitchhiking seemed very innocent.

***

Tilt a Whirl—One hundred feet of vomit

That August night was one to remember. The Fireman's Field Days were wrapping up and I had been able to come to the field of carnival pleasures for three nights in a row. In addition to the allowance and the summer money I had been making, I had a secret source no one else knew about. My father worked as volunteer treasurer of the Sodus Volunteer Firemen. In his volunteer capacity for the field days he was on duty in the main office collecting monies from various sources and keeping up with the needs of the vendors throughout the six-acre site near the school.

The secret source became evident to me at one of the first field days I ever attended. Dad was wrapped up in the business of the fireman's field office from 6PM until midnight or later each night. This was after a full day at his paying job. He was always hungry during these long evening volunteer hours! All I had to do was waltz into the office and ask him if he needed something to eat or drink. By doing these visits two or three times a night until I had to go home I was a caring son. I was also an opportunistic son. Dad was always hungry. I was never broke during field days because my father had a great appetite. What we had there was a beautiful relationship based upon his needs and my wants. Dad would give me some bills to purchase the food and offer to include me in the purchase and then allow me to keep the change. Dick never figured this one out, nor did I ever disclose the tactic.

On one of those summer evenings of my childhood, I had delivered Dad two different feedings involving Belgium Waffles and a drink followed by cheeseburgers, fries and a coke. Just as I thought he was full, he signaled to me out of the wide flap of a window in the office building. There was one more request from the treasurer. The evening would be just right with a piece of apple pie from the ladies auxiliary tent. Who could turn down such an offer? This would provide me with money for one last ride before heading home. It was also a piece of pie, and that wasn't such a bad idea, either.

I mentioned that on every visit for food orders for Dad he and I both ate the same amount of food. For every cheeseburger, order of fries, Coke, waffle or pie he ate, I did also. In between the father-related orders I also consumed cotton candy, hot dogs and whatever else was available. My source of funds was unending on those evenings. My appetite was also unending in those growing years.

After a night of my own indiscriminate eating coupled with the orders for Dad, I was "primed" for a ride. As I reflect now upon the end result of the Tilt-a-Whirl ride following all I consumed on that nasty night, it still gives me shudders of disbelief.

I mounted the magnificent Tilt-a-Whirl for a ride that would spin me around in a circle in a riding car while all the time being given a huge circular ride above the fireman's field. I was doing two circles at the same time. One circle occurred within the larger circle. I shall never know which circle motion caused the damage.

My youthful judgment that night was terrible. I never, ever should have gotten on the ride. The ride lasted forever and I puked my guts out. Fortunately I was sitting alone. Unfortunately, retch after fateful retch sent volumes of puke out over the space between me and the rest of humanity in the circle of life beneath the ride's path. My stomach contents flew all over the arc traced by the ride, as centrifugal force sprayed my vomit in a wide arc out from the ride's path.

The operator of the ride did not realize soon enough what was happening. The crowd received some serious discomfort. Ultimately, the operator saw the reaction to my distress and stopped the ride. The damage had been done. My stomach was empty and the mess around me was my only trophy for "finishing" the ride.

I don't know how many more rides were run that night on the device, because I beat a hasty, sickly retreat toward my home. I never shared the memory of the experience with my Dad since he would no doubt have commented on my sheer stupidity.

As I wandered home, the sounds and sights of the field days faded. But for most of my life I could not eat apple pie because the thought of it made the memory of the ride very vivid. Until recently, my taste for pie stayed on pumpkin or cherry—but certainly not apple.

The days of the Sodus Fireman's Field Days remain a nice memory of my Dad. They remain a nice memory of friends and fun times. Included in all of the positive reflections are the random episodes that were not so nice. The vomit-ride was certainly one of these negative events! Another was the inability to ring the bell on the attraction involving using a huge sledge-hammer. I could never ring the bell. This classical test of manhood eluded me in my developing years. I felt I was strong athletically, but could never ring the bell.

Also considered in the negative realm was the time I was trying to knock off some cloth dolls sitting on racks at the rear of a tent by throwing a baseball at them. A person knocking off three dolls would receive a stuffed animal. On the field day grounds that evening, a young boy about six years old wandered into my line of fire between the racks of dolls and my throwing location out from the front of the tent. I plunked him squarely in the back of the head with a fastball.

Unlike noisy peers in baseball games when I hit them due to my wild fastball, this young guy merely looked at me wordlessly; bit into a hot dog he was carrying and walked away. I followed to see if he truly was OK. His mother had missed the action so she was not concerned. The little guy did not cry and would not talk about what had happened. I told the mother about it and she could not get a reaction either. The mother would have been concerned if she had seen it. Did this turn the little guy away from baseball later in his life? Perhaps that was a young Chipper Jones out there before I plunked him in the head.

As I walked home after that particular evening I wondered what made the little kid so tough, because I would have yelled or cried or done something.

On the evening of the Tilt-a-Whirl I had some thoughts also. Someone should have hit me in the head with a fastball before I boarded that ride!

***

Wayne County Joy Rides—New perspectives

The joy rides of our youth came in three categories. The first category was when the guys just got together using a parent's car to go to a predictable destination. The second and third categories were joy rides with the guys, and dates with the opposite sex.

The purposeful destinations were limited somewhat by the parents loaning the car. They passed judgment upon the trip and the rules of the trip. They were, after all, loaning the car for a drive involving many miles and more traffic than the normal Wayne County type. Pro baseball and basketball games in nearby Rochester were common trips involving as many as seven of us in a car. Donald Virts got his father's big car sometimes. Sometimes our buddies merely drove us to school.

Some days the trip to school took on unusual twists and turns. Jake DeBadts was a constant with his big family car. He picked me up one morning by driving right up to my front porch across our spacious front lawn. No one ever had done that before. Isabel stood in the door telling me the ride was here. She got a laugh out of that as I had to crawl in a window since the door was too close to the porch step to open. Of course I could have gone around to the other side, but instead opted to crawl through a window. David Andrews had a station wagon during his high school years. Kingston, as David was called, won the hearts of the Sodus girls forever one day when he drove through huge puddles in the roads leading to school after a heavy rain. He splattered water over many young ladies on their way to school. He got guys wet also, but his intent was to aim for splattering females. None of us in the car connected that we were endorsing his rude behavior by virtue of our presence and our laughter. Kingston had a full crew of guys with him enjoying that mission. We were teenagers, and stupid was what stupid did back then, paraphrasing Forrest Gump.

My father allowed me to ride with the guys on some trips and not on others, but I never was given the family car. I really never bothered to ask because I knew the answer anyway. It was as if Dad knew what went on, and as long as I was a passenger things would go better for both of us in my journey to adulthood.

The second category of rides involved many or all of the guys involved in the "legitimate" trips of category one; but the trips in the second grouping were not really "legitimate" trips. These became joy rides in the true sense of the phrase. What went on during these rides might be as varied as riding around sampling hamburgers at three locations, firing fruit and vegetables at some roof or mailbox, or visiting some girl's home unannounced. Our cover stories for such trips were also as varied as the trips.

In all our high school years when the joy rides took place, the excuses to our parents enabling us to get together included studying, card games at a friend's house, and going to school for a meeting. We may, indeed, study or visit the school or even play cards somewhere, but ultimately we hit the roads for an hour or so. We then could legitimately report things to our parents about our cover story. Our other activities on those evenings were not reported to parents.

In a village as small as Sodus, an hour of joy riding could take a carload of guys to several locations. Not all rides I am describing in the prime of our youth were true joy rides. We got stuck in snow on one occasion, and froze our butts until we figured how to get going again. On another trip, we thought we were being chased by an irate person whose house had been plastered with tomatoes thrown from a moving vehicle. Don't ever try it, because you get tomatoes all over yourself and the car. In order to get away clean, despite having the inside of the car being covered with tomatoes, we drove with lights out down a dirt road and hit some skunks going across the road in the dark. That trip was messy and smelly and caused us great discomfort. We had to clean the interior of the car but could not rid ourselves or the car of the skunk perfume.

There was a third category of rides. This particular ride did not involve all the guys. There was a guy with a set of wheels and his girl friend. There may be another guy and his girlfriend. That was it for these outings. There was no room for horseplay with the guys.

This was a "date." Co-ed trips were fun and became more popular as we progressed further along in high school. What seemed like fun as sophomores with all the guys lost its allure as juniors and seniors. We had fun on double dates. It was a different form of fun on those dates also.

As with the other joy rides around the county there were limits on the choices available. The drive-in movie theatre in the summer was great. Bowling was always popular, as was going to the regular movie theatre downtown. We spent a lot of time on double dates slurping soda through straws. We also spent time sucking face either in a car or at some person's house. Despite the advent of TV in every home, we really did not spend much time watching the tube. In the 1950s we attended a lot of movies and played a lot of games involving many people. Socialization was evident in our dating. Double dating was quite common.

There was a scene in "When Harry Met Sally" where the characters were on a double date and midway through the date the double daters switched partners. Billy Crystal and Meg Ryan ended up together despite their well-laid plans. It seemed funny in that movie. It happened to me twice in my high school years, and it was awkward and not so funny. Once it actually left me dating a young lady from a nearby town whose family was reputed to be connected with the Mafia. Once I realized this, I vowed to be the perfect gentleman, since no one wanted to mess with a Don's daughter.

I got her home to her cottage at Sodus Point and then caught my ride back to Sodus with my friend and my original date of the evening. Before going home to Sodus I promised the Italian girl I would return another night to visit her. I was true to my word, and she was dressed up in her brief but pretty summer outfit when she waltzed out of her cottage called, significantly, "Romp." We walked over to the strip at the Point and things seemed to go well. Taking her home that evening I met her older sister, who'd just arrived from Newark, New York. The sister was my age, about seventeen. She would not have been my choice despite our common age because she had a lot more poundage on her frame than did little sister.

Her sister turned out to be littler than I had known. Big, big sister informed me that it would be wise if I left the cottage before the girls' father arrived from Newark. This was based upon the fact that the girl I had double dated with and then revisited was only twelve at the time.

She had to have been one of the best-developed twelve year olds ever, but that age scared the crap out of me. Her connection with the Mob may or may not have been accurate. I did not want to test that information. When I saw her a few other times when I was at the resort village, I would wave and she would wave but that was it for any relationship.

Once, when we were in college, I learned a body had been found out in our county by the side of the road. It was a suspected Mob hit. One of my chums from high school reminded me of the twelve-year-old girl and my junior year double date involving her. My buddy joked that probably the dead guy dated an underage Italian girl. The satisfaction of knowing my brain won the important battle over testosterone at that time in my life was refreshing. Those Italian guys do have a way of persuading a person to see their way of thinking. Some rides didn't work out as well as others.

***

Henry Comes to Town- What a recruit!

Henry Peussa arrived in Sodus in late summer 1955 to live with the Hungerford family during our senior year. David Hungerford became Henry's American host from our senior class, and became Henry's soul brother for life after sharing a year with him in our small village. Henry was from Finland and was a fine soccer player.

The bonus of having an exchange student from Scandinavia where football (soccer) is the sport of choice when there is no snow on the ground was evident the very first day of soccer practice. As we went through our typical, rather unorganized practices Henry was zipping balls into the nets, connecting on marvelous passes not ever seen on our field before, and raising soccer levels for all of us. Just two weeks into the fall season, we traveled to usual powerhouse

Wolcott and won the game 4-2 for our opening win of the season—
and our first win at Wolcott in several years.

Henry engineered the victory with his unselfishness and
creativity. He gave a great pass to his American brother David for
one goal and got the other himself. Back then, goals were two points
and penalty kicks were one point. The rules on scoring changed a
few years later, giving penalty kicks equal value as goals. I never
got over the upgraded scoring because I always felt an earned goal
should be worth twice as much as a referee's gift to a team in the
penalty box. This feeling stayed with me through a long career as a
soccer coach.

Henry did not take a penalty shot that day. Through the
season he would not miss a penalty shot. On Peussa's first day with
us and on our opening day together in Wolcott, the "new" Sodus
Cherrytowners outplayed and outscored the hometown boys.

After the game the coach from the opposing team came over
to our school bus and informed Burly Bill (the name we attached
to our coach) that Sodus possessed the best passing team he had
seen in the county in a while. This was a tribute to Henry and not
anything that Burly Bill had changed. We reflected in the glow of
the opening season win and the presence of Henry on our team and
in our lives as we traveled the twenty miles back to Sodus.

Henry could really play soccer and ended the fall season as
our leading scorer. We won more games that fall than we had in
some time. Henry was the greatest recruit at that point to ever to
wear the Sodus purple and gold colors. In the modern era there are
many more foreign students coming to our country, and every team
at every level of competition is immediately upgraded by virtue of
the foreign talent. There are private boarding schools that cater to
foreign students. There are even boarding schools specializing in
specific sports. What we had in the year 1955 is now commonplace,
but back then Henry's presence caused quite a stir in the county
soccer circles. Henry was the first of a long line of foreign students
to attend Sodus, but I don't know of another whose sport impact was
so great as his.

He was good enough to play in college, but back then very few college teams recruited as they do now. Most college coaches waited on campus for the talent to come to them. It is, of course, radically different now, as coaches spend weeks away from campus looking for the Henrys of the country.

The fun we had with Henry was not limited to just soccer. He taught us about his culture, and we tried our level best to corrupt him in ours. He came to appreciate the mobility an automobile provided. His presence in Sammy Junior's big four door DeSoto was a common sight around town. Henry did not play any other sport with the ability he possessed in soccer. We enjoyed watching him try basketball with us in P.E. He played tennis for a while with some of our tennis players. There were rumors that his American brother was teaching him how to drive.

Late in our senior year the Finnish kid had nearly finished his visit to Sodus when the huge lead sled called David Hungerford's car came head to head with a huge maple tree near the Sodus cemetery. The two "brothers" were on the way to school. Fortunately neither was injured badly; but Henry was hospitalized with a leg injury for a few days. Two rumors circulated around our senior class. One was that Sammy was having Henry drive the back road near the cemetery on the way to school that day. His driving lesson abruptly ended if that was the case. Rumor number two circulated that the young girls of Sodus were visiting the Finn in the Sodus hospital to cheer him up. The rest of that rumor was that some of the girls were "really" cheering him up during the visits to his room. I do not know first hand about either of the rumors, but feel the Viking will tell me the truth on these issues at our fiftieth class reunion coming up in 2006.

Henry returned to Finland where he completed his education and became an engineer. He revisited Sodus for a couple of reunions. I am told he visited David's family in Maryland over the years and entertained the Hungerfords in Finland also. Henry did not seem to change as we saw him through the years at the reunions. The healthy lifestyle in Finland kept him young and fit. He was certainly ready to roll when he arrived in Sodus as a seventeen-year-old recruit! I look forward to seeing the best recruit we ever knew in a couple of years.

***

Case the Joint—The key to success

While were shooting baskets in the gym the snow must have been falling in near record amounts. By the time we dragged our sweaty and tired bodies out the back door of the school, the cars were buried in a foot of snow. It took some time to get back to our homes. Those of us living on High Street ended up walking much of the way in the heavy snow, but we did enjoy the basketball. The reward far outweighed the price we ended up having to pay. Our parents knew we were safe and sound somewhere indoors that evening, and gave us more credit for common sense than we probably deserved. Contrast the panic related to a heavy snow and kids being out someplace in it during the modern era!

Our nighttime basketball ritual was a regular winter activity on weekends. We usually played our high school basketball games on Fridays and some weeknights. That left Saturdays to our imaginations and energy. Saturdays were date nights and recreation nights. One of our most popular recreations was to get Case Weist, Earl Carpenter or Harold Brown, all custodians, to let us use their master key to the school to get into the gym for basketball. These men knew about youthful exuberance and energy. They also knew we were far less of a problem where they could see us than the other way around.

Only one custodian was usually on duty and was really a watchman more than a custodian. There was a bleak history before the new school was opened when a watchman failed to detect a growing fire in the basement of the school. By the time he reacted the fire had set opening day back by six months. The three custodians rotated the duty and the rotation no longer had a spot for old Dave, the guy on duty on the night of the fire.

On some of our visits we would actually help do custodial work for the men. This was only fair since these kind men understood boys and basketball. Many of us ended up working summer jobs with the school at the recommendations of the custodians who were our co-conspirators in the easy access to our gym. A parent coming to the school during our basketball field trips would be surprised to see us volunteering to sweep the floors or dust mop the gym floor. We had to be reminded to do such things under our own roof.

There were some Saturdays where a few of us would meet at a designated time and place after our dates, and go to the gym to cap off an evening. Usually our parents knew where we were in the village—in a general sense.

Our games in the after hours of a weekend and after a Friday night loss took on new meanings for us. We would often revisit the spot on the court where we missed key shots or screwed up with an in-bounds play. It was as if by Monday our basketball demons of Friday would be exorcized. Our games in the gym were extensions of our love of basketball. We displayed this love on the blacktop playing court near the bus barns on the harsh surface when the court was available. It was under snow most of the basketball season. We did play outdoors during the summer when we were not in baseball activities. The court wore our Converse All-Stars out like crazy. The sneakers we got for eleven dollars a pair through the school were canvas and were not built for macadam surfaces. We played through blisters and torn sneakers.

We had basketball games in barns where the owner set up a basket where there was room. The barn games had all kinds of ground rules involving hay bales, animals, trapdoors and beams. Naismith would have given up his invention if he had played in one of the Wayne County barns.

There was a community center at Sodus Point with a short court and a low ceiling which was a great spot for games in the off-season. Where else could you swim, play basketball, boat and chase a girl all in the same round-trip of but ten miles? Some of the most fun we ever had was playing in the center at Sodus Point. For some reason the girls we went looking for after our games and swimming often came to look at the games in the center. It was as if they we were picking out the "keepers" from the pick-up games. It cast a whole new meaning to "pick-up" games.

It was the gym at Sodus that captured our boyhood attention. The memories were vivid, and walking through an empty gym was always an interesting experience for me and others like me so in love with sport. Even today as I depart a gym or stadium I am in awe of the electricity so connected to sport in our lives. An empty gym or stadium has a kinetic potential unmatched in society. Once the contest commences, the spectators and players are connected by invisible rubber bands that stretch and contract noticeably through the game. At the conclusion of such a game, the arena empties and it is as if we had imagined all that had transpired before.

Gyms in Sodus now number in the multiples since there are new schools, newer gyms and plenty of places to play. Back in mid-century America most places had but one gym, and it saw all the indoor activity in its confines.

Compared to the parking lot or the barns or the community centers of the world, Sodus Central School gym was our Boston Gardens or Rupp Arena. The real beauty of it all was that we could get into the place about anytime we wanted. The other beautiful thing about the experience was that on one really ever lost on a Saturday night in our whole high school careers!

***

Lester and the Boys Hang George—A nice touch
A bunch of the Sodus boys hung George Clark by his shirtsleeves in the horizontal windows in EBB's homeroom, much to the delight of EBB and the people in the classroom. This was but one example of simple pranks, done well, with innocence that were enjoyed and appreciated by all involved. No one was harmed or threatened. The educational process stayed on track but with interesting timeouts for fun.

There were numerous little things done to spice up the public school days in our school. Some times these little things came from the teachers. Many times they came from the students with the help of the teachers. It was a sure thing that during any given week, some person had fun at their own expense. This trait and practice seems to have lost favor in the modern era. Schools have become too serious for a multitude of reasons. Sodus turned out college-bound candidates and literate graduates without turning the school into a somber place.

In locker rooms it was commonplace to find clothes in places other than where they were earlier. In any season and at about any time in that season certain articles of clothing would appear or disappear as if by magic. There were times when boys' clothing would show up in the girls' areas and vice versa. How this was accomplished was always a mystery, but it obviously called for collusion on the part of the opposite sex, however it was accomplished. It was fun even when it happened to you—as long as your underwear was clean when the items were exchanged.

Putting shoes or gym shoes in a mix and match stage was done and this brought people together in a common cause. This routine was practiced at some parties as a mixer. There were times when students would find a teacher's car keys and would move the car slightly in the parking lot and then deliver the keys back to the desk top where the unsuspecting teacher left the keys.

There were thermostats in critical places around the school, and if a person could adjust the thermostat in the library, the library and study hall would heat up. It was quickly returned to normal, but this was a simple reminder that the inmates, at times, controlled the institution.

Science labs created unlimited opportunities for pranks. In chemistry, odious efforts would abound during certain experiments. Although the end result should have been something else, we did come up with home brewed odors that would strain the exhaust fans and the teacher's patience. No one was ever hurt, nor did the teacher lose his control—completely.

Dissection efforts would often create possibilities to harass anyone too squeamish to take part in the dissections. The parts of frogs turned up in lockers soon after the biology class ended. Where things went amiss with animal parts were when the legs went unnoticed until they smelled bad two days later.

Limburger cheese placed upon a car's manifold during a lull in any action would create a foul odor in the car until the food wore off. We always wondered how anyone could stand to eat the cheese anyway. It was made for manifold melts.

There was a hot story circulating when we were students about a faculty member sleeping in the nude in his boarding house in Sodus. The popular male faculty member was said to have had too much to drink one night after his basketball team won a big game. He was undressed by some peers and placed in his bedroom in a boarding house where several boarders shared a common bathroom. During the night he stumbled into the bathroom where he emptied his bladder. He then fell asleep on the rug just outside the bathroom. During the morning hours, as he slept, the other boarders used the bathroom as boarders are prone to do. The nude prone male figure was there for several hours according to the legend. The male and female boarders were able to confirm that the inert male teacher was comfortable and sleeping like a baby. Someone eventually covered the sleeping beauty with a bath towel.

This story has been verified recently by some who were involved in the episode fifty years ago, so we appeared to have heard it correctly. The male teacher finally was "aroused" after his long morning's sleep by a concerned boarding house proprietor. The nice old lady had not seen anything quite like that in all her years running the boarding house. The teacher recovered from his embarrassment to continue his career for another thirty years. The boarding house lady probably never recovered.

Streaking was just starting as a fad when we were in high school. On a dare certain students would streak at selected locations away from Wayne County. There were stories of future teachers, principals and doctors running naked along wooden docks and diving into fresh water bays and harbors around Lake Ontario.

Pranks were fun, and risk-taking was a part of the whole

climate then as now. The risks taken then were simple and involved skill rather than alcohol or drugs associated with the modern era. We challenged imaginations whereas many of our public school successors are busy challenging authority.

***

Building the Ark- Sodus style

Gib and I were in kindergarten or first grade. This seems reasonable to assume since there was no way in hell two second-graders would ever try to build a wooden ark in the basement at his Gaylord Street residence. We nailed some boards together and had grandiose plans that are still awash in the floods of our collective memories! There were numerous plans formulated by different ones of us during our growing years. Some came to fruition, while others still remain elusive. The thought of building a boat has vanished. All I aspire to do now is to own a boat someday. Gib owns a boat or two, so he no longer has to build any. We had many diverse interests growing up. Riding something usually was part of the drill. It seemed that we were rarely bored. Using writer's prerogative, the boat or arc we were building in my tale could correspond with all the other things we drove or rode around in during the developmental years. The buses carrying our teams were important "arks." The Virts boys and Robert Hicks had an old four-door car from the forties that friends called the "Mayflower" because, as rumor had it, so many girls came across in it. I remember many guys would ride around town in it.

Many of us thought we would be professional baseball players since that sport absorbed many waking hours during our younger days. Our dreams did not connect with the reality that one out of a thousand rural boys ended up in pro baseball. We played a lot of baseball, and some of us played beyond the Babe Ruth league days. American Legion and the Sodus Point Lakers afforded an outlet for many boys after Babe Ruth League. Despite our good intentions and the love of the game, we all ultimately settled into jobs, responsibilities, marriages, and other recreations that took us away from baseball except as spectators.

Boating was a big thing for us, and combining sailing, water skiing, power boat travel, fishing and just diving and swimming off boats into the fresh water of our lakes and bays, the hours on and in water were enormous. Our ears were continually filled with water and our eyes were red from the algae of the bays. We learned how to swim at about the same time we learned how to walk and slide down hills covered with snow.

A great facet of our childhoods, not realized or appreciated at the time, was that the continuous change of seasons made us very flexible and versatile. These traits came out of adaptations to climate that influenced sport and recreational choices. One had to be flexible due to the impact of weather upon jobs, industry, sports, school and travel. It is often said that certain climates make people" hardy" and I must concur with this thought. This truism recognizes the grit in the people along the "Ridge," as this part of New York State is called.

Gib and I may never have completed the boat or ark or whatever it was to have been. It was not because we lacked grit. It was more related to our inexperience as carpenters and planners. L.H. Sergeant, Town Clerk of Sodus, would have vetoed any house alteration to accommodate his kid's boat being removed from the cellar anyway.

Other fun things involved endless hours of card games. There were times when we would swim for two or three hours at the Point, and then go into some friend's cottage and play cards for three hours. Often these card games were hearts, spades or canasta. These three games were very popular during this era. No money ever exchanged hands even through the play was hotly contested. I contend that the games of youth can be a springboard to success in life and in school. We learned to discipline ourselves in our games. We settled most of our disputes without adult intervention, and our minds were as active as our bodies.

Isabel loved games, but I remember one time at Sodus Point when Dad's boss Ed Burns had a cottage rented for our family for a two week period. For most of the two weeks, the weather was fierce. Summer storms came across the lake from Canada and the waves were pounding thirty feet from the front door day and night. We jumped in the water and were pounded around for our efforts. The temperatures of the air and water were much lower than normal. Our mother did not venture out to swim or even sun bathe since the sun was scarce. After nearly two full weeks of inclement weather, and six to eight hours a day of eight to ten young boys hanging out in the cottage playing cards and table games, Isabel finally flipped out. I had never seen her do this before and only once or twice after, but this tantrum was a thing of beauty. She said the cottage was too small for ten boys and without good weather there was really no good reason to be at the cottage. She unilaterally made all of us move back to Sodus. This took the ambiance off our games. We loved the sound of crashing waves and wind whistling in the trees. Adding to the interesting time at Sodus Point was the sight of the trees bordering the road to the beach shedding white floating pieces like cotton. Pretty trees or not, we were driven back to Sodus.

Within two hours we were all cleared out of the cottage and rides were arranged for everyone back to Sodus. Isabel did not drive back then, so other parents had to deposit our family uptown. Dad came home from work that night surprised to see his family back up from the resort village by the lake. He had been staying alone in Sodus while we were in the cottage since it was a hectic time for him at his job. A day after returning to our house the weather calmed and the hot weather returned. We begged to go back to the cottage but we only had two days left in our two week allotment, so our mother decided it just wasn't worth the effort. We lived with the decision and went about our creative ways.

Many of our recreational activities were invented, and some were products of our connections in the village. Some of us had parents in the Masons and were able to get into the Masonic Hall to shoot pool. How the pool tables ever got upstairs in the Masonic Lodge I shall never know, but we did enjoy our time there. On other occasions we bowled. During most of our lives the bowling alley had hand-spotted pins. This meant that a pin-boy stationed between two lanes would hop back and forth between the lanes and put the heavy pins on little metal studs brought up from under the alley surface with the use of a foot lever. When the pins were all on the metal studs the foot pedal was disengaged and the work was done until the frame on that alley was over. There were hazards to the fun of bowling.

The bowling alley owner would let us set pins for each other on certain days. Some of us set pins in the leagues at night, so we knew the routine. When we bowled and set pins for each other we were always wary of flying pins from certain of our friends. Some guys fired fastballs down the alleys and the pins would splatter. Where did these splattered pins go? Many times they flew into the spaces between the lanes where pin-boys rested between frames.

Those setting pins during the evening leagues had two words that struck fear into their hearts. The two words were Tip Burkholder. The Tipper chewed on a cigar as a regular routine and he threw a bowling ball at fantastic speeds. When his strikes splattered the pins they carried two alleys away by way of the little spaces connecting the pin beds for the alleys. Often the pin-boys were victimized. This was no longer a recreation.

Riding our bikes was a vital part of our early mobility prior to the advent of peers with autos. We cycled all over and the ride to Sodus Point and back was our longest pedal. Remember, the bikes back then were typically one-speed, and leg muscles were taxed to the max on the hills between the two villages. Paper routes were easier to manage since we trained for the paper routes on our recreational rides.

Great times were available to us for most of our growing years. Whether we built boats, bowled, played baseball or rode bikes the effort was always worth it since we never got bored. Too bad the kids of today can't find safe space and energizing activities.

***

Streetlights—A stupid target

Teddie and I were good buddies. His mother was the librarian in the village and my mother liked to read. They knew each other quite well. The Smith family lived on the corner of High Street and Orchard Terrace. My family lived just down the street. My sister Donna and Ted's younger sister were friends. Ted's older sisters were very attractive. Many of us visited the Smith house with the high hope of seeing an older sister. We had fathers working in the food industry in the county. We had another common denominator in our lives. We each had streetlights right in front of our houses. At nighttime the light from the street cast its glow across the upstairs bedrooms in the Smith and Pearson family homes. Ted and I and our buddies worked overtime for a short period of time to keep the light from penetrating the homes at night. Probably we thought that people would sleep better without the intrusion of the streetlights. Probably we didn't think.

Using Red Ryder BB guns obtained by older brothers at the Western Auto Store, Ted and I were shooting out the lights with a high degree of accuracy. This shooting spree ended as quickly as it began when the police, electric company and adults living in the darkened house began asking critical questions. Credit us with greater intelligence after the first few blasted lights, since we knew enough to stop without serving any time. The guns were dismantled the last time Ted and I used them, and were stored in a cellar. They may still be in some cellar on High Street as far as I know.

Other stupid targets came and went in our youth, but the lights along the streets were the most costly. Our inherent interest in target shooting should have parlayed into something positive such as rifle championships. We also should have had fantastic pitchers in baseball since most of us spent the long winters picking targets and hitting them quite often. Some of the targets were moving.

Moving targets were human, vehicular and even sleds. Our group of young boys never lacked for targets. On certain occasions we broke a window or two or three. Usually these were accompanied by confessions, since people knew the snowball throwers quite readily.

Fortunately for life in Sodus, we were never armed with bows and arrows. We did develop a unique form of target shooting after some of us obtained cars.

The heavy, blowing snows of the winter gave us our new targets. Huge drifts were created when strong west winds blew the snow across the roads where there were no snow fences. Plows would deal with these drifts eventually but on cold, blustery days with light snow we gathered in someone's car and "drift busted." This involved driving through the drifts fast enough to come out the other side. The only damage a vehicle would sustain would be when the engine compartment filled with snow and the engine stalled. At this juncture we cleared the snow out, dried a plug or two and started the vehicle again.

Most of us did this one time and then headed for the barn. Stalling a car on a back road in the dead of winter was not the brightest thing we ever did. It astounds me today to realize that intelligence seems to grow after the age of twenty-one. The other corollary to that is the fact that parents really get smarter after their children reach twenty-one. These two facts eluded us as teenagers as we attacked the Wayne County drifts.

Water sports were critical to our development, and luckily for us we did not have jet-skis back then. The various powerboats we commandeered were put through their paces without any fatalities. There was one near miss when one rascal ran over a female water skier who had dropped off the tow. The lad driving the ski boat did not see the girl as he circled to pick her up. The prop cut through part of her leg and upper thigh. She survived and the driver recovered from the sight of the blood in the water. After things returned to normal she would gladly, upon request, show off her scars at parties the rest of her teenage years.

Snowmobiles came after we left the village as teenagers. This no doubt saved some of our lives. There were amazing stories coming out of Wayne County involving young drivers driving the snowmobiles over a huge snow bank on one side of a two lane road around Sodus and leaping the road at high speed. The machine and rider would land, usually, safe and sound on the other side. There were a couple of fatalities when the snowmobile and rider hit a large truck passing by on the road as a leap was attempted.

Streetlight popping was not a good thing. Driving into drifts was dumb. All of life is an adventure. Many seem to survive the curiosity and foolishness of youth.

***

Toye Pond- Skin deep

She was one of the more attractive girls then and her name always popped up when guys talked, as they so often did, about their "wish lists." She is probably a grandmother now and her name has been changed to keep her grandchildren from being unduly affected by an event that was a part of coming of age in our lives back then.

"Kim," as we shall refer to her,was driving; and we had arrived at what was referred to as Toye Pond. It had other names but it was one of the numerous spring-fed ponds all over the county. It served as a source of water for farmers to fill their spray rigs. It was a remote place also. If you followed a paved road for a few miles and then turned down the dirt road leading to the pond, it got very dark as soon as the headlights were turned off. There was no lighting out there at night. The paved road leading to the dirt road had no lights either. The nighttime at Toye Pond was unique.

We were going there to make out. This was quite common for our age group back then. It probably has its parallel now. The car was hers because I could not usually get a set of wheels as easy as my peers back then. I always had to share a car with Isabel. She got the vehicle eighty percent of the time. This episode might have been different if the car was in my hands.

I am not quite sure of all of the fine points, but my memory tells me someone suggested a skinny dip. That may have been Kim. I was a shy type. For the uninformed readers, skinny dipping is merely a swim without clothes so that you can have dry clothes when you get finished. Whatever swimming you accomplished would leave your body wet. It would be foolish to swim at night with your clothes on. Skinny dipping was agreed upon, and the doors on both sides of the car opened. There was a brief moment of light. The pond was filled with water and was within three steps of where the car was parked. A person could be swimming in a heartbeat.

The car doors slammed shut. The night was pitch black and I removed my clothes and dove into the watery darkness. When I broke the surface of the cool water, my head and shoulders were in the beams of the car headlights. Kim was so overwhelmed she decided to pull a great prank on me. The car backed up to a turnaround and, before I could react, she was gone. I was swimming alone in Toye Pond on a late summer evening. My clothes were up there somewhere but my partner in the potential skinny dip had departed.

I was very happy doing pranks and found clever things to do to people. Pranks were a part of the good life. This particular prank at my expense had serious ramifications! Not only was I swimming in the darkness miles from my house, but my clothes were going to be hard to find. Beyond those thoughts were others. What the hell happened to the co-ed skinny dip experience? What would I ever be able to tell my buddies relating to these events? Kim had all the wild cards in this joker's wild strip poker game, and turned it into solitaire. I was a nude joker.

As I was preparing this book for print I related the topic of this chapter's contents to my historical proofreader, Lester Harrison (alias Gib Sergeant) of Sodus. I informed him about the skinny dipping episode with "Kim," and even nearly fifty years later he was all ears for the rest of the story. He has the potential to be a dirty old man. Because he is a grandfather, I spare him any further notations because he has grandchildren also. Suffice to say Gib wanted much more detail. Suffice to say Gib wanted this episode to end differently also.

She left me there to swim on my own for over thirty minutes. For a while I thought maybe the skinny part of the dip turned her off and she had returned to her home for a swim suit. Perhaps I was too quick to participate?

After about fifteen minutes of swimming I sought my clothing from the shore. Luckily they were there. How in the hell would a naked teenager have gotten home in a case such as this? Would I have hitchhiked? Fortunately, I never had to figure that out.

After dressing I began the lonely, dark walk out on the dirt road. Toye Pond and its hope for a naughty swim were now behind me. I was vowing to be a more careful teenager now. I was also one whose ego had been shrunk more than anything else during the cool swim. As I neared the paved road a car's headlights appeared and there, driving towards me, was Kim in her vehicle.

True to her form she was enjoying the moment at my expense. I never quite knew where she disappeared to, but thankfully she returned and we shared some thoughts on the previous part of the evening. She drove me home after a while and our friendship continued for the summer. We went our separate ways that fall. Kim was a fun-loving girl and possessed a good sense of humor. This humor showed up many years later at a reunion of our classmates. Kim wondered aloud at the bar what would have happened if she had joined me in the swim that night.

How was I supposed to answer that? She was still attractive and had already gone through two marriages. I was still on my first—and my attentive wife was right there picking up most of my responses. What did I do? My response was carefully constructed. I merely told her the water was way too cold for any enjoyment that particular evening. I also told her I wasn't that great a swimmer. If something had gone wrong, she might have never lived it down.

The skinny dipping possibilities in any person's life are usually limited. The co-ed skinny dipping possibilities in life are definitely very limited. It was my good fortune that Kim used a hell of a lot more judgment than I that evening. Her prank was clever. I never shared my side of it until now, because it was so successful at my expense!

Gib waited nearly fifty years to hear this story about skinny dipping with Kim. Drearily for Gib, it turned out quite bland. Even grandchildren can read this segment and laugh.

***

STINKY'S TALES

A Long Walk Runs Through It- Sliding

I can not think of a place in modern children's play patterns to compare with what we did winter after winter in Sodus for entertainment. Consider that we took our sleds to the very top of Orchard Terrace, and then proceeded to slide down that steep street on the automobile tire-packed snow for what was probably a half mile. We then crossed a pre-packed small tangent across the yard behind the big Mill's house on the corner of High Street and Orchard Terrace, across the DeBrine yard and then my front yard to intersect High Street. From there, we continued down High Street at a sharp incline to School Street, yet another sharp incline, until we flashed across Gaylord Street into the huge farmlands between Gaylord and Mill Streets.

The whole run was exhilarating and could be dangerous at times. Once a sled got running on the runners at high speed the kid driving it was quite hard to see because of the high snow banks. There were several near misses each winter when cars and plows suddenly appeared on the run to the bottom. Part of the extreme natural high experienced was from raw speed. Part was from the wind and snow blowing in one's face.

There were times we raced to the bottom, and it was our version of the Olympic luge races seen every four years from some exotic winter setting. No matter what else was favorable about our entertainment there was one surefire reality with which to contend. When the mile long run was completed if you were in the mood for more runs, and who wasn't, there was the thing with the sled being pulled up to the top of Orchard Terrace by each winter sport participant.

In the modern era there are few natural highs such as I have described. There are fewer natural highs that are free of charge. There are even fewer natural highs that don't require a parent. Usually such parents get involved to make it easier for the kid(s). This seems to miss the point of reward and hard work.

My peers and I in Sodus would get together and slide down the streets because it was fun. Ted Smith, Fred DeBrine, Peter Moore,

Gib Sergeant, and older boys like Bruce Wood and my brother Dick would spend hours outdoors in the winter sliding down those streets. We always had to trudge our way back to the top of the run in order to get another dose of the three-minute thrill. Much like the ski run at nearby Brantling Hill later in our young lives, the run down was quick. The return to the top, even with a primitive rope tow like the one at Brantling, took much longer. We had no rope tow for our sliding.

The sliding was highly anticipated when the first snows arrived. The type of sliding I have described needed some good elements coming together. We needed some overnight heavy snows that brought out the plows but did not bring out any sanders or salt spreaders. Once the plowing caught up with the snow removal from the major arteries around the village, the same drivers that manned the plows then returned to spread salt, sand or small gravel in the streets where there were grades. Our sled run fit this description.

The heavy snows were plowed and cars would pack what was left after the plows removed most of the new accumulation. Plows could set their blades to a certain level to avoid taking up blacktop or making scars in the surfaces. What was usually left when the plows made their first runs early in the morning before daybreak was just about perfect for sliding. The first few cars out finished the course to our satisfaction. Our rush to get out of our warm winter beds was heralded by noise of plows going by the house. We filled up with oatmeal, hot chocolate and the wonderful breakfast creations from our mother's kitchens, and ten or twelve of us would appear almost in unison on the long trek up the hill with our sleds.

Christmas presents were often used in winter pursuits, so Christmas took on a very important function in addition to the normal celebrations. New sleds were high priority items. Ice skates, skis and toboggans were nice but the sled was the major tool of recreation in our village. The first good sliding conditions that appeared after Christmas were notable by virtue of the new sleds appearing on the streets and slopes.

The two or three person sleds were great since they allowed

for the sharing of the experience in an intimate manner. When two or three fellows got on a big sled, the bumps and the fear factor were all shared simultaneously. Sometimes a sled with three on it was tougher to steer, so that the sight of three guys sprawled on the street somewhere along the run was typical.

My thesis that the modern era youth does not have such an opportunity is true to the mark. I have read about a variety of things done to get wayward students back on track from juvenile delinquency and/or drug abuse. One common thread is that the successful treatments have some combination of forcing the young person to accept responsibilities for tasks and behaviors. The modern focus is often accomplished with some kinds of natural highs and sharing of these highs with peers. The natural highs are usually cheap or free and fill the voids left where drugs gave an unnatural high.

I cannot remember many or any of my peers suffering from drug abuse or being a severe juvenile delinquent. This does not give Sodus a perfect grade for these things at the turn of the last century. We had alcoholics, and some were developing in our school. Others were lawyers, teachers, doctors and everyday citizens of the community. The basic fact of life in Sodus was that the young people were outdoors a lot doing things in a seasonal manner. Winter called for more work than normal due to the chores of packing trails, clearing snow, making ice rinks, and pulling those sleds up the run every time we wanted a ride down.

Perhaps in the modern era we need to allow for children to experience work, planning, failure and being responsible for their own recreation. It is hard for me to imagine a drug abuser taking part in our winter frolics. For one thing, it was so cold the drug abuser would have a hard time getting to his or her drug of choice because the heavy winter wear would preclude all that. For another thing, how could any artificial high beat coming down the mile from Orchard Terrace to Gaylord Street?

***

Ernie's Indoctrination—A naïve newcomer

No businessman ever had a more unique indoctrination to a community than good guy Ernie Piekunka. Ernie was wise enough to wed Mary Guadino and set up residence in Sodus. Mary's father owned the Guadino's Dry Cleaning, and Ernie was set in motion to ultimately take over the business. During his first year in Sodus, as he learned the trade and moved around on the ground floor of the business, he and his family came up with an idea to develop a second location for the business. Ernie was given the names of some dependable, local boys to take to nearby Newark in order to distribute fliers for the new location in that village. We were solicited by our new businessman, and away we went on the dry cleaning mission. Little did Mr. Piekunka know he was being taken to the cleaners by some hellions.

After we distributed the fliers, Ernie manned the wheel on our return trip to Sodus. It was an education for him in good old-fashioned fruit tossing. We had taken a large supply of apples with us from a nearby orchard, and as the car carried us home we fired apple after apple at every stationary target between the two villages. Ernie was amazed at the accuracy of the throws as we leaned out the windows and made applesauce occur on mailboxes, barns, poles and signs. No windows or automobiles were included in this display of prowess. That would have been off limits and Ernie was, after all, new to our games.

We were having the time of our lives, with our adult driver doing a great job of slowing down and speeding up as targets dictated. Despite wasting a few good apples, an adult was sharing our juvenile fun. This was new to us. Ernie enjoyed our company and was really one of the boys that night. He did not have to do anything illegal nor did we damage anything with our throws. We were bonding, in the parlance of modern psychology.

Ernie captured our hearts and minds with his pleasant demeanor. Whenever we saw him during our years in school, it was always "Hi Ernie!" and he got to know us as friends. Our parents were some of the most well-known in the village, and they were his friends also. Business in dry cleaning was good, and many of us were Guadino's customers. The same clients would eventually be Ernie's customers, so he was astute to cultivate our friendship.

Over the years at reunions when we discussed different experiences of our youth the trip to Newark was one of the highlights. Our new neighbor and businessman made life interesting since he accepted some playful, rather innocent behavior and didn't get upset with us. We certainly couldn't ask our parents to drive us around throwing apples at signs, now could we?

As fun reflections about childhood come and go, the mainstays are the ones involving adults. This seems to be a pattern for many people. Fortunately for us, our town had a number of adults enjoying associations with kids. The number was sizeable. We all have read stories about bad adult influences and child abuse in the modern era. The numbers of positive adult companions seem to be diminishing. Many kids are distrustful of adults and with good reason. Some kids never learn how to behave reasonably when adults give them the chance.

Good adult guys were as abundant as hellions back in Sodus. It was a fine thing they could get together and cherish their roles. Thanks, Ernie!

***

Dancing to Disaster—Lester and the dumbwaiter
There were several riders taking turns in the cramped, dimly lit dumbwaiter connecting the kitchen in the school with the basement storage areas. The ride took twenty seconds from the kitchen to the basement. The riding was against the school rules of cafeteria protocol. There was trouble brewing in the kitchen one spring dance weekend; and my lifelong buddy Lester was smack in it. He was also stuck smack in the middle of the cramped device. His butt was stuck smack in the middle of the crosshairs of the principal's stern gaze.

Under normal usage, someone would press the button at either end of the ride and the dumbwaiter would travel up or down. This would deliver food items from the basement back up to the kitchen. The device was really a mini-elevator, and it came by its name quite aptly historically. It also hit an appropriate cord one spring night at the school.

One small problem connected to the operation of the device was that the operating buttons were on the outside wall at both ends of the ride. The cafeteria workers would oversee the buttons. If a rider ever squeezed inside the thing someone outside would control the rider's fate.

Normally the dim bulb in the 36" high by 18" wide compartment would allow someone to see what was coming up from the basement and help the loading process down below. The bulb would also show the eyes of perhaps the last rider in school history peering out from a narrow three-inch gap created when the dumbwaiter got jammed between floors.

Gib's eyes peered out from the three-inch wedge of connection with the outside world. As I share this memory, the great credit goes to the rider and not the writer. Lester (Gib) has shared this story with me from fifty years ago and my ability to share the story is a gift from the poor sophomore high school lad who was trapped in the dumbwaiter for well over two hours. For once in my high school career, on this night, I had departed the dance early and was not getting into trouble.

The fuse for the device had been blown when one of the previous riders, who happened to be a son of the vice-principal, pressed the UP button just after hitting the DOWN button. This dumb action by the son of a vice-principal slammed the dumbwaiter to a halt with just the cramped rider's eyes showing. Whereas this was highly comical to all involved *outside* the box, the rider was not comfortable. He was in the uncomfortable knees-up, semi-fetal position. This posture could be held for the twenty-second illegal ride that night, but not much longer. Consider more than two hours in the frozen position. Our buddy Gilbert was screwed big time.

The persons most responsible for his screwed position were top-ranked students in the sophomore class sponsoring the dance.

The vice-principal's son and the principal's son were riders earlier in the evening, and packed Gib into the device for his ride. When the switch was overloaded the damage was done.

After the usually laughter occurring in life during difficult moments such as this, the father of one of the riders who was Big Sam-Principal came to observe the sophomore in the muck. His eyes evidently met Gib's, and there was instant recognition. Whether there was excrement or urine in the dumbwaiter right after that, no one will tell. What did happen was that the handy custodian was summoned to make an escape possible. It turned out he received overtime pay that night, compliments of the three major players in the dumbwaiter deed.

Case Weist, custodian, merely replaced the fuse. Reports abounded that Case and the principal could not keep from smiling broadly at the plight of this future Sodus teacher/counselor. The severely cramped lad was finally pulled out by strong upperclassmen. In Gib's own words, he was severely cramped and despite the fact that the condition persisted the upperclassmen were humored all the way to Bill Gray's up the ridge and back. He gradually unwound from his newly discovered fetal position, and the attention from the upperclassmen helped him get over the exploit. Almost.

There was a matter of getting together with the principal in the main office the Monday following the weekend rides. The plural is operative in this story because young Lester (Gib) conceived a brilliant defense. He invited all the riders of the night to attend the meeting in Big Sam's office. Remember that the other riders and button pushers were Big Sam's son and the vice-principal's son. No body ever questioned Lester's grasp for quick thinking after this episode.

Other than having to pay the overtime for the custodian, the event came and went but left lasting impressions on memories. Once out of the fetal position, Gib stood taller than ever. He had stood the test in the principal's office without any corporal punishment. He convinced the other boys to stand up and be counted with him in his hour of truth on that Monday a long time ago.

Small events in big lives of service and community create opportunities to grow. The prevailing emotion seemed to be humor, despite Gib's personal ordeal for two hours. Sam Sr. showed his humanistic side as he stepped aside and smiled out of the sight of the eyes peering out of the dumbwaiter that evening. Gib's riding friends were compelled to fess up and stand tall. That was a good lesson. Gib's upperclassmen friends who took him under their wing that night were friends for life.

The overtime and fuse were a small price to pay for a lot of little lessons about friends and life that evening in the cafeteria.

***

Sailing Hellions—A freshwater approach to childhood
Wayne County Judge George Parsons was delivering a sentence to some poor man who was hunched over in front of the bench. The judge sat in the elevated judge's podium above the courtroom, much the same as a professor sits behind an elevated desk lecturing a class in some college. The parallel was very appropriate since the judge was mixing the messages for the Wayne County boys sitting in the courtroom behind the guilty man receiving his taste of Wayne County justice.

The guilty man was given a sentence. I cannot remember the sentence, but I do remember the edict at the end of the sentence. The man was never to set foot inside Wayne County ever again. That struck a chord with all of us sitting there. It was difficult to imagine never being able to venture into our home county again for whatever reason. The sentencing ended with the Wayne County law officers taking the man away to serve his time. The court session ended with the small details typical of ending a court day.

The courtroom cleared out except for the five of us sitting there transfixed at the Wayne County Judge. He had invited us in for the afternoon and we were entranced by the proceedings, but much more by the performance of the judge. The judge was our neighbor in Sodus who lived just around the corner and up the hill on Orchard Terrace. He was also the mentor for baseball in the village, as he continually arranged baseball leagues and fields for young men. Seeing him in the robes of a judge and being granted so much power was impressive to us. He decided the fate of the man banned from the county. Earlier, he allowed another man to serve his time outside of a jail term. He was powerful.

At the end of the session, while Judge Parsons was still in the robe of the court, he brought us up to the front of the courtroom. He asked us about our impressions, and then he looked us in the eyes and said that he never wanted to see us in the courtroom as law-breakers. This, then, was the message of the day. He performed his role as teacher quite well because we left the Lyons, New York Wayne County Court vowing never to show up in Lyons on trial for anything!

Judge Parsons was a local man who was elected judge in the county and worked as a lawyer in Sodus. His father, rumor had it, left a sizeable estate to George upon his demise, so George Parsons started out with a bit of a boost not granted other mortals. The neighbor was not a typical wealthy man. George bought boats and shared them with local kids, baseball players, and families in Sodus. This was his unique claim to fame. The judge/lawyer/father/neighbor was a boat lover. Every spring when the ice left Sodus Bay, his boat came out of winter storage where the locals had helped paint and refinish it over the winter. A ritual he practiced annually was to become the first swimmer in the bay each spring. As hellions, we never sought the questionable honor. As the "King of Hellions" he managed to swim in March or early April right after the ice had disappeared. No mortal sought to take the honor away. Once we tried to swim after we saw the judge go in, and it was a numbing experience with no fringe benefit at all.

His generosity was unmatched since he allowed people to use his boat in the bay, out in the lake, and, at times, on trips across the end of Lake Ontario to Canada. He would ride along and enjoy the sailing or boating experience. He would plot the course if that was needed, and would maneuver the various boats he owned over the years into docks or away from anchorages as needed.

He trained us well in these tasks and we became very proficient at these nautical operations. He entrusted us with boats over the years worth forty thousand dollars or more in 1950 dollars. It was said at the time that yachts of thirty feet or longer sold at one thousand dollars per linear foot. Judge Parsons always had yachts or sailboats of thirty-five to forty-five feet in length.

He bought t-shirts for a large number of Sodus kids in my age group. The shirts were simple white T's with one word on the front. The word was HELLIONS. This was a different George from the Judge we viewed in action in the courthouse. He recognized that we were teenagers and *did* raise some hell within certain boundaries. His goal was to provide baseball in great quantity and quality, and then add his boats to the mix. The HELLIONS would be his crew as the boat sailed around the marvelous waters of Lake Ontario and Sodus Bay.

The fresh water experience was unparalleled in most teenage lives. We were blessed by our neighborhood, our hometown and adults in the village. George Parsons was a young man at heart his whole life. He had two children later in his life who were given access to the same lifestyle we Sodus teenagers had already sampled with gusto. Judge Parsons gave of his wealth unselfishly. Upon reflection, I realize that much of what I know about sailing, boating, tides, docking, and nautical map reading come from the opportunity at Sodus Point to grow into manhood.

Lake Ontario was the training grounds (water) for many of us, and none of us will ever forget the Judge and the fun he encouraged. I remember times when we would dock at a Canadian port and spend the day exploring the area, play a baseball game in town and then return to the boat for our evening meal. After that we would collapse into bunks onboard and, as the waves lapped against the sides of the boat, fall into deep sleep.

Nothing can compare to the feel and sounds of sleeping on a cruiser or sailboat at anchor or tied up at a dock. We never had to pay a penny for the experience. George only asked that we bring some food from our own kitchens at home and some spending money for the Canadian stops.

During one stop, in an effort to maintain our hellion image, we managed to transform the white painted rocks spelling "Presquille" at one of our Ontario Province dockages to "Sodus Point." The change was made late at night in the dark. We knew we were safe since our departure was planned for 7AM in order to make it home late that day. We would be gone by the time the Canadians saw the change in their town name. One problem popped up to change all the plans.

Heavy fog descended upon the area during the early morning and we were unable to depart until 10AM when the fog lifted. During that time our creativity was evident to all. We were unable to sneak away to the safety of the freshwater. We were stuck in Sodus Point—oops—Presquille. With plenty of international negotiating by the Judge and with our tremendous work effort to replace the heavy white stones we were able to cast off from "Presquille" at noon. We were not in jail, and we maintained our hellion image, but the Judge was not too pleased. After a few hours of good lake conditions and fresh air, he got over his crew's dalliance in Ontario.

One thing stood out on the trip more than the rock incident. When we docked in Kingston, Ontario we went into town and met a new friend in one of the restaurants, where we wolfed down fish and chips like crazy. This friend introduced us to some of the local girls and we had a great dockage that was only necessitated because of our delayed departure from Belleview. The new friend's name was Sterling Virtue.

When we arrived back at the boat for our typical day-ending collapse into the bunks, we informed the Judge of our new friend. George Parsons got such a kick out of the lad's name that he wanted to meet him; he was sure we had fabricated the name. Before cast-off the next day, there was Sterling down at the city docks to wave goodbye to us. With Mr. Virtue were several of his female friends. Our reputations skyrocketed with the Judge over that episode.

I was able to visit with the Judge and his family when it was clear our great friend was dying. My younger brother Charley and I shot pool with the Judge's son Bob, and kibitzed with the Judge for an hour one evening. Although his memory and health were in serious decline, George brought up the fellow Sterling Virtue of Kingston.

He was able to dig into the depleted memory bank and share a great time with one of the hellions he had trained so well. None of us shall ever forget George Parsons—the number one hellion of Lake Ontario.

***

Orbakers or Bill Grays?—A classic question about hamburgers

Much of the time when trips were made to the west out of Sodus *the* choice had to be made in the summer months between Orbakers in Williamson, just ten miles away, or Bill Grays in Webster, thirty miles away. Orbakers was only open during the spring, summer and fall, but closed shop when the winter months shut down much normal travel in the county. Staying open would have been costly because heating and plowing costs would probably have doubled the hamburger costs. Grays became the only choice in the winter.

A person could get a great, full-sized hamburger at either place. The meat hung over the edges of the bun, and when smothered with all the condiments a person could handle, the whole thing seemed to melt in your mouth. Once winter weather hit and the Williamson choice was closed, the Webster option was the only way to go. No trip past Webster to the west could possibly be made without getting hamburgers at Grays. My father tried "sneaking" us by Grays once on the way home from a Rochester Red Wing game but Bruce Wood, my brother's friend, asked my Dad about stopping. If it were not for Bruce, Pete Pearson would probably have succeeded. The allure of a great burger might have tugged at old Pete's heart also.

There weren't any McDonalds, Arbys or Burger Kings. In those days the fast food chains were still over the horizon. Hamburgers were king of the kitchen for most travelers. They were cooked right on the spot and the portions of meat were much larger than you would ever get at home. For some reason, the hamburgers purchased at Grays were unlike *anything* cooked at home. I still don't know the reason. My best guess would be the logic of set and setting.

The set (or mindset) determines ahead of time what enjoyment a person might receive from an experience. Our mindset about Grays and Orbakers was that the nutritional experience would be fantastic. That theory seems to apply to many things in life. If a person looks forward positively to something and knows right up front that there will be enjoyment, then enjoyment it shall be. The setting is important also.

Setting is the actual place where you enjoy something. Once there with close friends, this setting seems to make the food just that much better. There may be fine hamburgers at home off the grill, but the mindset and setting just doesn't match that of Bill Grays.

Tragically, the set and setting theme is a huge reason behind the inability of drug addicts to break their habits. Once they get the mindset and then stay in the same old setting where drugs occupy a portion of their life, they are screwed. Their drug problem will defeat them nine times out of ten unless they can break the set and setting. That is why Betty Ford-type clinics—away from home and away from normal mindsets—work as well as any protocol on drug recovery.

When we were young our only addiction was to hamburgers served up at our two favorite places. That may sound simplistic and naïve, but that was a fact. We were not into drugs. Life was easier on kids back then because the consequences of hamburger eating were nothing like the consequences of drugs, tattoos, and promiscuous sex nowadays.

As I write this piece thirty years after enjoying my last burger at either place, I can almost sense the fatty beef giving my taste buds a treat. Nowadays I consider the cholesterol and saturated fat damage such food would do to my health. Times were simpler when I was a teenager. No mention of transfatty acids, triglycerides, or LDL ever crept into our discussions.

No matter what we ate, it was processed very quickly and we burned off whatever calories we took in. Ours was an active life style. Between the two s-words: spurts (as in growth—what did you think I meant?) and sports, our calories would be expended. Very few of us were heavy. I can only recall two or three heavy friends, and their weight was more a factor of genetics than overeating.

Bill Grays was the best place to meet friends after big events, and was the destination sought by guys on the prowl for gals. My guess is that gals prowled there also; we just did not realize this fact back then! Once we were able to drive and/or ride with friends, we sought out Bill Grays as if it were the only choice of destinations. Very seldom did it disappoint us. Many times we met young people from other nearby communities. It seemed that they were our friends at Grays despite the fact that they were our rivals on the fields and courts of the competitive county athletic leagues.

The same dynamic occurs on the world stage when athletes meet every four years in cafeterias in Olympic Villages. Despite sport competitions, these people enjoy one another's company. Despite cultural and severe political differences, these people meet over a meal without rancor.

Wayne County had more homogeneous than heterogeneous groupings, so we were not as challenged as young people in other areas of the USA or the world. Our task was pretty easy and most of our parents and friends shared common jobs, cultures and futures. We met over hamburgers, and that common fare merely made for an easier socialization process.

Dates seemed to go easier with hamburgers. Meeting young ladies was easier if the ubiquitous ground beef was there with us. Without making such a food staple bigger than life, it is noteworthy that for Wayne County residents it was the hamburger and not the hot dog that was more popular. There may be pockets of hot dog fans still living out their years in the county, and the hot dog may be America's food, but it was hamburger country. Typically the hot dog folks advocate a "white hot" and not a red hot. The distinction was appropriate locally. The white hot was a local favorite made by a local meat packing company. The white hot was a pork product that must have been one hundred percent fat. When grilled and packed into a hotdog roll and smothered with mustard and relish, the dog was a spectacular enterprise. It was always second to the burger, however.

It still does not compare with a Grays or Orbakers hamburger and all that went with such hamburgers. After all, how could a hot dog make a carload of teenagers drive sixty miles? The numerous trips up to Webster and back amounted to a sixty-mile binge trip for hungry teenagers. There were times when many of us could consume two burgers at one sitting. We never tried stopping at both hamburger places and I am disappointed that never crossed our adolescent minds at the time. It would have seemed a good idea.

The beauty of being young is that God usually looks over one's shoulder, because otherwise the life expectancy rates would be very poor. We sometimes rushed up to Grays and back the way people now go to the mall. Given the number of trips and the number of hamburgers, all of us lived a charmed life. The Orbakers and Bill Grays of my world probably occur in most lives. In Wayne County at Orbakers and just over the Monroe County line at Grays the burgers just tasted better. Call me a hamburger elitist!

You want to know something? Young people were a heck of a lot more social without designer drugs, unbridled sex, binge drinking, body piercing and/or body marking or delinquency. Maybe it was something in the beef that kept us from other sins.

***

Jake's Wheels—Our first brush with mobility
Donald "Jake" DeBadts possessed and still possesses the most infectious, hearty, wonderful laugh I have ever heard in my life! We called him Jake because that was his father's name. This was quite common then, for whatever reason young men do what they do. In addition to the great laugh, Jake had another special claim to fame. Jake had an auto before just about anyone else did; and he became the driver of our teenage dreams.

Jake was originally in the same grade with me and many of my peers. Somewhere along the way in elementary school Donald stayed behind for a repeat job. I am not sure why this happened, because back then things like this occurred in a shroud of secrecy. Donald became Jake in Junior High and it has stayed forever. His ability to drive was critical to our success as teenagers. It never mattered to us that he was a year behind us in school. He was years ahead of us in driving ability and experience.

In every era, learning how to drive is critical to one's well-being. Learning how to drive in the modern era is fraught with peril because driver's education is now out of the regular school curriculum. Driving in the modern era is difficult because adults are not as available as they were fifty years ago to step in and teach needed skills. The consequences of poor preparation as a driver today are enormous. Young drivers are out on the Interstate System. In my youth there was no Interstate System! We all took driver education for a whole semester. This involved wintry driving every semester. We were trained better than the current crop of young drivers.

Jake took driver's education, learned driving from family members, drove farm equipment when he was young, and became a chauffeur for his friends. Nobody ever had a better friend than Jake. He drove us around; he laughed and was a ready participant in all we did. Not surprisingly, he works with recreation now and has coached young people much of his life.

Some of the trips sponsored by a Jake-driven set of wheels would sound quite corny today to teenagers used to sophisticated malls, entertainment systems and even their own SUVs. Nevertheless, we were passengers for literally hundreds and hundreds of miles with Jake as we swam, ate, watched sporting events, played games, and even, on occasion, made out with teen-age girls.

Wayne County was a rural county and was therefore quite safe from the volume of traffic observed in and around modern cities. My wife and I have a niece who grew up in Atlanta, Georgia, and her teenage driving included some of the worst traffic known to man. Her parents had many more concerns than did mine and Jake's. In

Upstate New York we were blessed by the collective wisdom of our parents—and the fate that brought us together where traffic was minimal.

There were times when it became prudent to merely park the car and do something very domestic at the home of one of our friends. Snow and ice did this often. Other times, we just did not want to be seen for a few days due to some prank or mischief we were involved in, and staying low profile was a good idea. We tended to rotate to Jake's house more than others at times, because he had an older sister who was responsible for him when the parents were away. Jake was one of only a few friends who had an older sister, so this created the visit-Jake scenario.

Jake's sister was a distant supervisor for all of Jake's activities and he pretty much had the perfect situation. His sister had access to a car. She allowed Jake access to a car, and she seemed quite comfortable with Jake's entourage as we appeared at his place. Every kid growing up ought to have a friend like Jake.

The innocence of most of our activities would be boring to the many teenagers of the 2000s. Instead of a "rave" attended by so many today, we had roller skating and recreation basketball. Instead of drugs like Ecstasy served up at the raves (all-night, loud, dancing parties) we had homemade cookies during sleepovers at someone's home. We played poker, monopoly, hearts, spades, and other games.

Jake was the jolly leader of our pack and we could count on him to spice up our lives. There were times after high school when we started drinking beer in college as part of our entertainment. During high school most of us did not drink, nor did we have the urge to do so. Even after college, we rarely just sat around somewhere and drank. We usually tied whatever drinking occurred to some activity. We bowled a lot for a while. The bowling alley in the north during the winter months takes on a warm glow all of its own. The bowling alley in Sodus was next to the school as the busiest meeting place for young people.

Donald DeBadts was the son of a muck farmer, and around our

village that provided a set of pretty good credentials. The Dutch people who farmed the black earth did quite well for themselves and were key people in the community. Jake's father was a no-nonsense father and we enjoyed hearing him scold Donald. A typical rejoinder was "Gut damnit Don!" Many of our fathers had a significant phrase pulled out for maximum effect at critical teenage times.

My own father had a phrase that was a classic, and never once did he slip and utter the key "F" word he was paraphrasing. In front of me and my friends on certain occasions, my father would utter, "You had better stop *futzing* around." Other parents were more selective as to communications, but without fail most got their message across.

When Jake started picking on someone with a story about an embarrassing moment that person had endured, it was music to the ears of all the rest in the room. Whenever I heard a first sentence with "Stinky" in it I merely waited for the end of the story and then tried to defend my honor. In every case the ribbing was great.

Most of us could not get much over on Jake. This was difficult because he had driven his buddies around so much he, like most chauffeurs, knew a lot of information about all of us.

***

Dating Whirl- No place to go but plenty to do

Dates were simple and spur of the moment things. Many guys and gals went "steady," but this was often a flexible plan allowing for fun with one's own gender group. Girls knew the power of the "guy" thing, and usually did not mess with their guys once guys got together. Girls had their slumber parties and girl things, and guys stayed at a safe distance. There really were not many places to go on dates, yet dates persisted and succeeded. Compared to the modern era, even in Sodus, the choices in the mid-fifties were limited. We did not seem to notice this dimension of our lives.

The usual things were bowling, dances, parties, games, movies, swimming, and skating. The other things filling our lives were as varied as the list was long. Sometimes churches sponsored events such as church camps and youth fellowship meetings with specific activities. We enjoyed hay rides in the fall and boat rides in the summer. Some girls would get together and have a picnic where the agenda was to pair up people. Other times, parents would invite kids in for parlor games. It seemed that everyone played some variety of cards.

On a few weekends we arranged for trips to baseball and basketball games. Rarely did girls get invited into this male domain. It is interesting to note that during the construction of sport-related venues last century, fewer rest rooms for females were planned than were rooms for men. During a trip to any stadium built more than thirty years ago, check this fact out. My wife and I noticed that the twenty-five year old Omni in Atlanta displayed this feature before it was imploded and replaced by Phillips Arena five years ago. Phillips has equal number of rest rooms for each gender. The girls found few restrooms, even when they were able to go with us. They usually stayed home.

In a rare departure, even for us, we arranged a trip from Rochester to Cleveland, Ohio by train with the help from a parent. The parent arranged a ride up and back to the train station. We boarded a baseball excursion train and traveled through the early Sunday morning hours to see the Yankees lose a doubleheader to the Indians in front of eighty thousand fans. The year was 1954, and that was the year Cleveland won 111 games and beat the Yankees in the American League's only division at the time.

During the week before our excursion, Donald Virts' locker in the gym was robbed of his wallet and the ticket to the excursion. He bought another ticket and we spent the whole trip there and back looking to see who ended up with that seat in our group of tickets. No one ever showed for the seat. Coming back after the game on the all-night train ride was a drag. Our favorite team had been swept, Donald's robber failed to show, and we arrived in Rochester at dawn Monday. We had been awake most of the previous forty-eight hours.

Professional gamblers used the excursion train to ply their

trade in games of dice, poker and roulette, right in a couple of the railroad cars. The guy organizing the whole deal was called Tiny despite weighing over four hundred pounds. Tiny Coleman was a Rochester character right out of a novel. He was real and we saw him on the train. Any female on that train would have been out of place.

Girls joined us on a couple of outings to amusement parks in the area and to a couple of games in Rochester, but they seemed as though they were bored with our interests. If we ended up taking a girl to a movie, it did not require a vehicle. These dates were simple one-on-one deals. In the dark of the movies a one-on-one date became private. Sometimes we never gave a thought to what our buddies elsewhere in the movie or in town were doing that night.

We came up with interesting things to do involving scavenger hunts. As young kids we played a game called kick the can in the streets in front of our homes. Somebody was "it" and a can was placed in the street in full view for all to see. If a person kicked the can prior to getting caught then everyone previously caught would be free. The "it" person had to start finding other kids again and the game continued. As teenagers we altered the game to suit our hormones. We hid as couples and another couple had to find us. The can was there but the thing did not get kicked as often as before.

We drove around on double dates and instead of doing stuff guys would do in cars involving fruit and vegetables, we might go get ice cream at a nearby dairy. Girls seemed to think they had tamed the wild beast in us. I guess their less-rambunctious ways set the tone for most double dates.

Television was not the focus as it is today, but there were times when many of us would gather and share a program or two. This activity ended with some other activity taking over. We played spin the bottle, cards or even shot hoops. One thing was notable in its absence. Alcohol did not appear in our normal scheme of things until we hit college.

***

Drive-In Movies—Do you want hot and bothered?

Gib and I drove over to the restaurant just down old route 104 from his house during my recent summer trip to visit my home town. Across from the restaurant was the location of one of our favorite places during the summer months while we were growing up. The local drive-in movie theatre was not there anymore; but some artifacts of its presence many years ago were still visible. A small part of the entrance was evident, and a diner that went hand in glove with the drive-in was still there.

Gib is my friend of sixty-plus years. Despite the many years going our own ways, we have managed to stay in touch. His roots have been well-placed in Sodus for most of his sixty five years except for college and a few minor forays into other parts of New York State. My roots, by contrast, have been all over the United States including Rochester and Buffalo in New York; Albuquerque, New Mexico; Sacramento, California; Berea, Kentucky; and my current residence in Rome, Georgia. Despite our differences in lifetime locations, we both can come together on his home turf and enjoy the reflections. He merely paces himself during the time he spends bringing me up to date on events he has observed and/or lived in our hometown. There is much I have missed over the years; he knows this but he is patient and tolerant of my travels elsewhere.

We both vividly remember the drive-in theatre! As we sat eating breakfast recently, we were able to identify various locals like him who frequented the restaurant. As they saw me after literally decades of space between sightings, they were polite and we all then realized something about time gaps like this. A common reaction seems to be universal in situations such as these. The common reaction is being able to identify the voice first and then the eyes. Despite the effects of aging, people are able to establish a line of communication as though they had not been apart for all those years. The uncanny ability of old friends to pick up where they left off is a wonderful gift across the ages, and should be cherished more than it is in our lives.

The drive-in across the road from our breakfast that day was a common meeting place during our youth. Two friends eating at the restaurant fifty years later could no doubt remember things that went on during the nights long ago across the road from the eatery. As people ate their traditional Canadian bacon and eggs around us, one could only conjecture about what memories they had regarding the drive-in.

Could the people of the diner that current day be willing to talk about the events of those summers many moons ago? In many cases they would probably speak in hushed tones and respectful phrases, not knowing who was listening and who might still care. Gib and I talked about the old theatre in generalities but that triggered more specific thoughts. A chronic bug problem existed despite periodic spraying with DDT. This was a bugging reminder of the summer season in the north. Sometimes during a break in a double-header movie a truck would pull a sprayer around the car-filled theatre parking lot spraying insecticide to ward off the mosquitoes.

No thoughts were evidently given to the lingering effects of the spray upon the viewer's health, DNA or future problems associated with the now-banned spray! Despite the DDT spray, one could still enjoy the evening. Personal insect repellents were very popular in between DDT sprays by the management. The use of cigarette smoke in a car was a good repellent if the car carried smoking types. Windows could be rolled up on cool evenings. This would work as long as you could slam the car door on the speaker cord and have the speaker still work.

If a person could read lips on the screen or hear sounds from nearby speakers, then your car didn't need a small speaker provided by the drive-in. Cords connected the small speakers to the poles located all through the theatre lot adjacent to each parking slot. On occasions such speaker cords were cut, and then one merely moved on to another pole. Eventually upkeep on the posts became a serious problem for the owners of drive-ins as collectors starting taking speakers home with them and cords became ineffective.

As one walked from the car to the concession stand during the movie, interesting things were often observed. Sometimes, despite the heat, car windows would be rolled up and steamed up in what seemed to be a violation of common sense. In such cars the occupants obviously could not see the film being shown, nor were the occupants interested in the film. Common sense was not always evident. As I matured and learned more about life from my older brother and other older boys, there was always a question that begged an answer. The question was, were people actually "doing it" at the drive-in? In all my trips to the drive-in I felt the answer was probably "yes," but in those search missions "for popcorn" I could never positively visually identify such behavior.

What went on in cars that I was in going to the drive-in? That answer probably goes under the label "plenty of talk, a lot of commotion, and little substance." As with most adolescents the local talk was a whole lot more juicy than the actual events. Cars at the drive-in often went in with one or two persons evident to the ticket window employee collecting the admission fee. Sometimes there were additional passengers! Many times the ticket taker was a crony who no doubt knew what was flowing by him on any given evening. After getting inside the drive-in, several "free" people might possibly materialize from the trunk or from under a blanket in the back seat. This made for a cheap date. This also gave the occupants an option with the blanket later in the evening if the movie got dull. Many times numerous blankets were evident outside the cars on grassy areas between cars and at the rear of the parking lot. That would create problems with the blasted mosquitoes, but other priorities took precedence.

The best night ever at the drive-in in Sodus was a night when the northern lights were putting on a memorable display. The northern lights, or aurora borealis as they were called, were luminous bands or streamers in the night skies of the northern hemisphere. They appeared often during the clear nights in the northern hemisphere. Scientists theorize they are caused by magnetic particles moving in the atmosphere toward earth. On the particular evening that summer a half a century ago, everything at the movie came to a halt (and I really do mean everything) so all in attendance could view this extraordinary display. The colors and shimmering effect were profound. The projectionist stopped the movie and the windows were rolled down in the steaming cars.

The mosquitoes seemed to stop on this evening because it was cooler than normal. Some of the horny teenagers even stopped their evening of necking and petting in submission to something bigger, brighter and more profound. The display of color went on for over thirty minutes; most in attendance stayed interested in the display. As I recollect this evening five decades ago while writing in the new century, I did remember the northern lights and the young lady I snuck in with that night. I also remembered the couple that snuck us into the movie in their trunk. My date disappeared as the aurora borealis did likewise.

She evidently went home with her ex-boyfriend that night as I studied the skies over the drive-in. Once I realized what had happened, I ended up riding home with the couple sneaking me in that evening. As things evolved, my date ended up marrying her ex-boyfriend later on in Sodus. As with so many young marriages, theirs lasted about two years. I always rationalized for the sake of my wounded ego that by leaving me at the drive-in and going home with her husband-to-be, she was doomed to a life of folly. I ended up riding out of the movie with the guy and his date who did *not* get married later on. As it turned out I returned to the drive-in with that guy's girlfriend (ex) two weeks later and had a great, though uneventful night. Things seemed to be in transition during our youthful years. That probably was a good thing for a lot of could-have-been and would-have-been type marriages among high school guys and gals.

The drive-in is gone in my hometown. An era in America has gone, although there are some communities opening drive-in theatres once again in scattered locations across America. Maybe those places have tried to recapture the glorious days of yesteryear at the big outdoor screen.

***

Fishing Line—A mathematical miscalculation

Life is filled with interesting experiences, and the more one hangs around on this earth the more one realizes irony and humor can be found beneath the surface of almost any event. I say this out of the firm conviction, based on my involvement with teacher education as I write this book in the year 2004. My friends back in high school would not have picked me for teacher education as I involved them in my pranks in school. My first excursion into teacher education came many years ago as my associates and I helped train a student teacher in a math class during my sophomore year in high school. The school year was 1953-1954.

In a geometry class taught by Miss Lawrence that school year were banded together some of the most creative creatures Sodus had ever seen. There were faculty brats who were so-named because their parent or parents were on the faculty of the school. There were children whose fathers were preachers in the community. There were children whose fathers were lawyers, whose mothers were librarians, and some whose parents worked farms. Each of these creatures was unique, and some had more potential for deviltry than others. I would fall into that category; and my father was a salesman and my mother was a housewife. According to my mother, my expertise in deviltry came from a genetic link to a rogue grandfather named Ward. I carry his name as my middle name in some kind of historic deal with the very devil himself. When I reached puberty and tried desperately to impress Berniece Rawden, Esther Bohrer, and a few other pretty girls of the student body, there was no limit to my performances to score points with them.

During my first foray into teacher education in that school year and in the geometry class in particular, I had no idea that I would end up training teachers and coaches later in my professional life. I also had no idea I would be supervising student teachers in this era as they waged educational war against problems similar to the ones I and my friends at Sodus planned for the student teachers of that era. Looking at the whole development of my professional "style," I must conclude I anticipate problems young teachers encounter in their training due to my expertise as a "pain in the ass" as a student. It's the validation of that old adage it takes one to know one.

Our geometry class was taught by the wonderful Miss Lawrence, a stark, tall lady with a pleasant demeanor. She was almost at retirement age when we reached her classroom. Some people would say of her that she was almost at retirement age when they had her ten years prior to our encounter with her. We respected our math teacher and she was a fine teacher. We learned geometry and proved that fact by scoring well on the geometry Regents exam at the end of the school year. In the Regents exam Sodus students were matched against all other geometry students across New York State. These were exams authorized by the Board of Regents as a way of screening for college candidates at state institutions where tuition would be very, very low for those accepted.

During the school year a pretty, female, math student teacher appeared in our class with Miss Lawrence. The hormones in the males rushed around and our prank fever hit a high temperature. We wanted to impress the new teacher lady with our behavior as any adolescent would do in a similar situation.

When Miss Lawrence felt comfortable with our student teacher after a few weeks, the rookie was allowed to teach us solo, with Miss Lawrence doing other things outside of our view. We, also, were out of her view. On such a solo day for the new teacher, whose name I cannot remember, we mapped out a trick. I had brought nearly invisible fishing line to school for the express purpose of using it to string the desks together as our teacher was using the blackboard and her back was to us. This required the assistance of most in the classroom and there was no shortage of volunteers. We worked energetically stringing the line all over the room crisscrossing the aisles and connecting the desks many times over. If there had been a fire that day, we all would have gone down in flames with the classroom.

Our intention, I think, was to make the student teacher get flustered. Pranks don't seem to have a great amount of foresight. Sensing she was inexperienced in matters of classroom behavior and discipline, we predicted a fluster moment. We reached the point in the class where the student teacher began her walk down the aisles from the blackboard. She was going to check our work. This was the moment for which we had waited. It was at this same moment that Beula Lawrence came into the room.

As the key instigator of this prank and the person supplying the fish line from Honk's, I was aware my particular goose was cooked. Normally I would not have offered up my body so quickly but this was a different result than even I had predicted on this prank. Fearing that Miss Lawrence might fall over the line I told Miss Lawrence in a quiet voice that we needed to get some fish line out of the aisles that somehow had appeared there. She did not yell or scream because she was a nice, senior faculty member. She did not get flustered. Whether she liked to fish or whether she had seen juvenile pranks over the years resembling this I don't know. I would guess I would vote on the latter choice.

As the fishing line disappeared and as my classmates helped clean up my idea, the student teacher turned the classroom back over to Miss Lawrence. After class, Miss Lawrence brought me to her desk after the others left and told me she was disappointed in our actions. She did not say that to anyone else, so she intuitively knew the source of the line and the idea. As it turned out, the nice lady teacher did not report me to the principal but did make me apologize to the student teacher.

This moment was difficult, because the college senior was emotionally upset with her loss of classroom control to my fishing line. I apologized and then she asked the logical question about my motivation. I really could not rationally explain my actions. She then said she needed my help to make her student teaching more successful. Although her name eludes me and I don't even know if she went on to a storied career in math teaching or not, she was on the right tack with me by asking for my help.

She appealed to my better sensibilities, and usually when I screwed up I got a paddling at school or a smacking around the head and shoulders at home. After the fish line incident I became a model math student. I did it for Miss Lawrence and for the nice student teacher. I probably did it for my mother and grandmother, too, who would have been very displeased had Miss Lawrence informed them.

At the end of the school year after I had miraculously passed the geometry Regents exam with an 86, my highest grade for the whole year in the class, Miss Lawrence stopped me in the hall. She told me that I had answered one of the theorem questions in a way she hadn't seen before in her career. In telling me that, she said she was proud of my score. Not one word came from her about the fish line matter.

The incident taught me about the need to be nicer to student teachers. A student teacher had been instrumental in helping me comprehend her dilemma at a critical point educationally. It also showed me that it did not take much for one person to disrupt a class. My friends had gone along with this, but I was the leader. My efforts leading my friends should have been in other venues.

Miss Lawrence showed me her high level of teaching ability. She was able to overlook my temporary behavior lapse and see my potential to understand her favorite subject a little better than even I thought possible. Upon reflection, that story about my unusual success with a particular theorem answer was no doubt similar to when my mother would say I was one of her favorite children. Those sweet older ladies could make anyone feel worthwhile.

***

Snowballs From on High- The winter game

I knew about road rage long before it became fashionable. Road rage occurred during winter months on the old Route 104 passing through Sodus when trucks traveling the highway between Rochester and Oswego and other points were struck in the cab area by snowballs.

There were times when the corner wall on Main and High served as base for as many as fifteen armed and not too dangerous youths and their supply of pre-made snowballs. The wall stood ten feet above the street corner and another fifty feet above the main road further below on the next level below the armed corner. There was a set of steps coming all the way up the embankment from Route 104 to the area just below our throwing wall. There was also a set of about ten steps cut into our throwing wall leading to or from our throwing "camp." Keep these steps in your mind!

We would go to the corner whenever we became bored with other more reasonable snow pursuits. Once we were there, we would try to splat a snowball off the side of a moving target that was usually a trailer truck. A trailer truck becomes rather easy to hit if it is moving slowly due to traffic or snowy conditions. After seeing this occur we became more sophisticated and tried to throw a ball right on top of the cab of the truck.

On some throwing days we would accidentally splat an occasional auto on the roof or even windshield. This would create what we thought of as a scatter. We all would scatter and spread out closer to our homes to insure the driver of such a hit vehicle would not find us on the wall.

The snowballs coming from about sixty feet up and another one hundred feet away required a good arm and a sense of leading the target with our throws. Much like in trap shooting, or what we had seen in the movies with dogfights between planes and torpedo shots in the ocean, we developed and honed our delivery systems each winter. As a person lobbed a snowball off the wall at a truck target that was still many yards away from the spot where ball and truck would meet there was a great sense of anticipation. The reward was in following your particular throw to its target and seeing it hit if you could track it that far in the swirl of other snowballs and falling snow.

The snowball fights we held regularly probably, without design, became the answer to a baseball coach's dream. All through the winter months, young men threw regularly outdoors while, at the same time, playing basketball indoors. Since our school was quite small, with forty in a typical graduating class, most athletes became two or three sport athletes. The baseball players were able to stay in aerobic shape in basketball as they also kept their arms in great shape via snow workouts.

One day when our entire crew was throwing from the wall, we plastered a truck with a full volley of snowballs. Some hit the cab, many hit the trailer and a few even impacted on the windshield. Whether this truck had endured a previous run through snowball alley and was road raged over that run, we would never find out. But in the aftermath of his drive past the wall below we were shocked by the truck driver's appearance at the top of the fifty feet of steps coming up the huge embankment from the main artery. He must have stopped his truck farther down the road unseen by us and then walked back to the steps.

When he appeared at the top of the long climb of steps, all he had to do now to get at us was cross the extended Main Street, climb but ten steps built into the wall we were standing on and then reap his revenge. All of us calculated this proximity to danger in that instant he appeared. If there was any doubt that he meant us harm he shouted that he was going to "get you bastards." None of us were bastards, but we all knew enough to get the hell out of there pronto!

The snow-covered steps coming up from the main road below must have been very difficult to climb because as he ran across to the next set of steps leading to us we could see he was laboring as we hightailed it out of there. There is a saying about a wounded animal being the most dangerous and this no doubt added some adrenalin to our all-out sprint away from the wall. The wounded animal never made it to any of us since we knew the terrain and also the best hiding places. Youth triumphed over middle age as far as the chase was concerned.

The next major objective for us was to make sure we maintained a low profile over the rest of the day should the truck driver "hunter" get more aggressive in his pursuit of us. Reconstructing that day in my mind, we probably stayed out of sight playing Monopoly or Hearts in someone's home for fear that a return to the wall might trap us.

We returned to the wall many times after that; but we always remembered the day when a truck driver took up the challenge and nearly had some of us for lunch.

The moral of the story might be to practice safe snowball throwing. Another concept might be to avoid moving vehicles in such endeavors. Still another approach might be to keep adolescent boys confined until they reach eighteen years of age. All of them make some sense.

My view of the matter after fifty years is that the activity was harmless to begin with, but when trailer hitting became dull we should have changed activity.

At some point in my young adult years a car I was riding in got plastered with snowballs. Thinking back to the winded truck driver being unable to catch us in Sodus, my friend and I (both PE teachers) drove leisurely back to the area where we were hit and parked just out of view of the kids. We then leisurely walked up to the area where the throwers were gathered and for some reason they did not connect us with their previous attack.

Remembering my youth all we did was ask the kids to not hit cars. We even threw some with them at a couple of trucks going by trying to hit the trailers. This seemed to be one of those teachable moments that worked out.

They were not "bastards," nor were they going to be felons. As an adult with my own perspective on winter "fun," I merely put myself in their boots that day. It was fun catching them using our stealth technology of walking casually toward them rather than charging after them.

Fortunately, the truck driver back in Sodus did not employ the same tactics. I'll bet he threw snowballs at trucks when he was little!!

***

Lester Harrison—A Royal and a friend's new name
Les Harrison was a successful businessman in the business of sport. Back in the early days of the National Basketball Association

at the mid-century mark, Harrison was a typical owner, general manager and coach. He wore all three hats with the Rochester Royals and was quite successful in what was a small market city. There were other small market cities such as Ft. Wayne, Syracuse, Tri-Cities, and Minneapolis, but they also had to compete with Boston, New York and St. Louis.

The Royals were our regional team, and we traveled to see them play many times during their stay in the nearby city. As the years went by we were able to mingle with the Royals in many ways. On some occasions, they would send a player or two to an awards banquet for our school athletic program, Les Harrison would come to speak at Rotary or at a banque,t and the whole team came once to our gym to play against a local group called the "Beef Trust."

Les Harrison was smooth, and became very knowledgeable prior to any visit about what to say and what to do to promote our sports and his franchise.

After one visit, we concluded in our circle of friends that our buddy Gib Sergeant reminded us of Les Harrison. Gib was always organizing something; he had been a member of our basketball teams over the years, but had recently switched to management. In his new role as manager, he sat next to the head coach over the last two years of our high school career and performed many functions.

The most critical thing he did for his peers was look out for them when a coach was ill-tempered over something that may have been done or not done. Gib would quietly recommend a course of action short of the bodily harm that might have been called for under the coach we had as juniors in high school.

During our senior year when the coach was new and much more enjoyable as a coach, Gib's range of opportunities expanded. Much like his namesake Les Harrison up in Rochester with the pro Royals, Gib started making coaching suggestions to Swede Erwin, our new coach. In that realm Gib was able to influence certain decisions during games and practices. Coaches always vent to someone near them, and there was Lester Jr. right there for the asking.

Gib was an excellent soccer and baseball player and we all

enjoyed his new role as manager of our team in basketball. Here was a fellow athlete who was more than a figurehead/gofer for the coach to use. In fact, Gib wisely delegated the mundane duties associated with the team in the uniform realm to an assistant. His assistant was the more traditional manager type, and we had no problem "dumping" uniforms on the floor and doing what we felt like since Peter Moore was the recipient of all of that. Peter was a more typical manager type in that he did not play sports and had other interests not related to the sport world in which we lived night and day.

Gib went on to raise a bunch of athletes of his own and serve as a counselor for decades in the school system. His experience dealing with the fine line between coaching, playing and managing served him well over the years.

Anyone who could placate tough, hard-nosed Slim McGinn, who was our basketball coach during Gib's first year of managing, and then make the overnight adjustment to the personable, laid back Swede Erwin our senior year had to have instinctive counseling abilities!

Lester Harrison (Sodus style) became a fixture in the fun times we shared growing up in Sodus. Because his father and mother were so deeply involved with life and death in the community in their roles as Town Clerk and registered nurse, Les knew a lot about what was happening. We always could go to him to get an inside view in to something we may have heard about through our own pipelines of info.

In our own particular senior class, someone pointed out that they had not seen a class with so many parents having key titles and roles in a community. Upon graduating from Sodus it was evident that our collective parental involvement was unique. At graduation in 1956 at Sodus the parents observing graduation that day in June included: Principal, Vice-Principal, numerous teachers, mayor, doctors, lawyers, town clerk, registered nurses, ministers, and of course many fine adults occupying key positions in business, utilities, and farming.

It seemed back then that every parent had a connection with

their kids, the community, and with a thing called community integrity.

Les represents the actual core of Sodus and what was and has been good about it over the years. He pays his taxes, represents his school and family whenever it is called for, and also has spent his productive lifetime being a fixture in his home town. Fortunately, there are many Gibs around the United States to make a difference in their communities. Gloomily, we need many more now.

Among Gib's claim to fame is that he has many relatives, and at times that was a good thing in a small town. Most of his relatives lived within throwing distance of the Village of Sodus. In times when young guys and gals needed a guiding hand it was always quicker if it turned out to be a relative. In my case it became more of a challenge for me to exhibit good behavior when my father's mother and father moved out of Rochester to Sodus late in their lives and during my teenage years. My grandmother now had access to pipelines of raw data on my activities she had never had in Rochester. She activated that information network upon arrival, and I began to get an idea of how Gib had juggled his pranks and normal adolescent behavior with the knowledge his grandmother lived across the street from him!

As an era passed in the N.B.A., and Les Harrison sold the team he had nurtured over the years. We in the group of hellions (as the good Judge Parsons referred to us over the years) gradually drifted apart geographically and demographically. We could always come back to a common ground at any reunion through the efforts of our team manager—Les.

***

The Invasion of the Girl Scout Camp—Who said to leave?

The camp had been called something else over the years. It finally was taken over by the girl scouts of the area. It was located on a prime piece of real estate along the Lake Road leading to our summer "Mecca" of Sodus Point. The fact that we traveled past the area in cars, busses or on our bikes as a regular routine seemed to dull our senses to the possibilities inherent in the location. We were going to frighten those scouts.

We liked girls, but felt they needed some degree of hazing. Our Cub Scout and Boy Scout training often involved traveling to camps located quite far away from Sodus. This probably was done for many good reasons, but the best one was to get all the prospects located at one site and then watch over them carefully. The best-known camp for Boy Scouts was called Eagle Island, right in the middle of Sodus Bay. Since it was an island, the clients were easy to manage back then. Islands worked wonders for control and management principles. Nowhere, however, did the Boy Scouts train us for girls. The camp for girls' right under our noses was like a beacon of adolescent light. We were the moths attracted to such a light.

After a period of insensitivity to the potential overlooked in days past, we came to a conclusion. We must travel to the area sometime. The trip would best come after dark when our advantages would appear to be increased. Plans for using flashlights and stealth were part of the mission. It all started coming together.

Those of us involved knew we needed to go after dark so the counselors would not know who we were. Darkness would be our friend. Many of the counselors were our female friends and classmates. There were some other older girls in the camp staff. Our intent was to scare the younger campers and leave the counselors to sort out the after-effects of the raid. We were into military jargon since our childhood extended through the nation's involvement in two wars. We called it a "raid." It was to be a hit and run affair—with the emphasis on the run part.

After getting up the nerve to carry out our plan, we covered ourselves with a story involving a drive-in movie. After that fateful first step came the trip to the Lake Road. The car was secured on a side road. Using flashlights, we walked across the highway and down the steep incline to the stream's bed, around which sat the campground. Our ears picked up noises of the other gender. This, then, was the target of the mission. Those voices would be screaming soon in response to weird noises coming from us if all went the way we wanted it to.

The dark was a problem. Our flashlights gave us away on the trip down the steep incline. Using the flashlights became a nuisance. They gave away our approach. Once we switched them off, our eyes were no longer accustomed to the dark. Either way we were cooked, because walking through a wooded area at night was difficult. The surprise element had disappeared.

We gave our approach away. The campers were tipped off to a "band of brothers" coming their way. No noise from us was going to scare anybody. The Girl Scouts were not going to be fearful of us that night. If anything, their counselors performed admirably under the stress of the "attack." As we boys shared the peril of slippery footing, exposed root systems on trees, moss, and dead limbs snapping like crazy, the whole scene shifted from offense to defense.

One or more of the counselors yelled that we should get away from the camp since we did not belong there. To make matters worse, the girls from Sodus started yelling names into the dark, wooded area where we were beginning a hasty exit. Our attack turned into a hasty exit. Over our shoulders we heard familiar names echoing through the dark. "We know it's you Jake, we know it's you Bob, hi Charley, hi Herbie," and so on. They were brilliant girls. Our classmate Judy Rowe "knew" it was us. She was yelling our names.

The attack to scare them had turned into a disaster for us. Going up a slippery hill through the woods in the dark was a nightmare. Using flashlights now with abandon, we raced away from the site. There was no enjoyment on our part that night. We were the victims and our surprise for the girls became humiliation for us.

Later we heard tales from some of the counselors about hearing us in the woods that night. They said they chased us off. They relished the story since it proved, again, the superiority of the female sex over us. Our response was quite predictable.

We never admitted we were there that night. We did not have

any idea what the counselors were talking about. Our cover story for that night was the drive-in movie and we stuck with it. There was no reason to grovel in the harsh reality of an attack gone amok!

***

Sammy's Condoms—True or false?

The story was floated that one of our classmates employed at one of the drug stores in town was putting pin pricks into condoms, making them suspect as tools of sexual security. This was pure fantasy, according to the one who knew best. Sammy Jr. said he did not do the pin prick thing. Would he trick us and those men in the village depending upon a reliable condom? Would the Trojan be as good as its reputation?

We can let go of that particular story, but there were other stories running rampant in the village about the sexual encounters of the rich and famous. There were also stories about the not-so-rich and the not-so-famous. This chapter isn't an attempt to turn Sodus into a Peyton Place. That isn't the purpose of the book. It doesn't make sense to tell things I do not know and which, at the time, were rather far-fetched anyway.

It dawns on me now, given the fifty years in between my grandfather status and my adolescence, that a lot of sex was discussed and even bragged about. If all those sexual encounters discussed were real, they would have to have shortened the school day to accommodate all the sex and the other scheduled activities like sports. We did not see ads every day on TV for Viagra and Levitra. We also did not see any programming such as exists today showing vivid portrayals of sexual activity. When we went to a movie there was no PG or X rating. Everyone saw the same movies, and they were mild in a sexual sense.

But we were horny little devils back then. That lasted many years. It was the age of innocence running smack dab into the age of adolescence.

There were teenage pregnancies, but those were so limited in number that we can still name them at reunions on the fingers of one hand. There may have been illegal abortions back then, but we did not hear anything about those. There was a rumor once that a girl induced an abortion on herself by consuming some weird concoction of chemicals. It did not sound convincing then, nor does it now. If one believed all he heard in Honk's and the locker room, then everyone was sexually active.

Of the teenage pregnancies, one produced a senior year marriage for one of our friends, "Hunter" Clark. He did the honorable thing, however difficult it was as at the time. He was a fine basketball player and was graduated on time. He married the young lady a year ahead of him in school so she, also, was able to graduate prior to their wedding. George graduated on time despite taking a lot of verbal abuse from various people who did not quite grasp his greatly changed life. The person who gave him the most grief was Slim McGinn, our PE teacher and ex-coach during our senior year.

He asked George continually why he looked so haggard and why he was tired all the time. Another comment he made was very sarcastic. It was made in front of gym classes with thirty guys lined up getting words of advice from the garrulous gym teacher. The comment was that George could not possible wear out his newly found sex partner even though he was trying to do so. George took it in good humor and it seemed that old Slim was always good for a "boys only" type laugh or lecture.

An unusual pregnancy evidently occurred during one of our high school basketball seasons. One local cheerleader, who was friendly but not blessed with abundant beauty, was carrying a child created when her egg was fertilized by a star basketball player from another community. After the fertilization, our cheerleader grew into her pregnancy. The handsome young man responsible for the sperm appeared to lose his touch on the basketball court. This was good for us in basketball.

In his usual graphic analysis, Slim was heard to say that such a trade of services by our cheerleader(s) served the purpose of weakening opposing athletes. This struck him as a fair exchange. Others in both communities passed judgment on the coupling in less than flattering terms. In the real world of the boys' locker room, we assessed that it had to have been a mistake.

How the mistake occurred was a matter of conjecture since the villages were quite close but it was winter after all. One did not simply attend a dance and fertilize an egg at intermission in the cafeteria. Some of the sage older boys guessed that the star athlete from our rival school was either drunk (a rarity for an athlete in the 1950s) or he fell into a deep sleep while visiting a friend's house in our village and was compromised. That's when our cheerleader saw her opening, so the story goes. If the guy was awake and had his visual senses, the story went, there was no way he would allow himself to share the moment. I repeat that our girl was not our prettiest.

My buddy Gib called things quite frankly and with a possibility for accuracy. He theorized the lights went off at a party and the rival athlete crossed the room in the dark and grabbed a person he thought was somebody else. His haste in the dark using a punctured condom from the Sodus drug store allowed the sperm to travel farther than desired. Sammy Jr. had a technical assist in the matter. That, of course, is merely an opinion from five decades ago.

***

Streaking in Rochester—A future principal

The distance from our boat, docked in the Rochester Marina on the Genesee River, to the end of the dock was about fifty feet. Once again we were on a Lake Ontario cruise—compliments of George and Elsie Parsons. On the Rochester trip we were a male-only type cruise, and that created the climate for the challenge extended to a friend called "Deacon." His real name shall remain unmentioned unless he gives this away or unless that nickname is resurrected by one of his peers.

Our brave guy took a dare and completed a naked run down the dock at twilight one night and dove into the water at the end of the run. The boats berthed along the dock were populated by vacationers and fishermen, so the run did not go completely unnoticed. After the dive, into the relative security of the water, our man Deacon slowly made his way along under the dock until he could crawl aboard our yacht. He was proud of his accomplishment, and we were proud of our naked ninja.

As a future high school principal, Deacon's selective streaking of his youth merely gave him great insight into the behavior patterns of young people. In all of our travels together, we never put ourselves in serious harm. Our pranks were fascinating given the reflection of nearly fifty years. Others may give the pranks and dares some other descriptor, but we relished Deacon and each other as we shared our lives.

We had a good time almost every day in or out of school. Summer provided us with a wider geographical range for our activities. Those of us traveling with the Parsons visited special places up and down the lake and up in Canada. Even today, as I open up an atlas, memories come flooding back when the pages marked "Ontario Province" flip open. My wife and kids have heard so many stories about Canadian capers that the publishing of this book will probably force them to hear the stories all over again. We were called "Hellions" by Elsie and George Parsons. We are protected by two significant factors. Number one: Elsie is a kind, generous person who graduated from Sodus in 1939. We share the Sodus heritage. She witnessed our behavior through the years but has never disclosed the stories regarding all the future teachers, doctors, lawyers and businessmen frequenting her yacht. Number two: we managed to keep our activities well within the realm of legal parameters. Her husband was a judge and a lawyer.

Any streaking was offset by helping little old ladies across streets somewhere. Pranks and unusual behavior seemed balanced by the fact that we showed up in church with our mothers quite regularly. This was a brilliant strategy, since our mothers were really highly respected ladies. Who could second-guess any of us when we respected our mothers as we did? This respect was quite obvious as we moved through our formative years. My mother would continually tell me to never do anything she wouldn't want to see. She also threw in the one about having clean underwear.

The underwear thing was quite common for mothers in our generation, and I usually tried to keep my underwear clean. However, it was very hard to imagine my mother being able to see "everything" I did through my teenage years. Perhaps that is why she didn't go on double dates with me. Perhaps that is why none of the mothers, other than our friend Elsie, went on cruises with the Hellions.

***

Charley's New Salute—Future teachers

My little brother Charley was an absolute delight to our family. Although we were all convinced he was an accident, he was a great accident. Many of my friends thought Charley looked like Beaver Cleaver from the "Leave it to Beaver" TV program. Charley was a tremendous asset to the family and a source of great joy. He was also the guinea pig for some of the educational experiments performed by Gib, Jake, Sammy, Kingston, Neal, Ken and others. Many of the experimenters moved on in their lives to become teachers, so my brother Charley must have given them fertile grounds for future practices.

One of the more interesting things they taught him occurred when Charley was in kindergarten and we were in high school. There was a twelve-year separation between me and Charley, so he was a novelty to me and my friends. During kindergarten the little kids would move through the school at times in a long double line. The teacher was usually up front leading. Early in Charley's kindergarten career he showed the older boys he was trainable. The teacher was at the front of the line so she could not see Charley's new signal.

My friends had spent some quality time with the little tike and convinced him that whenever he saw me or them in the school he should immediately let us know he spied us by waving one finger at us. This would be a secret little signal between friends he was told.

For the greater part of a week as Charley came and went in the double line with the teacher up front he signaled to all his friends from the high school. His signal always brought big smiles to his friends, and he enjoyed this recognition by the big boys.

Sometime or other this new ritual was witnessed by another teacher who reported it to the teacher at the head of the pack. She asked the principal (who else?) to help put an end to the ritual by talking to the big boys. The kindergarten teacher was a woman of the world, and recognized the single finger signal for something else. She related to her five year old that he should not get that signal mixed up with a wave. The wave was more appropriate, she told him. I know because she came and told me that also.

Somewhere word filtered down to the aspiring "teachers" and me that the work with the kindergarten boy related to me must stop. We all realized that however humorous the "signal" was to older kids, it had no place in a primary school. We all saw and admitted the wisdom of that so no one got the usual "board of education" associated with discipline problems in the school. At least no one got the paddle for that transaction. The principal merely waited for the proper time to seek his revenge.

Little Beaver Pearson was not warped for life and is, in fact, quite normal. The aspiring teachers in the student ranks have all gone on to fine careers. They were not warped either. I was able to see some lessons in all of this. The obvious one was to keep high school kids away from the innocence of the primary school unless the high school students are there to really help with the kids.

Another really practical lesson from Charley's experience has applied to moving lines of students through schools from one place to another. Even today when I instruct student teachers, I encourage them to move up and down the lines they form so that they can see front and back and middle of each line they are moving. The kindergarten teacher probably could have snipped the episode mentioned right there in the bud the first time the "wave" occurred. She also could have seen the boys behind the training and could have given them better insight into kindergarten behavior.

No one overreacted to the situation, and even Francis Samuel seemed tolerant of the people involved at that time. There was a capstone to my career at Sodus that I think was related to the fact that I allowed my friends to subvert my brother. I say I think here because there never was a direct link to the wave and what happened later in the school year.

As President of the Student Council, I would lead the school in the Pledge of Allegiance done prior to any ceremony in the school auditorium. One day during my senior year, and after I thought I had been reformed as a smart ass by way of the physical urgings of the principal, I gave the pledge from the stage. There were steps on either side of the stage and this was the route I took upon going up to perform as student leader. Upon concluding I merely hopped off the stage and took my seat in the front row with my class.

After the auditorium ceremony concluded, I was paged to the principal's office. He said that I had been disrespectful to Mrs. Ingeson, the music teacher who was leading the performance that day, by jumping off the front of the stage. I should have taken the steps. He concluded that I would have to apologize to the music teacher. He also informed me that I should lean forward over his desk for one to make sure I appreciated the need for decorum in the school.

This had to have been a record of sorts for a student government leader during his or her senior year. I think, even today, that big Sam was getting a last lick in on my butt for the waving incident and for old time's sake.

***

Fruit and Veggie Car Tosses—Carry-over values were accidental

Sometimes things just happen in one's life with no planning, no purpose and no real carry-over values. There were times when my friends and I would embark upon some activity and events merely unfolded and we ended up doing something spontaneous but totally unplanned. Our car rides in a car loaded down with fruit and vegetables is a good case in point. These rides started out as target practice, pure and simple. Sometimes we ended up much better than we had started. Since none of us met an untimely demise in such joy rides we conclude, given the benefit of many years, we were protected by some lucky co-pilot.

The rides became a metaphor for our existence, it seems, because we always appeared to surface safe and sound doing something more productive or more in keeping with our age group expectations. One such time, we started out hellions and we returned to Sodus as scholars. This occurred when we stopped by teacher Bob Meneely's home during one of our rides. He was there, invited us in and ultimately took us out of the village in his automobile for a snack, and talked to us over food about the upcoming history Regents Exam. This exam was given in schools across the state in the spring of the school year. We would never have predicted this when we went out together "to play cards at someone's home." Meneely was a popular teacher, and an interesting mentor for the study of history.

Another interesting outing started one way and ended up with a large group gathered at a neighbor's house listening to his war stories. He never predicted our visit that night would evolve in the manner it did. In the two hours spent with us, the host showed us photos he had taken during the European war. After such revealing conversation, the man's wife said she had never seen the photos, nor would he speak of those times. How did all this transpire? We pulled in the guy's driveway to pick up the man's son—who was not there. While waiting for the son, the photos came out. When the son came in, he joined us in our history lesson from his father.

The same friend took me sailing in his Lightning-class sailboat in Sodus Bay. After an hour of glorious sailing in the bay, he said we should ride up to the St. Lawrence with his family and tow the boat along in order to sail it in the famous river. That started on a whim and turned into one of the greatest experiences of my young life. After arriving at the village of Alexandria Bay, New York, located on the St. Lawrence River, we launched the sailboat as his parents set up in a campground near the boat ramp. We were about to sail on the river for a couple of hours and then return for supper.

After an hour out on the river near some famous islands, we encountered a sudden change in weather. We were near Boldt Castle on one of the Thousand Islands when the weather became our adversary. The St. Lawrence River runs swiftly to the northeast out of Lake Ontario and flows to the Atlantic Ocean. Boats coming up-river or against the current are actually coming south/southwest. Most rivers flow north to south, but in New York State there are many interesting exceptions to the rule. The Genesee, Oswego, Niagara and St. Lawrence Rivers are but a few. People must sail or boat against a strong current to reach points southwest from Montreal.

We were being blown up toward Montreal, *down* river from our location, by the weather change. The rain commenced in sheets coming horizontally from the west. Our three sails on the sailboat were ineffective against the strong winds and rain. Sailboats are wonderful boats but when there is too much weather they become wet, wooden difficult vessels. We started taking on water and were drifting down the river.

Out of the storm came a powerful Chris Craft speedboat to tow us to a nearby island. We landed the boat, called the campground where we knew Bruce's parents would be concerned, and then dried ourselves before a giant fire in the Indiana governor's island mansion. This afternoon was memorable as we met the governor, his stunning daughter and attractive wife. When the weather improved, we were towed back to the docks in the village. During our stay, both of us had fallen head over heels in love with the daughter. We spent two or so hours in front of the fire smitten by a Hoosier teenager we would never see again.

In one of life's cruel ironies, she and her family were leaving for two weeks and we were heading back to Wayne County in two days. Neither of us ever saw her again, but her family did save our bacon that stormy day in the river.

Once, when we were in the community center shooting pool and behaving ourselves for a change, we were informed of an opportunity to play basketball in Palmyra in a church league. A bunch of us piled into Don Virts' car and headed to Palmyra to play in an unplanned tourney involving churches in the county. We represented four or five different religions in Sodus but we all became the same religion as the host church in Palmyra in order to get into the tourney. That Saturday we ended up playing two games before heading for home with an impromptu church championship coming out of a pool game in Sodus several hours before. The presence of a youth director, Paul Uher, who had good contacts with recreation leaders throughout the area, led us to a fine experience. Once again, an adult in the right place and right time had provided a window of opportunity through which we, again, traveled.

Our hastily joined team blasted through the two games in the church gym somewhere in Palmyra as we scored over one hundred points in consecutive games. Our same talent in the regular season of high school basketball that same year scored a team-high of seventy-two points. We could not explain the huge scoring of this tourney success because our skills were the same. We were also playing opponents we had seen in the high school battles earlier that year. Nevertheless, we returned home from what started out as a pool game at the recreation center in Sodus, and developed into an NBA-like scoring binge for us in Palmyra. Days such as that don't drop into one's lap very often!

During one outing we were treated to horseback riding at a friend's home when his mother turned up with two horses in a trailer. She thought her kids should learn to ride. I had never ridden before, so this visit to check out Barry Doreen's family house-girl gave us an unintended result. Barry's family owned the local Buick dealership. They had two children and could afford a high school junior as a prominent fixture after school and weekends as a housekeeper. The high school girl had prominent features and our junior high hormones carried us to Barry's house often for a cultural exchange.

In addition to seeing the young lady in her various working outfits we were treated, at times, to glimpses of her as she dashed between bath and bedroom where she stayed when working for the family. At the time we thought that was an accidental sighting of what awaited us later in our horny lives. This train of thought was dispelled later in our lives at a reunion where Barry mentioned the housekeeper Betty. It turns out that Betty loved displaying her prominent features for the horny little friends visiting the Doreen home. She confessed this to the boy she was sitting.

Additional visits to the Buick dealer's home on the ridge gave us chances to drive real cars (used), check out brand new cars as they arrived from the factory, drive motor-scooters and, of course, study anatomy. Later in my life when I had to take Anatomy and Physiology courses, I reminded myself of the junior high school lessons. Somehow they seemed more interesting.

In certain cases merely going out into the community led us to simple, fun things that would have been missed had we stayed inside. Once we shoveled snow for some neighbors at Isabel's urgings, and we ended up getting invited in for hot chocolate and home-made cinnamon rolls. If not for the good deed, my brother and I would never have been in the large home on High Street. On another work-related mission the widow we shoveled for treated us to similar treats. For years after that she bragged on us in church. We were compelled to live up to her expectations of us. Isn't that how high expectations seem to mold behavior?

If we did not go out into the social mix we called growing up in Sodus, we never would have had some extemporaneous experiences that help fill a special portion of a memory bank today. I wonder if kids of today get out enough socially. I also wonder if the community they call home has enough diversions to sway them away from hell-raising to more productive memory-raising.

***

Girl Friends- Good mothers

My school job as a student council member was to deliver the projector during my study hall. I was wheeling the cart carrying the projector through the school's main corridor as Berniece approached from the opposite direction. She was the girl I had met during the summer when a friend tried to fix me up with another girl. Berniece got all my attention that summer day and the other girl became, as they say, history.

I snuck a kiss from the girl right there within fifteen strides of the principal's office in broad daylight. That was a bold, surprising result for what was a routine day up until that point. As we dated after that, the pretty young lady became a prominent part of my coeducational outings for some time. Her mother was a prominent part of my dating cycle also. While Berniece's mother never accompanied us on dates to movies, dances, parties or other activities, she was always a presence. She raised three girls so she seemed to understand boys. She was also a mother at age sixteen, so she knew of other things.

My ex-date became a fine school teacher, and her mother deserves great credit for keeping boys like me from interfering with her completion of high school and her dedication in college. I met up with her while we were attending the same teachers college after my transfer there from Michigan State University. Although I had not seen much of her during the post-high school days, she was a refreshing friend away from home. The young ladies of my home town succeeded in fine fashion, just as did the young men. I happen to know much more about the young men, since we shared so many memories; but girls like Berniece were typical of Sodus. They were nice gals to start with, who then amounted to something better later in life. They developed along the way through their own interesting experiences.

Mothers such as Isabel and such as Gib's, Ted's, Neal's, Gail's and Esther's all played a great role in the shaping their kids and those other kids in the community. When Berniece's mother told her it was bedtime and visitors must leave, I was out of the living room after only one more reminder. If Gail's mother saw us acting foolish in the drugstore where she worked, she would straighten us out as if we were in her home.

Good women come from shaping done when they were good girls growing up. Some young ladies were a bit wilder than others, but most of the wild females seemed to make it successfully after age twenty. So did their male counterparts. Sometimes wild girls and wild guys ended up dating together and that was always an interesting dynamic. They seemed to try to outdo each other, and the romance or friendship flamed out quickly. Some of the best Sodus Point verbal exchanges came during the summer when a lot was evident in the summer heat. People were more casual and wore fewer clothes at Sodus Point during the summer months. In addition to the clothing, personalities changed during the summer. Some girls did a great job of tormenting their control-freak, high intensity boyfriends just by being different in the summer.

Dancing seemed to bring out the wilder side in some people. Boys would act much differently when dancing at Sodus Point in the summer than they behaved dancing in mid-winter in the gym at Sodus. It was the absence of restrictive clothing, I think. That was the same dynamic that separated the exciting female dancers in the summer from those at the proms. I usually spent my dances watching the show and slow-dancing when the opportunity came.

One gal's mother invited boys over to visit their home whenever we were bored. Her daughter Sylvia was one of our good female friends, and although none of us dated her, we enjoyed her company. We also enjoyed going to her house to visit because it seemed like a cool thing to do. The fact that Sylvia's mother was very friendly and very attractive had nothing to do with these visits. We spent equal time in other homes, even with less-pretty mothers prevailing.

Each mother related to our peers had a reputation. My mother was, of course, "Dizzy Izzy." She also had the reputation for providing food at any time day or night. Gib's mother was a registered nurse and was always involved in the current health issues in the community. She was friendly and rather quiet, but was in charge of Lester and her husband, Lawrence Henry.

Any person dating a girl with a dynamic mother got a bonus since things never got boring. Although Pat Parsons was much younger than I was, it seemed that boys of Sodus would be wise to date her since her parents were Elsie and the Judge. They owned a cottage on the bay and always owned a nice boat. Dating Pat would have seemed to be a no-brainer.

I cannot remember dating a girl to gain an advantage in ancillary resources such as cottages and boats. This was probably a tactical error; since it was evident my family was not going to possess a cottage or boat. There was a time in high school when I was invited to a coming-out party for a local girl. It required rental of a tuxedo. I did so and attended the event in Rochester. It was different from anything I had been at before or since.

The debutante's father owned a processing factory and had his name on various cans and frozen goods wrappers. This was a better opportunity than cottage/boat. This was a mansion/factory possibility. As I danced and socialized in the company of Kate and her father, it dawned on me that this life was there like a plum to be picked by the appropriate male. Somebody would eventually take the plunge in Kate's social pool. Fortunately for Kate and me, it was not my choice of lifestyles. She did find a volunteer for the tuxedo crowd a few years later.

Girl friends come and go through the lives of boys. Very rarely does one marry his/her high school sweetheart or steady. It is now apparent that each gender has pre-formed anticipations for these romances. My goals were always simple. These were: fun, simple activities, sport, outdoors, and freedom to run with my buddies at the drop of a hat. Young ladies who write about their younger years probably come up with somewhat similar lists with the addition of one more item. Their mothers should be able to like the young boy that they bring home, since it was the girl's home that entertained boys of my generation.

It wasn't that some girl's mother did not trust Isabel to supervise her son and the visiting daughter in the Pearson house. The girl's mother just felt better with her daughter right there under her nose, ears and eyes.

I was, however, able to sneak that first kiss in as a freshman right under the nose of Sammy's Sodus School Security!

PART FOUR
School

The class of 1956 reacted quite positively to the Sodus world we knew. Many of the events and people flowing through our experiences in Sodus helped shape a conclusion we have made many times over—and that was that something was being done awfully well in the school.

Without much hesitation, many of the graduates in those times had a firm grasp on what was important. The school and its teachers did a hell of a job teaching, mentoring, and being involved in our lives. Among other things, those teachers got to know us as individuals. This was evident by virtue of so many nicknames and so many close ties to the teachers. Whether this is evident in the modern era is debatable.

The forty or so graduates from Sodus Central School in 1956 were typical of classes before and after our graduation in that the graduating members went on in large numbers to successful lives. Many of their names appear on walkways, plaques, and donor lists at the school. A huge percentage of Sodus graduates from that era developed careers in teaching, coaching and services to humanity. Doctors, lawyers, counselors abound from the class lists. Many military success stories evolved from those class lists. Some of our friends and their families have sterling records of service to our nation.

Most graduates did admirable jobs raising their children and passing on values they themselves had learned, in part, in the school system. As reunions came and went, the success stories evolved and were heralded throughout the records of these events. The Sodus Record Newspaper is now combined with the local Williamson

Sun, but the stories of the past decades flow weekly from the newsprint despite having to share news with our old rivals up Route 104. The village and the school did a fine job. The newspaper keeps reminding people of this over the decades.

***

Swede Erwin- A new dimension

Prior to reaching eighth grade at Sodus, if someone had told me I would have a teacher/coach that would shoot hoops with me, tell me jokes, push me to higher expectations by virtue of praise and *be able to pole vault,* I would not have believed him.

But seeing it made me believe it, and there smack in my educational path was Jack Erwin. He was fresh out of teachers college at Brockport via the GI Bill, and came to our school with fresh basketball ideas and a unique classroom behavior. In fact, he was different from any teacher I had ever met. Are there such unique characters in the lives of current students in public schools? If so, such characters are limited in number and are limited by restrictive school protocols and rules. In an era when people shy away from jobs in the turmoil of public schools, the memories of such people as Swede Erwin may become rare.

Jack's nickname among his nearby East Rochester pals was Swede, and they immediately started showing up in our little village to see their buddy coach; and these friends also began telling us things about him. Some we could not use right away and others, like the nickname, we could try out on him without any fear of punishment. This was definitely new for us. It could have been dangerous for any teacher during that era, but we handled our new found privilege with great respect. He became as comfortable to us as a family member, and to basketball players he became our soul brother.

Jack Erwin taught in the junior high school and coached junior high and junior varsity basketball along the way. In our senior year we were able to enjoy our best season at Sodus in many years at the varsity level. Several of us reached within ourselves due to his encouragement and his basketball prowess. We also did some very good things we either couldn't do before, or were not allowed to do, under other coaches. In Sodus basketball, up until Swede appeared it was pretty much understood that our teams would be playing zone defenses. This created some tough situations for us when we were behind and had to play a more aggressive defense to catch up. It also allowed certain opponents the luxury of using some fine outside shooting to jump all over us.

Swede made us play man-to-man defense and also made us think about doing creative, fun things. Without boring the non-basketball readers, suffice to say each of us felt "free" to explore our personal basketball potential. This was done within a wonderful feeling of team effort, and in the closing two months of our senior year we lost but one game and nearly made the sectional play-offs. Our victory over the season champs at their court in nearby Marion late in the season was a sweet one, even though they went on to the play-offs and we didn't! Charley Mossgraber even made a hook shot at home one night to knock of Clyde, a team we had not beaten in seven years! Jack taught Charley to use the hook early in his coaching career. It paid off late in Charley's basketball career. Jack gave Charley the confidence to try the shot and Charley repaid the favor. Charley even stopped much of the stuttering that had confounded his communications during most of our school lives together. The confidence gained via a coach was transferred to real life situations!

Jack Erwin came out for a track and field meet in the spring one time, and much to our surprise he grabbed the pole and ran down the runway in his shirt and tie and vaulted over the bar. He walked away as if this was a daily occurrence for him. For those of us who were his fan club by that time, this was merely icing on the educational cake he had served up to us over the years. He was a breath of fresh air for overactive boys who had come into the junior high with only P.E teacher and coach Slim McGinn and sixth grade teacher Mark Scurrah as our male mentors.

Mark was our first male teacher in a classroom, and we crossed his path after six consecutive female teachers. Mark made an impact but he was a classroom teacher only. Whereas Slim was John Wayne in coaching garb and would not tolerate any nonsense in his gym class or teams he coached, it seemed that Swede was never reluctant to treat us as human beings first and foremost.

This has been a personal philosophy over the years and seems to have worked well based upon feedback from team members I have known and loved. Jack Erwin never felt threatened by adolescent behavior on our part, whereas Coach McGinn was "old school" during the old school days. Of the two coaching mentors I had for much of my Sodus experience, I attribute much of any success I have enjoyed as a coach and friend to students over many years to my coach and friend Jack Erwin. Coach Erwin was honest with us, encouraging at every turn and was the kind of guy who is called "a player's manager or coach" in today's sport jargon. Fortunately, I used his name for one of my sons.

During the fifties, he was way ahead of the coaching curve. In the fifties in Sodus, New York it took a high degree of faith and trust in a bunch of adolescent boys—and a high degree of courage—to raise a little hell with us in the context of our association together. It seems to have worked for him and for us. We still talk of him with humor and respect. He still rags on us and tells us his latest jokes when we get together. Kindnesses extended to young people seem to be good investments in time and energy. Swede Erwin must have a wealth of personal investment memories!

***

John Damn Wayne- Slim McGinn

If John Wayne were a coach at a small school and were to teach physical education classes for all the boys starting in the fifth grade, he probably would come across in much the same manner that Nelson McGinn did during his career in Sodus. McGinn was probably six feet two inches tall and had a ruddy and craggy appearance right out of a western movie.

We started getting physical education classes about fifth grade.

Prior to that we must have had recess and playground games, but I do remember being segregated by gender until about fourth or fifth grade. Nelson "Slim" McGinn did not put up with any horsing around. During the era when he was most prominent in our lives, his forms of teaching, coaching and discipline were accepted by a vast majority of the parents. Our worst fear in Sodus was that word would filter back to the parents about any discipline problems we might have had in school with Slim or any of the teachers. At that juncture our fathers would merely add on to the already administered discipline. There would be none of the second-guessing so common in today's schools.

Parents turned over the kids to the schools and the legal phrase *"in loco parentis"* was alive and well. It meant the school ruled in place of the parents for the school day. That has changed in education in the modern era. The contrast between now and fifty years ago is manifest. Part of the success of the schools back in my childhood can be traced to this concept, now overruled and ignored because of the actions of the ACLU and similar organizations.

Back to our guy Slim McGinn. He definitely had his ways. In basketball season our P.E. classes often consisted of three basketballs, three baskets, and forty boys. As he watched the time go by during such a class he probably formulated his scouting reports on the basketball abilities of the young boys. He could probably tell who was able to rebound and who could shoot the ball better than others as a result of the melee he created under the guise of a class. He would no doubt make mental notes about aggressive behavior—something he rather enjoyed in his teams.

I say all this now after having spent many classes fighting for loose balls and fighting for shots at the three baskets during such classes. When he retired from coaching, such gym classes diminished. According to students who came along when Slim was out of coaching, such trials by fire were a rarity. According to some, Slim himself actually got a bit mellow in his last years as a teacher.

Slim would run basketball practices with an iron fist. He would work the heck out of his boys, and much of the practice time would be spent on playing zone defense and perfecting his two-three zone. The second team would play against the zone played by the starters. This was great for the confidence of the starters, since the small school student body did not allow for much depth of talent on any team. The first team in any team sport could easily handle the second team almost any day in practice. Upon reflection, this worked against us at times, because we did not get enough trial by fire against strong opposition. We often played sixteen to eighteen games and did not have pre-season scrimmages against other teams. This was probably due to the overlap in soccer and basketball. We often went from soccer right into basketball without much of a pause. When McGinn coached all the sports, this was a year filled with Slim and his coaching tactics. Bare-fisted fights were allowed on occasion when Slim felt the two opponents needed this outlet. I never went for that, and was chagrined when I witnessed such an activity in our gym under the approving gaze of the coach.

We perfected a zone defense in basketball against less skilled players on our team, and when faced with a team of our equal or better they went through our zones easier than our substitute players could. It makes sense now, but it took a while to make that connection. Considering that we played offense against a second team playing a zone, we also suffered from a false sense of actual ability against a zone. Many teams played a man-to-man defense against us, and we were often ill-prepared for such a thing. For you see we spent an inordinate amount of time playing zone and playing against a zone in practice. We rarely practiced against man-to-man nor did we use it very often. Such details might be remedied in the modern era by a coaching specialist in basketball. When a coach coached all the sports at a school, it did not leave much room for specialization and detail work. In defense of McGinn, this was his case. It also showed a bit of arrogance to think opponents would not throw all kinds of man-to-man at us, which they ultimately did.

Our man-to-man reputation was not very good, and not until a change in coaches occurred in our senior year did Sodus really commit to something other than Slim McGinn's zone mentality. A person could talk basketball in the barbershop in Sodus and before two sentences were out the words McGinn and zone would be used. The barbershop scene in the movie "Hoosiers" accurately portrayed what went on in Sodus and many communities during basketball seasons.

Another thing about Slim was he lived during the Second World War, and whether he ever served in the military I do not know. What I do know is that he emphasized military training for the P.E. classes many weeks out of our school year for many years. This curriculum included close order drill for hours on end, running long runs around fixed courses, rope climbing, and horizontal ladder work. We never knew anything different, so we did it under the steady, approving gaze of the autocratic P.E. teacher.

None of us ever rebelled about all of that, because there was no rebellion back then. What seemed to doom every succeeding class to this military-type fate was the annual return of some alumnus from the school who would tell, truthfully, how vital the military training he had received during his high school years had been now that he was in the military. Many from Sodus went to the military. That would just put another in the notch in old Slim's military belt, and away the classes would go again in close order drill.

I experienced R.O.T.C. military training during the year when I attended Michigan State University in the fifties. I excelled at all aspects of the routines due to the training I had in Sodus. I did vow *not* to return to Sodus gym classes to brag about my prowess in R.O.T.C. in a small attempt to not be part of the "renewal" efforts on the part of military training in the gym at Sodus.

Once during one of my first high school basketball games under the coaching of McGinn, I had thrown a wild baseball-type pass the length of a gym somewhere in Wayne County. The pass had hit far up on the wall above the outstretched hands of the intended teammate. In the particular gym the teams sat on a stage edge across the gym floor from where all the auditorium-type seats were located. It was a gym/auditorium and seemed to be very popular at the time. The only problem was that the teams sat on the edge of the stage with their legs dangling off the stage. The players on the floor were within arm and leg reach of the substitutes and coaches. Sometimes legs from one team could slow down an opponent. Sometimes coaches could actually reach their team members.

After seeing my wild pass go astray I ran towards the other end of the gym to get into the typical zone defense posture. Before I reached mid-court I was removed from the game. I mean I was *removed* from the game physically by the strong arm of Nelson McGinn. He grabbed me bodily and yanked me onto the stage. A substitute was already going to center stage where the scoring table was in its elevated position, but for that moment we were playing a man short. Actually, we were playing a boy short. I remember being very shocked. The coach asked me why in hell I had done that pass. That shocked me, too, because I did not intend for it to be wall-bound and certainly did not do it on purpose. The question, therefore, had no logical answer. I don't remember what I said since I was in shock.

Coach McGinn did not suffer fools lightly, nor did he have much patience. This impacted upon me all through my own coaching career because I became the opposite of the man in many areas of coaching. I never felt I reached any satisfying level of performance under the man in any sport at Sodus; and I vowed this should not happen to a young man under my direction in coaching. McGinn was typical in the era of hard-nosed, no nonsense coaches, however.

On another occasion during practice, I turned to run at full speed in another direction in our gym and I ran smack into Coach McGinn. He was firmly planted, I guess, because I was knocked out and he evidently was not even budged according to his report later. I suffered some bruises on my face and was stunned. He seemed quite impressed that I "knocked myself" out for him in practice and for a long time he bragged about "Mayor's" hustle in practice. When I heard those stories attributed to him, I was quite proud in some perverse way. The guy just did that to us.

During some P.E. classes he would play volleyball with us.

Even at an advanced age of perhaps forty or fifty, Slim could still play volleyball. When you were against his team you were always on the lookout for one of his spikes. He could slam a spike down on your side of the net with great force. More than once, boys were bleary-eyed from a volleyball in the face. This was just another part of Slim's reputation.

One time in the heart of winter when I was in the junior high and still removed from his coaching scrutiny, I was walking alone to school in a heavy snow. Coach McGinn stopped to pick me up in his car and I finished the ride to school with the knowledge that it was me he had picked up and no one else on the long, open stretch of walk to the school. Although there were many walkers that day, I got a ride.

He could not have known it was me since under the winter coats and hats of the time no one was recognizable. I guess he chose one out of the many kids that day to show a touch of humanism in a career of toughness. To this day I am not sure why he stopped for one kid and no others. He did have a more mellow side, but it was not visible by many of us at that time. We heard later that when he drank with friends, was in his own home or with his wife, he exhibited a gentler side.

Every educational possibility in one's life cannot be engineered by an advocate of the John Dewey, learn by doing, humanism so desired in our teachers. I am sure Coach McGinn was a product of tough times, and he felt compelled to prepare his charges for real life. I can recognize that even if I did not prefer his touch as a coach.

After Coach McGinn had passed away, I was asked to speak to the graduating class at my home school. During the previous year a new gym was built at the school and Nelson McGinn's name was to be placed on the gym to honor him. Without hesitation I turned back the check that was offered for my appearance at graduation and told the superintendent to apply it toward the McGinn Fund.

I could still reflect positively upon what the man had done for me. He could have picked up any of the kids walking in the snow that one day but he got me. I thought about that when I signed the check over to the memorial fund.

***

Hey Dority!—A slap in the face

John Dority asked me what I had said as he moved down the length of the dugout toward me. I merely repeated, "Hey Dority, when is the umpire getting here?" For that repeated indiscretion, I was slapped once across the face.

John Dority was a history teacher at the high school, and I was a seventh grader working as an assistant to my older brother Dick, who was the manager of the baseball team. Dority was also the school baseball coach. He merely told me that, until I reached the high school status of the older boys, I should call him *Mr.* Dority.

I had already received the first of three Sodus career-paddling jobs during the seventh grade school year. That one and the other two were administered by the giant right hand of our two hundred sixty pound principal Francis Samuel Hungerford. The slap across the face was brief and less painful physically than the multiple applications on my butt by the maple paddle owned by the huge principal. The slap stung my pride, but it was 1951 and seventh graders took their blows at school and prayed no one at home got the word of any slap or paddling. If word were to reach home, more of the same would result.

I never called Mr. Dority anything except Mr. Dority, even when I was an upperclassman. The slap stayed with me well into high school. Mr. Dority coached many of us in basketball for a season and was baseball coach until our senior year. Just when we thought we were out of the frying pan of Dority's occasional temper, we got old Slim McGinn as baseball coach our senior year. Dr. Spock and the ACLU might shudder at some of the sport-related indelicacies delivered by these coaches during their careers at Sodus, but during the fifties that was acceptable.

Dority and McGinn reflected what was quite common across the land. Young men playing sports in the aftermath of World War

II and during the Korean Conflict were treated to the rude and sometimes harsh reminders of adulthood during sports experiences. Often McGinn would remind athletes of the greater battles going on in the real world. He figured boys should be ready. This accounted for the close order drill in his PE classes. This logic accounted for the paddling and even the occasional slap. Schools were different then.

Although I screwed up and called the coach by his last name in the dugout, I still was treated as a key member of the baseball group representing our village on diamonds around the county. As a seventh grader I learned about baseball from the older boys and Dority. He seemed to be an involved coach and the team usually did quite well. He never had to slap me again; but I do remember a time when he got irritated at the team during an indoor practice one rainy spring day. The practice was probably going poorly. People could tell this by looking at a red-faced Dority. He ordered the team to run lengths of the gym.

Experts in this type of thing in the modern era make sure any running done in a gym is done by touching lines and going back. Never should anyone run as hard as they can *across* the end lines of a gym and then into the end walls. The problem with that scenario is that the wall can stop the hell out of a running teenage ballplayer. We raced across the end lines several times and by the time we were done easing Dority's pain, we were hurting in our wrists, arms, shoulders and knees. It seemed that the competitive juices flowed, and in an attempt to appease the coach many ran with abandon into the end walls. Although they were padded in some places, the bare tile and brick walls were not forgiving.

The head coach ended up with a diminished return on that punishment because several were temporarily injured. In addition to slapping smart-ass seventh graders, Dority was typical of many in the coaching ranks back then.

As a seventh grader with the team I had some monumental moments that spring. Among other things I got to learn how to drive an old truck with a flatbed for baseball tools and lawnmowers. I was assistant manager of the team, and this meant Dority somehow got me out of the last period of the day so I could get the field ready for games and practices.

I learned how to drive when Case Weist, my buddy in the custodial department, gave me the key to the old truck and told me to drive it slowly from around behind the school out to the field. My brother crapped when he came down one day to see me shifting my way through the gears using the old-fashioned high shift stalk coming out of the old floorboards. I was on the way to the field with Case's blessing and I was light-years ahead of my peers up in the study hall! Dority had signed my excuse and I was in hog heaven.

My driving trips to the field were short-lived. Somebody mentioned to FSH (Francis Samuel Hungerford) that a seventh grader was practicing driving out on the road in front of the school. Although Case had given me the key and I had been driving for a couple of weeks, I merely told the principal that I took it upon myself to get the truck with the stuff on it to the field early so the work could get done. I did not rat on Case. I did not get a paddling. Big Sam, as we referred to the principal, seemed impressed with my grapefruit-sized balls and let me go with a warning not to drive anymore until I was older. He liked baseball. That literally saved my ass!

Sodus provided teachable moments often. I was a capable manual transmission jockey from the seventh grade, so that when I got into drivers education in high school I was prepared to shift gears. If a lad can shift a floor-mounted stick shift, anything else coming later is simple. I always considered my relationship with Case a blessing. I also considered that Dority and Case gave me a license to drive as a seventh grade. I got to hang out with the baseball team. I got out of study hall, got to drive a truck, learned baseball signals and strategy, and learned about teamwork.

It never crossed my mind that Dority did me wrong with the slap across the chops when I was a seventh grader. It was probably earned many times over by virtue of the things I did and got away with over the years.

Upon reflection, the slap could have saved my life somewhere along the line during all those times when I owned a four speed automobile and drove too fast. I could shift with the best of them. If it weren't for Dority's shaping and my ability to take his gruffness, I would not have been getting out of study hall when I did. It all helped me learn how to drive!

***

Francis Samuel—A formidable figure

How many school principals can throw in a two-handed set shot from mid-court on the first try? Francis Samuel did just that one day in the Sodus gym during the pep rally for the basketball teams. Another time, he was at a Little League dedication and he swing a bat at one pitch and drilled it over the outfield fence. It was a short fence at two hundred feet, mind you, but he required only one swat. The Swing Choir was comprised of students, faculty and alumni. Take a guess as to who anchored the bass section of the choir? You guessed it. None other than Francis Samuel Hungerford.

Our principal was an imposing figure and ran the school with a strong hand inside a soft glove. There was a vice-principal to deal with counseling and advising for college, but the principal ran the school. There was no superintendent then, and the Board of Education gave the principal free reign to operate as he saw fit. There was no second-guessing going on in the Sodus School System under the direction of Hungerford.

There is nothing at all similar to what we had fifty years ago in Sodus in the modern era. There are many administrators and too much back-stabbing and meddling by parents who do not seem to know how to raise their own kids. Almost everything wrong with kids today traces back to parents over-indulging and screwing up kids at early ages. The lack of discipline in the homes is reflected in the schools. The poor parenting or lack of parenting shows up glaringly in the schools. As we seek to find remedies for the problems in the schools, we seem to focus on the school.

As a teacher with forty-five years of experience, I say here and now that the problem is in the home.

Mr. Hungerford ran a tight ship, and depended upon excellent parenting during the hours when the school was closed. In the modern era we have village idiots raising unwanted children, who then get a lawyer and run to the school board when things go wrong at school. If Hungerford could come back and witness the evolution of his job at Sodus or elsewhere, he would no doubt be astounded by the encroachment into his power base by what my Dad would call idiots and do-gooders.

The liberalization of schools in America has been a profoundly effective way to diminish the power of the schools and the success of the schools. In Sodus, whatever Samuel Hungerford wanted—within reason—he got. He led by example whether singing, throwing in the mid-court shot or hitting a baseball. The school board was an extension of his power and served to liaison between parents, who cared and trusted the school, and the school itself. Not everyone liked the principal, but he sure had their respect and trust. Parents could visit the school and did so often for events. People were involved in the school in positive ways.

The lawyers in town were busy with wills, real estate deals, and contracts and yes, some divorces. The lawyers were not involved in the business of the school. Times have truly changed, haven't they?

Hungerford would prowl the hallways looking for things that needed his attention. He was a constant and supportive figure at games, dances, and musical events. His principalship was marked by awareness of all around him. He did not sit in his office and try to manage. F.S. was out and about in the school many hours a day. He managed by the seat of his broad pants and managed effectively. People who taught for him credited him with being fair. Students leaving the school marked him as a powerful figure in their lives.

Today there seems to be an abundance of administrators trying desperately to look good to those higher up the food chain. This posturing-effect, as I refer to it, produces serious morale problems and leaves teachers without strong advocates in the power structure. If the modern administrator fails to represent the little guy, then that administrator is failing in his or her job. Francis Samuel struck a harmony in the school by defending the little people and speaking straight talk to those on the boards. Little people were important.

There were times in the school when certain teachers needed a reminder from the "Boss," as they called him. These reminders might come in the form of a verbal jolt. This was reported to me by teachers when I was no longer a student. A couple of my teacher-friends reiterated that Hungerford was fair and very assertive. The indiscretions of the two were in the area of alcohol-induced behavior out of school but still within the confines of the village. This was always picked up on Big Sam's radar screen, and he dealt with the behavior very quickly and directly. Their drinking was somewhat curtailed, and one of the teachers in question reported to me and others later in our lives that Sam should have fired him but chose not to. The principal saw redeeming values beyond the drinking problem.

I reported in other chapters my dealings with the principal and his paddle. The "board of education" he wielded left an impression on my butt and my life. There were other times when he took an interest in my behavior and he did not need the paddle to press the point home. Once when I was making announcements on the school intercom in my role as student government treasurer, the "Boss" gave me some very crucial tips about speaking in public. He spent fifteen minutes prior to the broadcast informing me of protocol connected to the P.A. system. My time on the device was about thirty seconds a day for a week. I got a lesson in the operation of the P.A. from the Boss.

How many principals do such a service for individual students under their auspices? The Rotary Club used the school facilities for some of their events, and the principal was very active in the organization. He introduced his Rotary chums into the life of the school, and our connections with those professionals in the village made for better lines of communication. He was an active player in a group called the "Beef Trust"—an organization of ex-basketball players who played other old timers in the area on certain nights in the gym. Despite what must have been a busy job for him, the principal was involved many nights a week all year at the school.

As classes came and went in the school, our principal set a great example of how effectively a school could be run. For those of us going into education for our career work, there would be no better lesson than the administration according to Sam. In nearly fifty years of observing administrators and working under many, I conclude none were any better than Francis Samuel.

***

Where Were the Bad teachers?—Best of the batch

During a graduate class I took as part of my M.S. degree work, a question was asked of the class one night that provided insight into my public school education. The professor asked us to list on a page the names and numbers of the teachers we felt were truly outstanding in our educational past. The list could start in Kindergarten and could include all classes anywhere except the current course.

As each graduate student disclosed the list it finally came around to me. Up until my turn, the average number of truly outstanding teachers reported by the others averaged four to five in number. Later the instructor reported that it was his estimate that four or five was about the national average for this type of question.

My response was off the charts contrasted to all other responses. I recorded about fifteen to twenty teachers I felt were outstanding. As a person who became a career teacher, it might have been a "halo" effect I possessed for teachers. It also might have been related to the fact that Isabel was a teacher long ago in another world. I was the same age as my peers in the class, so I knew it was not a product of varied generations. What made my answer so radically different than those of my classmates in graduate school?

My conclusion and the answer to my question was that I truly was blessed in my education and did, in fact, have numerous outstanding teachers. Did Sodus have something unique working for it back when I was in the school system? Yes, it truly did. And it started with the top, where the principal was outstanding. There were board of education members who were responsible citizens and parents in their own right. Most board members reflected three basic facts of life in their service to the community. One, they were parents of kids in school or they had children who were recent graduates of the school. Two, they were farmers, business people and/or property owners (or both) so the success of the school was vital to them. Third, the board members were also graduates of the school, so they had enormous loyalty to the school. These types of boards were typical in the era under scrutiny, but not so typical anymore.

Once hired at Sodus, teachers were surrounded by mentors of all ages and levels of experience. In that era, mentoring was a daily, simple unstructured fact of life. In the modern era mentors are sought and often given compensation or release time. I contend that incidental mentoring allows for greater growth and enjoyment of the development as a teacher. One reason I found more outstanding teachers in my school experience was that the mentors were better back then. There were no unions. There was very little backbiting and little posturing for those in the ranks above.

The teachers of Sodus were career people and without their contribution to the educational network we would not have felt the way we did. There were teachers who taught two different generations of a family. This happens when teachers stay in a community and parents send their kids to the same school. This dynamic has changed in the modern era, but it occurred with regularity in the previous century.

I was fortunate to have several career teachers whose tenures at Sodus were marked by service to the school and the kids. It was a routine practice back then to invite your teachers to important functions in your family. At weddings and funerals, teachers would be present to represent the bond between teacher and student.

As I write this book there are two of my teachers reading and relating their insight into the stories. Although many of their peers have passed from the scene, the ones remaining are still invested in their careers by virtue of staying current, serving in the community and staying in touch with their students.

The lifespan of a teacher appears to be much longer than the average citizen. In studies relating to longevity, experts contend that reading, writing, playing word and card games and staying active all play an important role in longer life spans.

We had teachers who were vitally interested in our activities and proved this by showing up at events in the school year that were not part of their required teaching contract. Several teachers expressed the notion to me that they did their job as a "calling" rather than as a job. This was evident as I reflect upon their uniqueness. I always tell friends, students and especially the administrators I work with that I am never going to retire since my job really is my "hobby." It comes across as simplistic to some—and probably scares the hell out of administrators familiar with my outspoken manner—but nevertheless I am a dedicated teacher.

The experience with those outstanding teachers at Sodus and beyond has generated the ethic within me. I owe those numerous role models and fine teachers a great amount of thanks. If and when I leave teaching, it will still be important to me to follow up on my previous students and show them the spunk shown to me by EBB, Swede, Rubberhead, Big Sam, Coop, Ketch, Gert, Millie, Stelliano, Mark, Vitah, J.D. and all the rest too numerous to mention!

***

Holy Cow—A Mark-ed man in the teacher's lounge

Mark Scurrah came to Sodus after teacher training, yet another ex-resident who returned to teach. He and his family were Soduskans for many years. The returning alumns were a prized commodity, since they not only knew the system but were known in the community.

Mark Scurrah was a departure from the norm in the fourth decade of the previous century. By choosing to teach in the elementary school he became the first male classroom teacher at the Sodus School. This was to be a special claim to fame for us as students. We were his first class of his career.

During his time with us, we were treated to his interpretation of education according to Mark. His connection with boys was very different for us contrasted to the women in education for the previous six years. Women were great, and we enjoyed some very nice teachers, but once Scurrah took over things were very different. Boys seemed to be the gender of choice overnight.

Things must have been different in the teacher's lounge once he arrived. I don't know of his adaptations, but the women sure were forced to alter some routines. When I started my teaching career many years later and was one of two male teachers in an elementary school, my insight into my 6th grade teacher's life in my elementary school became clearer.

Our new teacher read books to us and established an emphasis in reading for every kid in class. Everyone seemed hooked on reading. This was a commendable accomplishment for a new teacher. He also played games with us on the playground, and that was certainly new to all of us. The applications of math and science took on new dimensions for our grade level as we did things differently. He invented games to help us learn math and science facts. Outside our homeroom was a pen filled with eggs that hatched and became chickens. These chickens were sold and the process began again.

Boys are different from girls, and Scurrah made a special effort to turn us into young men prepared for junior high school. He never made any of the girls feel slighted despite his efforts with us. There was no middle school concept back; then so elementary school was K-6, junior high was grade 7 & 8 followed by high school grades 9-12. As sixth graders got ready to go to the junior high level they needed special preparation. We got it from our guy Mark.

Women teachers typically take charge of their school and are territorial in nature. Their territory includes lounges, bulletin boards, classrooms, and even parking spaces outside. Mark Scurrah encountered many such territorial things, I learned later. We never knew it at the time, as he handled the situation with aplomb.

When I visited my first teacher's lounge as a teacher it was shocking to see so many smokers among the teachers at my school. Despite my training with the Sodus male teachers who smoked, it was new strange to me to see so many female smokers. I don't recall how many, if any, of my elementary teachers smoked at Sodus but at Thomas Edison Elementary School in Rochester, most of the women smoked.

The ladies of Sodus were good mentors, however, regardless of whether they smoked or not. Many were fine teachers enjoying distinguished careers. Mark's mother and father were established members of the community, so their son already was accepted by the teaching corps who knew the family. I never asked but probably our 6th grade teacher was a student of one or more of the teachers in the school. I should have explored that notion while he was my teacher. He was a good one!

***

Don't Throw Chalk—Rubberhead strikes

He turned from his position at the blackboard and tossed a piece of chalk so that it landed near the inattentive student. In an American history classroom with thirty students this feat with the chalk was awesome because the thrower was one of the most non-athletic persons in the school. The inattentive student was me at times.

Somebody gave him the name "Rubberhead" due to the uncanny swiveling of his head on his neck that preceded the wakeup chalk tosses. He could be writing on the board and whirl and toss. It had to be an instinctive feeling he possessed. When the chalk flew, it was for good reason. We were in awe of this talent. This teacher was like none other in our experiences.

The chalk never hurt anyone, and when contact was made on someone's head it was deserved. No one ever complained about him to parents as far as we knew. He served many years as a teacher and still teaches part-time. He even became a local board of education member. His real name was Robert Meneely, but over time that was overlooked in favor of the notoriety of the new name bestowed upon him. Respectfully, no one ever threw a piece of chalk back! There were times when we thought we had hidden the supply of chalk, but

Rubberhead seemed to come up with more every time! He could not be beaten.

When he wrote something on the board, that topic was followed closely because we wanted someone else to be a victim of his tossing ability. He captured our attention. He taught American and World History classes that were New York State Board of Regents Exams. This meant the test scores attained by his students in the 1950s were a measure of his success—and our collective success as students. The scores were critical to college entrance, as they still are today. His chalk and our attention created some very good scores. It appears that college-bound students were doing quite well in Sodus fifty years ago due to some good teaching. The state was asking for accountability even back then. The idea is not new to education.

The fun we had in the classes was respectful and in good taste. I also helped us keep from being bored. The fun we had in classes like Robert Meneely's helped us become very knowledgeable about history. Teachers such as he lived just a few blocks away from the central school and were present at most events during the school year. We knew we had teachers who cared about us because they went the extra mile with us many times over. They accompanied our journey through the public school education.

As we prepared for regents exams every spring during high school, teachers would go out of their way to assist us in the time prior to the exams. When the packets with the state exams were opened all across New York State at the same hour, on the exact same day for each particular subject, the Sodus kids seemed to relish the grand opening. We knew we were prepared and were not spooked by the opening of the envelopes. There were times when our teachers invited us into their homes at night for review sessions. This was a great opportunity for us to see a relaxed side of the teachers. This was also great for the students, because we enjoyed the special treatment once there.

I prepare students for national teacher exams offered several times a year at teacher training institutions like my current college. It is rewarding to see the success of the students as they come away feeling fulfilled by their passing scores. They give me credit, in part, because I organize study sessions for them and review past exams that are available in print and on the Internet. They achieve their passing scores because they take study advice to heart and pay attention to what is offered.

Whenever I get such successful feedback from students, I reflect upon the regents exams of my career and the help offered by people like Meneely. It appears that the chalk tossing of yesteryear paid off.

In a broader sense it is rewarding to consider this "passing of the educational chalk." What worked almost fifty years ago still has its impact on me.

I was the recipient of a chalk toss a few times. That bit of attention may have shaped me a bit as a teacher.

***

Periodic Elements —Teacher's favorite

Long before the advent of power-point presentations that are so much in favor in the modern era of education, teachers used other convenient tools. For many years, slide shows and super eight film were big in the classrooms across the country. VCRs took over for slides and super eight movies as more visual experiences entered the educational realm. Now coaches in schools commonly have videos of their teams in action, and these have replaced the more expensive and less practical sixteen millimeter movies of another era.

One science teacher in our school was a good teacher, interesting lecturer, and ran chemistry and physics classes quite ably. His career took off after teaching many years at Sodus by virtue of being hired by a state university college in Oswego a mere forty miles down the road to the east. Paul Shaver spent many years preparing students for the dreaded N.Y. State Regents exams in Chemistry and Physics. His students did so well over the years that his reputation spread to the university level. His competence was recognized in higher education, and away he flew to the university level.

I can remember trying his patience in chemistry labs as

our small group of aspiring chemists, gathered together in a lab group, kept expanding the horizons of caustic smells. Shaver would patiently explain protocols and then turn us lose with lab manuals. He finally realized some of us were merely altering directions from the lab books and coming out with new concoctions. His stoic nature seemed to accept our improvisations. Fortunately for his career—and our lives—we never blew anything up or injured anyone.

There was a piece of his classes that was a constant. The Periodic Table of Elements was hanging in the front of the classroom, and he used the table a lot. On the chart was the atomic weight of all elements known up until that point in time. Since the mid-century there have been additions to the chart, but for us in the early 1950s that was the world according to Shaver.

We did not have to memorize the thing but had to constantly refer to it and be able to explain it when called upon in class. There are modern parallels to the chart in education, but I would bet the old Periodic Table is hanging around Shaver's basement in Oswego where he still lives today. Paul Shaver used the tables regularly, and it reminds me today of my educational peers who depend upon power-point presentations.

As I understand the modern use of power-point, details from readings are outlined in projection form using a computer. By adding graphics and other clever visuals the student sits reading from a screen in the front of the classroom as the instructor lectures. In my current classes I encourage the students to employ the device as they lead me along with their peers through a new lesson. This flip in teaching procedure seems to work for me. Paul Shaver lectured from the Periodic Tables for many classes. His modern counterpart lectured from the projected material appearing in the front of the room. Both methods seemed to work. Shaver pulled his tables down from a rolled-up position over the blackboard and where they were quite secure year after year. The modern teacher pulls out the laptop computer with an accompanying projector and pulls down the rolled up screen. Class begins when the device warms up and if the laptop performs as it should. Assuming the five hundred dollar bulb is still working and, assuming the bulb life left in the projector's bulb is bright enough to be able to read the information on the screen, class rolls along.

No person at Sodus ever considered taking the Periodic Tables home or selling it at the local pawn shop. In fact we didn't even have a pawn shop. The contrast in the modern era is manifest.

Just within the past three months at my small, private college, we have blown a five hundred dollar bulb, had another dim bulb suspend the presentation at a meeting, have had two computers stolen right from our classrooms and had another taken from the hallway in full view of several offices. The cost of similar education appears to be greatly elevated in the modern schools.

Paul Shaver taught creatively from the Periodic Tables, used his labs well, and hosted study sessions for the state exams. We seemed to have done well, despite being deprived of the more modern tools now in abundance. Modern teachers depend upon modern tools whose educational value cannot be disputed but whose economic and security issues certainly create dilemmas. As I wander down the educational trail picking up random observations from contrasting eras, I am drawn to certain conclusions.

If parents do their job and the kids coming to school have a common core based upon discipline and respect, then learning can occur no matter what conditions exist. Consider the one-room school houses of American history as exhibit A. In the "no child left behind" promotion taking over in the United States, the emphasis seems to be placed upon the schools rather than on the homes. My conclusion is that the old Periodic Tables pulled down from the wall mounting sufficed nicely because we had a degree of discipline and plenty of respect. The flip side of that is that we may have five hundred dollar bulbs up the butt, but without respect and discipline the temporary brilliance of such bulbs won't accomplish the task set before all of us.

***

Mark S. Meets John Damn—Out the window with the noise

We were in the sixth grade classroom at the end of one of the downstairs hallways in the old Sodus School. The building was filled to capacity with all the kids who lived in the village grades 1-12. Our future seventh grade friends still out in the surrounding one room schools in the township of Sodus would join us the following year in the new central school being constructed in 1949. Our sixth grade class was unique in the history of Sodus and our memories were vivid of that school year.

This was the year that John Damn Wayne Sodus style would meet Mark Futzing Scurrah, newly arrived Sodus sixth grade *male* teacher. We would have a man teaching in the elementary school. This was a first, and the difference was greater than day and night. The difference was enormous! For one thing Mark Scurrah was going to defend his sixth grade classroom against the demands of Nelson McGinn. McGinn was the coach and physical education teacher for the boys in school grades 4-12. He did it all and his rule was the law. He did not tolerate any monkey business and he ruled with an iron hand. His rule was superseded only by that of Francis Samuel Hungerford, the two hundred seventy-five pound principal. Mark Scurrah was a six foot, four inch crane of a man who weighed one hundred seventy wet.

A young man named Richard Haslem brought the two distinctly different men together one spring day in a manner that no one would forget. I say young man because Richard had been around elementary schools for his whole life and must have been sixteen when "the incident" occurred. He had repeated so many grades through the elementary experience that teachers would admit later they couldn't remember how many times he revisited their classrooms. We were eleven years old, typical for sixth graders.

Haslem was bored with school and probably dumb as a rock, as they said back then. I guess in the modern era it would be said of him that he was intellectually challenged. Either way, he was dumb. Subsequent events would prove this fact without any doubt.

Mark Scurrah was a humanist and reached out to all students

in his first year on the job in Sodus. He was probably given Haslem in his class as a pedagogical initiation to the Sodus School. If that was the case, Mark did very well. Haslem seemed to like Scurrah. Two reasons I say that: Haslem sat after lunch daily and listened to Scurrah read to the class and did not ever interrupt the reader, and whenever the boards needed cleaning Haslem volunteered to wash them off. He had never sat and listened before, and he had never volunteered for anything before in school.

Scurrah found creative ways to involve all of us in the magic of his classroom. I reflect now, over fifty years later, that he was a great teacher. He instituted a reading club and students who could read fifty books in the school year got a prize from the teacher in June. That seemed to inspire the top end of the class. He also instituted play time above and beyond the gym classes McGinn would teach, and that inspired the bottom feeders because they loved games. I read fifty books and loved games, so my classification was with both groups although some of my books were short sport stories.

Mark Scurrah even got a group to ride bikes after school, and during the rides he would stop and treat us to a Coke or Pepsi. We had never had a teacher such as this before. Pathetically, some students did not have a teacher who inspired them like Scurrah did after the sixth grade. Our previous teachers were all female, some old maids mixed in with matronly mothers and wives, except for one. The exception to the rule came in our initial educational experience in kindergarten when we had Miss Marshall. That story is for another chapter, but suffice to say that all the little boys loved Miss Marshall. Back to the day John Damn met Mark Futzing.

Nelson "Slim" McGinn was tall, rugged and very much like our version of John Wayne. Slim lacked a horse but had the necessary demeanor to match the movie star's film presence. Scurrah, called Mark Futzing Scurrah by my father, was an educated man who enjoyed reading and outdoor pursuits and was gentle. My father called him "futzing" because my father couldn't believe a teacher would read to sixth graders and futz was a word used in times when old Pete couldn't quite describe where someone didn't fit easily into a certain category. It was a word borne of frustration and always came very close to the real "F" word, but never once did Dad say the real deal.

Richard Haslem listened to Mark read the Hardy Boys' latest chapters after lunch one day and then as Scurrah went into the hall to do something, Haslem stepped up to the huge classroom windows propped open and yelled out at somebody.

All of us were shocked because he yelled "Hey Slim!" I have already mentioned his intellectual potential briefly and this clinched the issue for sure. Nelson McGinn was below the window with some other class enjoying a game of some kind on the beautiful spring day. When Scurrah reappeared in the room Haslem had returned to his seat and things probably looked quite normal to Scurrah. They weren't.

Within in a minute or two at the most McGinn came storming into the sixth grade, intellectually stimulating domain of Mark Scurrah, new male teacher. Slim grabbed Haslem and began a systematic yanking, hitting and yelling pattern that carried Haslem out into the hall where more thrashing took place. Haslem was bleeding and McGinn probably could have killed the lad except for the presence of Mark Scurrah. Scurrah probably saved the lad's life that day; at the very least he saved McGinn's career.

Scurrah grabbed Haslem and sent him stumbling into the classroom filled with avid readers and impressionable eleven-year-old children. Scurrah then verbally bashed McGinn in the hall where everyone in the school was attentive to the whole episode by now. Scurrah yelled at McGinn to never come into his classroom again for any reason. McGinn could not be heard saying anything as Scurrah dominated the dialogue. I don't know where Francis Samuel was during this but he could not have defended the class setting any better than Scurrah did that day. McGinn left and Scurrah spent some time bringing his classroom back to normal.

Haslem screwed up by yelling "Slim" out the window. That was a gauntlet that had been dropped that could not be ignored. The punishment did not fit the crime, nor did the intrusion into the

Scurrah classroom make educational sense. Slim screwed up because he left a terrible impression on many of us that never really went away. We were always afraid of him on some level. Scurrah made a reputation for himself that day for being a no-nonsense protector of student rights and his classroom. He lectured Haslem about his actions but reached out to him as a human. Haslem wiped the blood from his face, cried and finally walked out at the end of the day. He never came back. I never heard what became of the young man.

The mid-century educational setting allowed for people like McGinn, and they seemed to dominate schools populated with a preponderance of female teachers. Parents seemed to like McGinn because he kept discipline in the school system. They may have badmouthed his zone defense in basketball or his conservative style of baseball, but they liked the discipline.

Scurrah would be a great asset in any school in any era. He was innovative, caring, intellectual, and fair. He liked students and they liked him. When our class went on to seventh grade, we parted with the man with sadness. He would not read to us again. He would not ride with us again or treat us to Cokes. The fifth graders would reap the benefit of his expertise the following year. We would pass into adolescence without his presence every day. We would go on to seventh grade knowing Slim McGinn coached most of the sports and taught all the boys physical education classes. We were subdued by the reality of that scene.

As I grew into my role as a teacher/coach over the years, I still remembered the day Haslem was the focus of ire in the elementary school. It occurs to me even now that students can choose to yell hello or yell go to hell. When they make that decision it usually is motivated by what they think, no matter what their I.Q.

***

EBB—Humor in the Classroom
Every day the English class moved along dealing with the big issues such as poetry, literature and modern writers. It was a required class as it was nationwide. Students took the subject every

year through the school experience. It had the potential for being a very dull required class. Horror stories abound about English being *the* course that drove students over the drop-out "bubble" and into the real world without a degree. It was not this way at Sodus. We enjoyed English classes because we had some good teachers.

Every year in the English curriculum, a different teacher turned up with a different twist on the English requirement. One year we wrote news articles for the student-generated paper. This went quite well, and things showed up in print that would not have been news elsewhere in Sodus. The teacher of that class made sure everyone in school saw his or her name in print for something. This seemed very democratic and probably was a great idea for any future papers.

Another two English teachers, Miss Moore and Miss Doyle, had reputations as party animals outside of school; and we enjoyed just being there letting our imaginations run amok whenever they spoke or came around the classrooms. The girls in class liked these two because they were smart, social and young at heart. They also taught in a manner that involved most of the girls. This put them light years ahead of their time.

We boys liked both of them because we heard the male teachers liked them. This made them very acceptable in our eyes. One other English teacher was a very attractive young woman, and although her time at Sodus was brief she left her aura behind when she moved on. The male teachers were sad to see her go, I am told. I even heard some of the students were sad to see her departure, but that news was very confidential. Her name belongs to the ages but Swede Erwin and others could help me remember the teacher's name. The English teachers of Sodus also included David E. Cooper, who was a great guy and merits his tale told elsewhere. Of all the subjects in the curriculum, English was certainly covered by the greatest number of memorable teachers!

A most interesting English teacher was a high school teacher whose name was Elizabeth "Bee" Bellinger. We called her EBB with great respect. She taught us typical stuff found in English classes everywhere, but she did it with great humor. Her eyes twinkled as she absorbed our inappropriate behavior and our hormone-driven actions. We knew there was a limit to how far we could go in our actions, and she seemed to know how to exploit that moment.

Once, when Charley Moss was reciting poetry as part of our senior year requirement an unusual event took over the classroom. Charley stood in front of the class reciting "My heart leaps up..." when a stutter took over his performance. Charley stuttered throughout school and, when he got in a tight position with the syntax he stalled temporarily. As he stalled this particular day on the word "up" in the classic Wordsworth poem, he unconsciously dropped one hand down to his crotch and proceeded to perform a typical sport scratch right there in EBB's English class. It was unrelated to the poetry, yet it was to be forever connected.

EBB was the first to burst out laughing as Charley tried to get the "up" of the poem out of his mouth as his hand worked feverously with his genital area. As all of us literally rolled out of our seats and laughter permeated the whole wing of the school. EBB merely stood by Charley to lend him support during the laughter. She did get him to stop the scratching motion. The pause for laughter lasted for many minutes until EBB finally encouraged old Charley to "finish." Even then the encouragement to Charley to "finish" brought gales of laughter and once Mrs. Bellinger realized she had authored this malapropism she just sat back and laughed again with us.

John Dewey spoke about educators taking advantage of "teachable moments" and the need for teachers to let lessons flow dependent upon the interests of the students. EBB certainly knew about this because she seemed to master it regularly. Her comfort with humor in the classroom has been a fifty-year memory for my peers and me. Many of us from the graduating class went into education, and we received good mentoring from this woman.

All too often, humor is lacking in modern education. It is almost as if the teachers of the modern era are afraid to let their collective hair down with their clients. If EBB was a litmus test for this trait, I would conclude she got more with humor than most teachers would have accomplished without humor!

My mother, who went to Normal School early in her life and was an informal teacher her whole life, said a teacher could get more with honey than with vinegar. She and EBB would agree.

On another occasion, EBB came in after lunch for her study hall with us prior to the next academic class in the daily routine. This study hall/homeroom situation would occur twice a day. We would meet first thing in the morning and then right after lunch. We all became friends since her humor and informality made for a relaxed atmosphere. On the particular day, she still would remember that she entered to find all of us sitting quietly in our seats. This was a rare departure from the norm. She should have suspected a prank.

She found George Clark hanging inside of the classroom supported by his shirt-sleeves, locked into windows that were long horizontal openings but that were shut tight with the shirt holding him up. Some of George's buddies had encouraged him to stand by the windows as they were systematically shut to accomplish the mission. They buttoned up his shirt so that he could not move.

George looked like someone being crucified, but this was Sodus in the mid-fifties last century and not Rome in the first century A.D. George relished his position because George was a true fun-loving soul. Although he was the first guy in class to get married (beginning of the senior year), he never lacked a flair for fun. EBB could see immediately that George was not in any agony.

"Hunter" Clark was enjoying the episode so much that EBB let him hang there for a short time as she appreciated the moment also. This truly was her forte. George had a reputation as a hunter, as he would hunt and trap furry things and then sell their pelts. He had been caught in his own traps at times, so he was a survivor. This window situation was not an indignity. He loved the situation, and Mrs. Bellinger finally had him "cut down" after everyone enjoyed the prank.

Of all the things that made an impact upon us about EBB, the greatest was her internal source of strength through difficult times. Her husband died prematurely and she became a young widow with two children in their teens. She continued teaching and raised her children. Later in her life her daughter was severely injured in a swimming accident. She was paralyzed for life as a result of this accident. Her mother, true to form, made the best of the situation and still could see bright sides of life. Many lesser persons would wallow in self-pity. Not EBB.

We met with her at various reunions over the years and her eyes twinkled as they did regularly fifty years ago. As I write this in spring 2004 EBB is alive and well. It is my bet and the bet of several of my classmates from Sodus that she is enjoying something going on in her life. I hope she can enjoy this piece. She probably would be shocked that Stinky had become a writer.

The legacy she passed on to me was that humor is really important, and everyone has some kind of load to carry. How a person carries the load is a measure of their basic nature. Teachers have the opportunity to allow humor to take a key role in their classes. Teachers also have an opportunity to *not* take themselves too seriously. Students can't relate to the teacher as a real person if the teacher is on a pedestal.

When EBB laughed with us and with Charley during poetry time, she proved to us she was a very special teacher. Our hearts truly leapt up because she and Charley made education fun.

***

Thelma and the Hospital—A contrast

Thelma Scott taught social studies to junior high school kids and had a reputation for toughness. Students would always refer to her when talk turned to toughness She still had her share of supporters who were alumni of the school. Many of the supporters were parents and administrators that appreciated Thelma's no-nonsense approach to things. She used the classroom for her form of the Spanish Inquisition, Sodus-style.

When she asked a question, a slow response from the student would get part of the answer from the teacher. It went something like this. I will use Gail Fitzpatrick as the student picked at random for this example. Actually I do not just pick her at random since I know Gail is still around Sodus somewhere and would appreciate being used in a Thelma Scott routine. They were combatants at one time.

Thelma would ask, "What southeast Asian country is being run over with Communists?" This was in the early 1950s so the answer would have been Viet Nam. "Gail Fitzpatrick, what do you say to that question?" Before Gail could get into any kind of correct answer, Thelma would start saying "V,V,V…" then "Viet, Viet, Viet…" and suddenly, right on cue Gail would say "Nam"—usually after someone in class had sneezed and said "Nam-chu!" This type of question and answer period would go on for forty minutes some days. Mrs. Scott would invariably lead the reluctant student to the correct answer.

Whether this made a lot of sense educationally, who can say? I know the students of Sodus went home to read their social studies books first at night for fear of being called upon in Thelma Scott's class the next day. I know I was well-read on Viet Nam and those other newsworthy spots in the world, so my answers could come quickly and not require her to amble down the aisle toward me.

There were students who did not gyrate towards this type of teacher. Some seemed to go out of their way to cause a confrontation. In any such endeavor where Thelma was angry over something, the female teacher usually won the battle. The word battle was operative because of all the female teachers in the school Thelma and a Miss Bates in the sixth grade (prior to Mark Scurrah's arrival as the only male teacher K-6) were the toughest. Miss Bates eventually retired after four decades of tormenting sixth graders. Fortunately, our class missed her by one year.

There were male teachers who would not mess with Thelma. Even Slim McGinn would refer to Mrs. Scott with great admiration. This was no doubt related to the knowledge that Thelma, on occasion, would drop the gloves (as they say in hockey) and have at it with a student. Slim appreciated that in anyone, and would even stage bare-fisted fights in the gym every so often just to ease the tension in the air.

I remember seeing hair pulled on girls and heads whacked with a book or yardstick in Thelma's classes. One thing she seemed to loathe was gum chewing. There were times when a gum chewer would wear the gum somewhere once discovered! Parents enjoyed the stories coming out of seventh grade social studies.

Mrs. Scott had one thing right on the money. In 1950, long before Dien Bien Phu, the French disaster in northern Viet Nam, and certainly long before our involvement in the 1960s and early 1970s after the French gave up the Viet Nam ghost, Mrs. Floyd Scott determined that our national fortunes would be linked with that Southeast Asian country. When we look back upon her fascination with Viet Nam when we were her students, it seems uncanny that she called the prediction almost twenty years ahead of many experts. She said there was no easy way to change the nationalism and communism evident in the country, and that our power would not be sufficient to stop the tide.

Thelma lived for a long time in the apartment in the cellar of the old hospital building in the middle of town. This was the Myers Hospital, where a person could walk by the hospital on Main Street and smell the whiff of ether and other hospital smells. There was no air conditioning, so the smells and noises escaped the windows regularly. The hospital was the scene for about every birth in the town of Sodus and probably all of the births inside the village A pregnant woman could get there in two minutes from anywhere within the village limits.

It seemed incongruous that Thelma lived in the basement of the hospital, since her reputation at school was one of toughness and the hospital enjoyed a different reputation. Whenever we went in to the hospital to visit a person, see a new sibling or even get a shot from the only family practitioner in the village (Dr. Thomas Hobbie), we viewed the place with a high degree of respect and awe. Mrs. Scott lived in the basement by virtue of her husband serving as custodian to the building.

There were times after we had passed the seventh grade when we could ease up on our normally harsh view of Thema's tactics and demeanor. It is always easier to be mellow on a topic once removed from the setting. A couple of times, some of us saw her on duty helping out in the hospital as a nurse, and she was a different person. We saw her at various reunions over the years and were struck by how friendly she had become in her older age.

Some teachers at Sodus were like those teachers everywhere who depend upon a degree of fear to make the whole equation of education work out in their classrooms. I never felt Mrs. Scott taught me a tactic, technique or method of teaching I would use in my career in a classroom setting. She did teach me that history was very important, however, and she has my deep respect on that note.

On the Viet Nam thing, she was right on the money. I wish she had lectured the politicians of the era when they were in the seventh grade. If Robert McNamara had been there in Sodus when all of us were there with Thelma Scott, I calculate a hell of a lot more Americans might still be alive that eventually had to visit Viet Nam!

***

Where the Boys Were—Smoke, cards and caring

Without a doubt the best play I have ever seen on any stage was one performed at Sodus Central School in the early 1950s. It was titled something like this: "If Men Played Cards As Women Do." The actors on the school stage performing before a full house two nights in a row were some of our favorite teacher/coaches.

The play's dialogue flowed around a card table, where four men played cards for the entire one act play. They talked in a manner similar to the way women talked while playing cards. I appreciated the play a great deal then because I had grown up playing cards with women. I enjoyed the heck out of the play because the four men were merely moving their card game from the coaches' office onto the school stage in the auditorium for the world to see.

Most male athletes going into the coaches' office back then to get a tape job or to whirlpool would encounter two distinct sensory experiences. One was an overwhelming blast of cigarette smoke caused by the fact that most coaches smoked. As a matter of fact, most people back then seemed to smoke. The other sensory experience was the sound of men in the midst of their dialogue with one another. Despite the presence of a student athlete, the men acted the same as if we were not there. We were expected to filter out anything we didn't need to know and be respectful in their domain. If we heard language unbecoming a coach, we realized it was under the stress of losing a hand of spades before practice. If we didn't like what we heard, we could go without tape or whirlpool. Young people behaved differently around adults, and this was one area where being seen and not heard was operant.

Our coaching staff was comprised of teachers in the school who took on coaching duties due to one or more of the following reasons: an interest in a sport, need for money, or the need for a teacher to take a team so the team could have a season. We were not judgmental of them or their behavior in the smoking/card area. Anyone growing up with New Yorkers or Yankees in general knows we are quick with a curse and faster yet with sarcasm. We tend to use expletives creatively. We can use any expletive as a noun, verb, adverb or adjective. There were times when a four-letter word was used several ways in the same sentence. The group in the coaches' office was friendly to us and it was fun to hear them. They never used a word we had not heard before.

When Jack Erwin (basketball coach), John Dority (baseball coach), Menelle Stelliano (Jr. High coach) and a guy named Bob Henry (a spirited supporter) got together on the stage, they were awesome. They had to curtail the use of words previously used in the card games in the gym office, but their performance was just fine. Those of us who were privy to the real games taking place in the gym area were fascinated to see the alterations to the game under the guise of acting.

The various lines taught to them by David Cooper, our resident theatre genius who also doubled as a very popular English teacher, were no doubt altered by the actors as they got into the flow of the play. After the whole thing was completed, Cooper was heard to say he would never work with such a group again due to their improvisations. That was interesting to hear, since the coaches on the stage liked it when their charges did stuff as planned out on the fields and courts of Sodus.

Whatever came of the card games as time went by, I do not know. Many years after graduating from the school, I asked about the card games in the office by the locker room. They no longer existed, according to a reliable source, since there was a change in principals and the new one did not like it when teachers spent time in this manner. Sam Hungerford knew these games went on during his time in charge of the educational ship, but never curtailed or interrupted the activity according to the players themselves. Perhaps the games served a collegial purpose in the school.

Those guys playing cards on the stage in Sodus a half century ago really cared about their clients, and I never viewed their card games as interfering with my education. There were times when guys would go whirlpool or get a tape job just to learn about our friends in the smoke-filled room.

***

Cider House Rules- Beware of the chemistry
Many of the lockers contained glass gallon jugs of cider. Up and down the hallway outside the study hall and library, a chemistry lab of sorts was brewing. This came about during my freshman year in school. The older boys in the school did such things, and that was all it took for us to try. The cider thing gives educators an insight into how drug and sex practices can spread through certain populations. We dropped raisins and other items into cider and within a short time the cider became "hard."

Whatever hard cider has over regular cider still eludes me. The older boys merely told us it made a drink that would be different from cider. They were absolutely correct; any sample of the "hardened" concoction did not taste worth a crap.

The mere attempt to make hard cider in the school lockers was enough of a minor teenage rebellion that it appealed to us. Before the whole thing came of age or turned out any great quality or quantity of beverage, the whole deal literally blew up in our faces.

Case Weist, custodian extraordinaire, reported to the main office one day of his discovery of cider in large amounts in front of a couple of lockers. It seems that the gallon jugs had blown their lids, so to speak, as a result of the hardening process. The seasoned liquid poured out over the floor and the jug—and jig—was up.

Francis Samuel declared all cider within the school a banned substance. He did not bring in sniffing dogs, police or have to open every locker with the assistant principal. He merely announced that the ban commenced the next day and within an hour after school the day of the proclamation dozens of gallons of the fruity mix were dumped outside the school. Empty cider jugs were reusable by the local growers so the empty jugs were carefully lined up outside the back door of the school. Respect for the local industry was very evident. Sam's mention of the ban was all it took to stop the hard cider experiment for good during my school experience.

I reflect that even if the jugs had seasoned to perfection, what would have come of it? The mere taste of hard cider was terrible. It actually was like vinegar. Would all of us have had a binge of drinking hard cider? I rather doubt that since most of us did not drink during our high school years. Sam spared the custodian a lot of needless work by preempting any further explosions. He was a masterful principal since he did not need to actually know who was involved. He cut off any discipline problem by not overreacting. His timing and demeanor were just right for the circumstances.

The cider "house rules" we encountered that year were crafty manipulations of adolescents experimenting with something of which they knew very little. Upon reflection, it dawns on me that modern administrators need to handle many situations with poise and patience. The kids of my era did not seem to need many adjustments to their routes through school. When Sam merely mentioned his displeasure in school, our general consensus within the student body was that his displeasure should never be shared with our parents. When Sam spoke, it was like the old E.F.Hutton ads on TV. When E.F.Hutton speaks, everyone listens. It worked that way in the Sodus Central School experience my peers and I shared. The absolute worst thing to happen would be for the principal to ask for "help" from the home with a particular student.

After each paddling at the hands of the "Boss" at school, no one at 20 High Street in Sodus ever knew of the recent paddling. That would have been stupidity on my part. The situation in public schools now is bordering on anarchy in some districts. Kids peddle drugs in schools and defy rules and laws against this activity. Lawyers and misguided parents have turned the schools into battlegrounds over rights pertaining to children needing more guidance and fewer privileges.

Our cider story can serve as a metaphor for the time we were in school. Oh how simple those times were.

***

Basketball Home Games—A coming together

The wind was howling outside the school entrance, and snow was whipping around the corner of the building as a drift formed right there before our eyes. The temperature was in the teens, and the wind-chill (although we never used that phrase when we were growing up) must have been less than ten degrees. If we stayed there another twenty minutes without an improvement in our situation, some of us were going to be in serious trouble. Frostbite was a definite possibility for the three or four dozen people out in the storm. Most of us were students easily recognized by the administrator on the inside looking out through the locked doors at us! But the doors stayed closed.

Was this a survival test? This was not a survival test, but it was an incredible Friday night for those of us outside the school. Many of us out in the cold were on the basketball teams playing the games that night in the Sodus Gym. We were waiting for the administrative official to open the doors of the school. On that night the doors of the school were locked tight in stark contrast to the usual protocol. Usually we were able to go into the school through the front doors at night into the front lobby. Usually the school doors, once opened on a Friday morning at seven AM, would stay open until the games that night were over. This was a surprising change.

The reason this incident stands out in a host of fine basketball evenings many shared at Sodus was that it was a deviation from the norm. The locked doors that night frustrated all of us on the outside because we were freezing out there. Many of us were going to be playing in the games that night and the absolute last thing the coaches wanted was to have half their teams standing out in the cold when there was an administrator standing on the inside waiting for the clock to tick to precisely five o'clock. The only conclusion we ever could make from this incident was that the guy inside the building was unable to relent and let us in despite being "in charge" that night. He perhaps reasoned that forty freezing kids allowed in prior to five o'clock just might take over the building. All we know is that the basketball coaches were pissed off and they told the school official as much. It turned out the visiting team had been let in a back door and they were in the warmth of our gym!

The reason this incident stands out is that it demonstrates the "up-tight" manifestation of leadership responsibilities by people in education. I have seen the "deer in the headlight" look that I saw through the double front doors at Sodus that winter night five decades ago many times in my educational career. The person who has a difficult time making decisions on the spot based upon the merit and circumstances of the situation should not be in administration. Dismally, there are very few colleges out there to teach a person how to be a good administrator. Sam Hungerford knew how to govern in an era when he governed by the seat of his pants. He governed broadly and well. Sam Hungerford was not at the front doors that winter night, or all of us would have been in the building.

There were many special people who made home basketball games enjoyable. Other than merely getting into the building and gym by virtue of an adult seeing to that detail, there were many other helpers. People associated with schools know of the many hours that are spent helping sports programs function. It may be the custodian working a double shift to insure that the rest rooms are always ready for big crowds. It may be the teachers who chaperone the event and who do so as a volunteers. How do successful programs get volunteers? My observation is that fine teachers make fine volunteers. The converse of that is crappy teachers make crappy volunteers. These people are often out of education before they can do much harm. Sodus had a bunch of really fine teachers.

At basketball games student athletes, cheerleaders and managers could see and feel the interest shown in them by other teachers and staff members of the school. Parents were usually around and liked being there. It was the sight of an English or Business teacher with no children that brightened the night. This dynamic is evident nationwide at schools and colleges, but I don't think it is happening as much as it used to.

The loss of the universal support for athletic events in schools is marked by certain changes. Money has to be raised by parents and athletes now, whereas a half century ago tax money made the programs stay solvent. There may be less money for each program now contrasted to before because women are getting their belated chance. More emphasis on academics in schools today is evident as sports, music, physical education, art and industrial arts get little or no support financially.

Here's the rub from all of this. The scores may be a bit better on certain standardized tests, but are we turning out a well-rounded kid in the public schools in the modern era? Are the kids as fit? Do people support the public schools as they did in the previous century?

The basketball games at Sodus were unique, special nights, win or lose. They brought the community together, and that sharing made the rest of the school really function as a unit. Mr. Bellinger was an agriculture and shop teacher in programs not even listed in today's curriculum. He came to ballgames and on occasion would come up to me and others and inform us he had bet a bundle on our team that night so we needed to play well. We knew he wouldn't even risk playing cards with the card sharks in the faculty, so we knew he wasn't going to bet on us. Other teachers would come up before games and let us know they were there and they wanted us to know it. Those were special people.

Basketball games allowed the girls a chance to shine despite being deprived of high school sports they deserved. Many were cheerleaders and band members who were able to be a part of the action. Other girls merely floated into the gym in their teenage splendor. Whatever was going on in the game would be ancillary to the uniqueness of a pretty girl showing up during a lull in the action.

The lobby of the school was the special place after a game, where people mingled and recounted the good, bad and ugly of the night just shared. As the final participants and spectators departed, there was no rush to go because those Friday nights only occurred six or seven times a season.

That brings up the deeply philosophic question going back fifty years. Why in the hell did we have to stand out there in the cold if there were only six or seven of those Fridays on the schedule and there were so many people who cared for us?

***

Wayne County Student Council—Watch out for those autographs

During the junior year in high school an idea floated for a county-wide student government, and lo and behold I was somehow elected the president of the fledgling organization. Its purposes were numerous, but in general it was an attempt to foster good will among rival schools using common bonds of sport, state exam preparation, school projects, sharing of speakers and student exchanges within schools for a day at a time.

All of the rhetoric was fine; but it boiled down to a good idea with very little time for gestation of projects and other activities. For me, at that point in my life, it was something else to do relating to student government, which was enjoyable. I was involved in the student government at Sodus for most of high school. I could garner votes in the other classes voting for candidates by mobilizing neighbors I bribed with Isabel's food. Even though one of our teachers told my own classmates that they should not vote for a screw-up like me for class office or school-wide government, things worked out for me. The teacher in question thought I was a screw-up because she remembered things I did when I was in junior high school. She truly felt there were more viable candidates. Her name will not be mentioned here, even fifty years later, but my classmates told me of her poisoning of my candidacy for class office. She could not foul up the school-wide vote since her private forum was only one grade level. Since student council votes came from the whole junior and senior high, her poison did not affect my election.

The particular teacher probably was accurate given some of my adolescent, hyper-active behavior; but I concluded that she had misjudged my more mature character and I set out to prove her wrong. This episode in my life made me vow to not "brand" a kid in any of my classes. I won the student government election, and coupled with the county office it gave my family two politicians at the meal table during my senior year. It was an interesting year because I met some new student friends and was able to find some interesting new recreations.

After meeting the new officers and traveling around the county to a few schools, I came face to face with two girls from church camp days when I was younger. These two girls were interesting, and one of them had a family owning a nice place on Sodus Bay. This was a place several of us visited for good times and some boating activities as a result of the re-connection from summer church camp. One of the other girls had written me notes after church camp, and the student government thing served to ignite a flicker but not a flame. After she married a guy from a neighboring community, they set up housekeeping on one of the Finger Lakes in a magnificent lake-side home. It dawned on me that I should have answered those letters!

My mother always told me to send thank you notes, answer all mail and wear clean underwear in the event of an accident. I think I failed her advice on all accounts periodically; but the one about not answering the lake-house girl's mail was dumb.

In another interesting development I made a point of trading autographs with all the student government officers from the county. We put together a handbook of county rules and our photos and addresses that disappeared in the landfills long ago. I assumed my autograph, name and photo had faded from view as I went away to college. After three years away at college I received a note from a female whose name I remembered from Wayne County days, but I wondered how she knew where I was. The note was in my personal box at Brockport State Teachers College west of Rochester. It had been hand delivered and not mailed. Attached to the note was my photo and four-year old autograph.

It turned out she was working in the same town and had heard I was in school in town. Her connection with me was through my elected office when I was in high school. I called her, and we dated for a time. She made a point of describing one of my campaign promises made during a time when I was but seventeen. Although none of my promises were too bizarre, she brought up the one about visiting every school in the county for some event.

To make a long story short, I ended up traveling to her home town to attend a play to keep an election-eve promise made four years earlier. Even my father would have appreciated my commitment to a campaign promise. It wasn't as if I had to kiss some ugly baby.

***

David Cooper—Humor the man

D.E.C. were the initials of one of our all-time favorite teachers. He was David E. Cooper, and even after his death I still could not learn his middle name. If I pursued the issue I am sure the artifact could be brought to light, but in respect for his attitude while he was alive I never tried.

"Coop," as he was called by his buddies, performed humorous things daily using his acerbic wit and quick insight into human frailties. He could reduce a situation to its very basic level and derive gales of laughter from it. I think he could have been a TV host in the current era since he could combine sarcasm and profanity with terrific results. One of the things we did with Cooper, commencing late in our high school years and extending well into our adulthood, was to visit his home and play poker with him, his brother and their eighty year old mother Grace.

She was much like her son David, and could entertain young guys sitting around the poker table in her kitchen with her wit. She chain-smoked, as did the whole family, (and I think they all died of lung cancer) but the smoke did not hide her love of the poker table fun. She and her sons entertained us by the hour. We would spend much of the evening belly laughing our way through draw poker hands.

David Cooper was a fine teacher. Unless he totally frightened a student with the initial sarcasm that hid his love of the kids, his classes were totally in his control. Kids learned and had fun. His job of teaching was blended in with other key roles around life in the school. He was the prototypical involved teacher. David Cooper kept the scoreboard at home basketball games. He directed many of the plays held in the school. He drove cars and vans for teams during away game trips when bus travel wasn't used. Cooper served as tennis coach for a time also.

If any of us wanted a laugh, we would visit his house after school or on a weekend evening when we were bored. Sometimes that prompted a poker game. Other times we just sat around joking and telling stories. The poker games were played for pennies so no real money exchanged hands. On some trips to his home, we would merely drop off a used toilet bowl from some bathroom conversion job at a nearby home. These porcelain trophies would typically be placed by the curb when a homeowner wanted to get rid of the old toilet. All we did was get them prior to the village trash removal crew and place them on Cooper's front porch. There were at least a dozen of these used trophies in David Cooper's barn where the items went after he was greeted by them the following day. When he moved from Main Street in Williamson to nearby Pultneyville during his career at Sodus, he had to part with the collection. His family told the story after his death that he could not stand to part with the sentimental gifts from his Sodus students. It was one of the toughest decisions of his adult life. Go figure that one out, you hard noised teachers who can't wait to retire! Here was a sarcastic guy with tears in his eyes over used toilets! It turned out he had to dispose of the used crappers, but his attitude toward them spoke volumes.

Cooper kept a scrapbook that was filled with his letters to corporations and the corporate replies. He made an art form of creating letters asking really stupid questions about various products advertised on TV. He might ask in hand written, poor English questions about why he "wasn't seeing the USA in his Chevrolet" because he didn't have the money to travel out of Wayne County. Would the warranty on the car still be valid? Another thing he asked would pertain to claims about cigarette smoking being cool. His letters asked the company to send him "cool" cigarettes since all the ones he smoked were hotter than hell.

On certain occasions he would pull out the scrapbook and beguile us with his creations and the really serious and condescending answers from corporate America.

I tried out for a couple of Cooper's plays, and to his chagrin I was the choice for certain roles, however limited. Our associations in these efforts tried his patience and made me laugh at myself over and over. The secret with David Cooper was to be original and honest. There was no bullshitting the man. He could spot that a mile away. His common phrase for anyone attempting such a brazen act was "they were a smiley ape-shit."

In one play, I was a warden of a prison. My only line in one scene was: "Hark—a pistol shot!" Now the word hark dates the play and my era in acting, but I figured a way to screw up one line. Cooper laughed for a day after hearing me come out in my suit and tie and say, "Hark—a shistol-pot!" It broke up the audience, the scene and the director. After trying the line again correctly, the play continued.

I never lived that down with the sarcastic English teacher. He taught us the art of not taking ourselves seriously. Teachers like

Cooper operate under tighter reigns in school districts now, for a multitude of reasons. We loved him and his style. It was perfect for adolescents and his detractors were usually jealous of his rapport with those of us who were his admirers.

His mother once told us that David was really a pain in the ass. This occurred during a poker hand in their kitchen as he played a winning hand, thereby taking the pot from his mother and her young guests. He said something to the effect that she was correct, but he was her creation. He was correct. There is a little of David Cooper in all of us, and it seems to come out when any of us play poker.

***

Do Good Teachers Yell?—Why not?

There are many teaching secrets. The teachers at Sodus were products of another era but their methods stood the ultimate test of time. Their students became teachers and administrators in vast numbers. Another litmus test for the success of the faculty was the return of the students to visit their lifelong friends—their teachers. Of all the criteria I have seen over the many years of teaching, "the teacher as my friend" appears to be very telling. Kids don't come back to see teachers they didn't like or respect.

Yelling at students is not a great idea, but when applied at the opportune time it can be a fantastic tool. Some of our best teachers did some yelling with great effect. A student-athlete expects to be yelled at sometime during the experience, and if it doesn't happen someone should probable check the pulse of the coach. When a yell occurs in a classroom it sparks a wake-up call, literally and figuratively.

David Cooper in English used the yell effectively. Bob Meneely would raise his voice during critical times in his history classes and none of us ever took it as a sign of disrespect. When women teachers gave a yell, it caught most of us by surprise. Some of our normally quiet teachers picked a time to yell when it suited the after-lunch naptime in various classrooms. The time right at the start of the school day and right after lunch in Sodus School mirrored what other schools found as a trend. Kids were not alert during those times. Sometimes the mornings were dreaded by teachers and students alike, for different reasons on a similar theme. Active people don't stay up late at night and then perform at their peak the next day. Teachers of first period classes raised their voices so the clients did not sleep.

After lunch the biorhythms slow down, and unless motivation is dynamic in that next class after lunch it can be a repeat of the early morning. When students had low blood sugar in the morning from not eating breakfast and drowsiness from excessive carbohydrates after lunch, teachers had to get creative. I don't know if Sodus teachers knew all this nutrition stuff, but our morning and early afternoon classes did not allow for naps or drifting off in class.

In addition to yelling out during times like those described, teachers threw lightweight stuff at us in their classes. No one ever got injured and the purpose was served.

Many of our teachers came out of New York State's Normal Schools and Teacher's Colleges. I would have to concur with my classmates and the adults in the village when the faculty at Sodus was adjudged to be excellent.

Our teachers were usually teaching from a "base" of personality that was their genuine persona. They did not alter their personality to suit a particular student or lesson or school marking period. Our teachers were themselves, and that remarkable description was a trump card for each. They did a great job of just being themselves. Contrast this to moodiness and personality changes, dependent upon who might be watching, as teachers tried to posture their way through a career.

David Cooper used to say a teacher could not be a "smiley ape-shit." (For a modern example of Cooper's mid-century phrase, see Al Gore.) When a teacher establishes his or her teaching style and basic personality, then students can deal with yelling and motivational tools. Students in Sodus were usually possessed of great common sense. They could spot a fake if and when a rare poor teacher showed up in the school. That type teacher did not linger too long in Sodus usually. I learned from my teachers to be myself in and out of school. It was a good lesson. It still stands the test of time.

***

Vital Vitah- Fifty years later

As the two of us went down the hall of the Cherry Blossom Nursing Home looking for a friend recently confined there in a wheelchair, we noticed the sun porch area filled with people either playing cards, watching the snow, or merely napping in upright positions.

As we passed the sun porch my friend and I found our wheelchair-bound lady in the middle of the hallway, bossing attendants around as she had done often in her public school career as a nurse in a nearby village. "Ma" DuVol, as she was known all over the upstate New York region because of her home visits in winter, her organizational abilities during crises, and her brusque manner with all, was the target of our visit, and we had found her. We had long overlooked the brusque manner once we saw through that particular façade for what it was. She was that way because she dealt with all kinds of people, and back then being politically correct with a village jerk was not necessary. Her brusqueness developed as an art-form over the years since some communities had their fair share of jerks!

After we'd been coaxed to have a cold soda and accompany her to the sun porch, we now knew we needed to find an exit strategy or we would be involved in cards for the rest of the afternoon. Cards were ever-present in the lifestyles of the region where I grew up because of the lack of TV for so long (my family got a TV set in the fall season of my tenth year) and because there had to be something to do during long winters and severe storms. Cards were the answer, and this entertainment permeated most lives then and even now in my own case.

Currently I am in the process of passing on card knowledge to many grandchildren. In this manner, I feel, I can pass on the heritage of the adults who were as active in my own existence as a child.

My friend and I visited with Ma Duvol for thirty minutes, and then we made polite attempts to get going. The heavy snowfall that started the day before and was continuing then gave us an excuse for departing even Mrs. DuVol would understand. She was, after all, famous for getting her Jeep Wagon through the drifts to medical emergencies all too many times in her career. She never underestimated the impact of the two to three hundred inches of snow that fell often in our region.

We were almost out the door of the sun porch when one of the ladies playing cards at the table by the door gestured us to her table. Bear in mind this episode occurred when I was in my fifties. The lady then told me *who I was!* She did not ask me, rather she told me. This lady, in her mid-nineties, was my first grade teacher Vitah Sims. The astonishment was further enhanced when she asked how my older brother Dick was, how my sister Donna was and, although she remarked she had not taught my younger brother Charley, she asked how he was! This was a teacher I had in first grade when I was six asking me about things as though we were in constant communication over the fifty years between the nursing home and my presence in her class.

Her knowledge of my family was keen and stunningly accurate. She taught three of the four kids in my family but she remembered! How many teachers can come up with a kid's name fifty years later and also know the kid's brother's and sister's names? This was a truly remarkable exhibition of the mind's ability to remain sharp. This was probably a tribute to Miss Sim's constant reading and card playing all her life.

Current research tells us we all can keep our mind sharp if we use it in our senior years doing games, cards, crossword puzzles and the like. As my friend and I stood at her table, we shared memories going back five decades. She was in excellent health for her years but was frail. Her decision to be in the nursing home was one with social purposes as well as with safety purposes. Many nursing homes in the north receive people who do not want the hassle of combating snow and ice alone over the six months of winter.

The other benefit is that you always have enough for a card game. Miss Sims (she never married as was the case with many teachers of my village and nationwide compared to today's demographics) was a delight for us, and we left the nursing home that day rejuvenated in a way neither of us could quite comprehend. The beauty of a life lived in service to others had obviously played a huge part in Vita's longevity. She was not self-focused at all, as are many seniors when they pass some unmarked point in their lives. She was not engaged in any self-pity for her feebleness, nor was she caving in to arthritis as she played cards for hours each day.

Her presence on the sun porch that day was lucky for us, because if she had stayed in her room, lonely and self-indulged as did many of the seniors, we would have missed this sterling exhibition by a classy lady. The fact that Vitah Sims had picked me up on her ninety-plus year old radar screen that wintry day was one of the most cherished memories I have of Sodus and the school that made such an impact.

***

Miss Marshall—A first love

My friend and proofreader Gilbert Sergeant and I attended Kindergarten together. We both enjoyed our first teacher, Miss Marshall. I have no pictures of her but she was the very first teacher I grew to like. In fact I loved her, since that became a necessary reaction to missing my mother during the first few weeks of the experience. My tears at seeing Isabel walk back toward High Street after depositing me at Kindergarten were real. Joan Marshall got me over the hump in my early days of schooling. She was Miss Marshall to us, and was Joan to all others in Sodus. My memory of her is dim, but I recall she was attractive.

Gib's memory is more vivid based upon our conversations and shared notes. He remembers her as average looking and, in fact, has a yearbook from the 1940s with her unflattering photo in it. I refuse to look at such renditions for fear of ruining fifty years of hype done by yours truly. Her long legs looked pretty to me as I watched her from my little magic carpet called my nap rug. Gib need not show me any photo depicting anything different.

My mother took me to school for several days in a row to insure I was handling the adaptation well. It was tough to see my mother leave when Kindergarten class began, but Joan Marshall had me on her radar screen early on and she "mothered" me early in the school year. Isabel finally did not have to walk me to school once the Marshall Magic took hold. This made her cry! Gib and I would walk home together and he and other friends made each day go nicely. Although Gib and I did not hold hands as Isabel and I had done, there were redeeming values for us as we meandered home each day. We were safe in a wonderful community and mothers could plan on, and feel secure about, their offspring walking a half-mile through the village home safely each day. It is my opinion that much has changed in the twenty-first century.

Kindergarten was not a regular thing until the year we started school. Miss Marshall's trial by fire was crucial to Sodus maintaining a class for the future. She must have done a great job, because Kindergarten stayed. Some kids we met in first grade did not have Kindergarten. We were ahead of them in many areas and Kindergarten class proved this point year after year. In the current era we have pre-school and sometimes a pre-pre-school.

Gib and I agree that we should have started school a year later. We were young for school due to our fall and winter birthdays. If our parents waited one more year to send us to Kindergarten, they and the school district may have incurred a distinct hardship. The parents were ready to send us and the school needed bodies to fill the prototype class for purposes of selling the concept to the district. Quite frankly, we became expendable at our cozy homes, and were sent out on a mission as four and half year olds.

Once we got into junior high and high school, we thought the girls were prettier in the grade below us so our thoughts drifted back and forth between Miss Marshall in Kindergarten to those beauties in the other grade nine years later. We should have flunked a grade for dating purposes. We should have done it for sports purposes also. Both of us could have benefited from an additional year of maturation. There was no reason to graduate at age seventeen. Our mothers were not concerned with these reasons back in 1943.

During the typical Kindergarten day we played a lot, ate our first school lunches and had naps on our own little private rugs. During the nap times on the rugs (magic carpets) I distinctly remember not wanting to sleep. There was a feeling that something was going on and I did not want to miss a thing. It seems this pattern has followed me all my life. It is difficult to "give up" during any activity. Even at my current AARP age, I still hate to ease off and shut down the engine.

Miss Marshall probably sits in a rocking chair somewhere in America, thinking how lucky she was to teach in Sodus in the early part of her career. She may or may not think she was fortunate to have our particular group first in her career. We all have pleasant memories of our "first lady." She set a tone for teaching that we encountered for the next twelve years and included many fine teachers. We were lucky to have a nice start.

***

Friday Rewards—An educational milestone
During selected Friday afternoons every month, our school dropped the formality of classes and allowed for mere fun. The fun came in the form of pep rallies, outdoor activities and, often, movies in the auditorium. During the World Series it was possible to go to the auditorium and "watch" a game involving the Yankees and some National League team lined up for the annual fall sacrifice. I say "watch" because it was more of a listen. The black and white TV was a very small screen, given the spaciousness of the auditorium, but the presence of our peers and the adequate volume made the experience memorable.

Most in our community appeared to have strong New York Yankee loyalty, so these auditorium visits found overwhelming cheers for any pinstripe success on the tube. Our principal was a baseball fan and supported the notion that good things happen in extracurricular activities. He must have included our Friday reward days in this category ,because we enjoyed many of them.

I can remember going into the auditorium to see the Three Stooges, Laurel and Hardy, westerns and even some sport newsreels, all compliments of the management. If a principal tried to reward his clients in this manner today during a busy school day, he or she would no doubt be pilloried by irate parents at the first opportunity.

There is an internal synergy in a school that comes from the top. If there is confidence and compassion coupled with assertiveness and empathy, then that school has something special. Sodus has always compared favorably with any place where I have taught or visited in the completion of my college duties as a student teacher supervisor.

The leadership ranks in many schools today seem to be comprised of highly educated personnel. This is a good start. The flip side of this analysis is that these leadership ranks are filled with people who posture like crazy and bend to a variety of pressures blowing through the schools like wind through the willows. Administrators should not be willows; they should be oaks.

In Sodus our oak was Francis Samuel Hungerford, and the forest of teachers around him were oaks and maples. Our Fun-Friday afternoons were the byproduct of the traits listed two paragraphs above. People had the guts to give kids some time on a Friday afternoon, and education was enhanced, not hampered.

One huge outcome of the Friday plan was a school cohesiveness and spirit that was real. Classes sat in the auditorium and cheered and enjoyed things and then left together. The end result was a tighter school and community. When there were ballgames, the Fridays of the school year helped generate the crowds at the games of the afternoon and evening hours.

We had pep rallies, and although some were corny it was fun. Once, while our cheerleaders were spelling our school name out by giving an "S", giving an "O", and so on the cheerleader responsible for shouting the "D" of our name, God bless her little blonde head, shouted out "U". This stopped the whole pep rally in mid-air. She was totally embarrassed and only a quick-thinking principal saved the day. He merely stood up and said to "start again girls," and no one had time to yell anything derisive about the blonde's first attempt. In order to preempt a bunch of hormonal teenage boys, a moment like this demands quickness of thought.

Who among us hadn't screwed up something and could, therefore, have empathy for the girl? School leaders protected us from ourselves many times over and, by using Fridays as a relief valve on a busy school schedule, they kept us all in the right frame of mind. The Friday pep rally could have been the Friday Follies for a nice cheerleader if allowed. Good leaders did not let anything bad happen to us. Fridays were special days at Sodus.

***

Case Weist—An educator

The class was dismissed and we moved quickly toward the lunchroom. The school setting for the village consisted of a large, old two-story brick school that housed all the grades 1-12. Children reached the building after attending kindergarten in one of the church basements in town. Little kids were mingled with big kids in the brick school. It was a large building with the big kids on the second floor and grades 1-6 downstairs. In the basement were the locker rooms, gymnasium floor level entrance, kitchen area, storage rooms and a large room that housed the boilers and hot water tanks, electrical and other services. We would walk fast across huge steel plates of the boiler room toward the entrance to the kitchen. We could make plenty of noise on the steel plates. Case Weist was the head custodian in the school and this was his domain. We were visitors to his world on a regular basis.

If a person took a group of second graders across the steel floor plates of a furnace room and past the huge furnaces heating a building in the modern era, some advocate group or lawyer would be all over the adult leading the charge. In our era this was something nobody seemed to think much about.

In our situation this represented the shortest distance between the elementary classrooms on the one side of the building and the food service. Rather than go across the long hallway to the stairs on the other side of the building, classes on our side did the path across the boiler room as the most direct route. And in doing this route day after day, year after year, school children could get their food quickly. After going through the kitchen line, we went to the gym to eat. Our tables and chairs were set up and taken down daily by Case and his workers. The gym was the cafeteria for an hour and a half each day. The two-story gym was the hub of the building, and performed its many duties adequately despite some dead flooring and low beams.

Considering the dual use of the gym it seems remarkable that we still had physical education classes, practices and basketball games going on there regularly. The only compromise was at the 11:30AM to 1:00PM time, when the ladies of the cafeteria controlled the gym.

Other than an occasional straw wrapper coated on one end with mustard or ketchup sticking to a beam, this was a clean gym. The straws became a great tool in the hands of expert, youthful marksmen. The condiments on one end of a straw wrapper gave it stability and added distance when blown. If a person aimed low other kids were targets. The teachers ate in a group elsewhere some of the time, and this is when the straws flew. Case Weist stopped the straw business by outlawing straws.

Case Weist was a man who managed the boiler room, custodial business of the school, and cleaned up the gym after lunch. Case became an icon in our school. Everyone knew him. We journeyed through his furnace room daily. We smelled his cigars regularly on our trips through his domain. He also possessed a unique manner of clearing his throat. It went something like a loud "ARRRRUMP" followed by a less pronounced "huurruuum." This announced his presence throughout the school. Some of us ultimately were able to imitate Case when our voices changed. Imitation was then and still is the greatest form of flattery.

Case was the most important man in the school, no doubt about it! His keys opened any door. This facet of his existence was to pay great dividends later in my teenage years. His word was law. His handprint was on everything in the school. If something went amok in the kitchen and food distribution was slowed, he could solve it. If winter weather lowered outside temperatures to under zero degrees, as it often did, Case merely fired up the boilers to a higher pitch. If the kids ran through the boiler room and made too much noise, then Case could change the rules. There were times when classes had to go on the long route to the kitchen because of raucous behavior in his boiler domain. It was unique to travel through the boiler room. It was as if we were in the engine room of a great ship moving to some distant destination. Case was usually there, smiling and waving at us as we traveled through his magical kingdom!

His position was powerful. The straws were finally banned in the gym/cafeteria due to his input. He got tired of seeing the straw papers fluttering down from the steel beams during basketball games when the temperatures in the gym dried out the condiments holding the straw wrappers.

He was a friendly man who did not suffer fools lightly. If he had to wait too long for someone's common sense to kick in, they would be on the "outs" with him. If in your dealings with him you tended toward naiveté, stupidity or disrespect, you could figure you had several years of trouble ahead. He hired older boys for jobs in the summers. He took care of the locker rooms and made things respectful for ball game nights. He took charge of the snow removal around the old building before the advent of contracted snow removal people at the new centralized school building and all the acreage of lots. He had the keys to the gym. In short, Case Weist was a character found in every successful school system across America, if they were so lucky.

Once during a class in college, the instructor told us to always befriend the custodian of the school to which we were assigned. This made good sense as a coach and teacher, because a custodian could make or break you. I learned this lesson long ago in Sodus. The lesson was taught by a friendly Dutchman when I was in elementary school.

During special times in any school certain teachers need assistance more than others. This can be a product of fate or it can be the product of irresponsibility. Case Weist helped those that were willing to help themselves. He also was a teacher to the teachers. He could solve problems quickly.

As a high school student we often went to the gym of our new school at night. We moved to the new school in the seventh grade. These trips to the gym were authorized by Case to let certain responsible boys shoot baskets after hours. This was very important since outdoor baskets in February in New York State were useless. We made many visits through the high school years to shoot baskets and play in the gym, courtesy of a man named Brownie who took his cues from Case.

There were times when we would see Brownie and Case out in the community, and it was like greeting an old friend each time we saw them in a different light. Brownie taught some of us how to bowl and would follow our efforts during his off hours from the school. He also became one of our best supporters at home basketball games. He and Case would stand near the end doors of the gym and get caught up in every game.

Case was critical to the success of our school. Case and Brownie deserved our thanks for being guides along the boiler room called life.

***

Driver's Education—Meaningful miracles

The teacher came into our history classroom and explained his purpose in the curriculum. He was the driver's education teacher and would offer a classroom session for that period all through the fall semester and then we would go outside into the car for the spring semester. We were all gathered in the vacant history classroom for the experience, since the history teacher was doing planning elsewhere. The first day, after the explanation of our year-long lessons in driving, we were brought quickly into the harsh reality of driving a car in New York State. He altered our somewhat sheltered lives forever, and the year-long lessons he taught were ingrained for life.

We had two different driver education teachers that we recall fifty years later. They worked the school with great effect. The man who taught our particular group of juniors was an ex-New York State Trooper. He brought graphic black and white photos from actual accident reports from his files as a trooper. We viewed the photos as they were displayed on the front desks. As high school juniors, just turned sixteen and just qualifying for a learner's permit under state law, we were given a wake-up call by the teacher. He was effective.

As I write this nearly fifty years after the experience I still shudder whenever I recall those grisly photos. Of all the driver education experiences in that junior year those photos remain the ultimate educational tool. They scared the hell out of me and my friends. Ironically the photos did little to completely stop the carnage on the highways around Wayne County. Within five years of our graduation from high school, three of our classmates met their fate on the highways in accidents.

Our driver education went smoothly in the classroom until we prepared to take on the snowy roads around Sodus. Since the classes were about fifty minutes in length, the teacher had to hurriedly gather us up at the rear of the school, designate one of us to drive and then start the short run around town. After the initial driver spent his/her ten minutes behind the wheel we stopped and made a switch. With four students in the car and seven periods in the day can you imagine how draining the spring driver education class must have been on our teacher? With about twenty-six juniors taking the course and each of us needing plenty of time behind the wheel, the logged time behind the wheel for each of us was critical. We were being groomed for taking the state license tests. The state tests were two-fold and were vital to us for our mobility. They were equally vital to our parents for a fifteen percent discount on insurance. Passing the driver education course meant we could drive at night at age seventeen. Normally one had to wait until the age eighteen to have the nighttime privilege. Once in Lyons, New York where all drivers' tests were administered for the county, a person had to pass two parts of the test. After taking a written test the aspirant driver went behind the wheel for a twenty-minute road test.

Our Sodus instruction prepared most of us for passing the tests the very first time. As I went through my testing my mother was very empathetic since she was a recent test-taker over in the county seat. Although she failed her first driving test and I was able to pass mine, there was no animosity on her part. She was pleased to have another driver in the family. This made her life easier and meant others would be able to check the oil and keep the gas tank filled.

During driver education classes, it never once dawned on me that I would become a driver's education teacher in the state. This occurred in my third year of teaching. My coaching peers in the Rochester school told me this was expected of each coach. It seems that in my initial teaching position the coaches did the driver education thing in summers rather than in the school year. It made for extra income and kept us off the snowy roads during the school year. Although the summer course was crammed into six weeks it did keep the students and teachers off snow-covered roads. This was easier for all but dodged the critical lessons needed in the winter months. Sodus students, again, seemed to be the beneficiaries of better teaching. Having seen both ends of the spectrum in driver education, I can conclude students need winter driving experience if licensed in wintry parts of the country.

The teachers in Sodus had to endure some very interesting driving experiences on snowy Sodus roads and streets. There were some days when the instructor would come in after a particular class and literally be shaking. With student drivers using clutch-operated transmissions, driving on snow became a crap shoot. I can remember slamming on brakes and sliding along a street at snow banks as the clutch-operated transmission stalled out. This happened as the clutch was overlooked by the novice driver. A car in third gear, on the typical column shift found in cars back then, jerks, grabs and then stalls whenever the clutch is not engaged. I know since it happened to me a few times while driving my peers and a teacher in the snow.

There was an episode in an adjoining community during this era when a student driver slammed the brakes on and did a slide into the rear of a garbage truck. A garbage man was pinned against the rear of the garbage truck and had severely damaged knees as a result of the slide. The student driver and teacher were no doubt changed forever. This was the tough part of teaching young drivers that always was in the mind of the mentor.

With the lack of emphasis on education for our novice drivers across the nation, is it any wonder that our teenagers are in so many fender benders? Given the safety measures built in to each modern vehicle including anti-lock brakes, airbags and crumple zones, it seems we protect the occupant better after fifty years; but we are doing a crappy job of teaching safe driving techniques.

We had to learn about controlled skids, pumping brakes (something you have to unlearn with anti-lock brakes), adjusting seats, mirrors and passengers in order to drive safely. In today's convoluted logic system parents toss the keys to an SUV or Mustang to a sixteen year old and send them out. They send them out with cell phones, CD players, and a breakfast buffet available in every car. Given the number of drive-through options and the traditional distractions such as friends, alcohol and speed, the modern teenager is programmed for disaster. Tragically, the disaster is visited at high speeds and by inattentive, unskilled drivers upon innocent drivers.

As I prepared for my career as a teacher it dawned on me that the longevity of driver education teachers was probably limited. My own career lasted two years, which was quite enough, thank you.

I did have great respect for Bill Dunn and Bill Bestrum, the two guys who were credited with teaching a large number of small town boys and girls how to drive.

They earned every penny they contracted for in the Sodus system. There were days when they merely cancelled classes on the road due to heavy snow, ice or, in some cases, because they had to go home early from school to change their underwear.

***

Library and Study Hall—Good ideas

One of the better ideas in the construction of schools was the location of the library right next to the room designated as a study hall. In such a room at Sodus, the desk spaces held over one hundred students. It was triple the space of an ordinary classroom and allowed for one teacher to supervise the whole room. In those days one teacher could easily supervise such a group because we were very manageable. It was mid-century 1900s.

Everyone was assigned a study hall period in the daily schedule unless there was a private music or specialty class preempting such a study period. While in the large room each student was expected to do homework, catch up on assignments missed or read. Whenever a head went down on the desk most teachers assigned to the room would gently tap the sleeper and direct him or her to a more meaningful use of time.

The library was adjacent to the study hall and, by merely signing a sheet in the front of the study hall, passage was permitted to that Utopia. The library was a quiet place but was also a less-structured place. A student could go in and read the sports pages of local and regional papers. This seemed to be a popular activity as the sports page would invariably disintegrate by noon of any day. I enjoyed reading magazines not on my parent's tables at home. Although my father was an avid reader and subscribed to Time, Life and Sporting News, there were many other options in the school library.

Reports circulated around school that certain students were able to sneak into the meeting room just off the library main area where it was rumored that necking occurred. (My, my how times have changed—in the public schools today the predominance of oral sex is one of the major discipline and supervision issues for teachers) Since the room was where student council met, and I was usually connected to student council, I could not perceive of such a use for the hallowed room. Only a barbarian would do anything out of line in the student government room. And besides, the key for the room was always kept in a secret location under the librarian's desk and she only left the library a few times a day for rest room and lunch breaks. A student worked behind the desk, in the absence of the librarian, and was responsible for the key and checking the books in and out. The system seemed foolproof enough.

The Sodus librarian was a kind, gentle lady with the name Miss Church. She was aptly named. She was always quiet. It seems most librarians take on a persona connected to their careers. Of course, the traditional coach and physical education teacher takes on the aura of the gym and locker room wherever he or she goes. I know this given the number of times my wife says, "You know, your voice just carries all over the restaurant." It is a gym voice. It is also a field voice, and that is a higher voltage than the gym voice. Hell, it probably is a neighborhood voice once I get outside on the patio and have a couple of brews after a busy day!

Good things usually happened in the study hall under the watchful eyes of our rotating teacher-supervisors. There were random times when the crowd gathered for a particular period in the day, and the teacher in residence was late to appear. Anarchy was possible with dozens of students from various grade levels all mixed in the same room. On rare occasions fights broke out over simple things; like blondes. On other occasions we planted seeds for pranks. The most common prank was to stuff paper into the little desk bell on the desk in the front of the room. Whenever a teacher came in the bell would be tapped and the ring would signal "get your butts in the seats assigned—pronto."

Without the signaling device the system broke down temporarily. We cherished our momentary victory and then dutifully sat down. Once we devised a system whereby a thumbtack was attached to the stem of the bell used to ring it. This was done by attaching enough pieces of scotch tape on the tack end to leave a very small tip of the tack. When tapped, a human ringing the device thought they had been stung by a wasp.

One day our buddy Donald Virts came rushing in just ahead of the substitute we knew was in the study hall that day and he rang the bell. His sting, intended for the young replacement teacher, took the air out of our prank. Replacement teachers were a rarity in Sodus as the overall health of the teachers seemed excellent. The longevity record for many of the teachers is a validation of that observation.

Another reason for the low number of replacement teachers was even simpler. Teachers seemed to enjoy coming to school as much, or more so, than we did over the years. This conclusion came out over and over as we watched our teachers laugh and enjoy our diverse personalities and corny gags. Even the librarian had a twinkle in her eye when she saw the "refugees" from the study hall flow into her domain. None of us ever knew where that key was either.

**

Donations—A theme for life

The influence of adults in a young person's life cannot be understated. For every successful passage from adolescence into adulthood, the positive influence of many important adults must be recognized. The parents are a crucial starting point. After the genetic links are established a young person still needs other adults to reinforce the lessons emanating from the home. For most parents in Sodus, the presence of such people made raising kids much easier. Passage through adolescence was less bumpy for the kids once the adults of the mid-century New York State stood tall.

Many of these older residents were members of the "finest generation," using the words of many historians and writers. These men came back from service during World War II in the military merely seeking peace and harmony. They had witnessed a world nearly come apart. In Sodus and America at mid-century it became possible to find tranquility.

Americans elected Truman, in part, because he was a tough

politician who had the guts to drop the bomb and end the war. He also did not have "that stupid mustache" displayed prominently by Thomas Dewey, Governor of New York and Republican nominee in 1948. The quotation marks are my mother's as she justified voting for only her second Democrat. Her votes went to FDR for four successive elections. My Mother returned to the Republican fold in 1952 and 1956 as Ike was elected to the Oval Office by an overwhelming majority. Isabel's vote was included in Ike's near perfect sweep of Wayne County.

Dwight Eisenhower set the tone for that period as his calm, fatherly demeanor provided a refuge for our anxieties. The post-war period in America was a good time to be a kid despite the Cold War, Korean Conflict and distant fear of "the bomb."

It was an era when people helped others find a new life after the war. The communities across America seemed to ascribe to the notion that, through community effort, good things could happen with cooperation. One thing I learned during this period was to be unselfish. The lessons came in waves as I matured in the pleasant village referred to by the Indians long ago as "Land of Silvery Waters."

The spirit hit me in several ways during my early teenage years. Many things came together in my life to leave an important imprint. For one thing I was learning how to be helpful at the grocery store carrying groceries for people. Another variation occurred as my family had assignments for each child old enough to do chores. I had very important duties in and around the house. Cub Scouts and then Boy Scouts hit a tender chord at about the same time. Everyone has heard what scouts do in the performance of their duties. During the same era, I was approached by three adults, for whom I had great respect, to help them.

The beginning of Little League Baseball in Sodus for 9-12 year-old boys came in the summer when I was 13. I had missed the new opportunity by virtue of being born in 1938 instead of 1939. I could not blame Isabel since there was no mention of this baseball possibility in the Sodus Record in early 1938 for her to use as a guide for her pregnancy.

Sponsors were obtained and the community rallied in support of the sport. It was to be the first uniformed baseball for young boys in the community. Sodus had high school baseball and a Sodus Point Laker team for young adults, but no organized kids' games. Up until then we did have daily "sandlot" baseball that was very competitive.

The three men came with a request and an offer. My Dad, the Mayor of Sodus; Judge Parsons, the generous neighbor who spent his life sharing his boats with the community; and Paul Uher, the outstanding Youth Recreation Director, all came to see me and some of my friends about a project. The request was simple: "Please go out in the neighborhoods and streets of Sodus to raise money for Little League Baseball." The offer was a promise of a new PONY League, with uniforms and sponsors, the following summer. Our turn at bat would come in the organized structure of baseball in Sodus. That was good enough for us, and we hit the streets in support of our younger friends.

There were several of us, over-age for the Little League but able to help raise money. We went out selling raffle tickets to raise money for the league. Our appeal, according to the three adults, was that we were raising money for our younger friends. Who could refuse teenagers who *did not* have a uniform or league raising money for their privileged friends? The logic was sound, and the cash poured in via the efforts of the street urchins.

The other thing motivated us also. The following summer there *was* a new addition for youth baseball in Sodus. As promised when we had gone to work for the "cause," the adult leaders developed a PONY League for 13-15 year old boys the following summer. This placated us and motivated us through the Little League's initial summer of competition. This made sense for several reasons, but the major reason was that we were a part of large numbers of baseball enthusiasts waiting for our turn, and we deserved the privilege of playing.

Another reason for the development of the PONY system was the fact that numerous 12 year-old boys needed a league to grow into, and the PONY League met their needs also. In helping the Little League I learned that I could serve a cause greater than my own. I also felt really good doing this service. I was donating my time for a good cause for the first time in my life and have never stopped since. My Mom and Dad praised my efforts. The other adults Parsons and Uher, praised my efforts. Doing something for others fit right in with the things discussed in the Presbyterian Church, Youth Fellowship, Church Camp, and in my family. For this awakening to occur at age thirteen was an achievement of which I was extremely proud. It was an extremely important turning point. Adults had brought me to a fork in the road of life and had given me a nudge down the best path.

A teacher has to live the ethic described above. A coach certainly has to do likewise. As a young man in Sodus I seemed very interested in arranging games for others. Sometimes I helped coach teams and even was a playing coach for softball in my late teens. There were times when I realized I had not yet entered the particular contest because the participation of my peers and the others was more important. I do not write this as any kind of self-tribute; but merely as a declaration of life's intent. It came right out of the Sodus experience. Those three key men motivated the instincts.

Even today as I serve the YMCA Board or Berry College, purposes more important than my own personal welfare, I remember my roots. We are a nation founded upon volunteerism and my hometown gave me many extremely valuable lessons.

The following summer rolled around, and my peers and I came out in large numbers to fill rosters for four PONY teams. For the next two years we flourished in the league. Midway through the second PONY season, some adults came to several of us and mentioned that we would need to raise money for the American Legion Team scheduled for us when we graduated from PONY baseball. The adults were our friends, and they got the same volunteer attitude from me and my peers as evidenced three years earlier. We started raising money for Legion Baseball. It was the best of times and we were invested heavily in its memories.

PART FIVE
Sports

You can travel anywhere in America, and sports stories will emerge quickly in any discussion involving memories. We are a nation of sport. We often spend time and money on sports to the exclusion of more logical endeavors. Sometimes certain things defy logic. These times are no different, as sports have a prominent place in society and in each community. During the early years described in this book, sports held tremendous fascination and interest.

Fortunately many sports figures and leaders were sources of great memories and fine mentoring. In Sodus there were many volunteer coaches during the summer months and many coaches during the school months. Some were better than others. Some coached for a stipend and to fill the void, although they themselves had little or no experience. There were also several coaches who loved their sport of choice. These people stood out and gave many interesting insights for those of us fortunate to join them for a season. Some of the sports of Sodus were unorganized, seasonal romps with our friends during tranquil times.

Organized sports had their place, but there was an abundance of just, pure old sport and fun. Fishing, skating, swimming, kick-the-can, work-up, snowball fights, climbing, biking, shooting hoops, and sliding down hill were but a few of the choices. Of great note was the fact that there were no engines or adults involved in most of these frolics. In the modern era the organization, sophistication, and parental involvement in sports appear to prevent spontaneous and unorganized peer group fun.

Do modern youngsters need a referee and a uniform to have a game? All too often this seems to be the case. Is this a good sign? My memories tell me these kids are missing out on an integral part of youth.

***

Religious Instruction—Were the Yankees Catholic?

Growing up in upstate New York gave us three options for baseball loyalties. One was the Brooklyn Dodgers; they were very good, yet seemed remote to the average fan. This was because they did not get the national coverage on radio and early black and white TV. Although the Dodgers had the first Black and White team structure in 1947 with the arrival of Jackie Robinson, they did not get much support where we lived. Upstate New Yorkers liked the Yankees and the Giants. Due to their great success and history, most of us seemed to be Yankee fans. The names of Joe DiMaggio, Mickey Mantle, Hank Bauer, Yogi Berra, Phil Rizzuto and many others were a legacy of success and ultimate greatness.

The Giants did capture our imaginations once the great Willie Mays joined their lineup, and they staged the Miracle of Coogan's Bluff in 1951. Coogan's Bluff was an area in New York City near the Polo Grounds that the Giants called home. They overcame a huge thirteen game Dodger lead in August to force a playoff at the end of the regular season. Bobby Thompson won the game with his dramatic homer. The Yanks beat the Giants in the World Series. For much of my early life in baseball and Sodus, it seemed that the Yankees were in the World Series about every year. It also seemed that the Giants and/or Dodgers won the National League Pennant every year.

I know all this because my friends and I played baseball were real fans. We enjoyed the Giants miracle in the National League during that memorable season of 1951. They faced the Yankees in the World Series, and our buddy "Ears" Davis and others were allowed to leave school early in the afternoon one day a week in the fall to watch a series game or two on television. Well that may be a stretch of the truth. Actually Donald "Ears" Davis (he had pronounced ears) was allowed to leave school on those afternoons to attend religious instructions.

What all of us knew, and what was a regular occurrence during the World Series afternoon televised games, was that Ears and our other religious buddies were watching the games over in the basement of the Catholic Church. Although my family was Presbyterian and my buddies were an assortment of Methodist, Episcopalian, Dutch Reform and other religious beliefs, we could not quite bring ourselves to convert for the purpose of being able to watch an occasional World Series game when it fell on the same day as Catholic indoctrination.

The conversion decision was one we had to live with, however, when Donald would retell the highlights of the game he had watched and we had only imagined! This was tough to take!

The Catholics always seemed to be ahead of the enjoyment curve in Sodus because they held raffles, auctions, and Bingo. They even had several summer picnics. The other churches were much more conservative in their approach to raising money and serving their worshippers. The Catholics had the fun. They even had real wine in their church services; we Presbyterians had grape juice.

Until I attended church once with Don Davis, I held the Catholics in high esteem. After sitting through a service, however, that lasted an hour and a half and involved two collections of money, communion and several other notable differences, I decided that I had a good deal up the street with my dull, grape juice drinking Presbyterians.

Despite the World Series bonus once or twice every fall, the Catholics had to make a greater commitment of time and money all through the year. It seemed that the Yankees and the Catholics were tied together in my youthful, undeveloped mind.

I liked the comfort of the Presbyterians because they had one service a week and they were notorious for getting the whole service over within a fifty-five minute time frame each Sunday. They even sent youngsters to church camp every summer at the height of our pubescence. This is fodder for another tale in the book, but suffice to say there were times during church camp when it was spectacular to be a Presbyterian. No one I knew at the church camp over in Geneva, New York during those summers ever mentioned the World Series or Ears Davis and his edge over us during the fall of the year. While we Presbyterians were frolicking forty miles from home, people like Donald were no doubt mowing lawns for the church or making confessions regularly. Everyone in town knew the Catholics confessed often and probably needed to do so.

Catholics seemed to be very active in their church by dint of all the special services, special events and lengthy weddings held in the church regularly. Parents of kids going to Catholic religious instruction were very much aware of what was happening in the afternoons during the World Series. This became apparent when some of our Catholic adult neighbors would join the kids in the church for religious instruction. It seemed that they must have known about the baseball connection and could get out of work if they went to church in the afternoon with the youngsters. We were aware of this one time in the fall when the parents showed up at church but the kids didn't. They had elected to stay in school with their buddies to watch the series. They no longer, for this special time, had to leave their buddies to enjoy baseball.

Whether it was the rebellious act of the Methodist part of our principal or the baseball part that was our principal, I shall never know. What happened was that a TV set was installed in the auditorium of our school and anyone in school could go down to watch the World Series game. At a time when we used to envy our Catholic buddies the tables were turned. We all had access to the series game of the day and did not have to undergo any kind of instruction after or before the game as did Ears and his buddies. We were at the series electronically without any strings. Things were flip-flopped on those Catholic guys! It seemed that our principal got tired of listening to the complaining in his own house. His son David was in our class and he knew about Ears and those Catholics. This was a new era in baseball and religion in Sodus.

The only drawback was that the year we had our TV in the auditorium the Giants played the Indians in the World Series. It was 1954 and the Yankees were not in despite a great season. The Catholic guys stayed in school to watch the series with the rest of us. Their parents watched in the church without them. Out of this event came the comment by one of the Catholics that when their TV was the only TV of choice in the afternoons during school hours, the Yankees always seemed to predominate. Once the principal made his move to equalize the World Series edge enjoyed by the Catholics in the school, he jinxed the Yankees. That became Catholic opinion on the matter. That was the year the Catholics appeared to be really connected with the Yanks.

***

Sliced Off the Team—Uniform discomfort

There were several moments in the pursuit of athletic endeavors where discomfort hit and sometimes it hit hard. Every athlete can remember the good stuff and can regale an audience with super moments. These super moments seem to get better year after year. At my advanced age, the good stuff has reached epic proportions when my grandchildren hear the stories. The home runs traveled farther, the soccer successes were better, the basketball shots get longer, and the time to cover distances keeps dropping. It is part of life to admit to the bad and ugly also. For the five consecutive shots made uncharacteristically from the corner of the Sodus gym in our last high school game, I must acknowledge the time when I missed seven in a row from the field over in Palmyra. They had the worst zone defense around, so basically they were saying go ahead and shoot, you can't hit a fifteen footer! For all the cheerleaders I kissed and was kissed by, I have to report that Bob Duncan, all six foot four of him, kissed me on the lips accidentally after a great victory over a Clyde Central team we had not defeated for four years. He wanted to hug me but in the melee our lips touched. No, it was terrible but we both knew it was purely accidental. You see, there is a humility that builds up despite the best memories. Without being humbled in sport, one can not appreciate the peaks.

My worst injury moment was the appendicitis striking me down in the freshman year right during soccer season. It turned out to be more than a moment; it was three months. As my appendix was removed so, too, was the first soccer season and a portion of the first basketball season. In effect I was sliced right off the team—two teams—before any uniforms were handed out. The recovery from the operation was finally achieved and I was in hog heaven as I took part in every sport existing in the village. We even played ice hockey on frozen ponds, tried golf, water skied, and became connoisseurs of tennis and volleyball.

People were rarely cut off teams at Sodus, as our enrollment in each class back then was about forty to fifty students. Half of these were boys and, drearily, none of the girls played interscholastic sports regularly. They had play-days and some intramurals, but Title IX was not yet the law of the land. Girls were cheerleaders, majorettes and could sing, dance, and play an instrument; but the boys got the uniforms and the teams to play other schools. This was incorrect and unfair, but no one challenged the logic until two decades later. Of the twenty-four boys in our senior class, almost every one of them did something in sports while at Sodus. Some of our best memories were of those less-athletically endowed guys rising up in one of the sports for their individual, defining moment.

As bad as I felt being "sliced" off the teams as a frosh, think about the girls who never got a shot at team sports. I can remember having only one serious injury in four years; that to a hamstring muscle in my senior year in soccer. It caused me to miss one game and there were none of the modern rehab tools such as electric stimulation, ice and hot treatments, nor were there trainers. Most Sodus athletes performed through small injuries and coaches probably did not want to hear about such things as sprains, strains or bruises.

There were times during each soccer season when I could hardly walk home after practice due to what I learned after high school was a "shin splint." There are stretches and treatments with ice and heat for such injuries, but it never once stopped me from playing soccer. In the less scientific and less sophisticated era I was in, such injuries merely healed themselves. Even today I bear a small protrusion on the muscle sheath running down the front of my leg caused by chronic use of the leg when it was afflicted.

Recently I heard some major league baseball players discussing the disabled list (DL) in the current season, and their conclusion was that the professional athletes were much "tougher" fifty years ago. I concur. I concur because the amateur athletes were "tougher" back then also. No one missed games as they do now at any performance level. Cal Ripkin's record is secure forever, based upon what the old-time baseball players reported during the recent ESPN interview. Look up some of the pitching records of the past generations in major league baseball and check out complete games, innings pitched and number of starts by pitchers. There were very few notable pitching injuries back then, it seems. Athletes had to earn money when they could. There were no guaranteed contracts and no five-man rotations. In high school sports we just played for the fun of it but we were did not want to miss a game. We were very, very durable.

Sodus had a whirlpool but the athlete had to endure twenty minutes of concentrated second-hand smoke for the typical whirlpool. It was better to go in the coaches' office in short visits to keep from polluting one's lungs. There were several broken legs due to the cavalier manner in which players tackled in the sport. There wasn't much science to the sport fifty years ago. Clinics and soccer camps were unheard of, so tackling technique was old-fashioned man-on-man to dispossess the other of the ball. The collisions were terrific because the techniques were unsophisticated.

Ed Toye was one of our typical athletes in Sodus. He was a competitor in soccer and basketball and would get into the games when Slim McGinn would look down the bench and figured it was time to get "Fluta" into the contest. Ed was very aggressive and provided us with some of the best collisions seen in the county. Just this year Ed was honored for fifty years of Wallington Fire Department service. He survived his man-made collisions in soccer and gained a few pounds but there he was, hale and hearty, pictured in the local paper. Thanks Lester, for sending it to me every week!

Uniforms were really big items to us, and the failure to dress out for a game for any reason was absolutely unheard of. We bought our warm-ups as seniors and there is a purple and gold basketball warm-up upstairs in the attic even today. I put it on when I watch the movie "Hoosiers" just to get into the mid-fifties mood. We tried to get the same uniform number in each sport we played. Numbers weren't retired as they are today, so the angst of seeing your number on some substitute player the following year after graduation really hurt. After our last home game in basketball in high school was over, we sat around in our uniforms almost in disbelief that four years had zipped by so fast. The manager asked for the wet uniforms so he could close up shop and go home but several of us refused. We spent almost an hour in there while manager Peter Moore waited patiently for the uniforms to finally come off the senior bodies.

As we journeyed the sports-dominated road through our teen-age years, we shared many wonderful moments on our fields of dreams. There were soccer games in snowstorms in late fall where the emphasis was on just making it through the ordeal and not worrying about the score. We had some basketball games in uncomfortable surroundings and the rare hostile crowd but we survived the experience. Our baseball season in the spring of the high school years was marked by typically cold New York State March weather. A base hit hurt your hands so much you almost would rather strike out.

Ever catch your foot under a chain link fence as you chase a ball? I have and it ripped open the skin and filled my shoe with blood, but the game went on and so did I. The award for sheer stupidity in a sporting event, whereby a competitor injured himself, went to yours truly. Just before a Soap Box Derby race down the hill in front of my house one summer I did some last minute repairs to my derby racer. As I sat in my derby at the starting line pounding the final three inch nail down through the top to hold a piece of the frame in place, the nail went through the 2x4 and went into my thigh above the knee. I was crammed into the compartment and could not move and the nail kept me from trying.

The race started two minutes later and I had about an inch of nail imbedded in my leg all through the race. The bumping of the racer on the blacktop jolted me with pain until I finally came to a stop at Gaylord Street. I pulled out the hammer and had someone dislodge the last piece in order to exit the contraption. After losing that heat, bleeding and hurt, I pulled my racer up the hill with blood running down my leg and into my sock. I didn't miss the race and I didn't even dare explain to my Mom what had happened. Sometimes mothers don't need to know everything. They were somewhat like the coaches we played for at the school. The less they knew about the injury, the better. Playing time was that important.

***

Broken Legs- Burning leaves and snapping tibias

I was raking leaves and burning the huge piles accumulated in front of our house. As a fourth grader this was a great chore by virtue of the accrued reward allowed at the conclusion of the rake work. I loved fire. It should not have been a shock to me as a young parent that my two sons loved fire also. One of them burned plastic soldiers in the furnace pilot light. The other burned candles and set his bedding afire once. My childhood fire was somehow safer and better in its application outdoors.

My leaf fires burned quickly with an intensity that was almost hypnotic. By adding in some horse chestnuts the end result was a loud, intense fire. This was really something for a kid in elementary school. My mother was inside and knew where I was and approved the fire under certain terms. No fires near a telephone pole, no fires in front of anyone's driveway and no fires in the yard.

As I burned leaves, in this approved fashion, I could hear crowd noises from the location of the athletic fields down near Fireman's Field. Our new school would ultimately be built near the fields, but at that point in time the school on Main Street did not have many fields around it; so our teams migrated to the green belt near the site of the annual field days.

The roar of two hundred people at a high school soccer game was significant in a community where this represented about ten percent of the whole population of the village. My family lived about a mile away from the games so the crowd noise was a fact of life throughout the fall season. Eventually leaf raking and building fires lost their appeal as I wandered to the fields. My life would never be the same.

For some reason the sport of soccer enticed me, despite its occasional violence. As I watched the older boys represent the school on the soccer pitch, my connection with the sport was set for life. One thing immediately intrigued me, and still does to this day. There were no timeouts and no lulls in the action. This appealed to me then and is the major source of the sport's appeal to active youngsters today.

Unlike the slow, predictable rhythm of baseball and the helter-skelter rhythm of basketball, soccer is uniquely controlled by the players. A coach in baseball uses signals and controls many aspects of the contest. In basketball the coach dictates so much now that it almost is boring to watch at times. Ever get frustrated with how long it takes to play the last minute of a basketball game? Soccer, even with the brief break in the action to treat an occasional injured leg, is fun for the players.

To offset the tremendous interest generated by the nature of the contest there was the random broken leg to sober soccer players. The techniques were often crude. The macho "play through pain" era in which my soccer career started was part of the whole picture. Soccer was a strong sport in the area, and many of the smaller schools did not play football. In our county there were three schools playing football, and three times that playing soccer.

In the mid-century there were very few athletic scholarships awarded but the cost of going to school was so reasonable that student-athletes could "walk-on," using the modern term. Wayne County soccer players showed up on numerous college soccer rosters. More high school soccer players played college soccer than any other college sport during that era. Our baseball and basketball high school experiences were very good but did not prepare many athletes for college. In New York and New England, soccer was king. My, how that changed once I moved to the South!

As alumni groups held their reunions in Sodus the topic of sports always came up. This was typical at most reunions, but in Sodus we discussed the personalities rather than the particular victories. We also discussed the wide variety of coaches we played under while in school.

Those of us fortunate enough to have a "new" coach like Jack Erwin in basketball were aware immediately of the change in the guard. Many basketball coaches in Sodus ruled with an iron hand and players did not ever reach a comfort zone. When an injury did occur under the auspices of a grizzled coach, we knew there would be no complaining.

We were practicing basketball one time in the gym and I turned to run up the floor at high speed. Just after my turn I ran smack into Coach McGinn, who was standing sideways and in a much-braced position. He weighed about one hundred ninety and was six foot three. I weighed in at about one hundred sixty pounds and was five foot eleven. The difference and his stance made all the difference in the world. My lights went out as I ran into his shoulder at full speed.

I came to looking up into twenty pairs of eyes standing over me. The mouths connected to the faces, whose eyes were staring down, were agape. Slowly McGinn offered his hand and pulled me up. He said something to the effect of, "Mayor, you were really hustling on that play." Not one word was uttered about medical, dental, Blue Cross or Blue Shield. No one called a trainer because there was none. No 911 call was made since this was long before that era. Practice continued immediately and I finished with a terrific headache, shoulder ache, and stiff neck. My nose stopped bleeding and I continued. The next day it was worse. I did not complain or even mention it at the breakfast table.

McGinn saw me sometime after that and said that his shoulder hurt and wondered if I had any after-effects from our shared embrace. Do you know what I told him? I merely said there was no after-effect and "Sorry about your shoulder."

That was how things were in the era of "burning leaves and broken tibias."

**

Brownie, Howard and others—Support for the team

In every community across our country, sports engender supporters called fans. The word fan is derived from the word fanatic. In Sodus we had our share of fans that were extremely loyal and possessed great appreciation for the athletes. Few were "fanatics" but brother, were they loyal! We were playing in what was called "B" classification sports, premised upon school enrollment. This scheme insured fair competition and, unlike Indiana's state-wide playoff system with all schools in one category as depicted in the movie "Hoosiers," Section V, class B allowed for play-offs with similarly ranked schools.

When we competed against other class "B" schools, our fans were there in large numbers. Soccer season flowed into basketball and basketball into baseball. Many boys played each and every sport and the seasons did tend to overlap so there were some interesting early season games when athletes were not in "game" shape. Some basketball games featured poor use of hands, and some baseball games sure had some air balls!

It did not affect our support system. Some of the fans that stood the test of time were school custodians, teachers, barbers, insurance salesmen, farmers, lawyers, doctors, businessmen and, of course, our parents. The custodians were our fans also.

One of the custodians named Earl Brown, who worked nights and often allowed us in the gym after hours, became one of our fervent boosters. He knew the details of every game played in the gym because he worked nights when the games were played. He cleaned up after the games, but during the actual game there he stood by the doorway observing everything. I can remember seeing Brownie during out of bounds plays giving his message of support to our player with the ball. The stoppage of play at those times allowed us to hear him. Another of the custodians hired athletes during the summer months to work in the school. Many of us worked portions of our summers with foreman Earl Carpenter and others. They were all fans.

Another fan was an insurance man named Howard. He was the type fan who sat and watched and then over the next three days he would stop a player from the team on the street or in a store to congratulate him on a particular play or moment from a recent game. Each of these men was a very typical fan.

Some teachers were very vociferous in support of our efforts. We developed nicknames for some of these fans. This became a ritual of sorts. We would refer to "Beefy" and all the athletes would instantly know who we were referring to in the lexicon of Sodus sports. Even though he passed on forty years ago, I would bet most of our team members from back then would instantly recognize the name. He did not know we called him that nor did his fine wife. It was our private "insider name trading." We had a "Burly," "Cookie," a "Zowie," and even a "Dingleberry."

I can remember a particular baseball game at Sodus Point, featuring a highly-touted left-hander pitching for the visiting team from Rochester. The pitcher came in with a good pitching reputation but it did not seem to matter. We hit him hard. Our Sodus Point Lakers team, comprised of high school seniors and college boys, won a big game in the last at bat against the thirty-year old lefty. It was the last day of the summer season for us, and it was a great way to conclude our summer together.

His pitches that day were framed by the huge green side of a two-story boat house located four hundred fifty feet from home plate beyond the center field boundary of railroad ties. Any right-handed batter, which I was, saw his pitches coming out of the dark green backdrop. The boathouse was a beautiful sight for right-handed hitters.

For me it was the best view I remember getting of any pitch ever in my life. Sadly, the boat house disappeared a year later and the backdrop advantage on that field went with it. After that summer, we had white sails and water instead of the boathouse as our backdrop.

Howard was at that particular game. True to his fan-ethic, he remembered everything. Due to the backdrop and a lucky day at the plate, I was three for four and my only out came as a line drive. The story of the game appeared in the Rochester paper the next day and my Uncle Don, in the city, called me and told me he had read about my three hits and the 9th inning victory over the ace of the visiting team. Howard approached me in the winter months at the local bowling alley and said, "Congratulations!" I said, "What for Howard?" I was then taken step by step through each at-bat that afternoon three months earlier by our real sports-nut local fan.

It was a real boost for my young ego, and I thanked him for his support and interest. He asked, "How was it that you were able to hit that guy's pitches so well?" I mentioned the boat house theory. He liked it and then informed me he was so impressed by the win and the hitting that he called the game in to the Rochester morning paper. What was a rare press release about Sodus Point in the city paper came via a rare fan.

Many Sodus athletes benefited from such nice tokens of affection and interest. We were fortunate that so many took such an interest in our lives.

***

Diving For Life—A sailor dive

The Sodus Point channel was a focal point for all who traveled to the resort each summer. We swam there against the better judgment of the Coast Guard and our parents. With the Coast Guard-maintained lighthouse at the end of a long concrete pier on one side, and with an equally long concrete pier across about six hundred yards of water, the setting was not only picturesque but very boat-friendly.

It was to become very swimmer-unfriendly one summer day.

The middle of the channel was kept dredged over many decades by the Corps of Engineers for the ease of passage for coal boats that came into Sodus Bay on their routine trips back and forth across the Great Lakes to ports in the U.S.A. and Canada. The "lakers" carried coal dumped into their holds from a trestle that supported coal cars backed out onto the one hundred foot high wooden structure located at one side of the huge bay.

Our bay has been referred to as the greatest natural harbor on all the Great Lakes by many living in Sodus and at the Point. There were other less biased judges of such things who merely referred to Sodus Point as "one of the best harbors in the Great Lakes." Either way, to those of us swimming, boating and fishing there by summer and fishing, ice boating and spinning around in older boys' cars on the ice of winter, it was simply great!

The coal came via train from coal fields in Pennsylvania, and was destined for industrial use in Canada less than a day away by boat across Lake Ontario. The lakers went to Canada loaded down so that a viewer on either pier would see very little of the sides of the boats in sharp contrast to how the boats looked coming into the bay. As the boats made their return trip empty of coal the waterline on the flat-sided hulls showed the red or brown bottom paint that extended several feet up the now-exposed sides of the vessel. These boats (actually Great Lakes ships because boat connotes a smaller vessel) were two to three hundred feet long and when resting against the coal trestle waiting for the many coal car loads to be dumped into their hulls, they did look mammoth.

The design of the laker was such that the pilot house was up on the front of the hull and that left ample space to load and unload across the flat expanse of the deck behind the pilot house. The design for building lakers was altered at some point in the sixties or earlier. A newer configuration had the pilot house (or wheel house) located in the rear of the ship. The purists on the bay insisted this was a way to save money and the newer design did not compare favorably with the pilot house at the front of the hull. Besides, the argument went; the captain could see things better from the front!

The many visits to Sodus Point each summer saw many

different ships plying the waters. Some like the "Fontana" made a daily run to Oswego and back just down the lake. Others with names such as "Valley Camp," and still others, named after previous owners and/or captains such as "Ernest Weir," became regular visitors. Some came into the bay only weekly, and others were more sporadic, which made us think they had long missions out there on the lakes.

The risky swimming behavior we engaged in focused upon the ships coming and going in the bay. Despite their best efforts the Coast Guard fellows were unable to patrol both breakwaters (piers), tend the lighthouse, and man their boat in the bay looking for whatever they looked for in the fifties. It was well before the age of terrorism and well after the era of smuggling illegal booze into the bay from Canada during Prohibition.

As we spotted the telltale plume of smoke from the stack of the ship approaching port, daredevil kids would jog over to the pier to prepare to jump into the huge swells caused by the three hundred foot coal boat as it plowed through the channel at six knots. This became great fun and at times the swells could lift a swimmer high up in the water almost even with the top of the pier. Without the swells the water was about six to ten feet down from the top of the pier. On any normal diving or jumping time without boat swells one had to face a slippery climb up the iron ladders built into the pier sides. On "swell days" a person could grab the ladder's top rung at the end of a wild ride.

We often used the swimming bus from the Village of Sodus to get to our destination unless the hitchhiking or biking modes were employed. Friends either did or didn't jump into the swells caused by the lakers. This did not become a matter of peer pressure because it seemed even then we did not want to have someone jumping into the swells unless they were strongly committed to the process. No matter what anyone did there swimming and diving-wise, the activity "stayed there." Much like the current advertising for Las Vegas detailing that what goes on there stays there, our group ethic held firmly in place—until one terrible day in July.

On that day I saw my first person die. Few of us knew his name until later and we only knew him because he did a "sailor dive" into a swell that was catastrophic. The sailor dive is so-named because it evidently resembles a sailor diving head first off a ship without using his arms in front for whatever reason. Why would a sailor dive into unpredictable waters without putting the arms out in front? Wouldn't a broken wrist or arm be preferable to a broken head or neck? Whatever logic was connected with the dive never made sense then, nor does it fifty years later. After that July day I never wanted another view of such a dive nor another fresh water swell in the channel.

The fellow diver did a sailor dive into the channel but he timed the whole dive poorly. The swell had gone an instant before and in its wake was a huge trough that occurs after each swell even after the ship had passed. The boy shut his eyes, did his "sailor" dive and clunked against the exposed rocks of the bottom nearest the wall. The Corps of Engineers did not dredge the areas immediately next to the walls of the piers because the big boats did not operate there. That fact set in motion the death of innocence and the Wayne County lad. The diver immediately turned a terrible blue color upon surfacing and as he was pulled out by two adults we gathered around in horror. Coast Guard men came running down the pier but there was nothing they could do as even then I realized I had seen death by a broken neck.

My swimming and diving pattern for the next several years involved the beach, the bay but *never the channel*. I finally summoned up the courage to cross the channel with a rowboat at my side. As a result of the traumatic experience, during life guarding duties, I have closed diving boards in pools with less than adequate depth clearances for fear I would witness a repeat of that terrible moment years ago.

Even today as I visit and stroll along the breakwater we dove off of fifty years ago, I still have a sense of dread at what I had witnessed there. The coal boats do not run anymore due to environmental concerns about coal-burning, but the memory of their visits remain in my mind. The beauty of the bay is never diminished in my memories, but the teenager lying in a grave somewhere in Wayne County because of one stupid, ill-timed dive never ceases to remind me about fate.

***

Is Fishing a Sport?—Peanut butter and bass

The twelve foot wooden row boat was tossing and pitching around in the channel. The sudden change in the weather had caused large swells to start rolling, and the wind change brought sheets of rain driving into the faces of the three people in the small boat. What was a pleasant outing for a grandfather and his two grandsons at Sodus Point one summer day had now turned into a life-threatening situation.

The grandfather was my father's father and he was probably sixty at the time. The grandsons were my brother Dick and me. The rowboat was filling with water, the oars were small use against the swells and the winds and we were visibly shaking with fear. My grandfather came up with a dialogue that took our minds off the weather and the situation. I can remember it well; it was a good bit of modeling for anybody in any seemingly difficult situation. He also had both of us bailing water like crazy, using worm cans from our fishing gear.

We had eaten peanut butter and jelly sandwiches for lunch and there were some left over. Herman Blaine Pearson Sr. recommended we eat the rest of the sandwiches to fill our bellies up with bread to keep from being seasick on top of everything else that was wrong at that point. We started doing his bidding and it became readily apparent that the sandwiches had taken on water and looked more like diaper do-do than food. He pointed this observation out to us and transformed a twelve-foot boat into a funny boat. As we were laughing and bailing like crazy, he rowed with all he had to the breakwater across the channel at Sodus Point from the lighthouse. Grabbing onto a rung of a metal ladder built into the breakwater Herman Blaine Sr. was able to keep us from rolling in the channel and give us a sense of safety in the storm. We sat through the storm in the rowboat, getting soaked in the summer rain.

Although he was a robust man, he was not a very physical man. He suffered from poor circulation at sixty and endured a series of heart attacks from age sixty to seventy-two when one finally took his life. He was the proud owner of a pot-belly that he would display after about every noon or evening meal. His typical scenario would be to stand, thank his wife Hazel for a nice meal (this was in sharp contrast to his son Herman Jr.'s typical post-meal statement of "Good try, Isabel") and then retire to the nearest couch to sleep for an hour. His body would be there after most meals, even if there was one couch and ten people looking for seating in the living room. He defined the phrase couch potato quite well. His idea of a workout was to walk around the block at a leisurely pace after waking up. He was not equipped physically to row us at age 10 and 15 into the Sodus Bay and out to the channel. Fortunately, I did not calculate all of this analysis back then, or I would have freaked out when he rented the boat.

Rowing in the channel that day took all he had just to get us to the relative safety of the breakwater. Out of necessity he taught my brother and me how to row as a tandem. We rowed all the way back from the channel to the boat rental place in the bay. We were worn out and our hands were blistered from the wooden oars. Grandfather Herman's endurance and strength had vanished so Dick and I were the twin motors to get us back. Herman Sr. sat at the big end of the small boat just looking at us labor away with the oars. He may have thought it but he never said it: "Why the hell did I get us into this mess to start with?"

As I reflect upon the episode, I realize that my grandfather did all he could do physically to give us a day of fishing. I cannot remember catching very many fish prior to the storm and rain. He really bit off much more than he could chew, so to speak, when he rowed us toward the channel from the boat rental place. It was probably a mile across water and even in the nice weather it was a chore. When the storm came up and we were at the extended end of the rowing trip, we were in trouble.

It was what he did mentally and emotionally that probably stemmed the "tide." His ability to make us see the humor in the peanut butter sandwiches and take our young minds off the true nature of our boating dilemma was the best lesson of the day. His heart must have been really taxed that day as he rowed. Fortunately for all of us, the heart did not fail him at that point. Otherwise we would have swamped, he could have died, and we could have drowned.

Sometimes when things get difficult in one's life it is important to see the ray of sunshine and use humor to ease the burden. I think we really would have been in trouble if my grandmother had made some other kind of lunch other than peanut butter that morning!

***

Climbing—Are trees sports?

In my current position at Berry College, I am deeply involved with what is labeled the "BOLD" Program. The acronym stands for Berry Outdoor Leadership Development. I mention it here because it is a big deal in our HPE curriculum and on our campus. Berry College has the world's largest campus in contiguous acreage. Despite the enormous land and timber holdings all around the major buildings, we have isolated several acres of land right in the midst of our main campus area for the BOLD ropes course.

Mike King, one of my close friends and a genius in the outdoor education realm, has planned, developed and operated the course over the years. All this is said to preface the content of this segment. It should not shock my relatives now to see a sixty-five year old fart up on the platforms and in the cables high up in the trees of the Berry College campus. It is merely a continuation of a fascination contemplated and explored my whole life. It started right outside my home on High Street.

The two huge Norwegian Blue Spruce trees, framing the view of our house from the street, were a climbing haven. There wasn't a BOLD Program or an equivalent Sodus Outdoor Leadership Program (SOLD), but boy did those trees serve us well! From the earliest age possible I began climbing trees. First were the apple trees, which were real easy due to abundant low limbs. Next were simple maple and elm trees with solid limbs, close together. The Norwegian giants became my rite of passage in the tree climbing experience. My brother and I had to get a ladder from our garage to commence the climb.

Unlike every other tree conquered up to that point, a ladder was needed for this job just to get to the large, sprawling lower limbs. As with any current climb on the Berry course, the journey begins with a single step up a rung, or cleat or foothold. Once a person starts, the end result will await after a steady, unhurried pace. In Sodus the end result awaited about eighty feet up using limbs covered with pine sap and very close together. In BOLD work the climber has a belay system, is spotted for the first several feet, and is always on some "support" system once at the top. Dick and I and our gutsy friends were thrilled by such a climb and did so without any belay, spotting or support once there other than our white knuckle grip on the last limbs.

Once at the top of the swaying green giant we merely hung out listening to the whistling wind and feeling the sway of the tree-top. Climbing trees was a thrilling experience for young boys. As we worked our way back down, with sap and sweat dripping off our bodies, it was if we had been at a team practice for two hours.

Now that I have the reflective ability related to my age and stage in life, I conclude tree climbing was one of the greatest sports available in Sodus. As I take part in the contrived and organized "tree climbing" at Berry College it dawns on me Mike King and his associates are merely substituting the man-made course of poles, platforms and cables for the trees the younger generation has missed out on in their own childhood.

The current crop of college students come to campus possessing great computer and technological abilities unheard of in my youth. They also come in with a sophistication based upon TV, travel and college-prep courses. They are great students, eager to learn and appreciate the BOLD course offerings. They usually have not had much climbing other than the occasional mall climbing wall. I do not think many of them spent as many hours in the trees around them as did the Sodus counterparts a half-century ago.

As we meet and greet the climbers at Berry, I always consider myself lucky to have had the natural and somewhat risky tree-climbs of my childhood. I also consider myself very fortunate to have the opportunity to re-live my childhood love of climbing under the protective umbrella of belay systems. There is no need to have survived childhood as I remember the risks, only to perish just as social security checks start pouring in because I fall from a forty foot platform or tree. I even get compensated for what I am doing now! What a life!

I love sport and do consider climbing a sport given my life climbing challenges at either end of the bookends of my life. If a youngster doesn't get the opportunity to climb as my peers and I did in mid-century America, those inspired souls should come to Berry and look me up. We will give them a great sport experience!

***

First Curveball—Sonny Hammond shocks me

My love for baseball had been fostered over the years by men in my family who took me to games when I was young. I started playing ball when my friends and I laid out improvised diamonds all over town when we were in third and fourth grade. My first uniformed game was when I was fourteen and the community could finally support Babe Ruth Baseball. At thirteen we had just missed the cut-off for Little League, and the Babe Ruth League was a year away. We trained during the summer of our unlucky thirteenth year wherever and whenever we could.

My summer of discontent over the apparent injustice to my own age group was marked by two significant acts. One was one of protest and the other was one marked by fear.

The protest thing took a very unusual turn. Several of us "aged out" of the current system set up our own summer league in and around our own rules and our own work schedules we had in various stores and on lawn jobs around town. When it came time to play the modified games on the field kept for the Little League boys we needed a new ball.

On a few occasions during the summer of our own discontent we picked up new balls at the Western Auto store in town. I don't mean that we went in and purchased a new ball at $1.25 or so, but instead we would wander in and without assigning the task to anyone in particular someone would lift a ball from the bin of new balls. The exit from the store was covered by a purchase by someone in the group, after which we'd meet outside and see if anyone had the balls to get a ball.

On some occasions no new ball materialized and we merely went to the field with what we possessed at the time. On a couple of trips a new ball came out of someone's pocket. There was one time when two new balls showed up as a result of the visit to the store. In the Western Auto a hand-written receipt was written for each item in the store purchased, no matter the cost. These receipts, we were told, were taken home by the owner and that is how he maintained his inventory. We had a friend on the inside whose summer job was as a clerk to restock shelves and help carry things for the owner. It was our opinion that David DeSmith, our peer, was aware of our ball source for some of our games that summer. As it turned out this was not the case, and when he was informed about how slick our ballplayer group was on our visits he was chagrined. The nightly receipts were showing up a shortage of baseballs. David was about to be blamed for the shortage since our visits to the store were to see him as well as check our other items. Mr. Skinner did business the old, old fashion way. He knew every piece in the store. He would "backorder" something for you but he did not believe in a huge inventory. Everyone in town tired of the word "backorder" since it meant a wait of two weeks while some item was shipped to the Western Auto.

We decided, I think without much fanfare, not to lift baseballs ever again since none of us felt any success in doing so—and if it put David in bad light that was worse yet. Our ethical behavior was tarnished for the short spell by a feeling of being messed over. There was a measure of being "smart-ass" teenagers in this behavior. Common sense and small community values prevailed. The one time I came out with a baseball bothered me. In two days I went in and paid for two balls when I purchased one and told David to put the money in the register. Wherever the money went in the bookkeeping of old man Skinner I shall never know. It seemed to help my conscience at the time.

That is how the two weeks of "ball movement" occurred in the Western Auto. The fear thing was different.

Sonny Hammonds was seven years older than me when I was about thirteen and getting ready for the PONY League. I knew of Sonny and had a chance to play catch with him and try batting against him. He had played baseball in a neighboring community for the high school with great success. He was picked by a major league scout to try out for the farm club at one of the local tryouts held back then at regional sites. There were plenty of minor league teams back then and the scouts never ran out of hot prospects from rural areas such as Wayne County.

It turned out that I was working in the summer on the baseball field as part of my duties with the local school. I was a young man and Sonny came by to sharpen up with some of our older boys as he prepared for a tryout.

I slipped on the big catcher's mitt and Sonny reminded me to wear a facemask. This was a good idea because I had no idea that the balls thrown by him would do what they did that day. He started slowly throwing medium speed fastballs that still popped into the glove and stung my hand. After several minutes of courage on my part and simple throws from him, he asked if he could throw some curve balls and a few fastballs. At this point I began thinking someone had to extract me from this sport hell to which I had agreed. If his medium speed balls hurt, what would the real fast stuff do to my hand? I had never in my young life actually felt a curve ball or seen it up close. I had seen them in Red Wing games in Rochester and watched the batters' knees buckle as the balls broke across the plate. Would I be up to the task?

Would I be able to handle the curve ball? Would I be able to find a way to handle the fastball? More importantly would I be able to hit these things when he pitched to me standing against the backstop?

I caught the first fastball and it hurt. I became afraid of getting hit even with the mask on. After catching a few more fastballs I slipped on the oversized catcher's chest protector and put the leg protectors on. The equipment made me look goofy but made me feel better. I was still nervous. Sonny then gave me my first half dozen curve balls. Even though Sonny developed arm trouble and never made it beyond minor league ball, he was very good for some time. His curve ball broke as it came in to me and I fought the thing to the ground several times. The curve ball was tremendous.

In that summertime I grew to appreciate the curve. I always looked at curveballs differently after trying to catch the thing that day. I then tried to hit the curve. After seeing the thing as I tried to catch it I calculated that the exposure as a catcher might give me a head start on trying to make contact with it as a hitter.

It would be fun to write that the balls flew all over the field from my bat. That would be an untruth. I might have made contact on two or three of the pitches but basically Sonny threw them by me into the backstop at Sodus. He was able to get his workout and I was able to better assess my potential for big league ball. My conclusions were that he was a potential major league pitcher. My secondary conclusion was that I needed a heck of a lot more experience with the fastball. The curve troubled me since no one had ever warned me about the weapon. It turns out that many coaches spend an inordinate amount of time trying to teach a strategy against the curveball every season at every level.

Curveballs seem to be the defining denominator in a ballplayer's life. We often read that the hitters having trouble with the curveball spend very little time in organized baseball. A good pitcher can make a good hitter look foolish.

In the summer of the Western Auto balls and the Sonny Hammond curveballs there was a parallel. Each particular pitch from Hammond gave me a challenge and a dose of reality. It took a very short time to realize the foolishness of the Western Auto ball. I took a very short time also to realize that my dream of big league success would have to be modified. My challenge in catching and hitting the balls thrown by the local ace helped me to reach a realistic view of my Mickey Mantle-like dreams.

***

Smelling the Grass—Gib, Soup, Jake, Junior, Ears and the boys of summer

In the summers of our youth back at mid-century, we played baseball about every day. There were scheduled games in the various leagues affiliated with Little League, PONY League and American Legion at the national affiliation levels. We also had a variety of pick-up games with each other and with groups that came together in a random manner.

The vivid memory that always comes across my thought processes when baseball is mentioned is an aesthetic memory. I can remember sitting on a bench waiting to bat during a PONY League game one summer at the Sodus field near the school. As our particular team cheered on the efforts of the batter at the plate, the voices were a part of a package of esthetic feelings. In addition to the voices of my friends on both teams, the smell of the freshly cut grass hung in the air and the brilliance of the typical high pressure (barometric reading high due to Canadian air mass) day made everyone just feel good. There were sounds of wooden bats on the balls, the smack of the ball into gloves, and the unique noises associated with people running the bases.

As I sat there mesmerized by all of these things and more, I honest to God thought that this was a great time to be alive and that this experience would be appreciated all my life. It shocked me to be so philosophical in my private thoughts there on the third base side of the field. It truly was my "Field of Dreams" moment early in the 1950s, long before Kevin Costner made the movie forty years later.

What made me think those deeply philosophic thoughts that particular late afternoon up there in New York State when I was thirteen? It did not happen to my age group very often. I never related the story to my peers for fear that they would think I was a goofy teenager. It was a touchy/feely moment that I enjoyed but could not own up to until much later in my life. It was real then and it is still real as I write about it. I think its gestation came via a great family and fine community in the tranquility following many tumultuous years. Those factors did shape me.

The motivation to write about the wonderful opportunities available to me in Sodus and the numerous adults making positive efforts on my behalf is certainly related to the baseball moment described. I knew way back then that I was lucky. I just didn't make a big deal of it back then. I *am* trying to do so in this book.

It was simple to see the effects of baseball upon our young lives. There were plush fields kept under a white covering of snow for almost five months. Once the snow was gone the grass took off as if to make up for lost time. We had to mow fields often and this accounted for the continual fresh smell of cut grass. There were great adults working as coaches, umpires, and league officials to make things work out as planned.

My own younger brother Charley does much of this type of adult baseball work where he lives in New Hampshire. When I visit and see the efforts he is making on behalf of young people in New Hampshire, I appreciate the whole picture. He is paying back the "debt" to the adults of Sodus who were there for him, even though he is five hundred miles from Sodus and deep in New England.

Baseball is truly America, as James Earl Jones states in "Field of Dreams," There may be flaws in the sport due to greed, steroids or other high level factors; but down in the small towns and villages I would guess baseball is alive and well. When I played the organized games I shared my hundreds of hours with Sodus originals. Larry "Junior" Davis was a man in later life who spent much of life in the school as a custodian serving the school and the kids. When we played he was a terror on the field and when I pitched against him I could never get a fastball by him! Ken Campbell, alias "Soup," was one of school's most outstanding hitters. He merely hit line drives every time up. Ed LaRock was a catcher for teams he played for in the summer and at the school level. He became a P.E. teacher and coach in Wayne County and coached several championship teams at his alma mater. He was my catcher one or two summers at the village fields when I got a chance to pitch. He was a worker behind the plate and adults would say of him that he would end up coaching. They were correct. Before he coached, he had to perfect the spin and chase maneuver typical of catchers when there were wild pitches. I kept him in great shape for two summers running to the backstop to get balls! I must have covered home plate on wild throws more than any kid in New York State!

Gib would show up with his two-tone Harry Walker-type Louisville Slugger wood bat and stand there in the batter's box waiting to spray hits all over despite looking more like the counselor that he would eventually become in the adult years. Looks can be deceiving. A player with the Rochester Red Wings named Don Richmond was a leading hitter in the International League, and when the bespectacled player was in the batter's box there was my buddy Gib.

We had a guy named Curly Waters who had a great curve ball, and I still don't know how he made it break as it did. His was a special pitch, so when you heard Curly you immediately thought curve. When you heard Smiley Ape you thought of Bill McGowan. Actually you thought of David Cooper, our English teacher who coined the phrase I think. Bill had the ability to smile through thick or thin and was smiling so much that we thought even back then he would certainly be a politician. Guess what? He was a political figure in a nearby community for many years. I remember one time when he was batting during the summer of his blooming love for Nancy, who would become his wife later on. His love was such that he carried her photo in his baseball cap for good luck.

After I had hit him for the second time in a game with one of my typically wild pitches he looked longingly into his cap, smiled and then ran to first. Now that was true love and a commitment to the smile. Not all the guys I plunked smiled. There were some in every game with me on the mound.

The interesting thing about our fields for many years was that there were no fences in most of the outfields. An outfielder could run forever to catch what would have been a home run. Conversely a line drive in the left-centerfield or right centerfield gap would roll forever and be an inside the park home run. It was always interesting to watch the poor third base coaches when balls were hit into the gaps. Nothing short of a tackle could stop a player from going for broke in an attempt to get a home run. I know, because I ran through some third base stop signs.

Baseball in Sodus was important. Kids played baseball against migrant laborers when picking seasons slowed down. At times there were Cuban players from nearby field jobs who showed up for unscheduled games. There was a team at Sodus Point called the Lakers and that is another chapter unto itself. The Lakers were organized to allow anyone in the area to play once the player had moved through the various age group opportunities leading to age 19 or so. There were men who were in their forties playing baseball at the Point who were an interesting collection of characters.

It figures that they would be interesting since they were those men in the community who helped younger players all through the week and then on Sundays they would bring out their uniforms. Although the uniforms were tight and worn the spirit of the men wearing them was terrific.

I can still smell the grass and see the sailboats out on Sodus Bay as I remember what those men did for baseball in Sodus.

***

Snow and Golf—A ride to remember for Charley Moss
The toboggan is a marvelous piece of winter apparatus. The six or eight foot long, two foot wide piece of highly varnished,

thin maple wood could take several people down a snow-covered hill in a hurry. It had no runners and the board was curved up at the front to facilitate a plowing effect through deeper snow. Unlike a sled or skis, the toboggan can not be aimed very accurately. By coordinating the leans of the many passengers behind the driver, slight course adjustments could be made. The emphasis should be on the word slight.

In Sodus winter lore, there were numerous stories about wild rides on the wooden devices. One of the classic stories still retold at reunions recounts the episode of a lad who flew down a steep hill in the new snow and went through a barbed wire fence unseen in the blowing snow. He was really never the same due to psychological stress. The poor plastic surgery back in the late forties in the previous century also made the memories linger.

A toboggan rides nicely on top of most snows since it has so many square feet of bottom surface. It seems that the flying saucers that came later in my life were single seat, round toboggans. They, too, were rather reckless in nature since they could not be driven accurately. All this discussion about lack of steering ability becomes crucial to a mid-winter ride many in our group of friends will always remember.

One of the best places to ride down hill in winter was at the local golf course located high on successive hills above beautiful Sodus Bay. The golf course was usually unused for the months of November through March by the local golfers. This fact of life for area golfers made the course great for the toboggans of the area. Sleds would not work on the golf course since the snow needs to be plowed or packed for a sled. Skiers did not frequent the golf course since there was a rope tow for skiers a few miles away on the biggest hill in the county.

So there we were one night, with two toboggans and twenty young people. The fresh snow was deep and the clear wintry night was highlighted by stars. Twinkling lights of far off year-round cottages and shacks of ice fishermen out on the bay added to the aura of the crisp, clear night.

Democracy ruled on the hill as all in attendance at the toboggan party got their chance to "drive" the devices. This was a tradition and part of the tradition was a test of the driver's courage since being up front was more hazardous. Riding was fun, but seated up front was twice the thrill since you got the snowy blast in the face. You also got any trees, bushes, and random things like fences.

The driver usually could finish the ride even as others flew off on the way down. The reason anyone flew off was that there was not much to hang onto, and if you were grabbing the person in front of you this could cause a convulsion of drop-offs on the way down. The only thing available to grasp was a rope down each side of the toboggan if you chose that grip. The guy or gal up front had the rope handles to grasp so they were the most stable even in their danger spot.

Our buddy Charley's turn to drive came up, and he was primed for the long ride down through the small trees on the hilly course. We had been there for nearly two hours and everyone was getting to the "hot chocolate" point for the evening. That was when everyone headed inside to warm up and debrief the various rides. Charley Moss (Mossgraber) was our tallest class member and was one of our unique friends. He loved basketball, and could shoot the lights out when his confidence overcame the pressure placed upon him by a sometimes overbearing father. Charley's father was not there this night to dissuade his offspring, and our basketball star's turn to drive was to be the event of the evening. His basketball prowess would not be of any assistance at this juncture!

The larger of the two toboggans was loaded up, and a push by others not doing the run got the last ride of the night underway. As a note of interest coming from years of snowy experiences, most accidents seem to occur on the "last ride" down or the "last ski run down." This ride was to prove the point. Charley was not a verbal person and, in fact, he stuttered some. On this run down, his lack of quick and accurate verbal cues about leaning, coupled with the normally poor steering, made for a hellacious ride.

I was about four people back from Charley near the end of the toboggan, so I saw little of our fateful course. Due to blowing snow stirred up by the toboggan and because of the people in front of me, only the rush of the speed on the snow and the wind were evident. Charley must have seen the trees coming up on the section of the course but due to the speed of the run and the occasional slowness of his speech pattern, we connected with one of the young trees poking up through the snowy surface.

Nothing stops seven people on a toboggan faster than an immovable object. If the tree were a couple of years younger perhaps we would have run it over. However this particular tree had made it through to its stout, young life and was not going to give in to a bunch of Sodus kids on a toboggan.

Charley Moss took the initial shot right where his legs were spread at the front of the toboggan as the toboggan split apart on the tree. He hit the tree and then all the riders piled on top of him in rapid succession. He, like all of us, was heavily covered with a parka and ski cap so damage was minimal. The rest of us were banged up here or there, but the hot chocolate and a couple of days rest took care of the damage.

We sat in the snow laughing with Charley after the collision, despite his temporary agony. No matter what happens in any sporting venue, the humors of seeing a performer get hit in the groin with a ball, another person or, in this case, a tree seems to bring on the laughter. The girls who were present did not quite understand the humor at Charley's expense. Guys seem to understand the humor evoked at the expense of some male's groin injury. Charley understood.

Life seems to be filled with memories of simple and sometimes painful situations. Long after the pain subsides the laughter can continue. A few years before Charley passed away, several of us laughed about "the" toboggan ride. He reaffirmed that he truly understood our laughter that night. God bless you, Charley Moss!

***

Bobby Thomson—A Sodus hero for anti-Dodgers

Bobby Thomson of the New York Giants hit a ninth-inning home run off Ralph Branca of the Brooklyn Dodgers on October 3, 1951. The date was memorable because the "shot heard around the world" decided the three game National League play-off after the teams split the first two games. The two teams were deadlocked in first place after the regular season ended. Remember, back in the fifties, there was a National League and an American League and the champ of each played in the World Series. It was pure and simple. No wild card, no divisional play-off and no games in November! The Dodgers were ahead in the National League by thirteen and a half games at the end of August 1951. The sterling comeback was a prelude to baseball history. Bobby Thomson's home run at the Polo Grounds in New York created quite a stir. The Giants then played the Yankees in the World Series and lost, but the National League pennant race was the most exciting in history.

My brother Dick and I were watching the end of game three on TV at home that particular day. When Branca's pitch changed direction at home plate and went sailing over the left field barrier, the two Pearson brothers charged out into the street in front of our house and started jumping up and down and yelling. "The Giants won the pennant, the Giants won the pennant!" That was a variation of the line used by Russ Hodges, the Giants broadcaster, heard all over the nation that day. We merely adapted it for our use in the street. Neighbors looked at us with amusement, and we had to tell them about the baseball game.

Why the great excitement? We were avowed Yankee fans interested in facing the Giants rather a formidable Dodger lineup in the 1951 fall classic. In my lifetime, up to the 1951 playoff, "my" Yankees were in the World Series seven times and the Dodgers were the enemy on three occasions. We were fearful that the Dodgers' time had arrived but the sudden elimination of the "Bums" made our vision for another World Series victory a bit more positive. Actually, the Dodgers time would come four years later in 1955 when they squeaked by the Yanks four games to three.

I return to 1951. In addition to the delight of meeting the Giants and their new star, Willie Mays, we were amazed at such a profound comeback by a team so far behind in the standings. The Giants became our favorite National League team. We had been to the Polo Grounds with our father, so it felt OK to be a Giants fan. The Yankees took them out four games to two in the Series, and our neighborhood resumed its normalcy.

When our father came in from work that historic day, he knew we were elated. We had called him to report the damage done by the Thomson shot. His take on the matter was that the Giants would be emotionally spent from their uphill climb in the N.L. and would succumb to the Yankees' well-rested pitching. Once again, Pete was correct!

My Dad was a great baseball fan, and he knew baseball statistics as well as he knew world and national affairs. His prowess was extraordinary when we started talking baseball. One of his missions in life was to educate his sons about baseball. His father, H.B.P. Sr. had done that for him. Both men would load up on cigars and nestle into a stadium seat and have the time of their lives. He passed the love, if not the cigars, on to his sons. He took us to the Polo Grounds, Ebbetts Field, and Yankee Stadium in New York, Briggs Stadium in Detroit and Municipal Stadium in Cleveland. We were fortunate to be able to travel as we did and get mentored by the "Mayor."

In my lifetime I have attempted to involve my own kids with baseball in the same manner as I had when I was young. They appreciated the attempt but neither stayed with baseball as a fan or a player very long. Maybe I should have used the cigars. Listening to games on the radio was a summer routine for me as I grew up. My father taught me to keep score at the games I attended. Most of my friends loved the game and we spent endless hours listening to and discussing the great sport. Often, as I listened to games on the radio, I would keep score. I had several friends also afflicted with the scoring "bug." Neighbor Ken Symonds would keep stats. Charley Moss would be a font of statistics. In the middle of basketball practice during a lull you could ask Charley what Don Richmond hit last season for the Red Wings and he would spit it out.

Sometimes on rainy summer days, we would sit on someone's porch and play a baseball strategy board game. With the rain pouring down, some mother providing us with treats to eat and surrounded by friends, this became a neat time for all of us. It was baseball love and we were hooked for life.

Once TV became commonplace, the radio broadcasts lost some of their appeal due to the new competition. I actually preferred radio over TV for a long time, since I could imagine the play and the early black and white TV broadcasts were not all that sophisticated.

My father would sit at night in our kitchen listening to a Yankee game or Rochester Red Wing game with me as we ate ice cream. He amazed me as he would clean out a half gallon of the stuff after I got what was my share.

His grasp for the details of the game was quite entertaining. He could remember what certain batters had done in previous games and then would tell me their batting averages just ahead of the announcer's declaration of the same information. I find myself doing the same thing sixty years later as I watch the Atlanta Braves on TBS.

Mel Allen was my Dad's favorite announcer and the "How about that?" trademark of Mel Allen brought a smile to the family's baseball connoisseur's lips. The Allen statement would usually come after a Mickey Mantle home run, a nice pitching performance by Whitey Ford or some similar accomplishment. Life was good in Upstate New York Yankee country. The Giants drove us into the streets with their unique, once in a lifetime comeback, but it was the Yankees who kept us enthralled season after season. Bobby Thomson and Willie Mays were really something in the fifties but, until the Yankees fired Yogi as their manager after just sixteen games in the 1985 season, I was a Yankee fan. Once that happened, I forswore my allegiance to those corporate pinstripes. Dad died in 1970, so he did not have to bear witness to the treatment of Yogi Berra. He would understand my switch in loyalties to other teams such as the Braves.

The Braves made a miraculous worst to first move from 1990 to 1991 in the National League. After finishing last in 1990 they won the pennant the following year. That was a great baseball achievement in the current era, though it did pale in contrast to the Giants' comeback and the Bobby Thomson homer of my youth.

***

Harry the Hat—Wonderful memories

"Harry the Hat" Walker played baseball in the major leagues for the St. Louis Cardinals, the Philadelphia Phillies and Chicago Cubs. He batted .363 to lead the National league in hitting in 1947, which was the same year Jackie Robinson integrated baseball with the Dodgers. A unique thing about Harry Walker was that in the year he led the league in hitting he was traded from Cardinals to the Phillies during that season! How many major league players can you mention that have been traded during their best season or won a batting title the year they were traded?

Another impressive item was that he batted .357 with the Cardinals in 1955 when he was almost 40 years old. He was the Cardinals' playing manager. This was the same role he played in Rochester for four years. How many AAA managers go up to the big leagues in the fall and hit .357? Walker hit .296 lifetime so his credentials as a hitter are documented. Harry the Hat won over six hundred games as a big league manager to go along with his successful minor league career as playing manager.

In between the batting title and the last at-bat in the big leagues, Harry managed the Rochester Red Wings as a playing manager in the International League. He managed from 1952-1955. During that time the Red Wings drew large crowds for a minor league team. Over the time Walker managed, the team drew about a quarter million fans annually. Many of these fans drove up the fifty miles from Wayne County. Many of us from our village went to Wings games often.

I saw the former N.L. batting champ pull off a squeeze bunt with the bases loaded to win a game at Red Wing Stadium during one of his successful seasons in Rochester. The move caught whoever they were playing that night completely by surprise. It caught the whole stadium by surprise also! After the game the newspapers reported that Walker gave the sign for the squeeze while in the batter's box. Surely he must have used something other than his cap to initiate the play.

Harry was called the "Hat," according to baseball historians, because he fiddled with the hat constantly between pitches. His nervousness with the hat was unique to the times. If, on the night of the game-winning squeeze play the hat was involved, it would have been a great deception.

We drove home from that game thinking Harry Walker was really something. It was unique to have a team's hitting leader unselfishly laying down a surprise bunt. Can you imagine a bases-loaded scenario in the modern era where a premier hitter would lay down a bunt in the bases loaded situation?

There was another interesting aspect of Harry Walker that I did not know until I read about Jackie Robinson. The paths of Robinson and Harry's older brother Dixie Walker crossed in Brooklyn in 1947. Dixie Walker was a lifetime .306 hitter, so it appears the Walker family turner out some good hitters. Dixie occupies an uncomplimentary niche in baseball history. According to many reports, Dixie Walker was one of several Brooklyn Dodger players that tried unsuccessfully to derail the Jackie Robinson major league express in spring training of 1947. The matter was resolved quickly as Brooklyn Owner and General Manager Branch Rickey informed Walker and his fellow petition signers that they would be traded if they could not work side by side with Jackie Robinson.

Baseball history tells us that things worked out for Robinson, the Dodgers and baseball history despite the awkward start in spring training. A close study of the record books tells us Dixie Walker was moved to the Pittsburgh Pirates after the 1947 season. Robinson was the N.L. Rookie of the Year in 1947 and stayed in Brooklyn for ten years. Baseball changed forever.

Dixie's brother Harry did not appear to have a color bias since his successful managerial career involved an appreciation of the skills of many men of different backgrounds.

Harry Walker used a two-tone bat in his successful batting efforts through the years. This became a common sight in our ball games in Sodus. It is interesting to reflect how a player's bat influenced young men across the country. Jackie Robinson used a thick handle bat and that bat appeared in sandlots in great numbers after he started in Brooklyn. "Louisville Slugger" wooden bats (made in Louisville, Kentucky to the specifications of major league players) were the standard fare in baseball for many decades. Times have changed and the company has to share the market with many other companies making metal and wooden bats. Back in the fifties every hardware and Western Auto store had a bin of wooden bats. For two bucks you could get your choice of particular player model in any length. The Jackie Robinson 32" bat with the thick handle seemed to last for a long time in our games. During that era players would share their favorite bat, so it was typical to try a Harry Walker, a Jackie Robinson, a Mickey Mantle and then a George Kell bat all in one week of play.

In the modern era it appears that the players' salaries, their use of steroids, and their undisciplined behavior have impacted upon young players much more than the wooden bats used by players in my childhood. A huge part of this is that metal bats predominate in all play below the major leagues. The two-dollar Louisville Slugger is now fifteen times as expensive. The fact that I can remember Harry's bat and know very little of any negative aspects of his career are refreshing to me. In my naivety associated with the era in which I grew up, I rarely considered that baseball players were as good or as bad as the society from which they came. It was better, I feel, not to know all the crap associated with private lives. We seem hell-bent to learn stuff like that now; and even if we aren't, the media is determined to spoon feed it to us.

I am impressed with wooden bats even today. Recently my wife Jan purchased a Louisville Slugger bat for me as a surprise gift. She had heard me tell a friend that I really liked two particular bats:

the Ernie Banks model with a thin, tapered handle and the Jackie Robinson bat with the thick handle. Lo and behold here I am in my sixty-fifth year of life with one of those bats. The Jackie Robinson model was not available anymore so my wife got the Banks model. It sits in my office at home with hundreds of potential hits still in its finely finished wood. It will never go to the diamond again to be shared with my friends in games, but it is a great reminder of some wonderful memories.

The bat seems to trigger a sensory overload. I can close my eyes and hear the voices and excited yells of my friends at play. I can smell the freshly cut grass and smell natural fragrances of the spring season in New York. I can see the blue sky and shadows across the diamond. I can taste the vanilla malted milk shakes we consumed after long hours on the fields.

Maybe Harry Walker's older brother Dixie should have tried the Robinson model bat in 1947. It might have prolonged his career in Brooklyn and helped him better understand and appreciate the game of baseball. I know that the shared bats sure were wonderful for me and my friends.

***

Luscious Luke—Easter came early
Luke Easter was a mammoth human being and he could hit a fastball farther than I had ever seen. Easter was a first baseman for the Rochester Red Wings for a time in his career. He played several years with the Cleveland Indians of the American League, but played at Rochester in the International League when his Cleveland career ended. Before a Rochester game once, several of us got an Easter autograph that was an esteemed collectible for each of us.

We had seen Black men before and went to school with a few Blacks but never had been so close to a Black professional baseball player. Luscious Luke, as he was called by reporters, stood 6'5" and weighed close to two hundred sixty pounds. Compared to the white boys from Sodus standing near him at the fence, Luke was a giant. Luke was a friendly presence for professional baseball. He was a presence because Jackie Robinson made his presence possible. I had seen Jackie Robinson on TV, but Easter was something else. Luke Easter was right here in the local stadium.

Sodus, New York was the temporary address during the summer months for many Black Americans referred to as migrant workers. They picked the many fruit crops in our county, starting with sweet cherries in June and concluding with apples in October, prior to their return south to pick citrus fruit in Florida during the winter. On occasion some of the migrant workers set up residence in the community and took permanent jobs. When this happened the children were in the school systems. Our schools were integrated thusly.

During summer months, migrant workers would occasionally play baseball on a rare day off against one another or against other migrant teams in the area. When these games occurred they were witnessed by many fans in the area. The talent of some of the fruit pickers was exceptional. These games took place against the backdrop of the post-Jackie Robinson era nationally, and during the Luke Easter era regionally. I can remember only one occasion when the white kids from local teams played against the teams of young migrant workers. As I remember the game it went about four innings and the score was not very good for the white kids! White boys should have played against those guys more often. Actually they should have played with them more often! Such were the times in the mid-century.

Easter hit plenty of home runs for Cleveland and twice attained the one hundred RBI mark in the American League. He finally had trouble solving the intricacies of the curve ball. While in the International League with Rochester and Buffalo, he continued his home run feats. Fans loved his presence.

Working in the orchards with the migrants was a job many of us did to make summer earnings. The workers loved Easter and men like him for their abilities. White young men would work in the orchards for the growers they knew and keep punch cards for tallying amounts of cherries that were picked by the migrants.

No one I knew could pick cherries like the migrant pickers. This skill was their existence. Whenever my buddies or I went picking anything, we did not make very much based upon pound picked. In and around the business of cherries were many discussions of baseball abilities. There were very few Black baseball pitchers during the era. There were many hitters like Easter that captured the imaginations of the fans. Baseball was a common language in the orchards.

The Easter followers were black and white. Talent was appreciated during the middle of the twentieth century despite skin color. One of the best discussions involved hypothetical match-ups of someone like Easter or Robinson against pitchers like the Yankee's Eddie Lopat or Allie Reynolds. When the Dodgers and Yankees played one of their many TV World Series games, people of any color could make their evaluations. Sport became the best road to integration.

There were times during harvest seasons when young boys in the county (including Sodus boys) would load up a car with vegetables and/or fruit depending upon the season, and ride around throwing these products at many targets. This was good for throwing skill development, but not a positive for community relations. Sometimes the targets were mailboxes. Sometimes the targets were signs. Sometimes the targets were barns. Sometimes the targets were rooftops and sides of houses, trailers and temporary residences set up for migrants. Despite the spirit of Luke Easter and Jackie Robinson and despite the presence of Black students in our schools, we strayed over the good sense line at times.

On one occasion, one of the riders in one of the cars on such a mission of mischief was a local Black who was a resident year around in the village. It seemed an irony that we were throwing at the migrant homes on the throwing rides. He pointed out that we also were throwing at white occupied targets. We were an integrated group of hooligans.

The rides diminished almost overnight when a car came back with shotgun pellet holes in the trunk area of the automobile.

These were said to have come from a fruit farmer who did not enjoy having fruit thrown at his property. He grew the apples but he sure as hell was not going to hear apples fall on his roof or hit his property. Suddenly new forms of teen-age fun developed. In a review of behavior, this form of juvenile behavior was pretty stupid. Fortunately the activity passed when we discover dating, weekend sports and other acceptable activities.

If Luke Easter said to us that this behavior was stupid, we would agree. The trouble with us is that we were adolescents and despite the myriad of good influences in the community, we still did stupid things. The overwhelming preponderance of good adult leaders in the adult community won the day. The guy who pumped shotgun pellets towards the car made his statement, but it was the other adults that made the difference.

An interesting development occurred one summer in Sodus when some Cuban migrant workers showed up to play ball against the white kids and then the migrant workers. The local youth recreation leader set a couple of informal games up, and the end result was a serious thrashing of the migrants and the white kids by the Cubans. The Cubans were picking a crop somewhere in the county, but in those games they picked baseball egos apart. We learned then what major league scouts have discovered over the past thirty years. Latino players were enormously talented.

Luke Easter probably would have enjoyed seeing the pick-up games, but he was already having his own problems hitting against Latino pitchers in the International League!

***

Bobby Wanzer in the Sodus Gym—Swish City

Bobby Wanzer stood near the circle around the center jump area in the Sodus gym and swished set shot after set shot from this incredible range. As his warm-up shots rippled the net and as his teammates performed their particular warm-up rituals, Wanzer was the focus of many in the gym, the marksmanship was so incredible and so beautiful to behold. The date was March 25, 1952. Everyone in town knew of this scheduled appearance.

The gym at Sodus High was packed for the exhibition game between the NBA Rochester Royals and a team of former Sodus High all-stars. Needless to say, all of us who were aspiring athletes in the Sodus system were eager to see how some of our Sodus legends would fare against the NBA stars from nearby Rochester. As we witnessed the Royals warm up it became quite obvious that our local heroes of the hard-court were going to be over their collective heads in this particular basketball pool!

Bobby Wanzer was a star player on the Rochester Royals professional basketball team in the NBA during the 1950s. He was the running mate of all-star point guard Bobby Davies. Wanzer would be considered a shooting guard in today's terms. Wanzer and his teammates traveled around upstate New York in the pre-season, generating interest among the small towns within a driving radius of the Royals' home court in Rochester.

The sports arena they played on was a one-hour drive each way for those of us in Sodus, and this was the confirming logic of pre-season games in towns such as Sodus. During successive years of such pre-season games, the numerous small towns hosted the Royals show in a rotational order so that the Royals would play in a particular gym once every several years. The Bobby Wanzer "show" being presented for all of us in Sodus that night was, therefore, a rare treat for all. The number of outdoor baskets increased in Sodus after that visit, it seemed, as all of us worked on developing a set shot as observed that evening in the gym.

The magic of Wanzer's two-hand set shot was so influential and compelling that many of us overlooked other mainstays of basketball such as rebounding, defense, and opposite-hand lay-ups to merely stand outside at various barn and garage supported baskets to fire endless two-handers at the hoops. It took many hours of coaching in our town and others, I am sure, to explain that such a shot was only a small part of the arsenal of weapons to use on the court. The thought that a mere mortal could cross center court in a gym with the defense retreating in front of him and then merely stop and pop a thirty five footer was incredible to consider.

Wanzer was living proof that it could be done, and we were seeing it right here in Sodus. Needless to say, the Royals creamed our legends, and Wanzer took and made many set shots from a more normal range during the game, and shared the scoring with his skilled running mates. The final score was never in doubt and Les Harrison, the Royals owner, general manager and coach was adept at keeping the score down. This kept the Royals from creating hostility among this huge crowd of potential Royal ticket buyers.

Think of what I have just written about Harrison. Three titles: owner, GM and coach. He had absolute control of the franchise and the players. Think of the endless problems in the modern era among the triad of leadership personalities as coaches and general managers are tossed overboard by bored owners. Those times fifty years ago were certainly different. Can you imagine a current NBA team visiting a small town and playing such a home town bunch as represented in Sodus that night? Each small town had their local legends, and fall after fall the Royals would generate ticket sales in this manner. The good will was evident, and the Royals generated plenty of tickets sales out in the other towns also.

The aura of attending a Royals game was part of our growing process in Sodus and other towns. We would ride into the city on route 104, watch a game and then stop at a fast food place called Bill Grey's on the way home for a giant hamburger, fries and cokes. What a wonderful life for aspiring basketball players. Consider what a treat it was then to see the Royals up close and personal in *our* gym!

On a couple of other occasions, before the Royals had to pick up and move to Cincinnati in the sixties for a greater fan-base, Les Harrison came to Sodus with a player or two to speak at awards nights at the conclusion of our sports seasons. He, of course, would say he was very interested in some of the Sodus products currently playing, and that would provoke great interest in our own game development and even more interest in the Royals. Realistically, we realized quite soon that no one from Wayne County would ever make the Royals, and certainly none of our Sodus legends ever did make the roster of the Royals.

For certain magic moments in an adolescent life, it sure made for great dreams. In the modern era the NBA is quite self-absorbed with their own pile of trouble and piles of money, and the little towns and villages of the country don't appear on the NBA radar screens. The Wanzer visit was intriguing for all of us, and the Royals and Lester Harrison became a part of our lore in the community.

Many of us started calling our buddy Gib Sergeant "Lester" in response to Gib's organizational and leadership skill in sports. Late in our high school years, when Gib hung up the Converse All-Stars for a manager position with the varsity basketball team, the name became his. Even today, many of us in Gib's memory bank still refer to him as Lester.

It was fascinating to reflect upon the Royals and their impact upon upstate New York. During that same time in NBA history there was a strong team in nearby Syracuse called the Nationals, led by Dolph Schayes and many other outstanding players. The New York Knicks were major enemies of the Royals, as were the Boston Celtics and Ft. Wayne Pistons. Some of these franchises have moved on to other cities, as did the Royals. Some possible trivia questions for sports buffs would be to answer the questions about where the Royals moved to over the years and where the Ft. Wayne team and the Nationals from Syracuse ended up.

***

Bare Foot Post—A Shoeless Joe from Irondequoit

Can you imagine playing first base in your bare feet? Can you also imagine getting into the batter's box in your bare feet? There was a time, and a man in that time, when these things occurred. The player was "Bare Foot Post," and he became a legend in the Monroe and Wayne County area at the middle of the previous century. I was fortunate enough to play against him and his team on two occasions.

Bare Foot had another name, but in all the years of his presence around the area as a player I never learned the man's name other than Post. When he batted, he would "dig" in at the plate—with his toes. I watched this ritual with fascination as I contemplated what a foul ball would feel like hitting *my* toes. Can you imagine getting hit by a low fastball without shoes on? When I was in my thirties, I played in a baseball game in Wolcott barefoot. A summer team came traveling by looking for a game one Sunday when I was visiting relatives and friends in the Wayne County village near Sodus. Despite not having played anything but softball for many years, I joined the Wolcott locals for the game. My part in the game was to play centerfield but, of course, bat. I ended up playing barefoot because there were no shoes to fit my feet and my Sunday clothing did not include spikes. My hitting did not suffer as I got a couple hits and, significantly, did not hit my own feet, did not get hit with a pitch and did not get stepped on during the game. My thoughts flashed back to my fascination with Bare Foot Post in the batter's box fifteen years earlier!

Post brought his team of all-stars to Sodus Point periodically to play an equally historic team called the Sodus Point Chiefs and Sodus Point Lakers. The name changed somewhere along the way, but teams traveled in from distant points to enjoy the unique setting. In the 1930s up until the late 1950s, a team using the beautiful diamond overlooking Sodus Bay challenged all comers on summer weekends. Many talented players displayed their wares on the field that was bordered by cottages on the left field line and roads along right field and in deep right centerfield. Centerfield and left field were the prettiest around. Sodus Bay framed that part of the field.

My peers and I joined the Lakers as they were losing their momentum as an attraction and a team. Many more leagues for youngsters were available, so many eligible adults were tied up with their kids. Another fact of life was the recreation industry. Baseball was losing out to boating, camping, travel, scouting and televised games. When the team did play over those glorious weekend afternoons (the field was not lighted) a hat was passed to provide money for the team's upkeep. None of the players were paid, but we still needed money for the expendables such as wooden bats and baseballs. Many balls disappeared into the bay and in between the cottages. We also needed funds to pay the umpires traveling in from other communities to insure objectivity.

Bare Foot Post was an excellent player who devised the bare foot routine to attract crowds and keep his name in the sport pages. Even when he was forty, when we competed against his team, his talents were obvious. The guy played first base and could handle a glove expertly. Everyone in the ballpark waited for some runner to stomp his bare foot sometime but it never happened. He was a good hitter but by the mid-fifties, when our group comprised the Lakers' lineup, it was evident his hitting ability had lessened.

Although our team at the time was a young team, we did have a couple of old-timers who played for us. Sodus Point had an illustrious baseball history and players such as Harris, Arney, Torrey, Rainey, Palmer, Parsons, Johnson and Sergeant representing the community on the famous diamond. A man named Oscar Fuerst did all kinds of things to make the games flow along smoothly as a kind of "defacto" general manager.

One Sodus man, Danny Johnson, was ten years older than we were, yet he pitched for us with great distinction. When he did bat, on days he pitched, he was an excellent hitter. He shared many important batting and pitching tips with his younger teammates. Danny had been a high school star and finished his amateur career with the Sodus Point team. This was a regular routine for twenty years or more as men in their thirties, forties and even fifties still did some spot hitting and pitching. It was baseball with a real local flavor. A player never really separated himself from the team. He kept his uniform handy for those moments when he would show up for an appearance or a pinch-hitting opportunity.

The truly remarkable thing about Danny was that he had lost an eye in a hunting accident after high school. His skill at hitting and pitching was truly outstanding in high school and stayed with him on the Lakers, despite the loss of one eye in his prime.

The older men shared their skill and love of the game with us. It was a distinctive honor to wear a Chief or Laker uniform. Once, during a high school team picture, I wore a Sodus Point uniform, not realizing the name was on the uniform front. It appeared in the yearbook later in the school year.

A game at Sodus Point on a Sunday had many traditional and unique baseball mores. When the hat was passed around there was never any doubt about making a contribution toward the game. Everyone got "in" free due to the wide-open nature of the field. No one ran from the responsibility of paying his or her fair share, however. Consider the possibilities of getting to the field. A boat could pull up in deep centerfield, pull up on the shore and walk twenty feet to the railroad ties marking the boundary of the field and watch the game from a railroad tie-seat. A car could pull in beyond deep rightfield and watch while eating some hotdogs. Cottagers came out their back door and sat in lawn chairs as the innings rolled along.

The cottagers bordering the leftfield area would provide hotdogs and cokes for the players between innings. The odor of the meat being cooked along the leftfield line was a terrific sensory memory. There were some attractive female cooks and they would be the source of food and dates all through the summer months. Sometimes baseballs would hit automobile windshields along the right field line. This was the field's only real problem area. The balls going over the railroad ties on the fly were home runs. If the ball bounced over the tie it was a ground-rule double. Railroad ties provided a ricochet-effect for a hard hit ground ball so the fielder had to be careful out there. On occasion the tie could be a real stumbling block.

An outfielder racing into the gaps for a fly ball had to be cognizant of the railroad ties at ankle height. Some spectacular spills were observed. Once I did such a thing during a game on the field. I made a running catch in left-centerfield, hit the railroad ties at full stride, and tumbled head over heels into the road and beach area behind left centerfield. I was OK and got up slowly, with the ball in the glove, When I completed my slow jog to our bench, my buddy Jake said, "Hey, Stink, we knew you were going to be fine, plus it was too far to come to check you out." Such was the love and concern of fine friends.

I never played bare foot at Sodus Point but I did experience a lot of fine mentoring. We had a grand time chasing those balls into Sodus Bay in order to use them over and over again.

***

Young Wyland Jr.'s Sprint—Out of the Arena with the Piston shirt

The security guards were in hot pursuit and the arena full of basketball fans were almost totally unaware of what had transpired. Was this an act of terrorism in a public arena? Why was the young man running? The young, redheaded teenager did not resemble a terrorist and the guards must have reached that conclusion because they gave up the chase as soon as the young man went flying out the exit doors at the end of the Edgerton Park Sports Arena in Rochester, New York.

This chase took place long before terrorism was considered a threat at sports venues in our country. Young Wyland (his father's name—a standard moniker for friends was to use their father's name) did not resemble a terrorist because those things were not yet on the awareness screen. More logically he should not have resembled any kind of threat since he was our quirky friend Neal, the Redhead. We watched in awe as he did what he had predicted. He wandered down through the crowd late in the Ft. Wayne Piston-Rochester Royals pro basketball game and calmly snatched a Ft. Wayne warm-up jersey and tucked it under his coat. This act was performed late in the game when the crowd was watching something at the other end of the court. He walked calmly behind the visitor's bench, picked up a jersey, keep moving toward the inviting set of numerous double doors at one end of the arena. And until he was almost halfway there no one noticed.

At some point one of the Ft. Wayne players noticed the snatch-and-grab performed behind his team bench and yelled at the red-headed lad. A security guard was alerted and then another, but it was too late. They were way too slow for one of Sodus' fleetest lads.

The security guards were also not too eager to chase the jersey out into the bitterly cold night air. Neal had performed an act of daring and had delivered the goods in the middle of the winter trip to Rochester.

At the time this was a fantastic act and was certainly brazen. It was, upon review, illegal. Recently one of our members of the group from that night so long ago noticed a vintage jersey from the now extinct Ft. Wayne Zollner (owner's name) Pistons (now the Detroit Pistons) advertised on EBAY. The object was bringing in hundreds of dollars!!! It was the same type of jersey snatched so long ago!

On the evening many years ago we were riding with one of the designated drivers for our group. Back in those days the designated driver wasn't essential for catering to the needs of his drinking buddies as done today. Most of us did not drink. Our version of designated driver was a person who could *get* a car to drive. The designated driver was usually Jake, because he could get his parents' car easily. He could cover the use of the wheels easily because he was usually "taking his older sister somewhere." Jake would usually dump the older sister or do whatever had to be done to make an excuse to borrow the car. Sometimes he merely told them the truth about where we were going. We often had to manufacture stories for our parents since they may not have been comfortable with a bunch of teenagers riding and driving to Rochester. Jake and guys like him could access the wheels the rest of us could not deliver. Therefore, Jake was a designated driver.

Rolling home after the snatch job on the thirty miles between Rochester and Sodus, we relished the fact that Neal had pulled such a great caper. It turned out that a second jersey appeared in the car on this ride home. My recollection is unclear but it seems one of the group had merely picked up a loose jersey and covered it with a winter coat as the Pistons were all warming up early in the evening. He had kept it under wraps for much of the game so the act would not be reported by an usher. Neil became the second of the group to perform a nighttime extraction under the collective gaze of ten thousand pairs of unsuspecting eyes! His grab had a flair the first snatch did not. Nevertheless there were two Ft. Wayne jerseys in Sodus, and we were all Royals fans.

This was about the most risky activity performed during such foraging missions. On some occasions we would eat at a spaghetti place near the arena and/or baseball stadium we frequented and someone from the group would go to the restroom at check time. While most in the group paid their individual checks and one of us finessed the tip with a pile of change to make it look bigger than it was, the restroom occupant would stroll right out without paying. This seemed to be a coming of age ritual. Once when it was my turn to do the rest room bit I merely strolled by the table to join my friends outside and dropped a couple of dollars there because I couldn't quite do the deed. There were other times when my courage was improved as I popped out a couple of streetlights with a friend's BB gun. I put a pebble through a window with a slingshot on a Halloween dare. In both cases I was not permitted to have a BB gun or slingshot by my parents, but could always borrow a device to prove my ability to be rebellious.

Such behavior would have disappointed our collective parents, but it was a teenage thing.

Ironically we had the collective "balls" to continue to return to the restaurant in Rochester despite the fact that the workers at Joe's Spaghetti House certainly would remember a group such as ours over the years. We were eight or nine teenagers who did bizarre things at checkout time. Why would we stand out? We ultimately spent a lot of bucks for spaghetti at the restaurant and many of us returned there as adults. We were willing to forgive and forget if they were!

During the span of years where we grew out of our smart-ass and hormone-driven teenage years, we all seemed to develop into good citizens in our communities. In almost every case, the power of adult supervision and caring put us back on track. Despite an occasional ripped off jersey and prank, we made it through the years. The problem today appears, again, to be the absence of course correction by caring adults as called for in the teenage journey into adulthood.

The jersey caper could be a metaphor for today. There are plenty of places being ripped off by professional franchises as taxpayers keep getting reamed by deals done by politicians. Despite all the suggested good will the politicians end up getting swallowed by the pros as the pros hop to a new city when more is promised than the current city can deliver. Neal was merely getting his share before the pros left town. In fact, the Rochester franchise was probably readying to depart town even as the redhead snatched the Ft. Wayne jersey. The Royals left the saddened Rochester fans and traveled like a carnival troupe over the years to Cincinnati, Kansas City, and finally Sacramento. Today they are called the Kings.

Some of our pranks were really harmless, but were cleverly done. In our immaturity we always seemed to draw attention to ourselves during the prank or shortly after, so the suspense never lasted long. It appears there were more funny pranks performed a half century ago. In my current teaching position, I create pranks or lead students to do them. The current teens in college are always amused at how corny my ideas are compared to their way of thinking. Many of the teenagers today have no idea of doing pranks because theirs was a prank-less childhood. The modern era is not a good base for prank understanding. Too many things preclude a good prank well done. Maybe it is fear of legal repercussions. Maybe pranks take the efforts of a group and group work is shunned except for gang-related work. That is something else. It would appear that our youngsters are culturally deprived in the modern era!

Our problem sixty years ago was there was never enough time in any one day to deliver the number of pranks we had in our minds those days. Why were we more creative in this realm? Would it be connected to today's lack of community? Could it be due to the absence of multiple friendships? Could it be because of the isolation-causing nature of computers and video games?

A couple of pranks really stand out because of the creative nature of the acts. Some of us were able to sneak into the cafeteria on one occasion and roll the portable ice cream freezer into a storage room removed from the cafeteria in the elementary school. We plugged it up again to protect the ice cream. We then returned wheeled the freezer back in a clandestine visit to the school the next night.

This revolt occurred because the principal had dictated that ice cream sales would be curtailed during noon meals in the school because the students had been too loud. This was a coup d'etat for the students because we had regained control of our cafeteria. None of the ice cream was missing because there was always a lock on the case. The whole nighttime scheme around our school was possible because we were friends with the nighttime custodian. He allowed us to do fun things at night using his master key. Basically we played in the gym. He did not know of the removal of the ice cream cooler nor of its return.

Another really exciting prank, we thought, was to figure a way to get the key to someone's car during the day and then go out and move the car to a new spot. Usually the car would be moved to a position relatively close to its original place. This really worked well in winter months since all the cars looked alike after a day of light snow. In rare cases we would target a student teacher, a new teacher or one of our favorites who wouldn't be too irritated at all of this effort. The beauty of the whole effort would be those moments when we could observe our target out there brushing snow off several cars in the area where the car was parked in the morning in an effort to find the right car. Forgive me but even today, fifty years later, I still chuckle about watching one of our favorite teachers going through the "search" for his car for fifteen minutes. Finally one of us went out and "helped" him find the car.

The Redhead was a great prankster, and he proved his worth at the Edgerton Park Arena that night many winters ago. The Redhead was also the victim of a prank or two. This was always happening to one of the group. One time at a baseball game in Rochester a bunch of us were sitting in the usual cheap seats out along the left field line. At a point in the middle innings when the redhead went under the grandstand for some reason the rest of us went en masse to the left field area where we blended in with the crowd over there in pairs. For two innings we watched as our buddy wandered around looking for his group. When he had suffered enough, we reassembled. That happened to each of us at some time, and since this was the Redhead's first time it was more enjoyable.

He was not grabbing anything that night, but in the end he was as much a success in our eyes in his wandering around looking for us as he was in the arena. It was a simpler time and it was a great time to be alive.

**

Line Drive Spaghetti—A new fare for Poopy

In my whole baseball playing and watching experience, one line drive comes back to me vividly when hitting is discussed. The day was bright and the blue sky was filled with puffs of clouds. It was one of those summer days made for being outdoors and made for baseball. The field had been laid out, the ground rules covered and the teams were ready for action. The teams were quite even and the score seasawed back and forth so that by the last inning many runs had been scored. It came down to a final at bat and the batter got the pitch he was looking for and drove a vicious line drive down the third base line. Fair or foul? The whole game rested on this call.

Since there were no umpires and since we were playing on a home-made field involving several unusual ground rules, the collective judgment of the players would decide the issue. This is the way kids played back then before the advent of parental involvement, paid umpires, uniforms and less-unique fields.

The line drive off my Jackie Robinson bat (thick, thick handle, 33 inches, Louisville Slugger—back then you remembered your bat because it lasted an entire summer—with luck) left no doubt whether it was fair or foul. I had caught it all, as hitters would say, and as it left the bat I knew it was foul. The ball crashed through a screen, a window and carried across the kitchen table of the Smith family on Orchard Terrace, where Jim "Poopy" Smith had just gotten into his lunch of spaghetti and meatballs. After clearing Poopy's plate off the table (his testimony) just as he had taken the first forkful, the ball continued across the kitchen to take out some glasses and then came to rest with a splat in the sauce pan. This journey was described by Mrs. Smith. This gave a whole new meaning to "hot-stove" league and also provided some sage advice from Poopy.

He was a baseball player, and although his meal had degenerated into a mess because of the foul ball he could still appreciate the nuances of the game. Poopy quickly advised me that a right-handed pull-hitter should not be hitting from the spot where we had set home plate. He was correct. Even though we had played for a long time with the same narrow, restricted field built around the position of home plate, we had screwed up and I was the major player in that aspect of the game.

It reminded me of my trouble with windows on the street. I had been involved in a snowball fight the previous winter. An errant throw blew through the Guadino's big window and did some damage to their dining room area. I confessed immediately and Mr. Guadino forgave me. I did not have to pay a penny for my damage but came to realize how wonderful a neighbor the Italian dry-cleaner was. Unlike the excited Mrs. Smith, Joseph Guadino was quite calm under the circumstances.

The Smith house's corner where the kitchen was located was in foul territory and the adjacent house down the right field line where the Moore family lived was foul territory. We had been playing on a field that was about forty feet wide and at least nine hundred feet long given that the next two yards beyond the Smith yard lay side by side across the back yards filled with trees. For the whole game we had been able to hit "up the middle" as it was with no problem, until my last at-bat.

In those days our improvised fields would often call for some creative hitting based upon the territory involved. As for the Smith Field it was our first and would be our last game there ever. I am not quite sure why we played there to start with due to the narrowness of the field. It may possibly have had something to do with Mary Anna Dye sunbathing in her backyard next to the Smith yard. Any balls hit up the middle were chased down in the Dye yard and the outfielders would then get a quick, apparently innocent and accidental view of our maturing female neighbor.

After Jim Smith explained the pull-hitting thing to me and my peers he was still excited about the line drive that ripped through his meal. He invited all of us into the remodeled kitchen to bear witness to the damage. This was not a good idea, but he insisted.

Mrs. Smith was not nearly as understanding as Poopy and we got advice from her that had nothing to do with pull-hitting, stances or field layout. Her advice seemed to pertain to intelligence and common sense.

Upon entering the kitchen we, like Poopy, were in awe of the results of my line drive. The spaghetti was all over the floor, ceiling, walls, table and even the stove. Glass crunched beneath our feet from the broken window and cabinet door.

The meal had degenerated with that line drive. Spaghetti was no longer possible that day because of the glass mingled with the ingredients. Poopy took the whole matter quite well, but Mrs. Smith was in no mood to put up with her son's awe of the damage done by one foul ball.

The game ended then and there and we saved our giggles about the line drive effect until we exited the house. Jim Smith would occasionally see me around Sodus Point in the summers and even a few years later we would discuss that magical day we shared.

As we played our way through our childhood I can remember many variances of baseball based upon our creativity and the grounds available for our ground-rules. One summer after Little League started in Sodus and we missed that first season due to our ages (13). We would go to the Little League field created by the community for the 12-and-under boys to play home run derby. The close fences for Little League were well within our more mature hitting prowess so we devised creative rules for this factor. Right-handed batters had to hit the ball out in right center and right field. Left-handed batters had to go deep to left center or left field. Failure to do so would void the long-ball. Another rule we came up with was any line drive or ground ball to the left of second base would be an out for a right-handed batter and vice versa for the left handed batters. We spent many hours playing thusly until we were evicted from the field because someone decided we were too old to play there.

Another unique place we played was behind one of the big homes on our street; the center field location on the field was a two-story barn with many of the dark, vertical boards missing from its side. We decided that any ball off the darkened monster (our version of the "Green Monster" in Boston) would be a ground rule double. If a fly ball could go into the gaps where boards were missing, it would be a home run. There were many ground rule doubles since the barn was located about 180 feet from home plate. There were very few home runs since the missing slats were few and far between.

During one game on that particular field I was able, luckily, to hit a fly ball that entered the barn through one of the gaps. I did my version of a home run trot. As I did a neighbor named Ernie Piekunka came running across from where he had been working on his garden in an adjacent field. He had seen the hit leave my bat and seen the end result. He had thought the placement of the ball was purposeful rather than accidental. His excitement almost matched that of Poopy Smith over the spaghetti line drive. Ernie did not have any baseball experience, so his excitement was different. There was a naivety to Ernie's reaction.

One of the other players near home plate merely told Ernie that we did that type of hitting regularly. Ernie went back to his garden shaking his head in wonderment at the abilities of his juvenile baseball-playing neighbors. He quickly realized he had been given the wrong impression as he saw no more balls disappear into the old Carpenter barn in centerfield. He watched for almost an hour, and none of us could duplicate the feat.

Ernie would be taken in by some of us again later in our lives, but he remained one of our favorite adults in town because he was a genuine article.

Another great field for us was the field at Sodus Point where the outfield for the diamond consisted of the bay with boat ramps and docks in left, the boat storage barn painted green in center and the road and fast food and ice cream places in right. It was a hitter's park due to the great green backdrop. It also was the scene of some very unique hits during organized and pick-up games on the field.

During a recent trip to the field, I was aware that the boundaries remained the same. The field suffered from neglect even if the memories did not!

One time a hitter hit a long ball that cleared the railroad ties in left-center, crossed the road leading to the docks and ramp, and then rolled out one of the docks and finally dropped into a fishing boat at the dock. I know since I was the fielder tracking the ball. It could have been the longest hit in the field's history if the fishing boat had taken off from the dock as the ball landed in the boat. That did not occur, and I jumped in the boat to fetch the ball. The batter had easily made it around the sacks but preserving the game ball was a vital act due to the historically meager number of game balls.

In organized games at the fields, there were ground rules on weekends about balls going under and around cars out along the road. Sometimes balls would hit cars and bounce back into the field where they would be in play. Once or twice irate fishermen got balls near their docks and kept them.

These sportsmen did not share the positive attitude towards baseball exhibited by Jim Smith the day his spaghetti lunch disappeared off the kitchen table.

***

Playground Pecking Order—Slim's way of choosing
"Everyone run around the block and the first two back here will be captains for the softball game." Thus a physical education class commenced at Sodus School. Ultimately every kid in the class of elementary school boys made it around the block of homes bordering Elmwood Avenue, a little cross street to Newark Road, and then back down Newark Road until we reached Main Street and then the dirt playing area adjacent to the old school. The run was about a mile it seemed. The year was somewhere between 1947 and 1950.

Slim McGinn was our P.E. teacher for many years starting about 1947 and extending all the way through to our graduation in 1956. We graduated, but he stayed on until his retirement sometime in the late sixties. His style was autocratic, and it fit the era like a hand in a glove. We did as he said and no one crossed him or his path intentionally.

As his methods extended from the gym class to the teams he coached, there really wasn't much difference between the two levels of expectations. His was not a sophisticated "touchy-feely" group seminar. He was open and blunt. *Like it or lump it* were the operative words of the day. Coming so close in time to World War II, his presence and manner was appreciated by the parents. We, as students, knew nothing else so we survived. At one time Nelson McGinn Sr. coached our three major sport offerings. His son, Nelson Jr., was a fun-loving young man who played for his father for a couple of years. These had to have been the longest years of his life. Nelson Jr. took the brunt of the normal coaching we all received when we screwed up; plus Nelson had to ride home to Williamson with his father. The father, being who he was, must have provided for some one-way observations of the son's efforts in the gym. Even Slim understood what happened when fathers saw their own sons mess up in practice. For some reason, McGinn allowed Charley Mossgraber's father into our practices for a time and poor Charley caught hell after those practices from a stern, demanding father. Finally, even Slim realized what was happening, and Pat Mossgraber stopped attending Charley's practices.

The nerds and the non-athletic types of Sodus pretty much avoided him in the coaching scene, and he them. One of the basic tenets of the gym class was competition. Whereas "challenge by choice," "every child a winner" and "education through the physical" are now great by-words for the sensitivity-related notion of what should and could occur in a physical education class setting, McGinn saw gym class as a form of basic training for his teams and for life. He did not do co-ed classes and the giant door separating the gym into Venus and Mars was the metaphor for his view of things. He did not suffer fools lightly. Common sense and hard work were two basic premises. We did learn to apply these tenants to our lives so we must conclude this basic training did not harm us and, in fact, helped toughen us for the real world. They served us well regardless of the fear thing. He truly did develop young men who were battle hardened for his teams. When our school fielded a team the training ethic of gym class showed through. Any Sodus student going into the military invariably returned to thank Nelson McGinn for the rigor of the gym.

In addition to the competition to serve as captain in a P.E. class early in our association with Coach McGinn, we learned many other little lessons. There were climbing ropes in the old school and, lo and behold, there were two climbing ropes in the new school gym once we got there in 7th grade. For a short time we thought the ropes would stay in the old school. They did, but we merely got new ones, a bit less frayed and thicker than the others. These ropes went to the rafters, about twenty-plus feet in both gyms. Climbing such a rope was a physical challenge as well as being a psychological Rubicon. Anyone climbing the rope wore out as he reached the apex of the climb. Just as a person's endurance was at its low point, a quick glance down the twenty foot hemp torture rack reminded the climber he was really high and out of gas. Most climbers had to come down under control or suffer a rope burn. It was Parris Island in Sodus.

Another subtle little "Slimism," as I call them now after he is long gone, was his absolute defiance about boys dating girls "steady." He lectured about the harmful effects of girls on the sporting potential in his boys. He did not hate girls, but he sure preferred we evade and ignore them until high school and our athletic years with him were over. There were times when we would literally duck out of sight if we thought he was driving by and we were with a girl. The girls, bless them, were our kindred spirits, and we discovered that athletic prowess was not permanently affected when we sucked face.

There was a matter of whistling. No one could whistle in the locker room or gym. Sometimes boys whistled by accident because they were cheerful. When the coach emerged from his office yelling to "cut out the birdseed," it was stopped instantly. We did not whistle much at Sodus.

Once we were having a race of sorts with a person carrying another on his shoulders down a long pathway on the playground. As our particular duo approached the finish line it was apparent we were losing the race badly. I was on the shoulders of the meanest S.O.B in school, for some unknown reason, and as it became apparent we were out of the race he merely grabbed my heels and threw me off his shoulders backwards to the ground. This was a headfirst flip, backwards off the rascal's shoulders, mind you!

I am writing this piece about the event so the reader knows the fall did not kill me. It did knock me out for an undetermined time and when my head cleared there was Slim telling me, "You should have picked a better horse for this race!"

The resident student S.O.B. was given a reprimand for dumping me but that was rather meaningless in contrast to the punishments he took for the animals he mutilated and kids he harassed over the years for lunch money. Everyone reading this book in Sodus in my peer group will immediately grasp who I am writing about here. Hopefully the fellow mellowed with age and became a sweet, old man.

We played a game in P.E. called "Beat the Duster." It was a variation of the old primary school game called "Duck, Duck, Goose." The essence of the game was to receive a towel with a knot in the end of it from a person jogging around a large circle of participants in the gym. After obtaining the towel in your hands (extended behind one's back) the receiver chased the original person who dropped the towel until the towel-dropper got around to the spot vacated by the receiver. If you could catch up with the other guy you could whip his butt with the knot-end of the towel until he got to your vacated place. The game placed a premium on speed and punished the nerds, the slow kids and the heavy kids. McGinn like to use the game as a warm-up to the real lesson for the day.

After playing the towel game or climbing ropes we might engage in "Battleball," a variation of Dodgeball. The beauty of "Battleball" was that the balls were playground balls or soccer balls that stung like hell when they hit. There were other "pecking order" games of our era.

I am convinced the veteran coach used basketballs in the classes to make up his mind about kids for his basketball teams. He would toss out three balls for the three baskets available in the half-gym allotted for the boys. With one basket for each ball, whoever got the rebound of a shot would get the next shot. Whoever got the most rebounds and shots was, therefore, a force in basketball. It was a variation of survival of the fittest. George Clark was a classmate who continually ripped rebounds out of the air and out of the hands of others during gym class shoot-arounds. George was also our school's best rebounder for our team for several years. Perhaps it was a case of the self-fulfilling prophecy at work.

The volleyball classes were interesting. Slim loved volleyball and was an excellent player, even in midlife. He could spike balls with accuracy and power. He was tall to start with and could still get into a spike. The team playing against his in a class was wary of those high-octane spikes!

One time, during one of the classes out on the soccer field, I was playing in the goal just for the heck of it. It was during a time when I already was on the varsity team as a midfielder, so the goal certainly was not my first choice. As the class flowed along, the team attacking my goal took many shots, and my body stopped most of them. The balls bounced off my head, knees, and elbows. One careened off my nose giving me a bloody nose. McGinn was very impressed and the next day in soccer team practice I was told the goalie job was mine based upon the gym class work on my part. McGinn did not coach the soccer team at that juncture, but he was advisor to Burly Bill, our shop-teacher/soccer coach.

The advice went to the varsity coach and Billy Palmer, the outstanding regular goalie, started on the front line against Wayne Central. This calculated gamble was premised on the sophomore "sensation" from the gym class shutting down the high scoring team from Ontario. Billy did his part by scoring our first goal. After about a quarter of the game we were tied at one. Somehow balls were kept out of the net behind me. It was only a temporary thing because the visitors scored on a pair of penalty shots, two other beautiful goals from long-range and then off a corner kick. The guy heading the corner kick by me was one of my buddies from church camp. "Duck," as we called him, merely asked what the devil I was doing in the goal. I really did not have a good answer. Billy Palmer scored a penalty shot, I think, and the score was finally something like 8-3 Wayne Central. Note: In the mid-fifties goals were two points and penalty shots one point.

After that gym class aberration I returned to the midfield and Palmer to the goal. At least Billy and I did not have to race around the block with the loser starting in the goal next game!

***

Swimming the Channel—Guts city

"Rite of Passage." That is the phrase used to describe an activity used to define courage or maturity during one's youth. Ultimately one of the litmus tests for us waited at Sodus Point each and every summer of our lives. The channel demarcations were the two concrete piers extended out into the lake from Sodus Bay. On one was the lighthouse and on the other were seagulls and graffiti from various visitors to the far side over the years. There was nothing at all outstanding about a grey pier bathed in seagull crap and names from another era. The only purposes it served were to keep the channel from filling up with sand and control wave action in the narrow body of water.

There was one other draw for the body of water. Although it served as a passageway for boats it also served as a metaphorical passage into adulthood for those willing to risk the swim. Many were able to swim the width of the waters and back against the wishes of the Coast Guard and against better judgment. For me the body of water was an enigma. I had witnessed a young man dive in and die there. I knew it was illegal to swim there. There were serious currents running through the passage due to the numerous big boats plying the waters in the era. The waves of Lake Ontario carried down the length of the channel on certain days when the winds were right smack out of the north. It was a stupid thing to try to do, and the benefits were very limited. Who gave a crap if you swam the channel?

That is precisely why a teenager would try to do it.

When I made the decision to try my hand at the challenge, my planning included a row boat, my brother to row and a calm day. There was nothing glamorous about my effort. Dick and I rowed out away from the near side of the channel after rowing up the bay from the dock. I slipped quietly over the side and merely swam next to the rowboat to the other side. I climbed up on the breakwater, took notice of all the seagull crap and the graffiti, and clambered back into the rowboat more mentally exhausted than physically spent. We took the boat back to the rental dock near the ball diamond and went back to Sodus. Dick wasn't interested in swimming that day. It probably came from the realization that I may not have been much help should he run into difficulty.

Unlike the efforts like those turned in by lifeguards who could swim over and back rather quickly I went slowly and methodically. I also did not "need" to swim back. One width was plenty for me, thank you! Certain lifeguards performed their feat under the collective gaze of large audiences of young ladies and other "beachlings." I wanted to try it in the presence of a rowboat operator in the event something went awry. Even then I possessed some degree of common sense.

One lifeguard called "Gorilla," with good reason, could swim over and back doing the butterfly stroke. This was the most exceptional swimming feat I have ever seen in my life. The stroke is very difficult and is limited to fifty or one hundred meters in pools. The lifeguard named John could do endless pull-ups on the beach while on duty. This entertained the young ladies and developed his upper body in an outstanding fashion. It also provided him with the upper body needed to perform the butterfly. The channel swim was his trademark, and the butterfly was his stroke of choice.

Even the Coast Guard guys once saw him and did not interfere with his remarkable passage over and back. They knew they were witnessing an unusual swimming effort. My timid, one-way trip next to a rowboat paled by comparison. I thought about my own mortality as I did my swim; "Gorilla" probably thought about all the nubile young ladies witnessing him.

This was summer life, full of choices, along the channel at Sodus Point.

***

Sodus Point Lakers—True baseball characters and the Judge

Don Harris was in his forties when he was one of our team's three starters on the baseball team. The other starters were a one-eyed man (sight lost in a hunting accident) and a short lefthander whose claim to fame was that he could hit a guy and never even make him mad because he threw so softly. We only needed those three starters since our team only played, at most, twice a week. Harris was a veteran of the Sodus Point Chiefs prior to the team being called the Lakers. His pitching style was right to the point. The batter got in the batter's box and Harris would make a fool of him. The Chiefs were a team loaded with local talent, and when they became the Lakers many of the veterans stayed around to play ball with the younger players coming out of the American Legion and high school programs. George Parsons and his brother-in-law George Arney were two of the major forces behind the success of a team in Sodus Point over the years. They were both involved with both "franchises" as they played in the popular resort.

Playing for the Sodus Point team meant having plenty of home games. It seemed, upon reflection, that there were two home games for every away game the team played in the summers. This made sense since visitors loved playing at the "Point" due to the abundance of spectators, plenty of food and beverage places, and the ambiance of the resort setting.

The characters stood the test of time and even today, fifty years after these events and people were current, you can walk down the street in Sodus or Sodus Point and mention some of the names and responses will be colorful. Dewey Rainey was a player-coach for a few years, and he was right out of the casting studio for the stereotypical baseball manager.

It was always intriguing to watch a veteran pitcher like Harris pitch to a high school star who did not handle curve balls very well. He could literally expose the hitter as an imposter right there in front of five hundred people. Great pitchers could do that to a hitter. Sodus Point residents watched Harris pitch for two decades on the diamond right in the middle of the community. He was an artist.

Jack Torrey could hit a baseball a mile. Since the Sodus Bay was about four hundred plus feet out beyond left-centerfield, it was always fun to see how often a hitter like Torrey could hit a ball into the bay. This scenario was way in advance of the popular stadium at San Francisco where Bonds hits balls into McCovey Cove. Torrey could hit a ball into the water, off cars, and across roads. Watching him hit when he was in his forties was a treat. We used wooden bats during the era, and Torrey would grab a bat from some young guy's hands, throw a lighted cigarette down on the ground, and demonstrate a hitting tip using the unfamiliar bat. Line drives sprayed off the bat for a minute and then big Jack would go over and pick up his still lighted cigarette and finish his smoke. So much for having a personal bat that is honed to fit one's hands perfectly!

Beer was a constant part of summer ball. Sometimes beer was consumed during the games at Sodus Point. It was not too unusual to see a pitcher cooling off after a particularly hot inning or two of work by downing a brew. There was a Genesee Beer fascination at the Point since the malt house for the brewing company employed many local residents. Although I could never quite get into drinking Genesee Beer, there always seemed to be some of it around the sporting events and beach activities at the Point. It was said that workers in the malt house could have a free six-pack a day while at work. This was further elaborated on by a friend who told me he drank as many as he wanted during his eight hour shift. When I started drinking beer Genesee was my last choice, despite its origin.

Not being much of a drinker during my younger years left me to imagine whether drinking so much on the job made any sense or not. I did not see any lessening of pitching abilities by the pitchers who had beer with their nine innings of effort. I remember seeing David Wells hurl a perfect game at Yankee Stadium against the Minnesota Twins in the summer of 1998 on national TV. After the game, in interviews and later in a "tell-all" best selling book, Wells admitted to being hung-over and under the influence of alcohol while he pitched the perfect game. It did diminish, somewhat, my fifty-year prudish view of drinking some suds during a game! Hell, it is now said that Coke is worse for you during a game than anything else!

George Parsons was the most visible member of the Chiefs/Lakers over the years by virtue of his multiple roles in the community. He was a veteran lawyer with a law office in the middle of Main Street. He was also, later in life, a prominent Wayne County Judge over in the county seat of Lyons. He lived in a home on Orchard Terrace for three seasons and spent the summers with his family down on the bay in a cottage. The homes were always open to neighbors and friends. The cottage was often inhabited by ten teenagers at a time!

During summer months many of us would congregate at the two-story green wooden structure connected directly to the magnificent Sodus Bay by a fifty foot L-shaped dock. I cannot count the number of hours spent on and around that dock; but suffice to say almost every trip to the resort included a stop at the cottage and the dock. This is where the boats tied up when they were not out on the bay or in the lake. This is where we did some of the needed boat work in return for our being asked to join the Judge on his trips. We gathered in a cold boathouse during the winter a couple of times to scrape and paint the bottom of the boat. This was a continuation of our responsibility to the boat's upkeep, and was a modest price to pay for the opportunities provided by the generous Parsons family.

Many trips to Sodus Point invariably involved the Judge getting out his first-baseman's glove for a game of catch. He could field and catch a ball with his ancient glove like a Gold Glove first baseman. On certain occasions George would insert himself into the lineup for fielding purposes late in a game. This was part of the mystique of Sodus Point baseball. A game's participants for the home team might number in the two to three dozens by the time the day was over. There were no limits on rosters and the number of players available at the diamond on any given day might very well be thirty!

The men associated with the baseball team playing on our memorable, personal "field of dreams" gave back to the community in several ways. They financed teams, coached teams and even made sure everyone wanting to play had adequate equipment and rides to games.

The characters were unique back then. They also displayed terrific baseball character for the sport that served as a common bond among all of us.

***

First Sport Ejection— Don Novelli then reappears

The soccer game was close, and in typical Wayne County fashion the players were playing with abandon. Not until I reached college did I learn any creative and strategic moves by virtue of playing soccer for coaches that liked the physical approach. We had a shop teacher as our coach for a few years and Bill DuVall saw the sheer beauty of soccer as being closely akin to chopping wood or cutting boards. Slim McGinn coached soccer the way George Patton would coach soccer. Attack in great numbers and do great harm on the way.

The soccer game that day was at Sodus and it must have been during our junior year since the referee for the game told me later that he did not officiate during the 1955 season (our senior year). In the fall of 1954 Wayne Central was atop the Wayne County standings and whenever a team played them it was usually no contest. Wayne Central always had a plan, had great talent and also had a coach who had played soccer. That made Wayne's coach stand out in the era of public school volunteer coaches from academic disciplines with little or no soccer experience.

We were playing Wayne Central and we were being defeated by a rather wide margin; hence the frustration levels were abundantly high for the Cherrytowners as we were called back then. As an aside: later the team's name would change to Trojans for a brief time and then finally, in a collective appreciation for the condom jokes being thrown literally at the teams, the name Spartans took over and still reigns today.

Wayne Central was closing out the victory at Sodus when a questionable call was made by one of the two officials. Before I realized it I had looked at the official and said something to the effect that his judgment was excrement and the call was excrement. I believe it was the second excrement of the afternoon that did the trick. He told me I was out of the game. This was before the advent of the red and yellow cards that went into universal use in the sport after the 1966 World Cup. I was gone and since this was my first sport ejection I merely sprinted off the field at the nearest sideline and then embarrassed, walked the rest of the way to our team bench. I did not realize that an ejected player should walk slowly to the bench in full view of the fans and the coach. Because there was no visible card or motion, no one on the Sodus bench knew I was out of the game.

I stood there watching the game with the subs when finally Coach DeVall spotted me. He was not aware of the ejection nor was he aware that we were playing a man short for about the last twenty minutes. I was asked why I was there and I told him that I had used some choice words. At the end of the game burly Bill, as we called our shop teacher/coach, went and asked the official for his version of the ejection. It was pretty much as he had heard from me. The official was a teacher at a nearby college and he merely said that the Pearson kid should shut up and play and he would be a better player. I would guess that was a fair assessment at the time. The official was

421

a man named Don Novelli and the only reason the name has stayed with me over the years is that he crossed my path again in my not so distant future.

After the soccer season concluded, many of the soccer players became the core of the basketball team. After basketball the same players usually were baseball players. Such was the situation in a school with a graduating class of forty or so a year! There were twenty-three boys or so in our graduating class and probably half of them played on some or all of the teams Sodus fielded.

Upon graduation I decided to travel to East Lansing, Michigan to attend Michigan State University. Part of the decision was based upon the fact that Fred DeBrine, a High Street neighbor, was there and he was sold on the school. "Ears" and "Deacon" (Donald Davis and David Beal) were going to attend from my graduating class, plus we knew a guy from nearby Marion who we knew from Sodus Point sailing experiences. The Marion guy was Bruce Curtis, and his greatest claim to fame was that he owned a Lightning Class sailboat he named "In the Nude." This created some great dialogue when sailing was discussed with the other gender. Michigan State was fine and I even had a chance to play some college soccer there; but I eventually decided to transfer back closer to home.

I ended up at Brockport State, where I concluded my undergraduate courses and soccer playing. There was an interesting episode related to Sodus and soccer when I settled in at Brockport. A teacher whose name was Don Novelli was an avid soccer fan and was also the supervisor of the student teaching experience during one's senior years at the college. He came by after a game one day and introduced himself. I recognized him, and he already had known of my presence at Brockport.

He felt I had learned to keep my mouth shut while playing soccer and told me so. I agreed and then apologized three years too late for cussing him out on the field at Sodus. He accepted it in good humor because he said that what happened that day in Sodus was mild compared with what he experienced in other communities where the schools had less discipline. Sodus evidently had a regional reputation for good discipline in the school. Knowing principal Francis Samuel intimately—as I did by my senior year at Sodus through an occasional paddling—I had to agree.

During my senior year Don Novelli took my career under his auspices as he assigned me to Lyons, which was ten miles from my home in Sodus. That was a great money-saver for me. Novelli even allowed me to offer the same savings to a college chum of mine, George Paulus, who was allowed to student teach at Newark— another village nearby to Sodus. Novelli went out of his way to be a good advisor and mentor. I learned a great deal about student teaching early on from the man.

The whole senior year experience in student teaching was nothing less than great, due to Novelli's efforts. He assigned a female supervisor to come visit me from the college and the two of us met over lunch in a restaurant in Lyons when she came to observe. Usually student teachers sweat out such meetings in a school conference room. He had told her to take care of me because I was one of his favorite guys.

That senior year was definitely not excrement!

***

Unusual Gymnasia—Character and challenge and weird boundaries

The inventor of basketball placed his original peach baskets on the ends of a gym up on a ten foot high running track at Springfield YMCA in Massachusetts. Naismith went with what he had available and fortunately for millions who have played the game since 1893 the running track upstairs at the Y wasn't twelve or fourteen or even eight feet high! It was ten feet, and that is where the basket is today. It was a bit of unexpected perfection. Playing basketball in the mid-century in upstate New York took us to some interesting venues. We also played in some interesting situations relative to ethics, sportsmanship and ground rules.

Many places during the last century tried to combine the auditorium with the gym in their school to save money. They got a compromised auditorium with a gym running through it. The stages in such places were usually where the teams and scorers table were located. All the fans and cheerleaders were across the gym in the auditorium. Usually the bands were also. In certain places the home team would allow pep bands the luxury of sitting right behind the visiting team. This, of course, created a nuisance during time outs for the visitors and was the plan of the home team all along.

In the combination gymnasia/auditoriums of our basketball time in high school we encountered some weird happenings. Substitutions were a nightmare since a sub had to jump down to the floor and run over to the middle of the stage area where the scorer's table was situated. If the person going into the game was adept, he would not get in the way of the game's flow. There were times when players were run down by officials running with their eyes on the play and wham—there was a sub knocked over!

There were other weird times when a sub jumped off the stage and immediately entered the game. This happened at the JV level once a year in predictable fashion. Once I was yanked right out of a game when I screwed up and our team was a man short. Speaking of man, it is noteworthy that the females in our school all through high school never got a fair shot at playing in sports other than the occasional play-day organized by the female physical education teachers. It never crossed my mind that this was very unfair until I got in college and realized that girls should have and could have played sports. Drearily, this was not localized in Sodus. It was a national blight that was eventually remedied with the advent of Title IX legislation in 1973.

The quirky gyms around the county included the stages at two or three of the schools. There were also schools with very poor lighting. Two stand out and in one, nearby Williamson, in their old gym we played there one night with a major light burned out over the basket we shot at in the first half. At halftime the custodian came out and replaced the big spent bulb with a new one just in time for Williamson to gain the advantage of the light during the second half.

One gym had such old baskets that when the fans in the balcony started stomping their feet in unison the basket would jump. This did not occur when the home team had the ball. In general there was better fan behavior in the gyms than we see displayed in gyms in the modern era. The cheerleaders even sat and watched the game while the ball was in play. This is in sharp contrast to cheerleaders dominating court space, under the baskets, in front of fan's sightlines and even on top of each other in two person pyramids while play is racing by them in modern gyms. I would vote for the modern cheerleaders to return to an auxiliary role to the actual game rather than becoming an event within an event.

The gyms of fifty years ago still are in operation today in many places. In Sodus, the new gym from the fifties is still being used by teams and for events. Recently my friend Gib and I ventured into the old gym of our era and even went into the locker room and shower area just to look things over during the summer when the building was empty. I could see very little change. In fact, I could almost hear Slim McGinn coming through the locker room yelling to cut the birdseed out.

There were some notable new gyms during our time in high school, and when they appeared the old gym was not missed by visiting teams. We felt very good about the newer offerings, because our own gym was new. Our old Sodus gym had two balconies running down both sides of the court and our old home court advantage was enormous due to the noise and the sightlines for the athletes below.

One place had a ceiling that was way below the twenty-foot minimum. The gym at Savannah was probably down to fifteen feet, and that precluded long shots and passes. Several times during games there, teams would hit the ceiling with the ball.

A routine occurrence at one school found a very bright light shining across the gym at the very middle of the gym floor. I was told this was for filming yet I saw no logic in the bright light at just the middle when the rest of the gym where the game was normally played was in semi-darkness. That gym at Marion still remains a mystery relative to lighting.

Sometimes home team scorekeepers finagled with the clock by starting it late if their team was behind and they needed more time to catch up. Conversely, if the home team was ahead the seconds on the clock could disappear as if by magic. On two occasions that I can remember, the book kept by a scorekeeper did not jibe with the score on the clock. Which score was correct? The one on the clock won out both times. Sometimes there were three point plays showing up on the scoreboard when the three point shot was not accepted for another thirty years.

Often teachers at the visiting schools kept the score, and the clocks so when something was fishy the teaching profession took a credibility hit. Our scorekeepers were so honest and fair minded; they took crap from local fans who expected them to finesse the visiting teams as we had been finessed on their courts. David Cooper, our English teacher and play director supreme, often was one of our key men in the middle of things. After taking crap from several people over a period of time merely because he honestly did his tasks, he finally told the coaches to find a new person to do the work.

Floor surfaces varied, and in some gyms there were dead spots that the home team knew about and the visitors would suffer with until they adapted to the situation. There was one place called Pal-Mac, which was a combined school from two towns called Palmyra and Macedon. Their combination was OK with everyone but every time we played there the game balls had PAL-MAC all over them on every side from every angle. It was no shock when the balls were, at least psychologically, difficult to shoot.

As I went my way from Sodus and all the unique old gyms of the county, I thought I had seen the end of old basketball gyms with severe quirks. Lo and behold I ended up in a college in Kentucky for a portion of my career where our home games were played in a gym nearly eighty years old with a running track extended out over the playing floor. Over each corner the running track actually prevented an opposing player from shooting a jump shot. The corners of the court were literally buried in under the running track just ten feet above. That was a super home court advantage. I was taken back in time to running tracks, balconies and stages in gyms around our hometown.

At Berea College, where this gym was used until just a few years ago for NAIA basketball competition, some of the home players were taught to shoot from these weird corners using a line drive delivery unseen anywhere else. One player became so adept at this that he made All-American status, in part, due to his uncanny shot. I can remember seeing shooters at old Savannah shooting from way out using little or no trajectory so they wouldn't hit the ceiling.

We also had the good fortune to be able to play in community centers, church gyms and even barns during the winter months. There was a time when a team of us went to Palmyra to play in a church against a recreation team of their boys. The game finally ended with the score in our favor by about ten points. The major revelation was that both teams scored over one hundred points. It seems that the scoreboard operator kept the time going *very* slowly in hopes his team would win out. It never happened, but the church is still standing, even if that scoreboard operator went to hell.

If both teams play the game by the same ground rules and the referees are impartial then all the little quirks in any gym work out. I wrote that just now to see how it sounded. I still don't believe it for a minute...or two seconds.

***

Generalization is Good—Specialization Stinks

During the period of time fifty years ago, there were scout camps, church camps and family camping. All of them provided a way of getting kids involved in a wide variety of activities. All of them built upon the family and then extended it by using adults and creative challenges. We still have such things but they have been displaced, in a large part, by specialty camps.

Contrast that snapshot of fifty years ago with what is occurring now. We have all kinds of specialty camps involving one kid with a specialty. The emphasis today appears to be more "me" than "we." The specialties range from sport-specific camps to space camps, computer camps, equestrian camps and even a camp for stamp collectors. As a person bearing witness to the proliferation of the specialty camps, I do have my private opinion of this phenomena.

Whereas we had group camps involving heterogeneous groups focusing on several common goals over a period of a week, the modern era sees an abundance of homogeneous groups meeting at a site to pursue very limited and specific goals. This cuts out the potential for understanding and communicating in diverse groups. An example of the typical camp from "my era" might be the old-fashioned scout camp involving water front training, knot-knowledge acquisition, canoeing, tenting, hiking, and preparation of meals. At such a camp the scout leaders ultimately came to grips with all shapes, sizes and interests.

An example of the specific camp from the current era might be the tennis camp. Parents send junior to a week-long experience involving tennis drilling five hours a day, tennis videos two hours a day, tennis rule clinics and guest tennis stars from the college ranks describing tennis success. The variety and elements of diversity have disappeared. What you have at tennis camp are tennis enthusiasts. Instead of learning how to prepare and share meals as kids once did in great numbers at scouts and church camps, the tennis "rats" show up at a cafeteria, sit there and play with their food and then load up on desserts since mommy isn't there.

I am, admittedly, a product of the old school of thought and action where we learned every sport amongst us and with the guiding, informal hand of an adult. We played seasonal sports and enjoyed the change in season and sport. The well-rounded athlete of my era was just that. He (and gloomily not too many she's) could flow from snow skiing to water skiing once the weather allowed. He could play soccer, basketball, and baseball, with some ice hockey or bowling thrown in for good measure. There was always time to play modified games, either invented or discovered, in and around organized team efforts. Most of us could do about every sport at some level of proficiency and were true generalists.

There were very few, if any, specialty camps for sports in 1950. This no doubt meant we were not very sophisticated in any particular sport offered during our childhood. I have learned much about various sports over my lifetime as a coach; by attending clinics and coaching a variety of teams I was able to improve my sophistication in sports. On occasion I have remarked quietly to others or admitted to myself that if I had known back then what I know now about hitting, fielding, soccer technique, basketball defense, off-season conditioning or psychology of sport, then I could have been much better in a particular sport at age sixteen.

After saying that, I immediately admit that the specialty camps and specialty mentality of the modern era bore me. My personality and versatility have been deeply rooted in the diverse opportunities available to me long ago. There weren't specialty camps and we probably could not have afforded them, even if there were such things. I am very fortunate for the wonderful experiences offered to me or created by my friends and me. It is my opinion that the youth of today have been raised in a culture buying into the theory of specialization. This trend has taken us to the individualistic attitudes in the family and in society. Whereas my brother and I might go to scout camp and engage in all the wonderful experiences offered therein, the kids today go away for a week of individual training to become more "expert" at *their* sport. It centers the family budget on "me" again, rather than "we" or "us."

Once we start sending individuals to specialty camps, we buy into the theory that the individual is ranked higher than the team or family. One can see this in some of the selfishness found in team sports. How can a kid, who is the focus of camps his whole sport life, easily evolve into a team player? I know this is a gross generalization of the fifty-year trend and that there are plenty of great camps out there doing wonderful things. Nevertheless, I contend the trend is off target. I like "team" camps much more, and they are quite popular on my own current campus. We even have had team running camps.

What are the advantages of specialization? For one thing

the benefit of better success in the sport of choice is invariably enhanced. There may be college athletic grants for the specialist making a significant impression upon a recruiter. The specialty may lead directly to job possibilities as related to computer camps and other specialty offerings. If you happen to operate a specialty camp, summer income is vastly improved over the typical summer teacher salaries.

Behind many specialty camp opportunities lurks another motivation. Parents place unpredictable and even unplanned expectations upon their offspring to achieve in an unreasonable fashion. There are many children experiencing undo stress premised upon parental dreams of stardom. Parents are often trying to glorify the kids to make up for their (the parents') athletic shortcomings as youngsters.

As a coach dealing with generalists and specialists over my many years, and as an admitted generalist in my sport resume, I do have a prejudice. It is my belief that if a coach has large enough groups of well-rounded, versatile athletes who have not been overwhelmed with their individual self-aggrandizements, then all things are possible. I can recount successful teams in my memory where the versatile, team-oriented athletes overachieve. Consider the recent movie "Miracle" re-telling the story of college boys beating the USSR in ice hockey in the Winter Games of 1980. They were a gritty team of over-achievers. There are many memories of very specialized athletes falling short in a team setting. Team expectations are enhanced by a team mentality.

Using major league sports to illustrate this point, consider the Seattle Mariners a few years back. They could field a baseball team with A-Rod, Randy Johnson and Ken Griffey Jr. Only after all three future Hall of Fame players were traded did Seattle become a powerhouse in the American League West. Another example might be the New York Yankees of recent seasons, who have failed to win the World Series despite possessing the highest payroll around. Anaheim and Florida won the title despite much inferior payrolls and fewer specialty players during the past two seasons.

I can remember thinking that if I, as a coach, could gather hustling, versatile, gritty players together in soccer, basketball and /or baseball, then we would never be embarrassed. This seems to be one of the common thoughts as coaches gather together. One amendment to that thought might be as follows: If a coach could have the team described above, coupled with a couple of super talented lads coming from a specialty camp in any of those sports, then the sky would be the limit. That might be the compromise needed in the year 2004.

***

Informal Play—Where is it today?

A contrast I see in comparing the teenagers of today with my own peers is that my peers and I could invent a game on the spot depending upon the time, space, equipment and season. Today fewer and fewer young people have a "feel" for inventing things to do for themselves. The common core of acquisition of many basic sports is missing in today's youth. The HPE programs are diluted in many places, and the specialization inherent in today's sports squelches creativity.

One of my college classes covers a wide array of sports and games within the scope of a one-semester course. This course equips future HPE teachers and coaches with a repertoire of selections for groups of students under their direction. My students learn to modify, modify and modify again and again. Many times it becomes prudent to change the games kids play to encourage participation by all in the group. Another reason to keep changing the games is to keep kids from becoming bored with the same old, same old stuff. A sport such as volleyball has as many configurations as can be imagined depending upon the ages and skill level of the group.

Reflecting upon games of our childhood in Sodus, it dawns on me that we generated our own entertainment much of the time. Of course, there were organized school sports and organized summer baseball, but in and around those offerings were found endless hours of our own creations. It only took two of us to start the ball, or balls, rolling. Once there were two it did not take long to generate a third and fourth participant due to the fact that many of us were outside for many hours per day. All it took to get a game moving was some interchange on bikes or by phone and, *voila*, we were involved in activity.

As I look out on the street where I live in Rome, Georgia, it is evident that children are not outside in great numbers much of the time. Because we live halfway down a dead-end street we see much of the dynamics of the life on the street. There are at least forty kids living on the street in the thirty homes lining our street. Other than one particular house where kids are outside much of the time, I do not see much evidence of children playing outside as I walk, drive or work in my own yard. The one exception is the family home for a physical educator in our county system. Most of the kids come back from school, go inside and stay inside. During summer months the local kids are not very evident. Where are they? The answer to that question is answered often by a word: inside. Another word also pops up in describing the neighbor kids: alone.

Contrast that dynamic to the streets of Sodus in 1950, and my conclusion is kids were out a whole lot more fifty years ago. This contrast is a by-product of the TV, computer and video game age. It is also a product of the economic and social times. Many parents raise children and the parent(s) are absentee for much of the day and/ or night. This may be a dynamic of parents working, single-parent families, or poor parenting.

The concept of playing outdoors was premised upon feeling safe outdoors and having someone to come home to when the games were over. This was the case fifty years ago as the number of at-home mothers was significant. In a small town, even if the mother was out of the home for parts of the day, the children knew where mother was and vice versa. Some mothers and fathers came home for lunch from work and expected children to be there for that meal *and* the evening meal.

We invented our games right around mealtimes and where we lived. I cannot recount the number of ground rules we thought up for versions of softball and baseball. We played in streets, yards, on hills, next to barns and even under the streetlights. One game required an honor code involving the throwing and catching of a ball coming over the high roof of a barn. Once the ball was thrown the other team got a point for each successful catch on the other side. When one team had a certain number of points they would run around the barn and declare themselves winners. This was a game of skill because the ball came over the roof at odd angles and took weird bounces off the highly sloped roof. This was a game of honesty since the catches made around on the other side of the barn were done without the opposing players seeing the result! Variations of this game were invented, and the game was referred to as "Alley, alley over."

A game we played on a steep hill involved hitting the ball *up* the hill. This created a unique dynamic for the defense and meant we would not have to chase the ball very far. The hill was quite steep and created a compressed game.

Another game, rooted in our love of baseball, was target throwing. We would set up tires, removes slats from barns and place coke bottles on boxes to throw at. We spent hours throwing in this manner. Is it any wonder we could raise havoc during winter months on trucks and trailers with our snowballs?

Football was popular, even though our school did not have the sport. We played modified games in our back yard whereby the field was shaped like a box rather than a rectangle. It was easy to run laterally, pitch-out or throw a pass in the "flat" due to the width of the backyard. The width of the yard also made it easy to score on any run. There were games where the field goal and extra point game decided the outcome. We learned to kick over the bushes at the end of the yard from down near the house. If you could do this your team got points before the other team ever got the ball.

Our love of the outdoors was manifest. We would play football in the deep snow. Often we would set up an obstacle course for our sleds and bikes. Riding a bike in the snow was tough, but we mastered it through our own slalom course. Another snow game was tag, but we invented trails and safety zones for staying out of a tag. The tag course in the snow-covered yard was enormous.

Swimming off the docks at Sodus Point opened up the prospect of races out to various boats anchored in the bay. We played a game of tag whereby going underwater kept a person from being tagged. This put a premium on holding one's breath, swimming under water and even hiding behind anchored boats. Certain colored boats were "safe" if a swimmer could get there prior to being tagged. There were times when, by nightfall, we could hardly move our limbs from all the swimming. During late summer, when the algae in the bay were more pronounced, our eyes would swell shut and our noses would drain endlessly.

We played a variation of water polo/dodge ball that was aggressive and fun. Playing in shallow water enabled us to throw the ball hard and accurately. When the ball missed a person it skipped a long way away down the waterfront. This game called for back-ups to catch errant throws. Once we got bored with that water game, there were others. The old-fashioned "chicken fight" with a person on another's shoulders was always fun. Several partners would alternate riding and carrying and fight to see which twosome remained standing the longest.

It is interesting observing college students making attempts to make up variations of games. One constant that is ultimately evident is that the current college-age students mirror young people in society as a whole. They are not as versatile as my generation and they haven't developed a high degree of creativity with their peers in entertaining themselves.

I enjoy teaching immensely, and can always come up with suggestions about modifying games. The college students have come to realize I spent most of my waking hours playing at something when I was a kid. My paycheck now is generated, in part, by my ability to share modifications from my memory bank. What a great life I enjoy!

***

STINKY'S TALES

Teddy, Herbie, Jake and Neal-new sport-Shooting food

Four of my friends and I were throwing spaghetti off the wall in one of the kitchens of our youth. We had heard that one way to check spaghetti's correct serving consistency could be determined by the act of tossing a strand against the wall. If the strand stuck there, the theory went; the spaghetti was ready to serve. We were sharing our judgment regarding the spaghetti as we continually tossed strands against the wall. Somewhere in all of this we started checking the sticking properties of tossed salad, spaghetti covered with sauce and hunks of bread. All were ready to serve as food stuck to the painted wall quite nicely. The host chef couldn't believe his kitchen was turning into a garbage bin. We were absorbed in the activity and enjoying the moment.

Our engagement in a full-fledged food fight evolved despite our love of the Italian food flying around the room. This was an aberration, but was intensively entertaining when it occurred! We did not have food fights in school although we did mix strange concoctions for display on the lunchroom trays and would toss an occasional roll or grape. The domestic food fight ended, we cleaned up the mess and then went on with our evening of entertainment. I conclude we were temporarily nuts.

For whatever reason, the dynamics involving this particular group always were unpredictable. We gathered to play, eat and travel together and all of us eventually became teachers. Our career success probably came as a great shock to many adults but most of our teachers seemed to consider us entertaining. Schools of Education across America should consider having a course in food preparation and appreciation as a prerequisite for graduation. The current educational models place a premium on getting groups of teachers to flow through the graduate experience together. We devised this idea as undergraduates in high school.

The nutritional aspects of childhood were often taken for granted, but all of us seemed to have a terrific appreciation for variations available in the community. When we went to eat and spend time with a family other than our own, the choices of food staggered us. My own mother deluged my friends with every leftover available in the house. This became her trademark. Any of my friends leaving my house feeling hungry had to take the blame for their own hunger. I know none of my family members ever went to bed with an empty stomach.

The rare times when we took over a kitchen invariably led to spaghetti preparation. This was our group identity and we loved pasta. Most mothers supervised our culinary efforts. This was very wise, given the mess we temporarily made of the kitchen described in the first paragraph.

Our eating prowess was tremendous and no doubt reflected all the calories needed in a given day by typical teenagers. There were times when we consumed two or three milkshakes at a time. Other times we would eat hamburgers four times a day. Summer was a great opportunity for us to engage in cookouts, and some of these efforts extended hour after hour, as the grill kept us in hotdogs and hamburgers throughout an afternoon of cards.

Hotdogs were popular in Sodus as they were nationwide, but in Sodus and Rochester we had "white" hots. These were pork hotdogs packaged by a meat company in Rochester. For a long time these were the only pork hotdogs available. People took packages of the product, packed in their ice filled coolers, as far away as Florida. Even today, despite their fat content, I consume a couple of them every trip I make to my home state.

I can remember attending picnics in summer months that lasted for several hours. The food stayed outside on tables much of the time, so our health risk was considerable. Given what we know now about leaving certain foods outside in summer months, we were always taking a calculated gamble with food poisoning. There may have been food poisoning cases, but the memory of such things is notably vague. I never had food poisoning but my constitution has always been strong.

Our noon meals during the school year were really quite good. Most of the students were much less finicky than current high school students. We received home cooked meals from the mothers who worked in the cafeteria. One reason no food fights occurred was the respect engendered by the ladies who worked the meals at school. They were mothers of our peers.

Of all the food-related memories, the events in Sodus involving weddings, anniversaries, funerals, graduations and/or birthdays stood out. During those times, friends and neighbors brought platters of food for the family or the event. Winter in the village found the naturally-refrigerated front porches filled with left-over food from events described above. Platters of food often found their way around town, as the original recipient family shared the largesse with many others.

My mother once received a clean platter from a lady in an adjacent community. Isabel had her name on the bottom with a piece of tape and although the full platter was taken to a neighbor several months previously, the empty platter finally found its way back to her.

Fortunately our gang of eaters did not borrow or even use big platters since we spent so much time eating with our hands!

PART 6
History

There are events in the lives of all of us that stand out as truly historic. We may not realize it at that particular time, but upon close scrutiny later on we realize we were involved or were witnessing something unique. History is fascinating to me, and seems to be so because of the early presence of a father interested in history, teachers who loved history, and a community and era when history seemed very important.

I grew up really liking history. The history of the nation and the community was something to be cherished. These feelings seem rekindled in the times following 9/11 in each community. Perhaps in the span of time between WWII and 9/11 we saw our collective interest in history and patriotism diminish. We should gain from the renewed feelings involving history and patriotism, and build upon these forces. The involvement was keen for me due to many factors.

Many of the factors evolved because my father was away during the war, I read a lot, and everyone seemed to have served some purpose. The people were very close due to the conditions in the world at large and in the village in particular. In the modern era we are seeing the resurgence of patriotism. In Sodus during the middle of the previous century, the Pledge of Allegiance, the flag and national pride were manifest.

***

Hello Governor—Tom Dewey visits
One of the most recognized governors of New York State in

history came to Sodus one time to open a section of new highway linking Rochester with Oswego. His visit occurred during a time when we were in elementary school. The reason for remembering his visit was that our classes had to walk out to the intersection of the new highway where a ribbon was being cut that day. The walk was over a mile each way, so hundreds of school children walked along the old route from the school to the Governor.

Dewey was popular in New York State for his reputation as a no-nonsense prosecutor of local crime lords. Dewey was so effective as a prosecutor that mobster Dutch Shultz tried to put a "hit" contract on Dewey. Historians put the bounty for the young prosecutor's life at $10,000. Schultz drew the ire of the mob for that indiscretion; the mob bosses had Dutch put to death rather than draw national attention to a mob hit on Dewey.

Tom Dewey grew political "hay" as his successes against organized crime grew. His election in 1942 and two re-elections in 1946 and 1950 to the governor's office attested to his popularity in the Empire State.

Tom Dewey ran for the Presidency against FDR in 1944 and lost as Americans weren't quite ready to unseat the popular wartime leader. Dewey did not even win New York State in the 1944 contest. He ran again, this time vs. Harry Truman in 1948. He squeaked by in New York State but he lost nationally when Truman won a shocking victory over the Republican governor despite losing Democratic votes from several southern states that ended up voting for a third candidate, Strom Thurmond. Thurmond is the same rascal from South Carolina that just passed away after seventy years on the American political stage!

My mother's theory of that election loss was the mustache-theory. Dewey wore a thin, trimmed mustache for most of his adult life. People in the USA and in the world, for that fact, were not excited about people with funny little mustaches right after WWII. New Yorkers were accustomed to the man and the mustache, but nationally it did not evoke voter loyalty.

When the man arrived in Sodus, he opened the highway with a little speech, shook some hands from the assembled group, and then disappeared in a big limo back to some airport. Among the hands he shook were several school children and a few teachers and village big shots. Many students were pressed up against the speaker's area for the event so they got a close look at the mustache. I was one of those kids. My mother was correct. The thing was distracting.

One elementary kid, who shook hands, was Martin Towne. He went on to a tumultuous career in school and in the area. He may have straightened out after graduation, but shaking Tom Dewey's hand did not impact positively upon the lad in the immediate time frame following the handshake. Interestingly, several of the remaining students, including me and some of my peers, were able to offer our hands but we got a politician's imitation hand shake. That is where he puts his hand out, someone nudges him toward a vehicle, and you may catch a finger nail. This was like a moving high five long before that was a part of the culture. Martin got the only pure handshake for a kid out of the man. I yelled "Hello Governor!" I couldn't call him Tom, could I?

His visit to open the highway was a prelude to taking the state in the upcoming 1948 election. He won the state by a mere 60,000 votes out of over 5,600,000 votes cast. Nationally, it did not work out well for him. He was beaten in the cities of America and only won fifteen of forty-eight states. The third party candidate Thurmond took four states. In a little-known voting fact, half of Tennessee's electoral votes went to Thurmond and half to Truman. Historically speaking, Strom did better in Tennessee than favorite son Al Gore did in 2000! Strom took over a million popular votes from Truman and the Democrats in the USA. Despite the four and a half states normally in the Democratic column and the one million votes, Truman still amassed nearly three million more votes than Dewey nationally. Simply put, it was the "Isabel factor."

From another purely historic point of view, I find it interesting that FDR and Tom Dewey were both New York State Governors in their political lives. FDR was swept to election for four terms, and Dewey couldn't get by Truman and a split Democratic Party in 1948, or FDR in 1944. I think it was the stupid, little mustache.

***

Black and White—Issues and television channels

There were three channels, with strong enough signals to be picked up by our rotating aerial strapped to the ancient chimney on the house. During the winter months we could receive a Toronto channel by some fluke of bouncing signals and stormy weather. By rotating the aerial, using a motor on the device, we could barely get the hockey from CBC. The three regular channels were from Syracuse (1) and Rochester (2). Everything was black and white back then, and our family did not get a color TV until I was long gone from our residence and into one of my own. When I see old-time movies and programs offered on DVD in "original black and white" it makes me smile. The technology of the current era mixes well with the processing of fifty years ago.

Every program was black and white so that when the first color came along it actually looked artificial. Life is color-enriched, yet we became mesmerized by TV and many of the movies in black and white. Once we got into junior high and high school we went to Saturday night movies and were treated to fantastic colored movies. I sat there, with my pretty date, watching the choice western of the week. I was impressed with the pretty women on the screen, in classy gowns, with their abundant cleavage. Even then I would ask my girlfriend if she thought women wore stuff like that while riding covered wagons as they headed west.

My girlfriend then, and others who would follow her, could never answer that question. My wife finally gave me the answer I sought all those years. She merely told me, "Bob, those women did not and *could not* have worn stuff like that going across country in a wagon." She then added, "Trust me on this matter and, it just didn't happen that way!" Since she doesn't dress like that while traveling west in our car, I must conclude she is accurate in her historic perspective.

The television programs fifty years ago were very conservative and did not show flesh as we see today. I kind of wished they would have, but it never happened. The language was very refined, in contrast with modern verbal exchanges. The black and white television sets were metaphors for life in 1950.

Things were black and white. Issues, decisions, viewpoints, attitudes and, pathetically, racial matters, were all black and white. When my father started discussing politics things took on a very traditional Republican viewpoint. In the matters related to abortion, death penalty, prayer in the school, Pledge of Allegiance and discipline in the schools the community and much of the area was conservative and traditional. There were very few liberals hanging around the village and, when they were exposed by their own actions and tongues, they did not merit much public consideration for these views.

Harry Truman, Democrat, was still admired by Republicans for his "Give 'em Hell Harry" attitude. When Ike became president, black and white still ruled the day. Spank the kid and ruin the rod was accepted instead of the generation following, where the rod was spared and the child was spoiled. Social history was forever altered as Dr. Spock's writings gained great favor. I did not realize until recently that the same Ben Spock was an Olympic medalist in rowing!

Blacks and Whites did not easily mix socially, and ours was a troubled racial history throughout the nation. In Sodus the migrant workers, comprising most of our Black population, stayed away from the village unless they needed groceries. This dynamic changed in later years, but in the fifties there were very few incidents between black and white populations as they stayed separated for the most part.

It seemed logical and correct to do the Pledge in school and pray during certain school activities. Our church attendance in Sodus was notable. Many churches appealed to a wide variety of constituents. There was a common core of traditional and conservative parishioners. I have heard various estimates of church attendance in the current decade and the numbers are not favorable when contrasted to the mid-century fifty years ago.

It is estimated that Catholics attended church at the seventy five percent-level in the mid-century. The current estimate, given on the "O'Reilly Show" recently, is only at the twenty five percent attendance rate for Catholics. Bill O'Reilly theorized this was a result of the secularization of America, the Catholic Church scandals, the breakdown of our moral fiber and the anti-religious rhetoric of judges and lawyers from the liberal left. I don't know what the stats are for other religious affiliations in America, but it does make sense that the figures are much lower for most religions.

My simple assessment of where we have gone off course in our country is in agreement with conservative assessments. There has been too much liberalization of our lives. There are too many lawyers searching for business or "trolling for bottom-feeders" as my father would comment. Too many frivolous lawsuits have eroded parental, institutional and legal clout. The legal system has gone bonkers over the past thirty years as the good are overwhelmed by the bad and ugly. We have trivialized institutions that used to mean a lot. My father had a phrase he used often: "Do-gooders will be the ruin of America." Never one to mince words, Pete did make his point to our family and close friends. Our close friend, George Parsons, was a lawyer and a judge. He was not categorized as one of the Dad's liberals by any stretch of the imagination. He was respected for his work with youth, his tough demeanor on the bench and his traditional legal practices.

Things were very clear in Sodus and our looking-glass was unclouded. Although our era had several issues that needed resolution, we lived a simple, constructive life. Our community was quite united on major issues and the citizens of Sodus made their lives meaningful for others. There was much less narcissism. Our generation evolved into a service-generation. The modern era is spawning a self-centered segment of our population with no commitment to anyone else's welfare.

I am fortunate that religion, school, family and community were so structured to assist me on the path to adulthood. I fear that teenagers in the current generation are failing to receive worthy notions of core values.

***

The World Comes to Sodus Bay—Dulles unwrapped

The two swimmers were going under the stern of the yacht belonging to the United States Secretary of State John Foster Dulles. They dove repeatedly under the props of the expensive cabin cruiser located in the bay. The yacht had come in during the day from the private island where Dulles vacationed during his breaks from Washington, D.C. and world events during the Eisenhower Administration 1952-1960.

These swimmers were not terrorists in some Tom Clancy novel trying to plant an explosive charge under the stern. They were two local Sodus Point residents who had been hired to clear the yacht's props of fishing line. These young men were hanging out at the Yacht Club when the boat came in and were summoned to duty by the Secretary of State. They were residents of the "Point"—Sodus Point. Many of us were swimming in the bay that day but did not realize the importance of the visitor until we heard the details.

Those of us living in the Village of Sodus six miles away were always envious of any of our friends living in Sodus Point. This envy occurred about four months a year. Their lives were much fuller than ours in the summer months. They were right where we aspired to be day after day. We journeyed to be with them during the months of May, June, July and August. When school started after Labor Day, Sodus Point was different.

Things were different during the other months. The Sodus Point friends journeyed on buses and in cars to be where the action was during the rest of the year. Up in Sodus! The central school was located in Sodus. Sodus Point in winter was very, very cold and desolate.

There were times in the winter when ice fishermen would venture out, cut holes in the ice and set up temporary shelters to sit in while they fished. The movie "Grumpy Old Men" with Jack Lemon, Walter Matthau, and Burgess Meredeth accurately depicted the set and setting for ice fishing. The scenes from the movie caught winter in a community on a lake quite nicely.

Food places along the roads leading to the bay and beaches

closed down during the winter. Because of the ice, boats did not get out of their hoists and/or storage or off their trailers for many months. Just about everything important occurred from April, when the ice was usually gone, until November, when it was too cold to be out. Sodus Point was a happening place during summer. Dulles proved this point.

One did not have to be a Secretary of State to get attention at the resort in summer. A beautiful girl would get much more attention than a Dulles. There were times when trips to the beach were like a trip to Fantasy Island. For young guys the idea of all the pretty girls gathering at one spot every summer was almost too much to handle. Our beach was one of the best on the lake, and our recreational offerings were much better than other, smaller areas on the lake.

The beauties gathered and the young men arrived in droves. This was a place for excitement in the summer. Dulles or no Dulles, the beach, roller rink, piers, fast food places, sailboats, golf course, rental boats, yachts, coal boats, fishing, water skiing, and summer romances all combined to make Sodus Point a great place.

Other than the normal excitement generated by all of the aforementioned things to do, we had a very unique place to hang out. Judge George Parsons owned a cottage right on the expansive bay. Tied to his large permanent dock was a boat of choice each summer. For several years he owned large sailboats then switched to cabin cruisers when he and his wife Elsie had children. Later he would return to sailing vessels. For much of my childhood George was a friend and a generous man. He shared his cottage, family, love of baseball and—uniquely—his boats.

Just down the bay from the Sodus Bay Yacht Club where the important visitors would dock, the Judge set up his summer retreat. His cottage was open to his neighbors up in Sodus, and as a part time baseball coach he became the "man" for team picnics, boat rides and even summer baseball on the diamond near his cottage. We were blessed to have so many fine adults in our lives that would map out activities for us and then be there enjoying the activity with us. The Judge was an exceptionally generous man. He was also a Wayne County Judge for many years, and on occasion he would invite his Sodus yearlings into the courtroom to listen to justice being delivered in nearby Lyons, New York where his chambers were located. In the courtroom he was a no nonsense judge. At Sodus Point he was a fun-loving adult with a reputation for drinking, swimming in March, and a love of sailing and Sodus Bay.

He would often say that Sodus Bay was the greatest inland harbor on the Great Lakes. No one could dispute him since we all believed it to be true. The world came to Sodus Bay.

When the coal boats stopped coming to the huge coal-loading trestle at the end of the bay, an era had passed. The bay became less worldly. The sight of the large coalers coming and going was always interesting. Fortunately the trestle was turned into a huge marina. This came at the time when the fishing made a big recovery due to pollution legislation in the Great Lakes region. Fish stopped dying off and now there were many more places for smaller boats. Things picked up recreationally and commercially.

The bay evolved and reinvented itself over the years. As I see the place during my periodic visits down memory lane, I see a unique place that existed fifty years ago with some changes. There are many more modern homes, improved recreational opportunities, and more places to eat. Dismally, there is no organized baseball for young adults after their youth baseball experience concludes. There used to be American Legion and Sodus Point Lakers baseball in the community for young men once they exited youth ball.

The Jet Ski has taken its place in the bay also. This fast, noisy and sometimes intrusive water craft is everywhere. Like their recreational winter brother the snowmobile, the Jet Ski can be rented or purchased easily and can take the driver about anywhere he or she wants to go.

John Foster Dulles would appreciate the beauty of the bay if he were around today. His security detail would no doubt be traumatized by the number of fast boats and Jet Skis in the bay. His journey into the idyllic summer haven many years ago to stop and refuel and get his props cleared of fishing line would be organized differently in the age of terrorism. He once flew into the bay in a seaplane when they were a rarity. That no doubt caused concerns for the traditionalists back then!

With lessons learned from the USS Cole's disaster in waters at the port of Yemen it is my guess a U.S. Secretary of State would be less likely to have unknowns clear his props even in tranquil Sodus Bay. John Foster Dulles need not have worried back then because it was a different world.

***

Sampson Naval Base—Largest building in the world

I walked into the building and was immediately awed by the enormity of it all. All along the curved ceiling were letters of the alphabet A-Z. The letters were critical to the quick connection of family members inside the hut. Families merely went to the areas under the letter appropriate to their last name to reunite with servicemen. The building was referred to as a Quonset hut later in my life, but for that moment it was the largest building I had ever seen. This has to be qualified a bit since the memory comes from the experiences of a six-year-old boy from a small town of less than two thousand people. The largest building in my life up to that point was the school, and the gym inside the school was the largest room in my young life. The hut at Sampson Base would hold forty gyms like mine at Sodus.

The building was a huge Quonset hut erected during the 1940s near Geneva, New York at a sprawling navy base called Sampson. My mother, brother and I were driven to the base by a family friend to visit my father at the conclusion of his basic training during 1943-1944. Basic training lasted about ten weeks, and after the brief visit my father was sent to his next destination. At the time of the visit I am not sure we knew that since my mother was in tears during the trip over to Geneva and back. The young people in the car rightfully assumed that their father was going to be going somewhere that could be dangerous. It was that time in

America and we already knew about the stars on tiny flags in many windows around town. The stars represented household members in the service of the country. We also knew of the stars with black on them.

If the stars in the windows weren't reminder enough for those of us left behind by the military men (and women), there was evidence of the loss of a loved one. The names of the missing were engraved on a board in the middle of town. There were local families with permanent losses, and we already knew this. My mother's tears were a clear awareness of the tribulations facing families during the war years.

The trip to Sampson Naval Base was a short forty-mile (each way) drive from Sodus to just beyond Geneva where the base had been built. I have photos of the base taken by my mother. In my father's mementos are artifacts from his service years including group photos of his training class. There were many sailors in the photo. The base trained thousands of navy personnel and along with the Great Lakes Training Base near Chicago and a base near Orlando, Florida these bases accounted for the most of the navy basic training in the war years.

The day we spent at Sampson was a brief glimpse into such training. There was an impressive parade followed by the reunions under the letters, and finally the parting of the family one more time. My father was impressive in the U.S. Navy uniform, and our photos depict a thirty-six year old sailor in probably the best shape of his adult life. He was our father; yet he "belonged" to Uncle Sam. He was as impressed with our growth spurts since he had gone to training as we were of his new home. The visit ended with announcements to clear the building, and Dad marched out the doors at the end of the arena-like building with his company. We headed home to Sodus. We were not sure where Dad was headed.

Such visits after basic training were repeated across America. In many cases the military personnel were allowed to visit their homes but this became a rarity due to the logistics of travel as the war progressed. There simply wasn't time to allow for large breaks in the routines with replacements needed everywhere. Men had to meet the schedule for the next station assignment. Sampson was the training base for northeast USA and our family had a forty-mile drive contrasted to trips of hundreds of miles by others in the building with us that day.

My mother's tears were not seen again during the war years. This was her attempt to be brave and was also connected to the fact that Pete was to be stationed in Washington, D.C. for the duration of the war. This was beyond the family travel reach, yet was well within a safety zone for military men on duty. Mother did not fear losing her husband in Washington. She knew her ordeal was much less than that of some of her friends in town.

In our history men and women have been going in harm's way in service to the nation. Whether the service is of military nature or that of a policeman or fireman, people have served without hesitation. The families of such men served that service ethic without hesitation also. In communities across America during the war years, we were in something important together. The images of service and love of country have never left those that served. It was the same for their families. It has impacted me in my life and has given me a solid sense of patriotism. The crucible of war made lasting impressions that brought people together in a common cause. Until the horrible events of September 11, 2001, I can not remember a similar surge of patriotism for such a length of time.

There have been historic events associated with the space program and sporting events, but the nation moved on in a different manner than we did during the war years. My father served for two years and then was home. He never had to go to battle, and he was spared having to go overseas. Although he had wished for a greater role in the events of war, my mother was pleased with the way things turned out.

Sampson Naval Base closed after the war and eventually became an Air Force Base, Community College and finally a state park in succession over the years. I have never returned to Sampson since that original visit as a six-year-old boy. Who knows the number of men trained there during the war years? Who knows the number of boys like me and my brother who went there and saw the huge buildings and witnessed the tears and felt the fears? The potential for loss was always there.

For many in our nation the aura of Sampson Naval Base has nothing but sadness connected to it. Many of the men meeting their families under those large letters of the alphabet disappeared forever from those families as they marched out through the huge doors at the end of the arena.

***

FDR, HST, IKE, JFK—Three-letter symbols for our use

When I first was cognizant of presidential elections it must have been 1944, since we went around the playground at Sodus School saying, "Phooey on Dewey!" Where we picked the saying up eludes me, but Dewey was running against an incumbent, war-time president. FDR was beloved in the nation, and even in rural New York State, the normal Republican bastion, he drew great popular support. The "Phooey on Dewey" theme was merely an expression of the times. America was not going to "switch horses" in mid-stream, according to my local political advisor—HBP. Dewey was the Republican candidate in 1948 and experts figured his time was nigh. There was no "Phooey on Dewey" that year, because in Sodus the governor was the favorite choice. Experts calculated Dewey was a "shoe-in" since the Democrats were a party in turmoil and, besides, who would vote for Harry Truman?

It turned out that many voted for Truman. Although Truman's election eliminated Dewey from the national stage forever, Tom Dewey left his mark on the state politics. The Democratic candidate got into the political spotlight via the succession amendment and not by an election.

FDR was replaced by Vice President Harry S. Truman when Roosevelt died suddenly in Warm Springs, Georgia in 1945. Suddenly the newspapers lost the subject of the normal headlines used for almost two decades. FDR was gone and now we had HST.

Harry S. made an impact immediately as he made the decision to drop the "bomb." In Sodus the general feeling, observed by a seven-year-old boy, was agreement with the use of the device. The atomic bomb became a fact of life through the next fifty years, as its use was always feared during the Cold War. Truman authorized its use twice and it ended a horrible war. The nuclear age jumped us into a fearful time unlike anything we had experienced before.

I can remember hearing about Japanese suicide planes at the young age of seven. My thoughts then were similar to the feelings I have now whenever suicide bombers are mentioned. It is absolutely abhorrent to think young men (or women now) are willing to sacrifice their life for an opportunity to kill others. The huge difference then, contrasted to now, was that the Japanese attempted to kill military enemies and hit military targets. As soon as the war was over, thanks to HST's courage under fire, the Japanese stopped dying for their country once the Emperor said to stop. No one person—or bomb—seems able to stop the insanity today.

Truman and FDR would not understand the horrible suicide bombings of the modern era. They would not comprehend the stateless nature of the terrorism. War was terrible to contemplate then, but the "religious" suicide bombers today are incomprehensible to this kid from Sodus, New York, grown up through both degrees of madness.

I liked Ike. When Eisenhower was elected to two terms in 1952 and 1956 our village, county and state liked the situation. Dwight Eisenhower was popular, was a war hero and understood world turmoil. He put us at ease because he seemed to be one of us. He was not at all unlike fathers, grandfathers and esteemed community males we all loved and respected. Eisenhower won the hearts and minds of the nation as he ended the war in Korea, keeping a campaign promise. Brother Dick served in Korea, so the Korean War was a Pearson family concern.

As I approached voting age, in time for the 1960 elections, I was very torn by the awesome responsibility. Should I vote Republican, as most upstate New Yorkers had done through the years, except, of course, for the FDR exception? Should I consider voting for JFK? He was running against Ike's Veep, Richard Nixon. Nixon seemed responsible enough and was tough on Communism. JFK did have something very different from Nixon. Kennedy was young, handsome and very smooth. Additionally he was a war hero, had a famous family and was wealthy. These aspects all had political flavors of their own. If a candidate was wealthy, Dad theorized, he would not be corrupted. The Kennedy family was, at times, an albatross around the neck of the family member who was a candidate. The sins of the father, Joseph Kennedy, were documented in upstate New York. War heroes were honored in the nation and in Sodus. The general consensus, according to Dad, was that Nixon was the man. Dad did not like Joseph Kennedy, JFK's father. After all, Nixon was an ex-Navy man also. HBP liked it that both candidates were Navy veterans.

In 1960 my family voted as follows: Dick went for Nixon, Dad went for Nixon, Mom went for Kennedy and I slipped an absentee ballot for JFK into the mail. If Dad had known Mom and I had gone to the Democratic side in 1960, we would have been disowned. I think Aunt Doris talked Mom into voting for JFK. My ballot was quietly mailed in, and Mom never knew she and I had cancelled out the Nixon voters in our family!

JFK was unique. He was "my" first president. Party affiliation was inconsequential in the bigger picture, as long as the man was honest, effective and created good feelings for our nation. He seemed to meet those criteria. The Catholic factor came and went as John Kennedy became the first Catholic President in our history. The fear of the Pope was never a huge factor. In Sodus, the Catholics had that religious instruction thing—and Bingo. What harm could that be on the national political scene?

As I summed up my early childhood political experiences I must confess Eisenhower was my favorite. He exuded a quality that was recognized by men going into battle during WWII, and by voters going into voting booths in the fifties.

The quality was confidence. People in Sodus liked a leader with confidence.

***

Red Glare—Red scare

Even though I loved fire at an early age, there was something very sobering about fire on a big level. The aura of leaves burning on a street was one thing. When the Sodus Theatre and adjoining restaurant went up in red and orange flames one night, it was a fearful sight. As a youngster whose father (along with many other fathers) was a volunteer fireman, it became a village-wide spectator event when a large fire occurred. The red glare on the night sky was evident the night the theatre burned. As Dick and I approached the scene, we knew our father was there with the other firefighters; so the red glare was especially fearsome. The red glare was our red scare.

There is something compelling about seeing flames and smoke pour out of a structure so prominent in the lives of village residents. I had seen barns burn down and once saw a house burn in the town, but the sight of the theatre was different. Were the seats on fire? Was the screen burning? When would we see movies again? Why did the fire ignite? The sky was the drawing card. Like lemmings drawn to food, the residents of the village streamed toward the blaze.

Sodus firemen were exceptional workers. All were volunteers and came to fires, at the sound of the centrally-located siren, from all walks of life. Our father would race out the garage, grab his boots, hat and black waterproof fireman's coat, and then race to the fire hall to catch the truck headed to the fire. Once the siren went off, normal traffic ceased in the village. Scores of cars raced to the centrally located hall and hastily parked and double-parked their cars all over. If the lot behind the fire hall was packed, some would pull up in front of a local business and race to the truck. There were two fire trucks in the fire hall and later more vehicles were purchased. These vehicles, purchased from profits from Firemans' Field Days and other charity events, would charge to the scene of the fire and begin their vital work. The trucks needed drivers and riders.

Dad was a worker. Whether he trimmed bushes, mowed grass, put up storm windows or fought fires, he had one work mode. Those working with him in the yard knew it would be an all-day job once started. Those fighting fires with him sensed urgency about the man at a fire. Friends of our family would relate Dad's performance at fires, and we would never cease to be shocked at his fire-related behavior. He loved the trucks and his association with the red beauties.

Firefighting takes plenty of work and teamwork. These things are evident among the men. The fire that night called upon plenty of those efforts due to the size of the fire and the location of the fire. A whole Main Street block was potentially fuel for the fire if it was not contained. In the history of the village, or any village for that matter, there was a constant fear about fire spreading rapidly through buildings sharing common walls and roof areas. There were fires that consumed multiple buildings in Sodus history, and I can remember hearing the stories about the blazes.

On that night, Dad and another man were evidently working the rear roof of the theatre/restaurant area to contain the fire. In the process of working the area HBP fell through a roof area adjacent to the fire. Whether it was a flimsy roof or whether it was undermined by the blaze, I do not know. By his own account he fell through the area on which he stood and dropped about ten feet to another platform below at the rear of the theatre, *but not into the actual theatre.* It must have been an annex to the rear of the main building. We stood outside the theatre, on the opposite side of the street, watching intently. The news flashed through the crowd that a fireman had fallen through a roof. This conjured up visions of a man falling through the ceiling of the theatre. That ceiling was about thirty feet up above the seats, so that thought was very sobering. Whose father or husband was in that terrifying fix?

Billowing smoke poured out of the building as residents watched in fascination. My mother appeared at our side sometime during the spectacle and mentioned that she, also, heard about a man falling through the roof. She amended her version of the story and said she was convinced it was our father. I do not know why she said that, except that she knew Pete Pearson's reputation. As it turned out, she was right on the money with her prediction. It, thankfully, turned out that the roof Dad fell through was the lean-to roof and not the roof of the high-ceilinged main theatre.

After the fire diminished and the men saved the adjoining buildings, Dad appeared through the turmoil of hoses, trucks, smoke and ashes in the air. He was blackened from his fall and his firefighting gear was a mess. His boots were torn; the black waterproofed coat was torn. He was smiling. There is no doubt in my mind now that he loved every minute of his fire department association. Whether fighting fires, doing parades, or working the main office as treasurer during field days, he was committed. On the evening in question, he appeared to be very much in "his" element.

Fortunately his only injury was a back strain, and after spending two days flat on his back on the couch he was back at his normal routine. It seemed very unusual to see the man in a prone position right there in the living room. Other than that time, I can not remember seeing Dad prone, except my final visit with him as he lay dying in Sodus Hospital in 1970.

Fires in the village were always a community effort. The firemen were our friends and relatives. They were honored and respected by all who were under the collective security offered by the volunteers. Some men in villages such as Sodus spend their whole adult lives serving fire departments in some manner. My own father finally stopped serving as a volunteer when he began his commute to Rochester when his nearby job at Alton, New York was absorbed into a larger company. He realized two to three hours a day of driving on top of long trips and extra hours required by the new corporation were too much for a fifty-year-old man. He also had a responsibility to Donna and Charley, as well as to Isabel, despite getting two older boys out of the family roost.

He could not respond to the red glares in the night sky, put his body in the red scares, associated with the duty, and still work sixty hours a week. He was truly a strong man, but the new corporation took on a different level of work-ethic. He was true to the task, as his associates with Curtis-Burns can attest, but the fire department lost one of their most committed workers. We all breathed a sigh of relief once Pete made that decision. The fires called for younger men who could handle the bumps, bruises and random falls. Donna and Charley did not need to stand outside the perimeter of a fire and wonder where their father was!

***

Burning Leaves—Illegal now but what a nice way to go
Back in the middle of the previous century, we burned leaves. In fact we burned about everything imaginable out in our backyards or in huge used oil drums. During the fall we burned leaves in *front* of our houses in the street. This act became an event on the street that was repeated many times over through October and early November. The annual end of leave burning season was marked by the advent of the first wet snow. After the first wet, heavy snow, burning leaves became impossible.

The leaves in Sodus were exceptional due to the numerous hardwood trees. The color produced by the leaves each fall was striking. In New York and in northern states all the way up through Maine and in Canada, the annual display of nature's coloring book was a tourist's delight. It was a resident's delight also.

Memories of burning leaves are forever ingrained in the senses. The smell sticks with you the most. On rare occasions during the fall or spring, the smell of burning leaves hits one's nose and brings back great memories with a rush. Although the burning of leaves now is illegal almost everywhere, the smells do escape from those random, illegal burns or from large controlled burns done to enhance new growth.

I can remember the smell of burning leaves permeating all our clothes. The whole house smelled the same for weeks on end. There was never any discussion about what the smoke did to our lungs. Of course back then people smoked without remorse or much awareness of the health issues. I would guess there were some cases of lung damage from prolonged standing in the middle of the smog wafting up from street fires, as we referred to our little creations in front of the house. The overall cultural and aesthetic values gained from the fires seemed to outweigh diminished lung capacity.

There were times when certain yards on the street had greater supplies of the fallen leaves. At times my friends and I would go with tarps and wheel barrows and grab leaves from in front of other houses just so we could "justify" having our own fires in front of our house. If there were leaves out there we could start a fire. This seemed to be the method of operation for the youth so inclined to practice their fire skills.

When leaves were ablaze, the creative juices flowed. Sometimes we burned horse chestnuts in our leaf piles. These little shiny nuts would pop like firecrackers when heated and the fire would be the source of tiny explosions until the embers of the leaves were almost out. Chestnut trees started vanishing from the scene in the last forty years of the previous century, so this treat has eluded new generations. Of course the new generations don't burn leaves. Maybe there is a sociological correlation between the lack of creative fires for fun in the modern era and the large need for Ritalin.

The popping of chestnuts reminds me of the time when my mother's purse was by the door and, in a story I have never divulged until now, I took what looked like fire crackers from my mother's purse and placed them in the weekly fire I was creating in the street out front. Needless to say the fire crackers were not fire crackers but were something else mothers carried with them in their purses. Things that had strings coming out the ends like fuses. My mother never asked me where her tampons went, nor did I have a clue as to what the things were. Logic should have told me my mother would not carry fireworks around in her purse during the fall of the year. When I finally learned of such things it was much too late to apologize. By now the statute of limitations is up on this type of juvenile misdemeanor, so the matter is a mere footnote to the great fires we sponsored.

There were other things thrown into the fires. Sometimes we would throw containers in the big blazes. Now that was pure stupidity, yet no one around Sodus was ever damaged to my knowledge. The things that went into fires were of many origins. Plastic toys were sacrificed for the pure pleasure of seeing them melt away. Old balls were set ablaze so we could see melting and hear popping of bladders. Of all the things perpetrated in the recreational fires we created, the most daring and dumb was the act of riding our bikes through a burning pile of leaves.

Considering that the bikes were our solitary dependable source of transportation way before we aspired to car travel, riding the bikes through fire was sheer folly. We stood a good chance of losing our transportation around town. There were times when bike tires would go bad. There were times when pant legs would smolder. There were times when sparks stung our hands, ankles and faces.

Reflecting about the whole experience from the safety of the word processor in my home, and insulated by a fifty-five year buffer, I now realize that kids do stupid things. Parents cannot possibly keep children from all harm no matter what. Parents back then liked the fact that we were outside building strong bodies, creating great appetites, and getting tired naturally, so that after a reasonable period of time we would drop into our beds exhausted at the end of the day. I calculate those results kept parents from worrying too much about some fires in the street. After all didn't everyone do fires back then?

There were never really any problems with fires until one of our buddies on another street started a bonfire near the base of a telephone pole in front of his house. After the fire died down and when the family was inside for the night they were rudely interrupted from watching their three channels of black and white TV when the fire truck appeared outside. It seems the telephone pole in front had cooked for the afternoon and finally was on fire. Flames were leaping up into the area where the wires were, and fortunately no further problems occurred.

In the words of my father, who was a volunteer fireman, there should be a fitting punishment for the imbecile child who started such a fire at the base of the telephone pole. Little did he know that little people living in his house had made the same mistake earlier in the burning season. Fortunately nothing caught fire as a result of the effort.

Little did he know that we had melted down ten pounds of plastic, had destroyed a bike tire, and had burned up the back-up supply of his wife's sanitary napkins.

***

Sodus Point Under Water—The new Seaway Project

During an occasional spring the cottages of Sodus Point located right on the bay flooded. The floods generated from the melting snow and ice along the Great Lakes became a bane of the cottager's existence. This was a severe problem in those flood years. Even then the insurance industry didn't like paying for flood damage, and many companies did not cover acts of God. This was what high water years were called at that time.

The Sodus Point high water always brought the sightseers out in great numbers. It was an eerie feeling riding around in water that was one or two feet over the roadways around the loop leading to the nicest cottages on the bay. The view was spectacular from the loop because one could see the lake out past the lighthouse over a mile away and still see vast reaches of Sodus Bay in the other directions. The owners of the cottages were usually quite wealthy, since these cottages were actually homes built on a peninsula stretching out into Sodus Bay.

On occasion teenagers would drive their cars through the high water, push a rider out of the car onto a small dry spot surrounded by the rising waters and drive off in some juvenile form of look what I have done! Some of us did this to Bruce Wood once, and when we came back for him he had disappeared. A cottager who had driven in to check his property had picked Bruce up and driven him back to Sodus. We spent two hours looking all over for him. We did not think he had drowned or anything like that, but after two hours we were anxious. He was dressed in his suit since we were out of church without listening to the sermon (as was our habit back then). Where the heck was he? We finally went home and were in trouble for taking the car out so long. There was Bruce eating lunch on his porch, waving and laughing at us!

From their homes on the water, the world actually flowed by in the form of huge coal boats, cabin cruisers from all over the Great Lakes and from destinations up and down the inland waterway. Boat owners could come up the east coast of the United States and reach Lake Ontario through a series of bays, canals, well-marked waterways and even up the St. Lawrence River. The St. Lawrence was a vital body of water, and even though the river flowed southwest to northeast out of Lake Ontario into the Atlantic Ocean a person piloting a boat from the Atlantic towards Lake Ontario was actually going up the river (against the current). It is rare to have a river flow generally north as does the St. Lawrence, but New York State has several that flow north as a product of the ice age and the geographical furrowing that was done when the glaciers receded toward Canada.

The St. Lawrence River was to become a bigger part of life on the Great Lakes. By 1959, after many years of negotiations with the Canadian government and the Provincial governments along the St. Lawrence, the Eisenhower administration in Washington, D.C. was proud to announce opening of the St. Lawrence Seaway. Through a series of locks and dams and via a process of dredging and widening, it was possible in 1959 to traverse the river in either direction with large ocean-going vessels.

The world literally could come to any port deep enough in the Great Lakes and the products of those ports' states could be sent down the river toward the Atlantic Ocean! This became one of the world's most vital waterways, and it affected Sodus Point in many ways.

Some fisherman felt the flow of lamprey eels would kill game fish in the five Great Lakes (Superior, Huron, Michigan, Erie) and Ontario-right there off the beach at Sodus Point. The various vessels were capable of bringing exotic growths on their hulls heretofore not present in the lakes. Other concerns focused on illegal trade goods now being able to reach Detroit and Chicago.

In Sodus Point the interest in the whole project focused upon a topic near and dear to all in the resort village. It was a resort village by virtue of a ten-fold increase in population in the summer. During the summer the cottage dwellers returned in vast numbers to spend their money all over Sodus Point and up in the village of Sodus six miles away. When there was no high water the previous spring, the summers went very nicely and the times were then quite good for all. The boat rentals were up, the fish bait sales were wriggling along, and the rental properties were bringing in vast amounts of money.

The topic near and dear to all was the avoidance of high water.

The new Seaway Project was just one more reason to really "like Ike"—the popular Republican president who was a favorite of the upstate New Yorkers. Ike had moved the seaway project to fruition during his two terms and the local residents of the Point liked the possibility now that the random high waters could be controlled by the series of locks along the St. Lawrence River.

As events flowed along, the waters were kept quite well controlled by virtue of the seaway devices. After a few years, a new problem surfaced dealing with fresh water in the lakes.

The St. Lawrence Seaway was beginning to allow too much water out of the Great Lakes and the water was flowing to the Atlantic even if it was going "uphill"! The by-product of this was the extreme opposite from what had occurred prior to the Seaway. Cottagers were coming down in the spring to launch boats, fix up the properties for rent, and get their docks in order. There was very little water!

The water was very low because of the seaway, and the floating docks were seen lying on the mud of the bay. The slips for the boats were empty of water and boats. The muddy bottom of a bay was not a pretty sight. Thus was the situation in Sodus Point during those times. A great furor developed about getting in touch politically with the same people who had worked so well with Ike just a decade or so ago! Much acrimony developed during these times, and the residents of the Great Lakes were now bound together with a common cause. They wanted higher water levels sooner in the spring season. Guess what? The Canadians on the St. Lawrence liked to let the water flow out to sea in great amounts during the winters since the ice damage on the river diminished.

Here was something new to the Sodus Point dwellers. After many years of this give and take and some mention of sending gunboats (cabin cruisers with hunting rifles) up to Montreal to sort things out, the situation seemed to improve through human and environmental events.

A series of conferences and agreements, coupled with low snow falls and less ice, helped create a more normal flow of water. The high water and low water crisis over a prolonged period has abated. Cottage dwellers are happier. Boating and fishing seem to be at their best levels ever. Fish are biting now and the industry is healthy. The hated lamprey eel seems to have gone. Natural rivals of the eel, under the surface of the water, have been developed in fisheries!

Men and women worked together across common borders with a common interest in shared water. Sodus Point was a focal point for major issues of those times. The issues were right there for all to see. History was being taught on the bay! Upon reflection, it now seems too bad that the countries and peoples of the earth can not resolve their issues in the refreshing manner that the American and Canadians did over the seaway. The folks from Sodus Point made their voices heard, and governments listened!

It did not hurt the arguments to have John Foster Dulles just down Lake Ontario on an island where he became concerned about water flowing by Sodus Point in unpredictable amounts. John Foster Dulles was the Secretary of State under Ike during the fifties! Dulles owned a large Chris Craft cabin cruiser that would venture into the beautiful bay at Sodus Point.

The world truly came to Sodus Point!

***

Paper is Heavy- Thursdays and Sundays

I delivered papers for my spending money early in my career as a professional. The main difficulty with the arrangement was the boss was my brother. His version of working conditions and fringe benefits were not in keeping with child labor laws of the time but it made me a better man, even as it made me a tired boy.

Every Thursday and Sunday, the papers were super heavy because of the advertisements and special sections. Fortunately we only delivered six days a week and that allowed us to miss out on Sunday's weight problem. I delivered Monday through Saturday and the subscribers got their Sunday paper through their own efforts or from another delivery person. My career in newspapers was to be limited. I enjoyed reading them much more than delivering them!

As I took on other jobs each summer, and in and around the school year, my associations with the customers were a pleasant memory. I now subscribe to our local paper each day and must confess I do not even know the delivery person. It is not a boy riding a bike as it was in my childhood. The delivery person drives a noisy, old car and gets his payment from the central office after I mail in the quarterly check. I hear him early in the morning when he cruises up and down the street stuffing the paper into the box next to the mailbox. Whereas I delivered right to the front door and beyond, the typical modern mode is in a box out front or in the driveway.

My father instilled the love of newspapers in us, as he made sure we got the local, regional and even nationally known papers. One of the biggest tasks for me at High Street, as a youth, was to bundle up the piles of papers our family accumulated. We all read the papers regularly. As the bundles accumulated we, too, accumulated a great amount of information. My father always brought papers back from each trip taken. Every Sunday he, or one of us assigned to do so, purchased the New York Times. This became an incredible treat to a family of readers. The Sunday New York Times was the largest package of newspaper ever encountered. I wondered, as a paperboy, how on earth delivery boys in the city ever were able to handle the task.

I devoured the Sunday paper from New York. As a Yankee fan, there was always insight into the team, unavailable in any of our other papers. David Cooper had developed an interest in Broadway plays during his productions at the school so the Times theatre section drew my interest. As a history buff the paper offered insight into current events, foreign affairs and diverse editorial creations.

There was a direct correlation, I truly believe, between my family and our newspaper habits and my success in world history under the watchful eyes of Robert Meneely, our history teacher. When our unique instructor wrote the name of a place or important person on the board for us to discuss, invariably I could recognize them. At the end of the year when we took the World History Regents Exam, and my score was 98, Dad was pleased. He helped me more than he knew.

Due to the reading of newspapers I believe my interest in writing was tweaked. History, sports and theatre were not the only sections perused. My mother enjoyed reading about books, authors and reviews of TV programs. This was all it took to start my lifelong enjoyment of those pieces.

Every day of my life I read at least two papers and with the Internet, I can read material from all over the United States. It is possible to check out Boston's best stuff when the urge hits me. I enjoy the USA Today because it contains stuff from all over in easy reading form. David Cooper once chided me for reading the Reader's Digest. To me the USA Today is much like the Reader's Digest, in newspaper form. Cooper may not like it if he was still here, but Meneely could give me a current events test and my score would still be very good.

***

Wind in the Trees—Norway comes to Sodus
The winter storm had reached its crescendo as I watched out through a hand-wiped hole in the layers of frost on our upstairs bedroom window. This was the same window we opened most of the summer to get refreshing, high pressure created air into the

one hundred year old house's upstairs. It was also the upstairs window we used to sneak out on the porch roof and descend to the lawn below using the trellis on the side of the porch. These were important missions of daring during adolescence. Some were stupid and some were entertaining. All were products of adolescence. No one was going to go that route that night due to the storm.

The storm was going to ultimately close down the school the next day, no doubt about it. With winds high enough to make the pair of one hundred foot high Norwegian pine trees sway and groan, there was no chance the mortals driving snowplows in the village below could defeat wind blown snow of such force. On nights like the ones recalled in this writing, the winds had the capacity of blowing snow at the horizontal plane at forty to fifty miles an hour. Once the Norwegian sentinels standing in the front yard started groaning and swaying we knew the winds had reached the magic forty-plus mark. This was our early warning system in the upstairs bedroom.

The groaning noises came from within the trees. The root systems must have been great because the winds were very strong. These fifty to sixty year old trees had grown to magnificent heights in our front yard. They were huge and must have weighed thousands and thousands of pounds Mr. Gage, who had sold the house to our mother during the war years, had informed her that these were two of the tallest trees in the village; he guessed their age at the time of the sale at forty-five years. We had lived in the house since 1944 so the age was now put at over fifty. The groaning was an incredible noise and one lacking appropriate description.

Once a storm hit the village and had the "lake effect" snow all so common with winter storms, we would wake up in the morning with two or more feet of snow on the ground. Consider the impact of two feet of snow on any village when the snow was driven by the high winds that made our trees groan. Lake effect snow came from off the moist reservoir called Lake Ontario, and the north-northwest winds would deliver it along the shores of the lake toward the eastern end of the lake. Welcome to upstate New York between Rochester and Syracuse!

Our trees were the visual envy of all because they rose up out of the modest front yard in front of a small, wooden house dating back to the 1800s. These trees were truly two of the highest trees in town by virtue of the fact that High Street was the second highest street in the village.

Once winter's storms and the March winds had subsided, my brother and I would climb up through the myriad of limbs in either of the trees during the summer months. The climb would take several minutes since a climber would have to contort his body around the mature limbs to gain the top of the tremendous tree. Once there you could literally see about everything in the village.

Every time we made the climb we would leave a message in a glass jar we placed there on one of the very first climbs. The jar cap had been screwed into the tree and the glass jar screwed on to the top. Each time we climbed the trees the messages from the previous climbs would be updated or replaced. I wonder if the messages in the bottles are still located at the top of the tree. We stopped climbing the trees at different times. My brother moved on to college, the military and finally his state police career. Once he got married, his tree climbing ventures were limited. I climbed the trees during one summer after my graduation and I think that was my last climb. There may have been climbs by younger brother Charley and his cronies but I am not aware of the bottle history.

The trees were great companions through the winter months. They had a great prediction value as described above. Once the winds topped the forty-plus mark we knew it. Even with the television set going, the trees were able to deliver their acoustical message. The normal winds of summer and fall were always a sweet noise with the windows open to hear the noise. No matter which direction any wind came from the trees picked up the movement with their growth of pine branches.

During such times the trees seemed to be nature's sleeping medicine. The greatest feeling of the trees was when the wind would pick up once you climbed to the top. As you held on you placed your trust in the strength of the Norwegian main trunk. This gave you a swaying ride to remember free of charge. I can write this now so these rides were not life threatening! The tree held me in its arms quite easily.

There was a winter treat that occurred during heavy snows. The Norwegian pines had lower limbs that would become heavy with snow and when this happened the limbs would touch the ground. We then could go under the limbs and enjoy a midwinter tree house, compliments of Mother Nature. At times the snow would last several days and each successive snowfall would bury the snow house even more.

One time when I was in high school, we had an ice storm and families had to hire professional tree surgeons to clear out badly damaged limbs from trees and take the limbs away. On a day that was remembered for a long time in our family, Isabel was home alone, Dick was gone, and the rest of the family all were in school or at work. As the tree surgeons completed their work in the damaged hardwood trees around the house and in the neighborhood, one of the workers approached my mother with a proposal to trim and beautify the pines in front of the house. She merely told them to go ahead and do what they thought best.

When family members returned home that bleak day we were vividly aware of a manifest change in the front of our house. Taking Isabel's verbal OK to do some work out front the tree people had removed the limbs on the twin trees up to about the twenty foot level. There would be no more snow and limb created snow houses. There would be less noise in the winter from the faithful friends. There would be less pleasant summer breeze noises coming from out front. Almost as a secondary concern, the front of the house could now be seen all year long from the street. This was never possible before. Mailmen and delivery people would come through the limbs of the trees on the sidewalk. We would always be immersed in the beauty of the trees every time we went up or down our sidewalk.

At supper in the kitchen that night hardly a word was spoken. The end of an era had occurred almost by accident. Mom's love of the trees was always evident ,so we know she had not dictated the twenty foot limit of defoliation out front.

We all recovered from the incident as families seem to be able to do. Every climb after that required a ladder from the garage; that had not been the case before. Once up in the tree, though, things still looked pretty nice. The noises still continue to this day because trees seem capable of doing this in their magnificence.

***

War Bonds—Banking lessons

My earliest memory of saving came when I was about four or five. As I crossed a large walkway over a busy Rochester, N.Y. main artery to ring a "liberty" bell in the middle of the suspended walkway, my mother explained that we had purchased a savings bond earlier in the day and that act would allow us to ring the bell. The savings bond was called a "war bond" since the money would help pay wartime expenses. The payback from the bond's accrued interest later in life would be a "reward" for helping win the war.

The crowd that particular day was quite large and memorable because we waited a long time in the line for our chance to signal our purchase to all who could hear that day. The day of the bell ringing, my mother had taken Dick and me to Rochester on the bus. This was our common form of transportation during the period of time my father was away with the navy. I guess his car was somewhere in storage, but my mother did not drive then so the bus from Sodus to Rochester was the accepted mode of travel. The bus stopped at every town between Sodus and Rochester to meet the needs of residents in those villages also.

We finally made it to the middle of the bridge over the street, and Dick and I rang the bell for the two war bonds. The war came and went and the war bonds were kept in the safe deposit box in the bank downtown. The Union Trust Bank has changed names many times over the years but it had the same name for a long time back in the forties and fifties. I knew that because my father was a teller there up until the time he went into the navy. He would be pleased that Dick and I had invested in war bonds at the prompting of Isabel.

The lack of banking knowledge on my part was due to my age. Dick was learning about banking since he was at the early part of managing a paper route on our street and two adjacent streets in our home town. He was very street-wise, it seemed. He told me somewhere in the surge of bond activity that we both would be rich as a result of this bond investment. As with most things, until I reached the age where I began to question Dick's insight, I merely agreed that it would be nice to be rich someday.

During my father's Union Trust days, he maintained a safe deposit box at the bank for him and Mom. When he went into the navy my mother kept up the visits to the box depositing the bonds, mortgage information and never ever told us of any other items in the box. When my Dad returned from the navy he managed the box again, I suppose and he changed jobs from the bank to Alton Canning Company in nearby Alton. He took me on his interview for the job up in Wolcott, New York at the Wolcott Hotel. The reason I remember this event is that he reminded me of this event over the years as his successes on the job gave him greater clout with the company. Often the son of the man who had hired Dad would say I was good luck since I had been along on the job interview with Mr. Burns Sr. at the hotel. Dad was out of the banking business, but he excelled in selling canned goods to large brokers between Chicago and New York. The safe deposit box remained in service.

Long after Dad's change of jobs and after he had passed on at a fairly young age of sixty-two, my Mom took us to the bank to check out the safe deposit box. In the box were the house papers detailing the six thousand dollar deal for our home Mom had purchased while Dad was in the navy. The deal was a rare no interest purchase with payments made to Mr. Porter over the period of the loan. Mr. Porter had loaned the money to Mom to give Mr. Gage so our family would have a place to live in the neighborhood we lived in from 1940-1944. Both men were rare men as they accommodated my mother's needs with very little thought to making a profit. The house was certainly worth more than the six thousand asked. The loan of that amount for no interest was definitely a great deal, no matter what era we lived in at the time!

As we looked at the documents relative to the house we came across some other items. There, at the bottom, covered by rare gold coins my Dad had collected while he was a banker, were the war bonds Isabel had purchased with us during the war. The year my Dad died was 1970, so the war bonds had more than grown to maturation.

The lesson in banking we learned from my mother was reinforced by my then-deceased Dad. Methodical saving paid off as did the investment in the bonds. The bonds returned a huge profit on their initial promised return. This delighted us since we needed funds. The sale of the gold coins helped finance family needs at a time when things were tight, and the price of gold was good. My mother sold the house around 1972 for a very fair price of twenty thousand to a young couple that "needed a break" like she herself did back in 1944. My mother taught us all the same lesson she had experienced nearly thirty years earlier when two nice men gave her a break.

Isabel "rang the bell" for her family when the bonds, coins and house all had been cashed in. True to form, she shared the proceeds with all four of us and then moved to a low income place in a nearby village. She was still comfortable and her kids were better off. The new family took ownership of a great, old house at a great price.

***

Busing to Rochester—Get out of town

We were on our way back from Rochester on the bus sometime in the 1940s. The bus made scheduled stops all along the "Ridge." This was the geographical path Route 104 followed. The locals called it Ridge Road. My mother, Dick and I were taking one of our periodical round trips into the city from Sodus during the war years. We made the trip to visit relatives living in Monroe County. One set of mother's relatives, the Nothaker's, did not even own a vehicle, so they either took the bus to see us or vice versa. Mom's relatives provided plenty of love and attention; but without a vehicle their collective range was limited once we arrived in the city.

Our other relatives had a car, but with gas rationing and Grandfather Pearson's traveling job, the Pearson's of Rochester did not travel to Sodus very often. We became the travelers in the family, and mother guided us nicely in the art of riding the bus. Once we got past Williamson, en route to Sodus, there were many empty seats, so each of us scrambled to obtain our own private seat. This was about the only luxury of our early childhood we enjoyed while traveling. I contrast this to the traveling habits of youngsters in my own family tree. Recently two different sets of parents and their children traveled to vacations in Florida. The SUVs in each of the family pulled out, in air conditioned comfort, with the kids already watching video tapes in the backseats of the vehicles.

It did not warp me when we traveled by bus, all jammed in one rather modest seat. There was a special treat. Because the driver took a liking to me, he often allowed me to sit right behind him where he kept his bag and jacket. The young loved ones in their SUVs of the year 2004 will have to make profound advancements in order to top the travel routine for which they are accustomed as children. When my Dad returned from Navy duty and we started traveling, it sure was not at all like the SUVs of this era. The children were jammed into the back seat, wearing no seat belts, using no car seats; and we drove until Dad was tired or we arrived somewhere. Dad did not get tired for hundreds of miles, had an incredibly oversized bladder, and smoked cigars as he drove.

The bus trips allowed for movement in the bus when seats opened up but in the Pearson Chevy we did not move around. I must amend that statement with the qualifier about needing to puke. That would stop the car quickly. I was the family puke-artist, and could be depended upon to get about thirty miles before needed to toss my cookies. It became predictable. Our car, traveling west toward Rochester, would have to stop at the bottom of what we called the "Dugway." This was the point where Route 104 crossed Irondequoit Bay. After I tossed my breakfast, and everyone else got some fresh air, we would resume the trip to the grandparents or ballgame.

Smoking in public transportation was permitted when I was a youngster, so a cigar in the car was not much different from a cigar on a bus. The only major difference was the concentration of the second hand smoke in the car. Consider a trip in a car, with the heater blasting full bore, throw in a lighted "White Owl" cigar and then toss in the kid in the back seat with motion and cigar sickness.

I can vividly recall my first airplane trip with two smokers in front of me and a cigar smoker behind me. That was not much different from a bus trip. My, my how things have changed! Smokers were finally brought to their knees by the system. At least on the bus trips there were plenty of stops and windows could be opened, despite the presence of smokers. When traveling with Isabel on the bus, there were always some apples, cheese, crackers or something else she packed in her handbag. Eating something actually helped keep the travel blahs to a minimum.

Our bus trips ended after the war, and the bus ceased its operation shortly afterward. Everyone had a family car and gas was very cheap. There were times when a gallon of gas was under twenty cents per gallon, so why take a bus? I did learn bus protocol during my childhood. As I began my coaching career and spent many, many hours on bus trips, the memories of our family bus trips lingered. I was always cognizant of the need to stop and move about periodically. There were toilets on the team busses, so Pete Pearson's non-stop, super bladder-travel ethic was not needed.

I always will consider my bus experiences worthwhile. My mother taught me to treat the drivers with respect and courtesy. The regular driver on the Sodus to Rochester run was named Ed Lund. How do I recall that name after nearly sixty years? He would let me sit behind him with the air blowing from his open window on my face during the trips. My own father did not even do that for me in his Chevy!

***

The Ontario—Across and back in a day

Public school in New York State commenced each fall on the day after Labor Day. This mark on the calendar was the end of summer for all of us and marked the new grade level in school and the chance to see all the faces we may have missed during the busy summer months. The Labor Day of my Brother Dick's senior year in high school was marked by a rebellious act on his part. He and several of his friends from Sodus traveled to Rochester, New York and caught a ride on the Ontario I—twin to the Ontario II—the two ferry boats running straight across Lake Ontario from Rochester to Cobourg, Ontario in Canada daily. The trip took about three hours each way from Rochester. It was a one-hour auto trip to the port at Rochester. In a span of about ten hours residents of Sodus could take a boat ride across the lake, spend some time in Canada and then be back home. In brother Dick's trip the return trip did not occur until two days after Labor Day.

Dick and his buddies came up with a plan to travel to Canada, miss the last ferry boat out of Cobourg and then come back the following afternoon. This would have them miss the opening day of school and start their senior year with a unique statement. The story they all concocted was that the ferry left without them as they were eating somewhere in Cobourg, Ontario Province. Service was slow and the boat left. That was the story Dad heard two days later and that is the story all the boys had for Francis Samuel Hungerford, principal extraordinary, when he got in his licks on their butts.

Life was simple back then. If a person screwed up, and someone was always screwing up somewhere in the school system, the paddle was brought into play in the principal's office. After that gesture of discipline, the parents took their children home where they got more of the same. Back then this was called double trouble. It was almost a sure thing. Today the ACLU and the liberal applications by too many lawyers and judges have reduced the control schools have over their clients during the daylight hours. Fifty years ago discipline and control was swift, usually fair, and very much appreciated by parents. The boys of the Cobourg incident paid for their folly. They then began school two days late and all of them graduated from high school as planned.

In the history of the class of 1951 the Cobourg excursion by several of its members was hardly mentioned again. The trip made a lasting impression upon me. As an eighth grader who enjoyed school and would not miss school on purpose, the whole thing looked, again, like my brother's foolishness while challenging authority. The fact that he went on to become a New York State Trooper is interesting given his rebellious attitude for so many years.

The "illegal" Cobourg trip was probably hatched during the summer of 1950 when many of us took the ride with our grandparents and parents. Dick and his buddies were on the boat that summer. We had taken the same trip when we were real young with the Rochester relatives we visited on occasion. The trip was inexpensive, and gave everyone a brief taste of Lake Ontario during the summer. Seldom were there bad winds or waves and the short distance across the lake was relatively simple for the two identical ferries. One would be coming as the other was going. They would pass in the lake at times and on weekends they would make several trips. There were automobiles on board and, darned if there weren't railroad cars in the middle of the ferry where tracks allowed for their presence. The autos parked on either side of the freight cars.

Cobourg, Ontario was and still is a small place. Population figures in 2002 placed the population at about 16,000. In the era of the Ontario ferries the population was much smaller. The Ontario I and II stopped running there in the early 1960s when auto traffic predominated due to the modern four lane highways. People from upstate New York could get around the lake by way of Buffalo, Hamilton and Toronto almost as quickly as the ferry could. They could do it much cheaper at fifty cents a gallon for gas. The boats were scrapped, and I remember seeing photos of them being dismantled. It saddened me at the time. The era ended but the memories live on. Just recently there was a story in the Williamson Sun/Sodus Record about a hydra-foil making the trip to Toronto from Rochester in two hours in any kind of seas. I look forward to trying that!

When the ferries were at their peak the boats could transport plenty of people who merely went along for the ride and did not bring an auto. Meals were available on board, and the trips were the first experience for many of being out of sight of land. Normally in our childhood we could see land wherever we boated since we stayed close to shore with sailboats and power boats. We sailed in and out of the huge bay near our community and kept the lighthouse in view in the event of sudden bad weather.

In my brief experiences on the Ontario ferry I don't remember bad weather, and that is fortunate. During a couple of boating ventures involving Judge Parson's yacht and a friend's sailboat coming out of Sodus Bay and traveling east toward the St. Lawrence River, sudden wind shifts and heavy seas occurred and in both episodes the trips were very scary. Those memories are indelible as I still remember large, fifteen-foot waves and the troughs between the waves. The troughs between waves become the real ominous part of the experience because all a person can see is water everywhere as the boat rides its way down and then back up the wave.

One thing I learned from traveling on the Ontario I and II was that a person should eat plenty of bread or rolls to keep the stomach filled up. This can keep the juices from broiling around in the stomach. Although we never had to employ such stuffing during an Ontario trip, I did have to try the tactic later when I was on the yacht and sailboat. In both cases the loaf of bread I consumed kept me from being sick. Sitting outside on the deck was also a great help. For rough seas it is prudent to be able to see the sky and be out in the weather as contrasted to getting below decks. Once below decks the world turns your inner ears and stomach upside down and inside out. Being seasick is one of life's worst experiences, according to those who have gone through such an ordeal. I have been close and have experienced the near- puke state. Being on deck and eating a ton of bread saved me. This bread trick was taught by a loving grandmother whose knowledge on the matter, she said, came from a friend who had sailed the Atlantic Ocean.

Dick and his buddies were not seasick from their Cobourg trip during the early part of their senior year. They did experience the wrath of their fathers, and something more. As each leaned over the bare desk top on Francis Samuel's desk and got three blows on the behind from the "board of education," visions of the pleasant boat trip did not dance in their heads.

***

Prisoners of War- A moral dilemma

When my mother hooked a ride with Fauney Knapp one day in the apple season during a fall in upstate New York, it became an outing I would always remember. Fauney lived across the street from our home on High Street and she possessed a pre-WWII Packard coupe that was sleek, black and very well kept. The mystery woman called Fauney was always a bit scary, and behind a wheel she became much scarier! Miss Knapp was a single woman for as long as I remembered and kept to herself even though she was sister to the personable Rexall Drug Store owner, and sister to the most eccentric woman in town called Gertie Knapp.

Gertie appears elsewhere, but sister Fauney was a real case study. She drove my mother around when needed and due to gas rationing during the war her Packard sat in the garage for long periods of time.

On the apple-picking day we were driven to the Sodus Fruit Farm where we were going to gather apples rather than pick them since apples taken off the ground were free to those wishing to gather them. We arrived at the orchards via dirt roads lining the perimeter of the huge three to five acre plots filled with abundantly fruited apple trees. The harvest was going to be a good one, and there were many apples on the ground already so our job was going to be easy. After stopping the car, we walked through several rows of trees to work the ground under the trees being picked that day. The foreman of the farm was there and some other workers were already in the trees as we worked our way under them to gather loose apples off the ground.

My mother started talking to some of the workers and before long I realized she was struggling to communicate since the pickers were, as it turned out, German prisoners of war. They usually were in a stockade just down the road towards Sodus Point, but on this fall day they were out and earning fifty cents a day, according to my sources much later on in my life. Their choice was to stay in camp or earn money just down the road serving a useful purpose. For those Germans picking that day, it was a chance to meet my mother, my brother and me—as well as good old Fauney Knapp.

In what was a truly multicultural experience long before such experiences were thought to be good for the soul and for one's education, my mother was treating me, again, to some of her school teacher wisdom and worldly attitude. We mingled with the men in the trees and were able to gesture and make small talk in German and English. My mother's guardians the Nothakers taught us all some German and helped develop in us an appreciation for 'foreign" food. These Germans were merely workers to me and my brother. Not once did we consider the fact that they were, in fact, POWs.

These POWs were kept in American camps away from communications, railroads, major cities, and large populations by design as it now turns out, according to historians writing about the period. The upstate New York area on Lake Ontario with the five to six month cold climate was great for preventing possible escapes and made for a difficult freedom should an escape be made successfully. The POWs were also those higher echelon type prisoners who needed to be removed from Great Britain and other allied areas so they could not easily be recycled into the German war machine. These men were pilots, seamen and according to some historians, U-boat personnel.

We picked up a couple of bushels of apples that day for our domestic purposes, and got some help from our new friends in the trees as they dropped some picked apples down to the ground. Upon departing the orchard after the German-American "hour" we waved goodbye to some interesting men. These men seemed very interested in us at the time. As I reflect upon this interesting episode in my life it is now apparent that these prisoners were no doubt lonely and homesick for their own kids and women.

After the war years and as the POW camp was turned into a series of enterprises such as a campground, a trailer park, a recreation area and home sites over the years, many of the war kids would reflect about the prisoners. There are records of some of the events and activities but the memories faded rather quickly. My Dad returned home after the war, and he and others like him did not talk too much about the experience. Fortunately my father served in Washington, D.C. for most of his time after finishing basic training at Sampson, New York. Sampson was one of the largest training facilities for the navy and was built for the huge need for sailors in the war. It was located only fifty miles away in Geneva, New York so we were able to see my father a couple of times during his training.

We had an interesting discussion one time around the kitchen table when my Dad finally explained some of his duties in the navy during the war. Among other things, the unit he was in helped predict weather patterns for the Atlantic Ocean and tested weather equipment to use on ships and at bases. It came to me during that discussion that the POWs in the orchard several years earlier (while my Dad was in Washington predicting weather and testing weather balloons) were often plucked from the Atlantic Ocean that my father's unit was trying to make calculated decisions about for the safety of our own sailors. It seems ironic that the friendly and benign apple pickers were at odds with what my father and millions like him were trying to do on behalf of the USA!

Isabel was certainly an interesting mother and was doing her patriotic bit by riding around with Fauney within gas ration limits. Those limits included a fruit farm only three miles away from our house. After the orchard encounter was complete, we drove on a dirt road along the bluffs overlooking Lake Ontario. Fauney seemed intent on placing us in danger as she navigated her coupe along the very edges of the bluffs along the perimeter of the orchards.

Upon reflection it appears we were in greater danger from our neighbor than we were from our avowed enemy.

***

Cold War O.P.—Mom was a patriot

Long after my father came home from navy service during World War II, our family was still involved in service to the nation. My mother volunteered to work in the Civilian Patrol observation post at the very top of the Orchard Terrace hill at the very end of the known road at the time. The time was the late 1940s or early 1950s, and Orchard Terrace was not the lengthy street it is in the twenty first century. Back then once you reached where Paul Shaver, a chemistry teacher at the high school, and Mrs. Alling of Alling and Lander corporate fame built homes on the street, you were at the end of known civilization!

Beyond the last homes and up a dirt road was found a water tower and an old silver metal-skinned trailer. The water tower kept the water pressure at acceptable levels on the steep street during the summer months when water was used heavily by canning factories and homes. The reservoir was across the village on the other large hill called Green's Hill. Green's Hill and Orchard Terrace were the two natural landmarks between which the village nestled.

This water pressure and a chronic low summer capacity situation were both remedied when the water was pumped from Lake Ontario during the mid-century. This change from dependence upon the spring fed, old reservoir came after a voter referendum was passed to allow for pump stations and pipes to come across farms along the lake and to the village.

As an aside it was this event that brought the greatest satisfaction to my father when he reflected upon his public service as mayor of the village. He and others advocated such a plan, and it took a lot of wrangling to get the finished product.

Let's go back to the trailer on top of the windy hill. It could be reached by driving or, as my mother and I did several times, by walking up Orchard Terrace. The trailer was a small Air Stream look-alike and had a phone, electricity, a small heater and little else. When a volunteer would report for duty in 1948, the enemy was communism and volunteers would be looking for the planes of the USSR. I am not sure how long it took for the people in charge of manning the trailer to decide how futile the duty was, but perhaps it came when the United States established radar lines across Canada. The early warning line, as it was called in the cold war, was an early warning string of radar stations developed to prevent a surprise attack from over the North Pole from the USSR.

My mother had served during World War II in the same trailer. At that time she was looking for Japanese or German planes attacking from out in the lake or from Canada. Historians point out how impossible that would have been for the enemy; but during the war caution took priority over all else. During the time she spent there with binoculars and charts of enemy planes Isabel saw nary an enemy plane. I say that with confidence because Dick and I or I alone would accompany Isabel to the trailer each visit. Sometimes I remember other ladies of the village going with her. Sometimes they would have a car. The long walk in all kinds of weather was merely a short drive in second gear for Mom's friends.

The closest enemy was not in a plane but in the prisoner of war camp on Lake Road on the way to Sodus Point. Realistically, we had a greater risk of them escaping than we did any plane coming in with a bomb for some factory. The Cold War began after 1945 when the USSR erected an iron curtain across Europe in the words of Winston Churchill. America feared nuclear attack over the pole, so the observation post was the destination for Isabel and her kids and friends.

At some point when radar eliminated the need for the post, my mother stopped going there and all the other volunteers did the same. However, the traffic to the post was not over completely.

For some reason attributed to either apathy or forgetfulness the observation post lingered up there in the four seasons, taking a beating from the wind and weather. The trailer stayed there for several years, a lonely sentinel and reminder of a time past. The kids of that side of the village would go by and write their names or other's names on the body of the trailer. Some hunters and/or target shooters had begun using the trailer for target shooting. How ironic it seemed then and now that the trailer stood out there on the top of the hill through the hot and cold wars and never suffered any damage until American guns tore the trailer apart.

Over time the damage was completed when large numbers of us merely took a page out of the vandalism already begun and emptied hundreds of BBs from our gun collections at the remaining windows and the metal sides. The noise of a BB hitting the metal trailer was significant. The noise of shattering glass also had a special ring to it to the practicing juvenile delinquents of High Street, Orchard Terrace and other streets.

Although my parents would let me buy cap guns, they were adamant against me owning a BB gun. This was a hurdle I had to surmount if I wanted a piece of the observation post or any other suitable target. As with the modern era when gun dealers and collectors are always able to get and use guns, there were boys who could get BB guns without any problem. Teddy Smith (Gumpert), Peter Moore (a name even I can not use after fifty years), Bob Pearson (Stinky) and a few others rented or borrowed BB guns from Jim DeBrien and other older boys in the area. We then staged shoot-outs where rules of engagement were to shoot at legs and butts only. This went along swimmingly until several of us arrived at a logical conclusion on the same day. Three people had taken BB's in the facial area. Fortunately no eyes were lost but our common sense finally took charge over hormones. We stopped the gun fights, and went after stationary targets.

The trailer was one of the targets and we finished the job started by the more sophisticated fire-power. We then went on a two-week shooting spree that included streetlights near where we lived, mailboxes, and glass bottles placed on fence posts. During the time when the BB guns were most active, they were dismantled at the end of each outing and stored in cellars in the neighborhood. No one wanted to be caught with a BB gun.

My father brought the topic of BB guns up in a discussion one night. Local streetlights were being destroyed and his curiosity was piqued. Probably it was more like his intuition was piqued! The night before his query three or four lights in a row went dark. He said he was placing Police Chief Con Loveless on the case since Dad (remember, he was mayor) felt there was something organized about this power outage and it was *not* normal breakage. Chief Lovelace lived right down the street and ironically he lived near a pole with a missing light. The glass from the light in the street in front of Con's home was no sooner swept up when the light was taken out again. The second vandalism was witnessed by Con, who was outside his house at the time. He snared the culprit.

Fortunately for those of us in the neighborhood, the captive shooter was a kid from across town. He was merely enjoying a bike ride that night shooting out streetlights in someone else's neighborhood. The critical news for all of us in the neighborhood was that Con was pinning the previous shootings on the lad. The bad luck of the new kid on the block was evident. Although he was much more adept at his reasoning than were we in attacking lights away from one's home turf, he did have to pay for the one light Con saw being blown away. It finally dawned on us that our two-week binge was pretty stupid. It was also delinquency. All of us were under age. The captured lad and his parents paid for the light, and the shooting stopped simultaneously. It was all it took to wake us up. Lights were no longer targets, nor should they have ever been. It was work to replace a bulb. Our neighbors with the electric company were made to perform unnecessary work because of us.

Con felt that he had solved the crime. We had dodged a serious bullet (or BB). The RGE enjoyed the return to normal maintenance on their pole lights. The trailer was a different story.

Isabel would have been chagrined had she seen the remains of the trailer when someone finally dragged it away on a flatbed trailer. It seems the tires had been blasted away with hunting guns. The windows and door were gone and the names on the trailer outnumbered all of those living in the village. There were also hundreds of tiny dot-like indentations in the metal skin of the trailer.

Many were put there by a lad who, at one time, had helped his mother search for enemies in the sky above Sodus. She would have been disappointed with the ground attack against her former cold war bastion.

***

Driving Miss Isabel—Fauney and her old classic

The Symonds' house across the street was occupied by Fauney Knapp for many years. During those pre-Symonds years of ownership old Fauney kept to herself most of the time but would occasionally stir from the nest and get out. Getting out meant backing a black Packard coupe out of her barn out into High Street; then Fauney would navigate the huge auto through the village to her destination.

I knew this routine because preceding such a venture was a phone call to my mother from Fauney to get my mother to accompany her on the trip. Inherent in accepting Fauney's request was the fact that my mother took me along on many of these trips. Whether my mother knew I would be an asset in an emergency or merely a companion for the duration, I do not know.

I did not, nor do not now, feel I was a "Mama's boy." I did, however, accompany my mother everywhere. I am not sure how older brother Dick dodged many of the outings since there were just three of us living together at that time. My guess is he begged off or was busy as a ten year old, and I, at five, had to go along for the ride. My mother and I did "bond" at this point and the educational opportunities for me to learn how to relate to my elders was good for me my whole life. Instead of "Driving Miss Daisy" I did the "Riding with Miss Fauney and Mrs. Isabel."

The rides were usually a simple trip to get sweet cherries in season, apples from the ground free of charge, some fresh vegetables from a stand out on old Route 104, or a trip to Sodus Point for some ice cream. Isabel was not a driver until she was in her fifties, but

Fauney evidently was a driver of long note in the village. People would take close note of her trips and stare at her passengers as though we were curious companions for an eccentric old maid. People also admired the black, pristine late thirties Packard in mint condition.

I was not into cars then, and did not know much about Packards vs. Chevies and Fords. All I knew was that my mother would sit up front and I would sit in the rather small rear seat. The upholstery was probably as clean as it was from the showroom. We never ate in the vehicle. My mother was nervous about spinster Knapp's driving abilities because she kept up a steady stream of talk to the driver and even to me, behind her in the rear seat. My mother talked continually when she was either nervous or agitated. This was nerves, in my reflective judgment.

The time Fauney drove us along the high banks along the Lake down at the nearby Sodus Fruit Farm gave us both a thrill! That trip even made me nervous. I did not talk when I was nervous like my mother. I buried my face in the felt upholstery, and waited for the noise of the impending crash.

Other times Fauney merely drove slowly toward her ultimate target and other drivers seemed to make way for the vehicle. Once she drove into a fruit stand with her front bumper and scattered apples and peaches all over the place. The owner of the stand was probably quite patient as I do not remember any harsh words or actions. My mother did buy more apples than intended, and took them from the spilled offerings. She was a notable peacemaker in times such as that, and could always come up with a gesture or word to smooth troubled waters.

On some trips Fauney would get gas and in those days someone pumped the gas for the driver. The service person would inevitably open the massive hood and check the fluids. I am not sure where the car was serviced but wherever it was those guys probably had a field day. More interestingly I wonder where the car ended up when the lady died. It must have been a "little old ladies car."

She had a brother who ran a drug store, so my guess is he

inherited the car. I never remember seeing the car again. Whenever a person opened her hood at the gas station that person would make a big deal of the power train. I felt quite honored to be invited for my periodic rides. I felt as though I shared ownership of the auto on those rides. Since Fauney did not drive more than ten miles on any of her periodic outings, she did not need much gas. Gas was rationed during the war years so she was probably way below the average in gas consumption. I never remember her driving my mother to Rochester or farther than the fruit farm or Sodus Point.

My mother got her first driving lesson courtesy of Fauney. Fauney got Isabel behind the wheel of the car somewhere in Sodus where there were no vehicles and plenty of room. As I cowered in the rear seat, bearing witness to my mother in a completely new position, I was also amazed to see our reclusive, eccentric neighbor spending time patiently explaining the controls to Isabel. I vividly remember the clutch! It had a clutch that made the lesson all that more difficult. In New York State at the time and for many years, people had to take driver's education with a clutch-operated car. My mother avoided the formal driver education and she ultimately drove only automatic transmission cars. There was too much else going on while she drove to worry about a clutch also!

I had never seen Fauney Knapp except behind the wheel of her car, and an occasional glimpse of her on her front porch. Fauney reached out to her neighbor Isabel with a kindness unmatched in her dealings she had with all others in Sodus. Isabel took another decade to get into driving but the black Packard was her first drive.

As I reflect upon my memories about the Knapp lady across the street, I remember that she had an older sister named Gertie who was a village "fruit." Everyone thought she did not hit on all cylinders, and she reinforced that notion in by virtue of her unbathed, unkempt, and barefoot appearance around town. For reasons I never could understand, my mother purchased rotten fruit from Gertie as she peddled the fruit door to door in her bare feet during the summer and fall months. I now conclude that Gertie probably got her supply of fruit from the trips Fauney and Isabel made. Gertie's delivery and storage systems were as bizarre as she was so a month later my mother would be purchasing fruit from a goofy lady as a favor to her driver education teacher.

That seemed to be how people took care of the fruits back then.

***

Slavery's Legacy—Underground railway and migrants

When my mother worked out the business deal for our family home at 20 High Street in Sodus, we merely moved out of the rental house on the corner of the street and crossed the street diagonally to our new home. Our new home had a very old, damp cellar. When Dick's older friends came and looked over the cellar they commented that it probably was part of the "Underground Railroad." For days after that I would go down the steps to the damp, musty cellar and try to figure out how a railroad could go through the space. What were the guys talking about?

Finally teachers and other adults were able to explain the nature of the railroad system. Our house at 20 High Street was built in the late 1800s so the "Underground Railroad" label applied to it when we moved there was impossible to validate. Our house was built after the Civil War.

In the time period leading up to the Civil War 1861-1865 and during the war the "Underground Railroad" functioned as an escape mechanism for slaves escaping from their bondage. For many years, at mid-century in the 1800s, the social movement, sympathetic to the notion of freedom for slaves, helped approximately sixty to eighty thousand slaves reach freedom in the North. The movement took on the name, "Underground Railroad." Many of the slaves reached Canada, and ultimate safety, from bounty hunters trying to capture the individuals for return to the owners in the South.

There was no actual railroad, as I had looked for in the cellar. It was, instead, a series of individuals willing to conceal runaways in their homes, barns, cellars, or on their property. The stopping places were referred to as "stations" and the friendly sympathizers were called "conductors." They had railroad terminology but no rails. There were routes leading north out of the south through Maryland, Kentucky and Pennsylvania. The "freight" was guided by sympathetic abolitionists, as the slaves made ten to twenty miles a day, usually on foot or in a wagon under farm products.

There were Underground Railroad Stations along the Ridge serving as the last stop before getting into boats bound for Canada. Wherever there were natural harbors such as at Rochester and Sodus and Oswego, slaves made their way to Canada. Pultneyville, N.Y. was the historic site of a known abolitionist named Cuyler. During our time in school we visited various museums and homes having connections to the movement. I remember going to Pultneyville with my mother and some other ladies to learn about the system. It fascinated me to consider people were hiding others and guaranteeing them safe passage. Something we take for granted all our lives, was not guaranteed to others in their lifetime.

As I worked my summer jobs in the orchards owned by the Fruit Farm, my association with migrant laborers was a critical part of the employment. In my mind's eye the migrants were symbolic of the migration north by many of the ancestors of the Sodus migrant workers. They were determined to make a living by traveling back and forth from the south to the north, depending upon growing seasons.

My travels in trains, cars, and busses, at that point in my life, were nothing contrasted to the travels of the migrants. They started out in the backs of trucks and in run down, old busses and covered over a thousand miles. This made my trips of forty miles to Rochester look like a short hike. To think I got impatient sitting for that Rochester trip! How about the migrants, loaded into a bus going three to four hundred miles a day?

Think about heading north with bounty hunters hot on your heels, with only the clothing on your back, and with the notion that sympathetic people along the way were there when you needed them. The "Underground Railroad" was not the answer to the problems of slavery and/or racial relations, but the notion that white folks one hundred and sixty years ago went out of the way to help Blacks is an historic marvel.

***

The Ridge—Plenty of history about Indians and lore

New York State is called the Empire State with good reason. The history of the state is compelling. The early Dutch settlements, the Hudson River, the Erie Canal, New Amsterdam... all are topics entwined in the lore students learn at early ages. As a school child in Sodus I was always made aware of the illustrious history. We were very intrigued with our regional and local history as it played a part in the mosaic of our education. Teachers did a great job leading us to an appreciation of our heritage and that of the first people coming to our area.

My love of history comes from a series of exceptional teachers whose own love of the subject brought things alive. Included in my list of teachers was, of course, Isabel and HBP, whose own interests were manifest. I can remember having to learn the counties of the state while in 7th grade. Our teacher seemed surprised that many of us could recite the counties and even point them out on a map. Little did he know we used to do that in our home as a form of family contest! With the advent of TV and other family activities, historical trivia and table games diminished in importance. I think the interest in history diminished with the trivia and table games. How many homes have National Geographic maps from the past twenty years? How many grandparents had National Geographic Magazines going back twenty years?

There was history in our area that was fascinating and predated the early European settlements, the Revolutionary period and subsequent history. We learned about the Iroquois Confederacy.

The Iroquois had a culture and a common code of laws, long before any European set foot in what became New York State. It was estimated that the Indians were so organized that their governmental system, or confederacy, persisted for over two centuries before our Revolution occurred. We take pride in our

Declaration of Independence and Constitution with good reason. It was predated by Indian writings about government. The Iroquois Confederacy survived tribal conflicts, withstood early attempts by others to encroach upon the tribal lands and, ultimately, was able to negotiate with established countries. They ended up being shafted by unscrupulous traders and foreigners, but the Iroquois were remarkable.

We learned, early on, about the Indian names given to local towns and bodies of water. Sodus was an Indian name meaning "Land of Silvery Waters." The five tribes comprising the Iroquois Confederacy were the Oneida, Cayuga, Mohawk, Onondaga and the Seneca.

As we looked at maps and studied about Indians, we were overwhelmed to think just how many places there were around Sodus using those tribal names and much more. Sodus Point was the water-way used by the Cayuga Indians long before the coal boats and the recreational industry hit the bay. When we went to Babcock-Hovey Scout Camp, we were divided up into campsites named for the tribes of New York. Tuscarora was a name given to a campsite used by some of us from Wayne County. This was despite our wish to be in one of the sites named after one of the tribes of the Confederacy we had learned in school. Thus was our schoolboy logic, of which the schoolteachers of Sodus would have been proud!

It turned out the Tuscarora Tribe was a late-comer to the Iroquois Confederacy after being chased out of North Carolina by settlers and other tribes. Once I learned that fact, well after the scout camp debate, it was evident that some of us were a bit anal about our location at the Geneva campground.

Whenever we took trips around the state with our family the trips became extensions of the history classes at our school. There were forts, harbors, reservations and trails. The reservation visits were very annoying to me. It seemed repulsive to me then, and even now, that such proud, vibrant peoples, such as the Indians of our region, were ultimately relegated to reserved lands. The reservations were what many historians referred to as the White Man's leftovers after the white settlers claimed all the prime real estate.

During a recent trip to New York my wife and I came across an Indian Casino right outside of Syracuse, New York. It is a fairly recent departure, but a significant one, that allows Indians to maintain and operate casinos on "their" lands. This is happening nationwide. Any Iroquois Confederacy member being reincarnated for a day would smile at the irony of it all. The white men are flocking to casinos operated by tribal owners where they are being "fleeced" by descendents of the five tribes—right there in Upstate New York!

***

Our First Exchange Student—Henry the modern Viking

Henry Peussa was our first foreign classmate and he left an indelible mark on our hearts and minds during his all too brief stay with us in 1955-1956. His return to native Finland was our loss. He did come back briefly on other occasions but he remains in Finland today. Wayne County was the ultimate destination for many foreigners and Henry was but one of the many Scandinavians making the trip.

A famous local writer, Arch Merrill, wrote about Upstate New York history while he worked at the Rochester Democrat and Chronicle newspaper in the 1940s. According to him there were many Scandinavians who came to our area much earlier than Henry, our happy Finn. One name that caught my eye was that of Clang Pearson. Clang was a Norwegian man with my family name.

When I read about old Clang back when I was in school and shortly after Merrill wrote his books about Lake Ontario's Ridge Area, I was ecstatic! Here was a man from Norway with our family name and perhaps we were related somehow going back to the 1700 and 1800s. Merrill's book called "The Ridge" had it right there in black and white. I was historic and was only in elementary school. Merrill wrote that book and several others involving exhaustive research and travel to the actual sites he wrote about in the popular books. My family had a couple of books that were autographed by the author but those editions have disappeared in the many moves and deaths in the clan.

According to the Democrat and Chronicle reporter, who traveled the region broadly collecting historic briefs on the Upstate New York region, Clang did not settle in the area near Rochester after landing here. Clang and most of the Norwegians moved on toward the west beyond Rochester. My disappointment was manifest when my Grandmother Pearson could not recall a Clang in the family tree.

As a grade school child at the time, it felt very compelling to be connected to a relative who transited the Atlantic Ocean, reached New York City, navigated the Hudson River to Albany and then came west on the Erie Canal to our area called the Ridge. Grandmother Pearson, ever the realist, merely said she did not remember seeing that name in any family bible and besides that she and her husband moved to Rochester *from* Indiana. If anything, she and grandpa crossed paths with Clang as he headed west.

She did tell me about Indiana and Anderson, where my father was born and raised until the family moved to New York State. If Clang was part of the clan. then his descendents came east after a sojourn in the west. My grandmother told me a very interesting story about my father when he was a small boy. My father fell into water over his head one day at a river near Anderson, and a Black man fishing on the bank pulled him out and blew air into his lungs to revive him. There wasn't much training in CPR back then and Black men during the first decade in the 1900s probably wouldn't be allowed to receive such training anyway. My father owed his life to an anonymous Black man who brought him back from a drowning fate in 1908 using common sense and a makeshift protocol. As my grandmother told me that story, she was emotional about the near-drowning. She was equally emotional when she told me she did not get the man's name and address for appropriate recognition. As I have gone through my life it dawns on me that the Sodus Pearson connection owes its existence to an unknown Black man from Indiana.

By nearly drowning in the river in Indiana, it pointed out his swimming shortcomings were not typically Norwegian. If Clang was our relative he would have been perturbed since Viking-types must know how to swim. My grandparents got their son swimming lessons, and Dad went on to become an excellent swimmer in his high school years. Even later in his life I was always impressed by the barrel-chested man called "Pete" by his friends as he ran into Lake Ontario's waves and swam out several hundred feet before stopping. He could swim well and he made sure I did also.

There were other Scandinavians among our Sodus residents. They were hard-working and added a tremendous flavor to the village. One of our close friends, Alan Cedarvall, was the son of Swedish parents. He was a late arrival to our class during our fifth or sixth grade years. Over the remaining years together, he formed a lasting bond with us based upon loyalty and a quiet nature. My mother would say of Alan that "still water runs deep." Isabel always had an eye for the quiet kids who, at times, would be overwhelmed by some of the more boisterous kids in town. That group obviously included her son Stinky, who was counseled to look after the quiet boy when we were out. Isabel was a teacher first and foremost.

Tragically, Alan succumbed to childhood leukemia after graduation from high school. He and Donald Virts became our first close friends to pass away. Both died much too young. They lie in graveyards on opposite sides of the village, and the trauma of seeing these lads go so early was severe on those of us who knew them through sports and school.

Alan took some of us to meet his parents one time and during our first visit we discussed the history of the area and they started teaching us some Swedish words. Some of us had learned Italian words from our dry cleaning man and wife. I had learned German from my maternal great-grandparents and now we were adding Swedish to our repertoire. We were multicultural way before the fad swept American education.

Alan was a fine young man, and the last time we saw him alive was in a hospital in Rochester where they were trying their best to figure out a protocol to help him live. While we were talking to him a lab technician came in and proceeded to take blood samples from his ear lobes.

Our friend muttered something foreign to us and after the technician departed we asked the bed-ridden friend what he had said. He said the guy came in three times a day for similar activity and three times a day he swore at him in Swedish. It seemed to help him. He was a Viking to the very end.

As I reflect about the lore connected to Clang Pearson, think of the wonderful associations with Henry Peussa and Alan Cedarvall and consider I owe my existence to an unknown Black man from Indiana, it dawns on me that we are all fortunate to be on this earth, and we are all of one blood one way or another.

I have one other thought associated with these Vikings of my past. They all would be pleased if they knew I have spent nearly a quarter of a century at this point at a college called Berry College. We are called the Berry Vikings.

***

One-room Schools—A birthright

Ed Toye was recently honored in Wallington for his fifty years of association with the Wallington Fire Department. Ed was a classmate of mine and is a regular at one of the roadside restaurants in the small village. Gib and I saw him there a year ago and my bet is he is there right now as I write this piece. He and I were class of 1956 at Sodus and we, and our peers still around and kicking, will celebrate our fiftieth anniversary of our graduation in June 2006. Ed was a one-room schoolhouse kid.

The Wallington Cobblestone Schoolhouse, 6135 North Geneva Road, Wallington, New York is still there. According to Wayne County's website, the schoolhouse is still alive and well and is visited by school children of the area regularly. Ed Toye and his classmates moved out in 1951, to travel by bus to Sodus Central School. Their teacher came along to continue teaching in the school at some grade level. Up until that juncture the Wallington teacher was "the" teacher for all the kids, big and small.

One-room schoolhouses were an integral part of the educational landscape until the mid-century. I find it very interesting that many schools in the nation are employing a "looping" system for their teachers and classes at the elementary levels. Looping is the name for the system whereby one teacher stays another year with her class as the class moves to another grade level.

I know a fourth grade teacher locally who will "loop" with her fifth graders-to-be as they move out of fourth grade. She is looking forward to doing the looping because she already knows all the students and can start her fifth grade year at a brisk pace. There will not be any wasted time associated with getting acclimated to a new teacher or vice versa. She has identified the problems and can anticipate trends so there will be very little "pulling the wool over her eyes." Looping seems to be held in high favor in some schools.

Isn't that interesting? That is what Eddie and his classmates had in Wallington year after year after year! Looping was commonplace. As my classmates and I developed friendships with the new influx of classmates in 1951, we were indeed fortunate. The new kids on the block were well-behaved, versatile, fun and, importantly, their arrival doubled the number of girls hanging around the school every day! The arrival of the new students was a highlight of our school year, but it was the number of pretty girls that was most rewarding.

Were the one-room schoolhouses a progressive approach to a series of problems plaguing education today? Educators are continually talking about mentoring as a part and parcel of learning. In Alton, Wallington, Sodus Center, Sodus Point and Joy there were mentors for the younger children. The mentors were the older brothers and sisters, and a "family" existed at most of those schools. I have spoken with the kids coming out of those systems over the years and although some of the teachers were "older," "tougher," or "too strict," the over-all consensus about their teacher(s) seemed to be favorable.

If family is lacking in schools today, the old-timers had plenty of that by virtue of the fact that every member of some families was found in the one schoolroom. Another advantage of the old system seemed to be that teachers were not micromanaged by administrators. Test scores were not the driving force as they appear today. Despite the fact that test scores were only a small part of the total package back then, it appears more kids knew math, history, and science and also possessed more common sense. Where did those things come from? Something must have been inherent in education at mid-century missing today. Discipline, parenting, values, community and more are just a few answers to the question.

Unlike most schools, the kids at the old schools did chores to make the school system work. I can remember what a big deal it was to wash the blackboards for various teachers. It seemed to be a treat to do that task. Kids attending Wallington, and other places like it, did a little of everything. Sometimes they had to get firewood for the stove. Shoveling snow was a routine task that wasn't needed once the new students reached Sodus "Central." Sodus had bus drivers, custodians and absorbed the teachers from the outskirts readily. Other people shoveled snow.

It must have been quite a change for those teachers to have their own classroom for one grade level in a school where most of the work was done for her. We got into activity with our new classmates easily. Sport was one of the common denominators, as it is everywhere, for allowing an easy mix of people.

Specialization in education has also delivered us into a system where experts develop theories behind the invisible walls of intellect and elitism. These so-called experts make me nervous. We seemed to have an abundance of generalists in the 1950s, both outside the village in the unique schools, and inside the village, in our Sodus faculty. Nothing against a specialist, but a person needed to be quite well-rounded to survive in those special schools of the previous century. I still think we need more people in education with common sense and a broad range of experiences.

Thank you for your interest in my "Tales." God Bless America!

Stinky.